"The most massive souls are seared with scars."
– K. Gibran

* * *

This is for the teens whose souls are already scarred. May they use these titles to heal, to grow strong, to succeed, to overcome, and to achieve their dreams.

This is also for the courageous authors who write books to help soothe those scarred souls, knowing that their work may be challenged, even as it helps and heals the teens for whom they wrote it.

Finally, this is for the equally courageous librarians and teachers determined to make sure these difficult titles are available to the teens who need them and willing to fight battles to overcome the challenges these books will face.

📖 Contents 📖

📖 Tips for Writing Effective Book Reports 📖

- Write down everything you will need to know about the assignment when the teacher tells you about it. Ask questions if you are not sure about something.

- Go to your school or public library or a bookstore and get at least two or three books. Look in the library catalog for books on subjects you will like reading about, or ask a librarian for help. Most bookstores are arranged by subject. Ask one of the salespeople for help in finding the subject or subjects you are interested in. Select more than one book in case you don't like the first one you picked out. It is very hard to enjoy reading or to write effectively about a book you really don't like or that doesn't hold your attention.

- Read a little bit every day and take notes on what you read as you go along. Jot down the characters' names and a brief description of each of them, a summary of the plot line, and any important scenes or ideas from the book (with the page numbers so you can find them again).

- Try to set aside a special time to read. Make sure you have something to take notes with; and plan this time for when you are not too tired. If you read when you're very tired, you might easily miss something important.

- Organize your notes. Use a separate sheet for each topic in your book report and keep them in order in one place so you will know where to find them. Putting them with the book is always a good idea.

- Write your first draft using these four sections: a brief plot summary; the author's main idea or ideas (including why you think the author wrote the book); a discussion about the characters and the setting (with an evaluation of their realism and believability); and your own opinion of the book (why you either liked it or didn't like it, what kind of a person you think might like it, and to whom you would recommend it).

- Check with your teacher to see if you are on the right track and doing what he or she expects you to do. Be sure to find out if you need to include any other information about the book or the author.

- Revise and edit your first draft. Carefully check the spelling and ensure that your grammar is also correct. At this point you may also want to change what you have written in the body of the report if you have thought of a better way to explain what you want to say or if you have thought of something else to add.
- Make your final draft and proofread it. Don't forget to put your name and class information on the top sheet; and, if your paper is handwritten, be sure that your writing is clear and easy to read.
- Turn in your paper on the due date.

These ideas are partially based on *Scholastic's A+ Junior Guide to Book Reports* by Louise Colligan (Scholastic, 1989, $2.50), which has much more information and also helpful forms in it which you can use to make sure your book reports are easier to write and easier to make an A on.

Richard Peck, a well-known and prolific writer for teens, has the following questions to ask yourself about a novel, which could also give you book report ideas.

1. What would this story be like if the main character were of the opposite sex?
2. Why is the story set where it is?
3. If you were to film this story, what characters would you eliminate if you couldn't use all of them?
4. Would you film this story in black-and-white or color?
5. How is the main character different from you?
6. Why or why not would this story make a good TV series?
7. What one thing in the story that's happened to you?
8. Reread the first paragraph of chapter 1. What's in it to make you read on?
9. If you had to design a new cover for the book, what would it look like?
10. What does the title tell you about the book? Does it tell the truth?
11. Are there characters in the book who wear disguises of some kind, and if so, what are they, and why do they wear them?

And here are ten generic questions which can be considered when planning a book report for any of these titles:

1. What is the most important thing you learned from reading and thinking about this book?
2. Would you recommend this book to a friend? Why or why not?
3. If you could talk to the author of this book, what questions would you ask about it?
4. If you could talk to one character from this book, who would it be, and what would you say and why would you say it?
5. How would you tell someone about this book? What would you say to make him or her want to read it?

6. What scene or situation was the most important to you, and why did you choose it?
7. What scene or situation made the book's theme or plot most clear, and why did you choose it?
8. Will you act or think differently as a result of reading and thinking about this book? Why or why not?
9. What did you like most and least about this book, and why did you choose it?
10. Would you read another book by this author? Explain why or why not.

📖 Tips for Writing Effective Booktalks 📖

1. A booktalk is not a book report, but a kind of commercial for a book that persuades the listener to read it. Therefore, it doesn't tell the ending and doesn't evaluate the book in any way. It just tells a little about the plot and the characters and stops without telling what happened next. In addition, a book report is mainly something that you write and the teacher reads (although you may be asked to read it in class as well), while a booktalk is usually spoken. It is really talking about the book. It is basically the kind of thing you'd say to a friend when you've just finished a book you really liked and want to make sure that your friend reads it too.

2. Never talk about a book that you didn't like—how could you convince someone else to read it if you didn't like it?

3. Never talk about a book you haven't read all the way through—you might miss something crucial, or your teacher might ask you to talk with him or her privately about the end of the book. Plus, in a booktalk, you are introducing your audience to the people in the book, and if you haven't read the book, you won't know who they are—they'll be strangers, not friends.

4. There are four basic kinds of booktalks based on what you thought was exciting in the book.

    Plot summary is the first kind. You just summarize the plot, leading up to an exciting and climactic moment and stopping without telling what happened. The last sentence for a talk like this could be "To find out what happened next, read. . . ."

    Character description is another kind of booktalk, one based on talking about one or two or more of the main characters in the book. You can pretend that you are one of the characters and write your talk in the first person, or you can just describe the characters in the third person. The more characters you use, the less you can say about each one of them because you don't want to make your talk too long.

If you are writing about a book that is a collection of short stories or is written in an episodic style (the main character might have a series of adventures or problems to deal with, each contained in one or two chapters), you can use the **short story/scene** kind of booktalk. This talk simply tells the whole story or scene (or one adventure or problem) from beginning to end. The last few sentences of the talk let the audience know that there are other adventures or stories they will miss if they don't read the book.

If the author of your book has a unique writing style or if the book itself has a mood about it—mysterious, scary, or suspenseful—then you will want to write a **mood-based** booktalk. This kind of talk lets your audience know what to expect from the book and sometimes includes an excerpt from it that demonstrates the author's writing style. In order to communicate the mood, you'll need to use your voice, including variations in pitch, pace, and rhythm, to convey the mood.

5. A booktalk shouldn't be too long: usually between two and four minutes, depending on how much of the book you have to reveal to convince your audience to read it. This means you will have to leave out either most or all of the details about the book and just put into your talk what is absolutely necessary.

6. Take notes while you read your book, including the names of the characters and the page number of any special scene or quote you want to use in your talk.

7. Make your first sentence exciting so it will hook your audience immediately. Start in the middle of the action, and include more action than description, because most audiences find action more interesting. Once you have gotten your audience's attention with your first sentence, they will be more willing to listen to what else you have to say.

8. After you've written your talk, time it while you are practicing to make sure that it isn't too long (no more than four minutes). Be sure that you do practice, and that you practice not only what you are going to say but also the way you're going to stand, how you will handle the book itself and your notes on it, and whatever gestures you will use. If you don't practice everything at once, you will be more likely to forget something you really wanted to say when you deliver your talk. Also practice projecting your voice so everyone in the room can hear you.

9. Don't memorize your talk! Use slightly different words when you practice so that if you forget the exact words you have written down, you will have some other familiar words to fill in. This means that you shouldn't look at your notes too much while you practice after the first two or three times you read it aloud. This will force you to find different words to use.

10. Wear comfortable clothes. (I always make sure that I have pockets in my skirt or pants so I have somewhere to put my hands to keep from waving them around.) And remember to speak slowly, because you may be nervous and thus more likely to speed up without realizing it. But most of all, remember to have fun! That's one of the main purposes of booktalks—to have fun sharing books you've enjoyed with other people who will enjoy them too.

And there's an extra bonus to doing booktalks. People are more afraid of getting up in front of a crowd and talking than anything else. If you learn how to do this, while you are learning how to give booktalks, you'll have an advantage over all of them!

There is more information about how to write and present booktalks in my book *Booktalk! 2* (H. W. Wilson, 1985, $32.00). Most public and school libraries have copies of this book. In addition, your librarians may be willing to share their own hints on how to do booktalks.

📖 Guide to Abbreviations 📖

The following abbreviations are used in the book for different reading and interest levels:

MS   Middle School, sixth through eighth grades

YHS   Younger High School, ninth and tenth grades

OHS   Older High School, eleventh and twelfth grades

📖 Acknowledgments 📖

There a lot of people to thank for their contributions to this book. First of all, Ed Kurdyla, whose patience made this a better book, with more recent and more controversial titles than the first edition. Ken Haycock, Director, School of Library and Information Science, San Jose State University, who supported my work by approving my requests for graduate assistants to work with me. Patty Campbell, Beth Wrenn-Estes, and Teri Lesesne, who went over title lists with me and suggested what to include and what to omit. Patty also graciously sent me copies of the titles she recommended. Cathi Dunn MacRae, who encouraged me to "Just finish it!" when I badly needed to hear that. Dana Weber, Jonathan Hunt, and Sarah Kimmel, SLIS graduates who worked with me on the first part of the project, transcribing entries and locating reviews and awards. Casandria Crane, a SLIS student who located the bibliographic information on all the various formats for the titles, transcribed entries, and looked for reviews and awards for several semesters—and never complained when I dropped titles she'd worked on and added new ones to be completed. She also updated the bibliography of articles on the value of controversial literature for teens, helped me find "lost" entries, counted titles over and over, was incredibly patient, and never let me know if she was tearing her hair out about my unreasonable demands! Her contribution to this book cannot be overstated. And finally, Blair Andrews at Scarecrow, who promised me the cover would look *radical*—and came through on that promise in spades!

📖 Introduction 📖
The Value of Controversial YA Literature

Today, teens know about violence, drugs, sex, and insidious predators they must be aware of, both online and on the street. They know about death, divorce, conflict, and homelessness. They know about bullies, prejudice, rejection, and hatred. They know that survival can be difficult, and success isn't guaranteed to anyone, no matter their age or social class. They watch TV, go to movies, surf the web, listen to music, and talk to, text, or IM their friends—and the ugliness of life is right there in front of them. Many of them know firsthand how much more "controversial" our society has become—it is their truth, their life. And they demand that it be reflected in the books they read. If YA literature doesn't reflect today's reality and look ahead to tomorrow's reality, it will fall by the wayside. Our society has begun to edge toward the extreme in a variety of ways and, as a result, so has the literature for the part of that society who is most willing and least equipped to take risks of all kinds. So if we are going to defend and protect these titles, and keep that door to the real world open, we have to understand them and why they are controversial.

Today's YA literature is controversial because it reflects reality, in all of its ugliness and all of its beauty. Teens want books that reflect reality without sugarcoating it, books that can help them find out what experiences, good and bad, are waiting for them and for their friends. They want a chance to experience reality vicariously before meeting it head-on, and they know the safety of having those experiences through books. But today's reality is far more intense than the reality of previous generations. Teens have access to more information, more quickly, than any other generation before. They don't live in a bubble, protected from the knowledge or the experience of things like drugs, rape, abuse, homosexuality, mental illness, and teen pregnancy. Nor should they. Within a few years, they will all have to find a place in this world as adults. The teen years are the last chance for them to have one foot in childhood and the other in their future adulthood.

Today's YA literature tells the truth. It doesn't lie. Our world and our society are far more complex and harder to navigate safely than ever before, and teens need all the help they can get in order to understand the world, the culture, and the times that they are living in. Books can do that. Providing teens with books like those in *Radical Reads 2*, books that reflect the darkest and most difficult parts of our society and show them ways to deal with those dark shadows and difficult decisions, can be one of the most valuable things we do as YA librarians, teachers, parents, and youth advocates.

But some teens aren't lucky enough simply to be *learning* about these life challenges: many of them are actually *living* them. Teens in tough situations will need particular help in their journey to adulthood. Books that reflect their world can be resources to help them work through their problems. But these are also the books that create the most controversy. Josh Westbrook, branch manager of the Prescott Library, Walla Walla County Rural Library District, Walla Walla, Washington, says it in one sentence: "Kids are living stories every day that we wouldn't let them read." Books can help those teens feel more understood and valued when they find characters and stories that truly speak to them, that can give them hope, an inspiration to move forward, to succeed, to transform their lives.

It's controversial because it's incredibly well written. Adolescence is a time when everything is black and white, when emotions are intense, whether displayed or hidden away. YA authors know that they must hook their readers by inspiring those intense emotions through their work. Teens, unlike the adult readers they may become, have little patience with unrealistic characters or situations, conversations, or emotions. It is the reason why the best of young adult literature is usually considered to be as well written as some adult literature, and better than much of it. Teens are far more discriminating than adults, and will not hesitate to put down a book they label as fake, or lame, or yesterday. Characters, situations, and emotions are real, vivid, believable, intense, allowing the reader to identify with them. These authors respect their readers, and don't pull their punches, or tack on deus ex machina happy endings to difficult stories. If these books didn't elicit such a strong response from the reader, there would be far fewer objections to them.

And here is the paradox: if controversial novels for teens were more poorly written, more banal, didn't inspire such an intense emotional response in the reader, they would raise far fewer red flags. Skillful, well-crafted, thoughtful writing that respects the reader enough to depict reality accurately, including all the dark corners and subjects that some adults would prefer teens remain ignorant of, is much more likely to draw the censors' fire. YA authors know they have a great responsibility, because teens read their stories and respond to them. They have to tell the truth—they must cut straight to the heart of the story. Characters and plot can be complex, but emotions must be clear. And not all of their stories can end happily, or resolve every problem, which allows readers continue the story in their own heads, creating their own solutions.

It's controversial because it makes adults uncomfortable. It reveals things that adults would prefer stay hidden. It introduces subjects and characters that are difficult to read or even think about. It doesn't protect readers from the darkest parts of reality, and presents those realities with intensity, validity, and power. It allows teens to see the good and the bad side of the question "What if?" which can be threatening to adults who care about them and don't want to see them hurt. Teens deserve well-written books that make them think, feel, wonder, hope, and that show them reality, no matter how uncomfortable it makes the well-meaning adults who want to protect them from it. These are the books that open the door to real life, a door many adults wish would stay closed. But the fact is that protecting teens from reality may do far more damage than letting them read about it.

It's controversial because it changes lives and empowers teens—they read it and respond to it. It gives readers new perspectives and new insights. It can promote a cathartic response in the reader, which can lead to new thinking and new action. Sometimes teens may not even realize they've made a change in their thinking until they are faced with a situation similar to one they've read about. It gives them the information they need to make their own decisions about what's right or wrong, good or bad, create their own philosophies, live their own lives, make their own mistakes and pay the prices, achieve their own triumphs and reap the rewards. It gives readers the knowledge that they aren't alone in the world, that someone else understands their feelings and experiences. It suggests new solutions to problems that readers may not have seen or considered. A character's mistakes can educate the reader about the wisest choice of action in the future.

And even if none of the above were true, YA lit would still be so controversial simply because adolescence, by its very nature, is controversial. How could the literature that reflects it be anything else? Adolescents want to explore the forbidden subjects, the secrets, the conflicts, the darkness that they see almost daily—and they will. Isn't it safer by far to learn about those things from an author who tells it like it is, straight from the hip, rather than getting a skewed or less honest story in a dark room or on a street corner?

And Chris Crutcher, one of the most challenged authors of YA literature, a family therapist who works with at-risk teens, and one of the most passionate defenders of teens' intellectual freedom, does what he does best when he tells like it is:

> Our schools are filled with kids who have been treated badly all their lives. They don't tell anyone, because there is shame in being treated badly. Many, girls and boys, have been sexually mistreated. Still others struggle in fear with sexual identity. They respond with eating disorders, cutting, suicidal thought or action. I can't tell you how many letters I've received from kids who found a friend in one of my books, a character who speaks to them. And if I get those letters, think of the letters Walter Dean Myers, or Lois Lowry, or Judy Blume get, thanking us for letting them know, through literature, that they are not alone. In light of all that, there's really only one thing to say to the censors. Shut up.

Radical Reads 2 is a celebration of authors who have the courage to treat adolescents as true young adults, and resist those who attempt to censor them, and continue to publish their dark, difficult, inspiring, insightful, and educational books. If these books can help even one teen to feel new hope, ask for help, find a solution, or know they aren't alone, it will be worth it.

REFERENCES

Bowler, Tim. "Let the Young Decide What They Read." *New Statesman,* July 17, 1998.

Crutcher, Chris. "I Don't Give a Damn About My Reputation." *Book Standard,* September 23, 2005.

Westbrook, Josh. www.google.com/profiles/jcwestbrook.

Novels

📖📖📖

33 SNOWFISH. Adam Rapp. Candlewick Press, 2003. $15.99. 192p. ISBN10:
0763618748. ISBN13: 9780763618742. Candlewick Press, 2006. $6.99. 192p.
ISBN10: 0763629170. ISBN13: 9780763629175. Realistic fiction. Reading Level:
MS. Interest Level: YHS, OHS. English, Ethics, Psychology, Sociology.

SUBJECT AREAS
abuse, sexual; crime and delinquency; death and dying; friendship; love; self-knowledge;
travel; substance abuse; child abuse; family relationships; grief and mourning; homelessness; illness, mental or physical; lying and deceitfulness; poverty; runaways; secrets; sex
and sexuality; survival; racism; manipulation; intimidation; revenge.

CHARACTERS
Custis: he never had a real home or family and has spent most of his life on the
    streets
Boobie: seventeen years old, his parents kicked him out when he tried to set the house
    on fire
Curl: a teen prostitute, she's Boobie's girlfriend
The Baby: Boobie's little brother, who's to be sold to the highest bidder
Old Man Turpentine: he took Curl fishing and looked out for her
Bob Motley: he makes horror and snuff films, and he used to own Custis
Sidekick: a child molester, he makes movies with Bob Motley
Aunty Frisco: Curl's crippled aunt who talked her into being a prostitute
Seldom: he's an old man with a good heart

BOOKTALK

They're disposable kids, throwaways, kids no one wants or cares about. And they're going to try to survive on their own.

Curl's fourteen or fifteen, but she's been a prostitute for years, and the clap she's had for most of those years is finally beginning to shut down her mind and her body. Custis has no idea where he came from, what his last name is, or even how old he is. He's lived mostly on the streets, but the last four months he's been owned by a guy who makes porno and snuff films. Custis hooked up with Boobie after he realized he was going to be the next kid to get snuffed. Boobie's got wealthy parents, a big house, a baby brother, and a lot of problems. He's fascinated with fire and his parents kicked him out when he tried to set fire to the house. He almost never speaks; he just draws strange pictures and his eyes are almost hypnotic in his ability to draw people to him just by looking at them.

And now they're on the road and on the run. Boobie's parents are dead and the kids have Boobie's baby brother with his beautiful violet eyes to sell to the highest bidder, hopefully for five hundred dollars or more. But with Curl jonesing for her next fix, a baby who cries entirely too much, Boobie screaming because he got the clap from Curl and it's burning him up inside, and Custis paranoid about staying away from the cops, how far will they get? Can these four throwaway kids figure out how to survive on their own?

MAJOR THEMES AND IDEAS

- When you're warm and fed and safe, even the worst place can seem like home.
- When you aren't safe, it's time to leave.
- You can get used to almost anything. When you do, it seems normal after a while, even when it's not.
- Making a pledge, a commitment, means you're in it for the long haul.
- Talking about your problems can sometimes make them feel smaller. Not talking about them can make them seem to howl inside.
- Not talking doesn't mean not communicating or not caring.
- When the pain gets too big and too bad, running away might seem like the only choice.
- Eyes can say more than words.
- You can't run forever. Sooner or later, the highway runs out and you have to turn around and look at what you left behind.
- A man who hits a dog today is likely to kick it in a month.
- Once your life starts spiraling downward, it's very hard to change directions.
- Babies have an amazing ability to survive.
- Kindness and friendship have nothing to do with the color of your skin.
- When the coldness is inside you, you can't ever get warm.
- If you've never been loved or treated kindly, it's hard to know what to do when you are.

BOOK REPORT IDEAS

1. Speculate on how the story might have been different if it had happened in the spring or summer instead of winter.
2. Once they were on the road, was there anything Curl or Custis could have done to make their situation any better?
3. What do you think happened to Seldom, Custis, and the baby after the story ended?
4. Boobie is an enigmatic character. Based on his pictures and the others' views of him, what kind of person is he? What are his strengths, his flaws, his problems? What do you think happens to him after he disappears into the woods?
5. This book seems to say that children can't survive on their own without adults. Is this true? Why or why not?
6. Discuss the concept of home as Custis defines it. What's necessary in a home? What isn't? Compare and contrast the homes Custis has experienced in his life.
7. The adults in this book are almost all negative characters who intimidate and manipulate children for their own profit. How close to reality are these characters? Compare and contrast them to similar people from your own life.
8. Boobie, Curl, and Custis are all "throwaway children." Discuss how parental figures in each of their lives discarded them and why.
9. Custis is a racist, and yet the person who treats him most humanely is black. Discuss how Seldom helped Custis to find a new perspective on how blacks and whites are different and the same.
10. Custis tries to run from Seldom but comes back. Why did he change his mind?

BOOKTALK IDEAS

1. Write your talk from all three points of view, using Boobie's pictures and Curl's and Curtis's words.
2. Write your talk as if it were a TV news item.
3. Choose the most significant scene or event in the book and center your talk around it.

RISKS

- Teen drug use
- Teen prostitution
- Teen kills parents and kidnaps baby brother
- Runaways
- Street slang and vulgarities
- Racism
- Manipulation of children for adult profit
- Children participate in pornography and snuff films
- Most adults depicted very negatively

STRENGTHS

- Lyrical language
- Realistic language, including street slang and obscenities
- Believable, multifaceted characters the reader can identify with
- Narration from multiple points of view allows reader to see the characters from different perspectives
- Shows the strength of the human spirit and the drive to survive
- Well-written; characters evolve throughout story
- Ambiguous, unresolved ending allows reader to speculate on outcome
- Wrenching, involving depictions of forgotten or thrown-away children
- Portrays a part of society many teens are unaware of

AWARDS

ALA Best Books for Young Adults, 2004
New York Public Library Books for the Teen Age, 2004

REVIEWS

"Readers are exposed to the realities of the young and poor, for whom survival is a singular preoccupation. The novel ends hopefully; however, the salvation described might not be the fairy-tale ending readers have been taught to imagine. This novel might not appeal to all readers, but it deserves a place beside young adult classics." Amy S. Pattee, *VOYA*, 4/03

"With his customary ear for the language of the marginalized teen, Rapp . . . allows his characters to present themselves with total unselfconsciousness, frankly and powerfully laying out the squalor of their existence without any seeming sense that life can be anything else but squalid." *Kirkus Reviews*, 2/03

"Spare descriptions and stellar characterization reel readers into the dark and violent world of these dispossessed and abused young people. This book will be controversial, but for those readers who are ready to be challenged by a serious work of shockingly realistic fiction, it invites both an emotional and intellectual response, and begs to be discussed." Joel Shoemaker, Southeast Junior High School, Iowa City, IA, *School Library Journal*, 04/03

📖📖📖

ACCELERATION. Graham McNamee. Random House, 2005. $6.50. 224p. ISBN10: 0440238366. ISBN13: 9780440238362. Realistic fiction. Reading Level: MS. Interest Level: MS, YHS. English, Creative Writing, Psychology, Sociology.

SUBJECT AREAS

crime and delinquency; friendship; family relationships; problem parents; secrets; working; self-knowledge; reading; rites of passage; anger; death and dying; dysfunctional families; ethics; fear.

CHARACTERS

Duncan: he works at the most boring job in the world until he finds the diary of a serial killer

Jacob: Duncan's supervisor at the Lost and Found

Vinny: one of Duncan's best friends, he's a brain and doesn't have a summer job

Wayne: one of Duncan's best friends, he works at a fast food place and isn't all that bright

Mom: Duncan's mother, who's into exercise and learning new things

Dad: Duncan's father, who works graveyard shift at a factory

Kim: Duncan's ex-girlfriend

Roach: the arsonist and potential killer Duncan is searching for

BOOKTALK

It wasn't the best summer job in the world, but at least Duncan didn't have to wear a uniform, and fifty feet underground the summer heat wave didn't have much effect—it was always cool. Working the Toronto Transit Commission's Lost and Found was actually not a bad job, if you didn't want to do much—and Duncan didn't. All he had to do was sort through the stuff left on busses and subways, tag it, store it, and look for stuff he wanted to score as soon as the expiration date rolled around. His favorite find so far was a black leather jacket in perfect condition. But it was when he was browsing through the books that he made his most frightening find—a small, thick, plain brown leather book—someone's journal. Someone's journal with notes on bizarre and deadly experiments with animals, experiments with starting fires that get bigger and bigger and more and more costly, all documented with newspaper photos. And, finally, notes on how he's been stalking Cherry Bones and Clown and details on where and when they ride the busses and the trains. He's moved on from the kid stuff, the animals and the fires. Now he's going after bigger game—human beings.

A potential serial killer is stalking the subways of Toronto, and Duncan is the only one who might be able to catch him.

MAJOR THEMES AND IDEAS

- There are no coincidences. Things happen for a reason.
- You can't go back and fix a mistake from your past. You can only deal with it and go on.
- It's hard never being able to answer the question "What if?"—but you'll never be able to.

- Sometimes problems or situations we can't or won't deal with come back to haunt us in dreams.
- Guilt is usually futile. It accomplishes nothing.
- Doesn't matter who starts in front. It matters who can close the distance. It matters who can finish first.
- You can be programmed by life to fail. But you can also choose to reject that programming.
- Pay attention to the details—they can reveal large chunks of information.
- When it's time to make your move, don't hesitate; go for it!
- Some ghosts *can* be exorcised.

BOOK REPORT IDEAS

1. Guilt plays a large role in the actions of several characters. Explain how this emotion changes their behavior.
2. Speculate on what you would have done in Duncan's place.
3. Examine Wayne's flirting with illegal activity and how that affected his relationship with Duncan and Vinnie.
4. At one point, Duncan says he "swallowed the hook" in searching for Roach. What does he mean by this and when did it happen?
5. How did failing to save Maya change Duncan into the person determined to stop Roach? Did that change occur at once or gradually? When did it happen?
6. The question of what is right and ethical is a central part of this story. Discuss your reaction to these questions as they are seen in the book and contrast it to your own beliefs.

BOOKTALK IDEAS

1. Use a plain brown leather book as a prop.
2. Write your talk from Duncan's point of view, focusing on his increasing horror as he reads the journal.
3. Write your talk, as much as possible, from excerpts from the journal and newspaper clippings.

RISKS

- Teens show risky and criminal behavior
- Descriptions of gruesome crimes
- Serial killer suspect stalks women
- Parents uninvolved with children

STRENGTHS

- Multi-dimensional characters readers can identify with
- Characters grow and mature during the story
- Not all questions are answered—some ambiguity in the ending

AWARDS
ALA Best Books for Young Adults, 2004
ALA Quick Picks for Reluctant Young Adult Readers, 2004

REVIEWS
"McNamee . . . pulls no punches in this thriller. . . . This novel will intrigue *Silence of the Lamb* fans, but McNamee offers much more. The dark symbolism surrounding the subway and the rich character development are as intoxicating as the adrenalin rush." Ruth E. Cox, *VOYA*, 12/03

"Characters are more than stereotypes here, though it's the mystery and the boys' repartee that give the novel its page-turning punch." Stephanie Zvirin, *Booklist*, 9/03

"This is a well-written, read-it-in-one-gulp thriller." *Kirkus Reviews*, 9/03

📖📖📖

THE ADORATION OF JENNA FOX. Mary Pearson. Henry Holt, 2008. $16.95. 272p. ISBN10: 0805076689. ISBN13: 9780805076684. Macmillan Young Listeners, 2008. $29.95. ISBN10: 1427204438. ISBN13: 9781427204431. (unabridged audio CD) Science fiction. Reading Level: YHS. Interest Level: YHS, OHS. English, Science, Ethics, Biology, Psychology.

SUBJECT AREAS
illness, physical; lying and deceit; secrets; family relationships; self-knowledge; environmental issues; ethics; friendship; love; school; rites of passage; anger; computers; fear; legal system; survival; grief and mourning; politics.

CHARACTERS
Jenna Fox: she's seventeen and has just come out of a coma and doesn't remember anything about her life
Clair Fox/Mother: Jenna's mother, who's with Jenna in California
Mom/Lily: Jenna's grandmother, Claire's mother, who lives with Jenna and her mother
Matthew Fox/Father: Jenna's father, who lives in Boston
Clayton Bender: he lives near the Foxes, on the other side of the pond, and is an artist
Kara and Locke: they were Jenna's best friends
Father Rico: he lives at the Mission San Luis Rey and is a friend of Lily's
Dane: a boy who lives in Jenna's neighborhood

Mitch: the facilitator at the village charter school
Dr. Rae: Jenna's principal teacher
Ethan: Jenna saw him at the mission; he goes to the village charter school
Allys: another student at the charter school
Gabriel: he's also in Jenna's class
Edward: a childhood friend of Matthew's whom he knew he could trust
Victoria: Allys's mother
Senator Harris: he had a twenty-five-hour filibuster against a bill that would drastically reduce the power of the FSEB

BOOKTALK

Jenna Fox has just awoken after being in a coma for eighteen months. She doesn't remember who she is. Her parents and grandmother aren't familiar. Her parents show her home movies, but neither the child nor the teenager she became are familiar. She knows facts—history, mathematics, science, literature—but she doesn't remember anything personal about herself or her life.

How could a coma wipe away her whole personality? Why doesn't she remember any of the celebrations her parents recorded for sixteen years?

Her body feels strange as well. Her hands and feet don't work quite right. She's clumsy and awkward. And her parents are hiding something. Why isn't she allowed to leave the house? And why does her grandmother look at her as if she hates her?

What has happened to Jenna Fox? What happened after the accident that left her in a coma? Her parents have told her they'd do anything to save her—but what did they do and who is she now?

MAJOR THEMES AND IDEAS

- How can you love someone you don't know?
- Time heals.
- Everyone should have at least one friend. What kind of person is someone with no friends?
- People can reinvent themselves and their lives.
- Sometimes we don't know when we've gone too far.
- When your life is uneventful, every encounter seems to have extra significance.
- Some things take time. Sometimes, too much time.
- Find your way. Make it your business.
- Friends help friends.
- "I went to the woods because I wanted to live deliberately." —Thoreau
- Life is a collection of moments, shards of memory.
- Just because we *can* do something, doesn't mean that we *should*.
- It's essential to consider the long-term impact of new developments and discoveries, not just the short-term impact.
- Look at the *worst* case scenario, as well as the *best* case.

- Sometimes there is just no choice. You have to do what you have to do.
- When you're perfect, is there anywhere else to go?
- The mind is not the brain. It is the energy the brain produces.
- Wanting can't make something happen or change the truth.
- Life is lived in only one direction. You can't go back and start over. You must keep moving ahead.
- In an instant, life can flip and change forever.
- "If one advances confidently in the direction of his dreams, and endeavors to live the life which he has imagined, he will meet with a success unexpected in common hours."—Thoreau
- If you use bits and pieces of yourself to fill up the holes in the people you love, soon you won't have any to fill up your own holes.
- New information means new situations and new rules to deal with them.
- Given time, people change, laws change, maybe we all change.
- One small change can make the world spin differently in a billion ways for one small family.

BOOK REPORT IDEAS

1. Jenna always goes to her room when someone tells her to. Explain what that means, and what would have to happen to make Jenna disobey that order.
2. Birds won't land on Jenna's hand to peck the seeds she holds. Discuss what some of the reasons for this might be.
3. Explain what Lily means when she says she doesn't have room for Jenna.
4. Lily and Father Rico are passionate about saving plant species by preserving their seeds. What has happened in the world that makes this so important?
5. What makes a person human? A real person? What is the essence of humanity?
6. Explain why Jenna is so bothered by the fact that she has no friends. What does having friends mean to her?
7. Discuss the meaning of the title and how "adoration" is used.
8. Explain Jenna's feeling of "wrongness" about her body. Have you ever felt something similar? If so, describe the feeling and where it came from.
9. Discuss the problems that may result from the overuse of antibiotics in the future and how their current use predicts that future to some extent.
10. Allys says the FSEB is "trying to preserve our humanity" by limiting how much an individual can be replaced or enhanced. How appropriate, how ethical is that, and how artificial? How much of our original genetic material do we have to have to be human?
11. Jenna says she has power over her parents. Discuss whether or not this is true, what that power consists of, and how she can use it.
12. Discuss the scene when Jenna tells Ethan the truth and how he responds. How do you think you might have responded if you had been in Ethan's place?
13. Discuss the price Matthew and Claire had to pay to keep their only child. Speculate about what you would have done had you been in their place. What would

you do to save the life of the person you love more than anyone else in the world?

14. Both the old Jenna and the new one ask themselves, "Am I enough?" To what are they each referring when they ask this?

15. Discuss the idea of perfection, as experienced by Jenna as she watches the DVDs of her life. Explore the kind of pressure she was under.

BOOKTALK IDEAS

1. Use the text in the shaded pages to write your talk.
2. Focus your talk on the idea of memory.
3. Build your talk around the question "What makes us human?"

RISKS

- Parents go to medical and ethical extremes to save their daughter's life
- Some vulgar language
- Didactic about medical/environmental issues
- Some medical advances are portrayed negatively
- Parents lie to their daughter
- Parents authorize extreme medical procedures on their daughter against her wishes

STRENGTHS

- Examines the essence of humanity and what it means to be human, to be an individual, a person
- Suspense is maintained by revealing very slowly what happened to Jenna
- Examines the idea of secrets and why people have them
- Narrator's voice is clear and authentic
- Characters are three-dimensional and realistic
- Examines the bonds between parent and child
- Provides many opportunities for discussion
- Resists giving easy answers
- Characters develop, change, mature, and rethink decisions
- Provides a glimpse of one of humanity's possible futures

AWARDS

ALA Best Books for Young Adults, 2009
SLJ Best Books for Children, 2008

REVIEWS

"Pearson creates an extraordinarily fine novel. There are clear explanations of how the new Jenna is created. The ethics of biotechnological advances are debated and seamlessly woven into a well-developed story. . . . In this beautifully written novel, Pearson deals with the heart of what it means to be human." Hilary Crew, *VOYA*, 8/08

"Pearson has constructed a gripping, believable vision of a future dystopia. She explores issues surrounding scientific ethics, the power of science, and the nature of the soul with grace, poetry, and an apt sense of drama and suspense. . . . This is a beautiful blend of science fiction, medical thriller, and teen-relationship novel that melds into a seamless whole that will please fans of all three genres." Meredith Robbins, Jacqueline Kennedy Onassis High School, New York City, *School Library Journal*, 5/08

"Outstanding examination of identity, science and ethics. . . . Pearson reveals the truth layer by layer, maintaining taut suspense and psychological realism as she probes philosophical notions of personhood." *Kirkus Reviews*, 3/08

📖📖📖

ALMOST HOME. Jessica Blank. Hyperion, 2007. $15.99. 256p. ISBN10: 1423106423. ISBN13: 9781423106425. Hyperion, 2007. $7.99. 272p. ISBN10: 1423106431. ISBN13: 9781423106432. Realistic fiction. Reading Level: YHS. Interest Level: YHS, OHS. English, Psychology, Sociology.

SUBJECT AREAS
runaways; homeless; survival; friendship; problem parents; love; betrayal; substance abuse; sex and sexuality; homosexuality; incest; drugs; lying and deceit; sexual abuse; addiction; fear; anger; animals; violence; self-destruction; betrayal; self-knowledge; rape; revenge; poverty; guilt; crime and delinquency.

CHARACTERS
Eeyore/Eleanor: she's only twelve when she runs away from home
Rusty: he ends up alone when his boyfriend dumps him
Squid: he's survived too many foster homes to count and wants to create his own "street family"
Scabius: he's a rough, delusional punk from Utah
Critter: he's a heroine dealer who looks like a movie star
Laura: she's come to Hollywood to find something, she's just not sure what
Tracy: she's got hard edges that hurt most people who try to get close to her and is a little bit scary
Jenny Kirchner and Julia Birmingham: two girls who like to torment Eeyore
Linda: Eeyore's stepmom, who's clueless

Brian: Eeyore's stepbrother, whom she hates
Dad: Eeyore's father, who's also clueless
Matt Dilkus and Marco Rollo: two boys who give Eeyore her nickname, "Tits"
Jim: the choir director at Bakersfield High School, and Rusty is in love with him
Bianca: a transvestite prostitute who hangs out near the liquor store

BOOKTALK

Eeyore was only twelve when one day she didn't come home after school but walked away into a new life on the streets of Hollywood, where she didn't have to be afraid her stepbrother would sneak into her bed every night.

Squid had been in too many foster homes to count. He didn't really trust anyone—he'd been betrayed too many times.

Tracy was all hard edges, squinty eyes, and an in-your-face attitude. She was a survivor who'd been on the streets for years.

Rusty was in Hollywood because he fell in love, but you can't have an affair with your teacher in your hometown. So Jim gave Rusty a bus ticket and some money to head for L.A. He promised to follow him—but Jim never showed up, and when the money ran out Rusty was on the street.

Critter had the face of a movie star—he was beautiful, even in Hollywood. But he was a drug dealer, an addict, and he lived on the street.

There are 1.5 million kids living on the street in this country. These are the stories of seven of them.

MAJOR THEMES AND IDEAS

- Loneliness is supposed to be like a vacuum that sucks in other lonely people until it fills up and you aren't lonely any more.
- Bullies aren't strong, they're weak. They pick on other kids to make themselves feel stronger than everyone else.
- Living on the street can feel safer than living at home, where you are never really safe.
- When someone abuses you, it's *never* your fault, no matter what you said or did or looked like.
- Living on the streets requires a whole different set of skills that only someone else who lives there can teach you.
- Survival is easier with friends who can watch your back. There's safety in numbers.
- You have to believe in love before you can find it.
- Love, and lovers, aren't always forever.
- Sharing your pain and worry can make them smaller and more manageable.
- When someone dangerous notices you, it can be very scary.
- When someone hurts you, your first impulse is to hurt them back, any way you can.

- Sometimes it's way too easy to do the things you hate, the things you promised yourself you'd never do.
- Sometimes, you do to someone else the same horrible things that were done to you.
- Parents frequently have no idea what their children are doing or how badly damaged they may be.
- When things on the street get dangerous, you're almost always on your own.
- Friends don't let friends go into a fight alone.
- On the street, you just do what you have to do to survive, physically and emotionally.
- Sometimes you have to hurt someone in order to protect them.
- When someone's mind matches yours, and you can both see it, and then they go off and do the opposite, they gotta have a really good reason.
- It's amazing what you can put up with when you know something else is coming.
- When things happen with strangers it's different from when you're with people you know.
- It's best not to expect anything from anyone—but it's not easy. Sooner or later, you slip and get slammed.
- Being with someone you care about makes everything different and new.
- Things that don't make sense when they're happening to you look like part of a plan when you look back at them.
- Places don't change you; people and events change you.
- When home isn't a safe place, you at least have *try* to make people understand that.

BOOK REPORT IDEAS
1. Discuss how each of the main characters ended up on the street.
2. Tracy leaves Eeyore very suddenly. Explain why she did that.
3. Speculate on what might have happened if Elly had walked home the day she was attacked and told her parents what happened.
4. Discuss how Eeyore was different from the other kids she hung with.
5. Could Eeyore and Squid have convinced Linda that Eeyore was telling the truth? Why or why not?
6. Discuss why the group of teens stayed together and what they each got from it.
7. Different members of the group shift alliances and connections, deciding who they will be tightest with. How and why are those connections formed or ended?
8. When Scabius tells Eeyore to go home, was he doing it to help her or to stop her from getting between him and Critter?
9. Rusty confides in Tracy, telling her all the reasons he ended up in L.A., and then leaves her the next morning. Explain why he left and what his confession meant to him.
10. Speculate on what happens to each of the main characters after the book ends.

BOOKTALK IDEAS

1. Describe two or three of the main characters and how they ended up on the street.
2. Describe each of the main characters in one sentence each and a little about how they connected.
3. Use some facts about homeless teens as part of your talk.
4. Write your talk from the point of view of the character you most identify with.
5. Use pictures of street kids that look like the ones in the book as props.

RISKS

*   Homeless teens
*   Runaways
*   Teens smoke and drink alcohol
*   Substance abuse
*   Teen drug dealer
*   Homosexual characters
*   Sex and sexuality
*   Bullying
*   Obscenities
*   Homeless teens lie and steal to survive
*   Teens are prostitutes
*   Streetwise teens teach new runaways survival skills
*   Parent denies that daughter is the victim of incest
*   Teen makes porn films in exchange for drugs

STRENGTHS

*   Accurate, graphic view of teens' lives on the street
*   Multiple narrators make story complex, allowing reader to see situations from different perspectives
*   Gritty, dark tone
*   Realistic dialogue, including street slang
*   Author doesn't pull any punches
*   Plot line pulls reader into the story and doesn't let go
*   Characters teens can identify with
*   Unresolved ending allows for discussion and speculation about what happened to the main characters afterward

AWARD

ALA Quick Picks for Reluctant Young Adult Readers, 2008

REVIEWS
"Blank's book is gritty, graphic, and realistic. . . . It is a difficult but necessary book that will raise awareness of the issues surrounding homeless teens." Jenny Ingram, *VOYA*, 10/07

"Calculated emotionless presentation of the street-sex trade helps communicate the bleak circumstances in which many homeless youths find themselves. . . . The author's note offers resources for both at-risk and street teens. Examining the ties that bring people together and force them apart, this is a harsh and honest view of home-less teen life in the city of angels." *Kirkus Reviews*, 9/07

"Blank writes with gritty, urban poetry that reveals the heartbreaking fracturing of selves, from vulnerable child to hardened street kid, that allows the teens to survive. . . . The characters in this accomplished, disturbing debut find hope by speaking devastating se-crets aloud and feeling heard and believed." Gillian Engberg, *Booklist*, 11/07

📖📖📖

ALT ED. Catherine Atkins. Putnam, 2003. $17.99. 208p. ISBN10: 0399238549. ISBN13: 9780399238543. Puffin, 2004. $6.99. 208p. ISBN10: 0142402354. ISBN13: 9780142402351. Tandem Library, 2004. $15.80. 208p. ISBN10: 141765659X. ISBN13: 9781417656592. (library binding) Recorded Books, 2003. $51.75. ISBN10: 1419301772. ISBN13: 9781419301773. (unabridged audio CD) Recorded Books, 2003. $30.95. ISBN10: 1402559054. ISBN13: 9781402559051. (unabridged audiotape) Recorded Books, 2003. $41.75. ISBN10: 1402559046. ISBN13: 9781402559044. (unabridged audiotape, library version) Recorded Books, 2003. $51.75. ISBN13: 9781428185623. (unabridged audiobook) Realistic fiction. Reading Level: YHS. Interest Level: MS, YHS. English, Psychology, Ethics.

SUBJECT AREAS
bullying; interpersonal relationships; school; self-knowledge; psychology; therapy; homosexuality; persecution; friendship; death and dying; anger; revenge; animals; betrayal; problem parents; fear; family relationships; gossip; intimidation; love; peer pressure; stereotypes; abortion.

CHARACTERS
Susan Callaway: an overweight sophomore at Wayne High and the daughter of the varsity football coach

Kale Krasner: he torments Susan and others constantly

Jason Schrader: Kale's friend and fellow tormentor

Brendan Blater: school freak because he's gay; he is being boycotted by the entire sophomore class

Roy Duffy: the school counselor and one of the campus jokes

Tom Callaway: Susan's older brother who is one of the school jocks

Scott: Tom's best friend

Randy Callahan: a popular and handsome football jock who's in the Alt Ed group and the boy Susan has a crush on

Tracee Ellison: beautiful, popular, independent, and a Christian

Amber Hawkins: she's one of the school sluts; she's tall and tough

Coach Callaway: Susan and Tom's father, the varsity football coach and athletic director at Wayne High

Justin Wright: star quarterback and Tracee's boyfriend

BOOKTALK

It wasn't fair that I was getting punished. I hadn't done anything. Brendan did all the work—all I did was watch. I didn't care that he was trashing Kale Krasner's beloved truck. Kale had made my life miserable for years—mine and anyone else's who was different. Brendan was one of his victims. If I could have gotten back at Kale, I would have. But as the fat daughter of the varsity football coach, there wasn't much I could do except try to ignore him. And then Mr. Duffy made that impossible. Six of us ended up in his Alt Ed program, forced to sit and talk for an hour after school every Wednesday. It was either that or we'd be expelled. Not a hard choice.

I knew why Brendan and I were there, and there were endless reasons why Kale might be, but the other three were more of a mystery. Randy Callahan was a football jock, drop dead gorgeous, and popular. I'd had a crush on him for years. Tracee El-lison was the prettiest girl in school, a cheerleader, and someone everyone wanted to be friends with. She was dating the star quarterback Justin Wright. Amber Hawkins was tall, tough, and everyone said she was a slut. And we were going to get to know each other and share our secrets? I don't *think* so. No way was I talking about myself, or my family or even what went on at school. All that would do was give Kale even more stuff to torture me with.

But Susan does start to talk and so do the others. Maybe they have more in common than they thought they did, and maybe Mr. Duffy isn't the school joke they all thought he was.

MAJOR THEMES AND IDEAS

- Recognizing someone in the hall at school means you know their face but not who they are inside.
- Bullying someone always makes you look bad.
- Ignoring a bully puts you on his side.
- Homosexuality isn't a choice, isn't a lifestyle. It's a biological fact.

- Those who are bullies actually show their weakness, not their strength.
- Sometimes being invisible is a blessing.
- "No justice, no peace." — Malcolm X
- There are always bullies, no matter where you go or how old you are. You just have to learn to deal with them.
- We all want to feel safe and move toward that which is least threatening.
- People are innately territorial.
- The best defense is a good offense.
- People can be cruel, and sometimes it's the ones with the most to hide who attack the most viciously.
- Bullies get satisfaction from others' pain.
- Bullies put down others to build up themselves.
- Words hurt just as much as actions, and sometimes more.
- Sometimes it's important to do what's right for you, even if you will be harassed about it.
- Gays come in all shapes and sizes—including jocks.
- People are responsible for their own mistakes.
- Sometimes bravery isn't enough.
- When you have been fooling yourself, hearing the truth can be very painful.
- When bullies are confronted about their actions, they usually run away. They pick on the weak, not the strong or the assertive.
- You can't know why people do what they do or how they think and feel on the inside. But most of the time, if they are honest with themselves, they know.
- Therapy can be effective and help you change, if you want it to.
- Being gay isn't right or wrong. It's just part of who a person is.
- A friend doesn't judge you, but tries to understand you.
- Take responsibility for your actions. No one ever *makes* anyone do anything.
- No one's perfect. Try to give others the same understanding you want for yourself.
- It hurts when you can't fight back. After a while, all you can do is hate and hate and hate.

BOOK REPORT IDEAS

1. Discuss why Kale has tormented Susan for so many years.
2. Is bullying something that is more or less innate in humans?
3. Discuss your opinion of Tracee's comments about Susan's appearance, and April's reaction to them. How genuine do you think Tracee was?
4. Susan says Shelly, the fat cheerleader, is a "mascot." Explain what that means and how frequently cliques of girls have one.
5. Tracee says she disapproves of gays and wants to heal them so they don't sin any longer. How is her perspective similar to and different from Kale's opinions of gays?
6. Explain why Kale likes to be hated. What does he get out of it?

7. Susan's father doesn't talk to her about anything. Explain what you think this means. How does he feel about his daughter?
8. Susan's father seems oblivious to the way she's treated at school, especially by his jocks. How realistic is that? How aware are faculty of what's going on with individuals in the student body?
9. Discuss why members of Mr. Duffy's group attack each other.
10. Compare each of the group members and how they changed from the first til the last session.

BOOKTALK IDEAS
1. Have each person in Mr. Duffy's group introduce themselves and say something about themselves.
2. Focus your talk on the idea of bullying and why some kids are targeted.
3. Have Susan introduce the group members as she sees them at their first session.

RISKS
- Vulnerable teens are bullied and persecuted
- Homosexual character
- Vandalism
- Homophobic characters
- Father is unable to accept his children for who and what they are
- Frank discussions of sex and homosexuality
- Parent ignores and marginalizes his children
- Teens are violent physically
- Girl brags about beating up on other girls
- Teens verbally attack each other in cruel and vicious ways
- Teens are sexually promiscuous
- Boys have sex with drunk girl after she passes out
- Brother ignores his friends' bullying and harassing his sister

STRENGTHS
- Two persecuted teens become friends and grow stronger
- Teens learn to trust each other
- Teens grow and gain insight
- Characters, although somewhat stereotypical, can provide behavioral examples for readers

AWARD
ALA Popular Paperbacks, 2005

REVIEWS

"Skilled writing, on-target dialogue, and sharply drawn characters bring this thought-provoking story to life." Diane Tuccillo, *VOYA*, 4/03

"Carefully nuanced connections between characters plus insight into the adolescent ability to use low self-esteem as a cruel weapon catapults this novel of troubled teens well above the familiarity of its trappings." *Publishers Weekly*, 9/04

"The characters . . . come to life in new and interesting ways, and Susan's story is strong, because she is reinventing family relationships as well as trying to communicate with her peers. . . . Kids will be drawn to this novel about teens they'll recognize, sometimes too well." Ilene Cooper, *Booklist*, 1/03

"Atkins. . . offers an anxious and tender story, excellently written on a theme of peer acceptance. . . . A complex and stellar work." *Kirkus Reviews*, 4/03

📖📖📖

AMERICA. E. R. Frank. Atheneum, an imprint of Simon and Schuster, 2002. $18.00. 224p. ISBN10: 0689847297. ISBN13: 9780689847295. Simon Pulse, 2003. $7.99. 256p. ISBN10: 0689857721. ISBN13: 9780689857720. Thorndike Press, 2004. $21.95. 288p. ISBN10: 0786264845. ISBN13: 9780786264841. (large print) Tandem Library, 2003. $16.95. 224p. ISBN10: 0613664760. ISBN13: 9780613664769. (library binding) Recorded Books, 2003. $36.95. ISBN10: 1402528906. ISBN13: 9781402528903. (unabridged audiotape) Recorded Books, 2003. $51.75. ISBN10: 1402528892. ISBN13: 9781402528897. (unabridged audiotape, library version) Realistic fiction. Reading Level: MS, YHS. Interest Level: MS, YHS, OHS. Comunication, English, Ethics, Psychology, Sociology.

SUBJECT AREAS

abuse, sexual; adoption; anger; bullying; child abuse; cooking; crime and delinquency; cultural identity; death and dying; dysfunctional families; elderly; ethnic groups; family relationships; fear; friendship; grief and mourning; homelessness; foster care; love; lying and deceit; manipulation; poverty; problem parents; runaways; secrets; self-knowledge; sex and sexuality; substance abuse; suicide; survival; therapy; working.

CHARACTERS

America: he fell through the system when he was about five and at fifteen ended up in residential treatment after he tried to kill himself

Mrs. Harper: she tried to adopt America and was a stabilizing force in his life
Browning: Mrs. Harper's half-brother
Lyle and Brooklyn: America's older brothers
Clark Poignant: Mrs. Harper's close friend
Dr. B: America's therapist who is determined not to give up on him
Liza: she's in America's class at school
Tom: their counselor
Mrs. Patterson, April: therapists at Applegate
Ben, Kevin: they live at the group home with America
Phillip: social worker at the group home

BOOKTALK

His mother threw him away when he was two days old. His first family threw him away two months later. When he was six, his mother wanted him back, but then promptly threw away him and his seven- and eight-year-old brothers. When he was nine, his guardian's brother, who'd taught him about baseball and cooking, also began to teach him to drink and sexually molested him. When he was about twelve, he finally fought back, set fire to his molester's blanket while he was asleep, and threw himself away. At fifteen, he tried to kill himself and ended up in a residential treatment center, where he found the one person who wouldn't throw him away.

America is a boy who's been a lot of places. He's a boy who can get lost too easily and isn't worth the trouble of finding. America is a thief and a murderer who didn't learn to read right til he was almost ten years old. America's been told he's bad and broken and ruined so often, he's decided to believe it.

But now he's met a man, Dr. B, who's decided to change America's mind. Can a fifteen-year-old boy who's been rejected since he was only two days old, who has had to survive mostly on his own, who has never been taught to believe in himself, ever recover, mend, and grow up whole and healed?

MAJOR THEMES AND IDEAS
- In a depressing and chaotic life, one positive connection can overcome many bad ones.
- When you are on your own, you'll do what's necessary to survive.
- Adults sometimes manipulate children in their care to fulfill their own selfish needs.
- Consistent rejection can convince anyone of their own worthlessness.
- It is possible to turn your life around from negative to positive, but it is also difficult and time-consuming.
- Family connections are important and should be maintained.
- A child who has been sexually molested will grow up confused about sex and sexuality and needs the help of a competent and caring therapist to recover.

- As individuals begin to heal the broken parts of their mind and soul, they grow stronger and happier and are more willing to let others get close to them.
- One caring, supportive adult can help a child have enough strength and resilience to overcome horrifying circumstances.
- While a therapist can help you redefine yourself, you still have to do a lot of work as well.
- It's not okay for adults to break the rules.

BOOK REPORT IDEAS

1. Discuss how the relationship between Dr. B and America changed over the years.
2. America was thrown away over and over again. Explain how that rejection made him feel and act.
3. Dr. B wasn't a perfect therapist. What are some of the things he did right with America and some of the things he did wrong?
4. Speculate on what will happen to America in the future. Where do you think he will be in five or ten years, and what will he be doing?
5. Which relationships helped America cope with the chaos of his life and how would his life have been different without those people in it?
6. What was the most important part of the book for you? Why?
7. Discuss why shoelaces are so important to America. What do they represent?
8. What were some of the turning points in America's therapy, times when he learned something important or made major decisions?
9. The book is written in alternating chapters between Then and Now. Why do you think the author used this style and how does it affect your understanding of America and his life?

BOOKTALK IDEAS

1. Write your talk as if it were a part of a therapy session between America and Dr. B.
2. Let America tell his own story, in first person.
3. Focus your talk on the loss and rejection America feels.

RISKS

- Sexual abuse of a child by a person he trusted
- Negative portrayal of the social service system
- Children are abandoned by their parents
- Crime and delinquency
- Children smoke, drink, curse
- Destruction of property by minors
- Child deliberately sets fire that kills someone
- Manipulative, evil adult characters

STRENGTHS

- Writing style draws reader into the wrenching story
- Characters evolve and grow
- Main character survives and overcomes incredible adversity
- Realistic portrayal of a long-term therapeutic relationship
- Chilling and realistic portrayal of a manipulative sexual predator
- Shows and explains that sexual abuse is not the fault of the child
- Shows that the effects of sexual abuse can be overcome
- Characters are realistic, not stereotypical
- Demonstrates the healing power of love and respect
- Realistic dialogue
- Writing style gives clear portrait of the main character's childhood in contrast to his current situation

AWARDS

ALA Best Books for Young Adults, 2003
ALA Quick Picks for Reluctant Young Adult Readers, 2003
ALA Popular Paperbacks, 2005

REVIEWS

"The story is not only about America's past but also about his attempts to salvage his future. . . . The whole of America's story is a powerful one." James Blasingame, *VOYA*, 2/02

"A powerful story of forgiveness both of oneself and of others." *Publishers Weekly*, 1/02

"[Frank] creates an extraordinary character in America who, with the help of his doctor, confronts the deepest betrayals and, finally, lets himself be found. A piercing, unforgettable novel." Gillian Engberg, *Booklist*, 2/02

📖📖📖

A BAD BOY CAN BE GOOD FOR A GIRL. Tanya Lee Stone. Random House, 2006. $14.95. 228p. ISBN10: 0385747020. ISBN13: 9780385747028. Wendy Lamb, 2007. $7.99. 240p. ISBN10: 0553495097. ISBN13: 9780553495096. Wendy Lamb, 2006. $16.99. 240p. ISBN10: 0385909462. ISBN13: 9780385909464. (library binding) Verse novel. Reading Level: MS. Interest Level: MS, YHS. English, Creative Writing, Psychology, Sex Education.

SUBJECT AREAS

dating and social life; friendship; school; manipulation; anger; gossip; lying and deceit; love; self-knowledge; sex and sexuality; secrets; rites of passage; revenge; peer pressure.

CHARACTERS

Josie: a self-confident freshman in high school who is fooled by *Him*
Kim and Caroline: Josie's best friends, also freshmen
Lindsay: a senior who's popular and throws great parties
Him/T.L.: a senior, he's the original bad boy out to nail every girl he can
Nicolette: a junior who's into control until she lets *Him* control her
Aviva: a senior, she falls hard for *Him* and his lies
Amanda: a friend of Aviva, who warns her about dropping her girlfriend when a hot
   guy shows up
Kristen: one of the popular girls; she acts like she wants to help Aviva

BOOKTALK

Josie was the one who started it—outing him for the first time in the warning she put in the back pages of the school library's copy of *Forever*. She was a freshman who couldn't believe a senior and a jock would want to date *her*. Soon, *He* was all she thought of. And after promising her friends they'd stick together, she didn't hesitate to leave them in the dust to be with *Him*.

Nicolette likes guys and she likes to be in control. She decides who and where and when, and *she* has the power. She likes being with a boy, the way he smells and feels and tells her he wants her so bad. When she heard about the scene Josie had with *Him*, she decided to check him out, even though Josie told her to take a look at the copy of *Forever* in the library. But *He* didn't give her a chance to grab the power—he was the one who decided when and what in their relationship, and before she was sure what had happened, Nicolette was in over her head.

Arriva was a Criss-Crosser, someone who wasn't part of any clique but sort of floated among them, accepted but not a member. She was surprised when *He* noticed her and asked her out. Soon she was hanging with the A-list kids and going to all the best parties with *Him*. And then suddenly, it was over. *He* said she got too serious, too fast. He was gone.

That's when Aviva found out about *Forever* and what one girl after another has had to say about *Him*.

Love hurts sometimes, but that doesn't mean you can't learn from that pain. Sometimes, a bad boy can be good for a girl.

MAJOR THEMES AND IDEAS

- Falling in love makes you do things you normally never would consider doing.
- Boys can say one thing and mean another or tell lies to persuade you to do what they want.

- Leaving your girlfriends high and dry to run after a boy you're infatuated with is never a good idea.
- The best relationship is between two people who like each other for who they really are, deep inside.
- When you've loved and lost, it's important to remember how it felt, good things and bad things, and to take what you've learned into the future with you.
- No one has to let anyone else make them feel like nothing.
- "No one can make you feel inferior without your consent."—Eleanor Roosevelt
- No *always* means no.
- Don't wimp out about things that are important to you. Stay firm on what matters.
- No matter how well you know yourself, you can always be surprised, finding something new about yourself.
- Wisdom stings, but innocence is *not* wise.
- The one who cares least in a relationship has the most power.
- Parents aren't always your friends, but they can be.
- If someone says he likes you but still doesn't treat you with respect, he's lying.
- If he tells his friends about how far you've gone with him, you aren't really as special as he says you are.
- Everything happens for a reason.
- You can learn something from even the worst situations or experiences. Figuring out just what that lesson is can help ease the pain.
- When your best girlfriends warn you about a boy, listen to them. They're on your side, and they just may be right.

BOOK REPORT IDEAS

1. Compare this book with *Forever*. How are they alike and how are they different?
2. Discuss what each of the three main characters learned during their relationship with T. L.
3. How do you think T. L.'s life will be affected by what girls wrote about him? Do you think he'll ever change?
4. Analyze the comments in the front and back of the book that were added to *Forever*. How do you think the girls who wrote them were affected or changed by what they wrote?
5. Discuss the questions Nicolette asks herself at the end of her section: "Am I a whore because I like sex? Or because I did it too soon? Or too much? Nobody ever calls boys whores. Why is that?"
6. Do you think the three main characters will see the next bad boy they run into for the user he is, or will they be fooled again?
7. Discuss what you think is the most important scene or idea in the book, and explain why you chose it.

BOOKTALK IDEAS
1. Use a copy of *Forever* as a prop.
2. Use the handwritten pages in the back of the book as a prop.
3. Use some of the comments from *Forever* as part of your talk.
4. Write your talk from one of the three main points of view and have her introduce the other characters.
5. Write your talk in first person, from all three points of view.

RISKS
- Boy deliberately manipulates girls sexually
- Teen nudity and petting
- Teens are sexually active
- Teens enjoy sex
- Boy gossips about the girls he's "nailed"
- Boy shows no regret or shame for the way he uses girls

STRENGTHS
- While some teens are sexually active, others are not
- Supportive, positive parents
- Three points of view show characters from different perspectives
- Tackles a subject not often written about
- Very quick read
- Blank verse format makes emotions feel more real
- Girls gain wisdom and insight from their relationship with a "bad boy"
- Girls reach out to help each other get over a broken relationship
- Realistic characters readers can identify with
- Realistic language
- Ending doesn't tie up all the threads, allowing the reader to speculate
- Genuine voices of teens
- Vividly shows how many girls can be fooled by a loser
- Excellent use of "graffiti" pages at beginning and end of book

AWARDS
ALA Quick Picks for Reluctant Young Adult Readers, 2007
New York Public Library Books for the Teen Age, Winner, 2007

REVIEWS
"Written in three distinct voices of poetry prose, Stone's intimate and honest work accurately depicts both the agony and ecstasy of teenage relationships from the inside out. . . . Each [girl] learns difficult lessons from their bad-boy experience and come

out stronger, proving that a bad boy, in some cases, can be good for a girl." Michele Winship, *VOYA*, 4/06

"The free verse gives the stories a breathless, natural flow and changes tone with each narrator. The language is realistic and frank, and, while not graphic, it is filled with descriptions of the teens and their sexuality." Susan Oliver, Tampa-Hillsborough Public Library System, FL, *School Library Journal*, 1/06

"Stone's novel in verse, more poetic prose than poetry, packs a steamy, emotional wallop. . . . The lessons learned here . . . are important." Cindy Dobrez, *Booklist*, 1/06

ᨏᨏᨏ

BALL DON'T LIE.   Matt de la Pena. Delacorte, 2005. $16.95. 288p. ISBN10: 0385732325. ISBN13: 9780385732321. Delacorte, 2007. $7.99. 288p. ISBN10: 0385734255. ISBN13: 9780385734257. Delacorte, 2005. $18.99. 288p. ISBN10: 0385902581. ISBN13: 9780385902588. (library binding) Realistic fiction. Reading Level: YHS. Interest Level: YHS, OHS. English, P.E., Psychology.

SUBJECT AREAS
sports; self-knowledge; crime and delinquency; suicide; friendship; mentoring; sexual abuse; physical abuse; foster care; legal system; dysfunctional family; love; sex and sexuality; anger; drugs; ethnic groups; homelessness; lying and deceit; obsession; poverty; rites of passage; secrets; substance abuse; school.

CHARACTERS
Travis Reichard/Sticky: he's a white seventeen-year-old foster kid who loves to play basketball
Dreadlock Man: he's a regular on the court at the Lincoln Rec Center
Hawk: a big black man who looks and acts like he might be somebody
Dante: the best basketball player at Lincoln Rec; he played pro overseas for six to seven years
Jimmy: he manages the Rec, the best place in LA to play ball
Ol' Man Perkins, Johnson, Rob, New York, Big Mac, Dollar Bill, Dallas, Trey, Slim: they're also ballers at the Rec
Anh-Thu: Sticky's sixteen-year-old girlfriend
Crazy Ray: a homeless man who sleeps on the homeless side of the Rec and used to play ball

Baby: Sticky's mother, who named him Travis
Laura: a friend of Anh-Thu's who works with her at Miller's
Georgia: Sticky's foster mom
Coach Wilkins, Coach Reynolds: Sticky's high school basketball coaches
Counselor Julius: Sticky used to beat him at foosball at the foster care center
Maria: Sticky's friend, who's also in the foster care system
Carols: a short Mexican homeless who likes to watch the ball games
Fat Chuck: he shows up almost every day to watch but never plays
Mico: he lived with Sticky and his mother for awhile when Sticky was six
Francine: Sticky's first foster mom, when he was nine
Reggie, Fat Jay, Sinclair, Dave: members of the high school basketball team
Manuel: the gym custodian who lets Sticky practice at night after the gym's closed
Carmen: Sticky's second foster mother, when he was twelve
Counselor Amy: she was one of the counselors who worked at the foster care center
Ruben: Carmen's husband
Mr. and Mrs. Smith: they were Sticky's third foster parents, when he was fourteen
Tammie, Jamie, and Johnny Smith: the three Smith children
Milo: he runs a liquor store in Venice and doesn't ask for ID
Wong and Rolando: two of Sticky's foster brothers
Julie: Sticky's foster sister

BOOKTALK

Sticky is a three-time loser. He's seventeen and he's been in four foster homes since he was seven. He's tall and skinny, and all he's ever wanted is to play pro basketball. That's why he's at the Lincoln Rec Center every Saturday and Sunday, and every day during the summer. It's the best place in LA to play ball.

It was hard to get a game at first. Not only was he a kid, he was white, in a gym where every other face was black. And the men who played there were just that—men. But Sticky was good, better than some of them, and soon he was playing more and more. Even the high school coaches noticed him, and he ended up on the JV team.

But even though basketball was all he ever wanted to do, today was special. It was his girlfriend's sixteenth birthday and he knew just what he wanted to give her. There was a stuffed bear she really wanted, and to go with it, he was going to lift a slinky gold bracelet at Macy's.

Shoplifting was just as much a part of Sticky's life as ball was. It was how he got his clothes, his shoes. His foster parents hadn't really been willing to bug him much, and while he knew stealing from a person was wrong, stealing from a store where they'd never miss it didn't seem like a big deal. But wearing a couple of extra pairs of pants out of the dressing room, or trying on some shoes and walking around the store to see how they fit, were way different from walking out the door with an expensive gold bracelet. He couldn't take it away from the counter without paying for it, and it didn't require a fitting room. Was this the time he wouldn't be able to pull it off?

MAJOR THEMES AND IDEAS

- Bring your A-game. If you're gonna run with the big dogs, you can't pee like a puppy.
- Stealing from an individual is wrong, but stealing from a big store is no big problem.
- Obsessive-compulsive behavior isn't something you can decide to stop doing. You are under its control, and not vice versa.
- It's not the game, it's the win. It's all about beating someone.
- A basketball gym is a whole different world, with its own rules and customs, and the guys who come to play or watch come for a whole variety of reasons.
- Each of us has a destiny, a reason we're alive.
- You can think yourself out of the game.
- There's no time for reflection when you have to react to the situation.
- Keep your mind clear and your eye on the ball.
- Stealing is a risky business. Sooner or later, you'll get caught.
- In urban areas, there are day people and there are night people. Sunlight fades, and the whole face of the city changes.
- Why worry about something that's completely out of your control? You can't change anything.
- Cops are just normal people dressed up.
- Anything can be addictive—even basketball.
- If you're poor, and a foster kid who's a five-time loser, and all you have is ball, it's not likely you will make it big in the NBA or anywhere else.
- Laws are by the rich, not the poor, to protect the rich, not the poor.
- This is *not* a righteous world.
- You have to live with your bad decisions. You can't go back and take a different path.
- Sometimes everything you're holding inside just gets too big and has to come out, one way or another.
- Sometimes crying does help, it helps wash away the emotions so you can see more clearly what's left behind.
- Look around you; you may not be as alone as you feel you are.
- Family isn't about the color of your skin, but the ties that connect your lives.
- Stand up for yourself. If you don't respect yourself, no one else will respect you.

BOOK REPORT IDEAS

1. Compare Sticky's four foster homes, and explain how he both was and wasn't the reason why the first three failed, and how the fourth was different.
2. What do the regulars at Lincoln Rec get out of the weekly games?
3. Trace how Sticky gained the respect of the other regulars. What kind of a relationship did these men have with Sticky?
4. Discuss Sticky's ethics about shoplifting.

5. Explain why you think Anh-Thu put up with Sticky's stealing and didn't try to stop him.
6. What does Sticky mean when he says, "There's spirituality here. On this court. With these guys. Holding this ball."
7. While we know what happens to Sticky after he gets out of the hospital, we don't know about Anh-Thu, whether or not she was pregnant, and if she was, what she decided to do about it. Speculate on what you think has happened in the three months since the shooting.
8. List four turning points in Sticky's life, and explain why they were important and what they meant.
9. Speculate on what Sticky will be like in the future. In five years? In ten?
10. What was the one thing in Sticky's life that was most important in helping him change? Explain its importance.

BOOKTALK IDEAS
1. Use a ball like Sticky's as a prop.
2. Write your talk in first person as Sticky.
3. Have some of the Rec center regulars describe Sticky and how he plays ball.

RISKS
- Uses street language
- Characters steal and shoplift casually
- Mother makes her son panhandle for food
- Child abuse—burned with cigarette
- Neglectful and drug-abusing mother
- Alcoholic, homeless characters
- Prostitution
- Sexual abuse and molestation
- Teens drink alcohol and smoke
- Vandalism
- Teens are sexually active without birth control
- Teen gets pregnant
- Foster parents reject boy over and over

STRENGTHS
- Realistic language, including basketball slang
- Non-sequential plot/timeline, shows glimpses of the past to explain the present
- Details about main character are revealed slowly
- Accurate and graphic portrayal of several minorities
- Precise descriptions of basketball games and plays show characters' passion for the game
- Realistic characters with realistic voices come alive

- Unique characters infrequently seen in YA literature
- Unresolved ending leaves room for speculation and discussion
- Basketball players are mentors to teen—positive male/male friendship and bonding

AWARDS
ALA Popular Paperbacks, 2008
ALA Best Books for Young Adults, 2006
ALA Quick Picks for Reluctant Young Adult Readers, 2006

REVIEWS
"Marked by inner-city slang and profanity, the dialogue and pacing of the story has a hip-hop rhythm much like change-of-pace moves performed on city basketball courts. Stunningly realistic, this book will hook older readers, especially urban teen males, and they will share it with friends." Rollie Welch, *VOYA*, 10/05

"Jumping back and forth in time, this first novel has a unique narrative voice that mixes street lingo, basketball jargon, and trash talk to tell Sticky's sorry saga from a variety of viewpoints. . . . Sticky is a true original, and de la Pena has skillfully brought him to life." Jack Forman, Mesa College Library, San Diego, *School Library Journal*, 11/05

"Teens will be strongly affected by the unforgettable, distinctly male voice; the thrilling, unusually detailed basketball action; and the questions about race, love, self-worth, and what it means to build a life without advantages." Gillian Engberg, *Booklist*, 11/05

📖📖📖

BETWEEN MOM AND JO. Julie Ann Peters. Little, Brown Young Readers, 2006. $16.99. 240p. ISBN10: 0316739065. ISBN13: 9780316739061. Little, Brown Young Readers, 2008. $7.99. 240p. ISBN10: 0316067105. ISBN13: 9780316067102. Realistic fiction. Reading Level: MS. Interest Level: MS, YHS. English, Sex Education, Sociology, Psychology.

SUBJECT AREAS
homosexuality; family relationships; problem parents; divorce and separation; love; anger; manipulation; betrayal; rites of passage; self-knowledge; fear; animals; school; bullying; cooking; depression; ethics; substance abuse; sex and sexuality; secrets; prejudice.

CHARACTERS
Jo: she and Nick's mom have been partners for years, but they are starting to have problems
Nick Tyler: he's fourteen and has always had two moms, and likes it that way
Neenee and Poppa: Mom's parents, who don't like Jo
Mom/Erin Tyler: Nick's mother
Uncle Derrick and Aunt Lizzie: missing
Matthew: one of Nick's kindergarten classmates
Mr. Hasselback: Nick and Matthew's kindergarten teacher
Mrs. Ivey: Nick's third grade teacher
Ms. Gault: the elementary school principal
Jessica: Nick's neighbor who babysits him occasionally
Kerri: she teaches cooking classes
Reiko: Kerri's partner; they are both Erin's friends from college
Takashi/Taco: Kerri and Reiko's son
Sasha McLaren: she's in Josh's class at his new school in the city
Mrs. Mendoza: Nick's high school vice principal

BOOKTALK
It's always been the three of us, Mom, Jo, and me. They told me it would always be that way. I believed them. Oh, they'd fight sometimes, but they always made up. Kids gave me a hard time about having two moms, but it wasn't anything I couldn't handle. We were together. We were a family. We were forever. And then, suddenly, we weren't. I didn't have two moms—I didn't have anyone.

How do you choose which parent you want to be with? You don't want either/or, you want both. But it isn't up to you.

MAJOR THEMES AND IDEAS
- Some things you carry with you forever. Some things leave permanent scars, on the inside and the outside.
- Words do hurt you. They hurt on the inside, where you can't see it. And they keep on hurting, because the words keep cutting and reopening the wound.
- What you see on the outside of a person doesn't always reflect what's on the inside.
- Even if a married couple fights, it doesn't mean they don't still love each other.
- Sometimes it seems like forever is a myth, and nothing goes on forever.
- It's hard to know how to respond to a homophobe. Should you just avoid them, or stand and fight for yourself and your rights?
- Some people don't have to learn to hate—it just comes naturally to them.
- People make fun of what they don't understand.
- Some things are too painful to be forgiven or forgotten.
- Kids don't have to be stupid like their parents.

- No one can tell you what to believe in. As long as you know in your heart that something is true, it is. For you.
- Until you're old enough to see your parents as they really are, you can't trust a word they tell you.
- "A Defining Moment"—the memory that stays fresh in your mind and marks a turning point. Sometimes you know it as it happens, other times you realize it only as you look back at it later.
- People handle pain and fear differently, sometimes in ways that can be incomprehensible to others.
- If you are wondering if you're gay, you probably aren't. If you were gay, you'd know.
- Sex without love is wrong.
- If you have love in your life, you have everything.
- If you love someone enough to have sex with them, respect them, cherish them, and marry them first.
- It's only in retrospect that you really appreciate the best times you ever had.
- You can tell when someone you love is in pain, even if you don't know what caused it.
- You're never prepared for death. You have to make every day of your life count.

BOOK REPORT IDEAS

1. Nick's scrapbook is a unifying theme in the book. Discuss what he put in it and why each item was significant.
2. Trace the dissolution of Erin and Jo's marriage. What held them together, and what pulled them apart?
3. Discuss how alcoholism runs through families and how Jo's parents impacted her own life.
4. Explain why Nick felt like Jo was "his *real* mom." How did his relationship with her differ from his relationship with Erin?
5. How is Nick's situation both different and the same from any child whose heterosexual parents get divorced?
6. Jo's departure was a total shock to Nick. What are some of the warning signs he missed?
7. Homosexuality is presented as a biological fact rather than something someone can choose or not. Explain how you agree or disagree with this idea.
8. The family's pets are very important to them. Explain the roles that each had: the dogs, the cat, the fish.
9. Speculate on what happened after the book ended. What will Nick's life be like, and what roles will Jo, Erin, and Kerri play in it?
10. Discuss why Erin kept Nick away from Jo. What kind of emotions and facts contributed to that decision?

11. Why did Jo leave so abruptly, without telling Nick? What might have happened if she and Erin had talked to Nick together, ahead of time, before she left?
12. How did Erin's changes over the years create a rift between her and Jo?

BOOKTALK IDEAS
1. Focus your talk around the scrapbook entries and what they mean.
2. Focus on two scenes, one happy, one angry, and show how Nick felt as he watched his family fall apart.
3. Center your talk on the idea that even when families expect to be together forever, they aren't always.

RISKS
- Two lesbians have a child
- Very butch lesbian works construction—stereotypical characterization
- Realistic language with obscenities
- Homophobic characters
- Alcoholic parent
- Homosexual, lesbian characters
- Scenes of lesbian affection and love
- Homosexuality is presented as something that is biological and not a choice to be made
- Parents ignore child's pain and cries for help

STRENGTHS
- Married couple fights and makes up
- Depicts homosexuality as normal
- Shows the problems a child with homosexual parents will face
- Conveys the narrator's wisdom gained from reexamining his life
- Powerful family bonds
- Love outlasts divorce
- Realistic portrait of how a strong relationship is slowly eroded
- Narrator's perceptions and beliefs change as he grows, matures, and gains insight
- First person/flashback style makes narrator's experiences and emotions very real and graphic to reader
- Characters love each other and are willing to make sacrifices for each other

AWARDS
Lambda Literary Award Winner, 2006
ALA Rainbow Reads, 2006

REVIEWS

"Peters again works her writing magic in this perfectly structured and exquisitely written novel. . . . Because of this family makeup, many librarians will self-censor the book. . . . But the novel needs to be read. Doing so takes one step toward helping this kind of family feel less invisible; doing so represents one step closer to recognizing and supporting their very real existence." C. J. Bott, *VOYA*, 2/06

"This novel is a timely exploration of the struggles faced by same-sex couples and their children, and while the issues are significant, the story is never overwhelmed by them. . . . This coming-of-age novel powerfully portrays the universal pain of a family breakup. It also portrays what is still a 'weird' situation to many people (as reflected in the behavior of Nick's babysitter) as totally normal from one young man's point of view." Beth Gallego, Los Angeles Public Library, North Hollywood, *School Library Journal*, 4/06

"An unromanticized look at divorce and parent-child relationships, as well as an addition to the tiny canon about gay parents." *Kirkus Reviews*, 4/06

ꙮ ꙮ ꙮ

BIG MOUTH & UGLY GIRL. Joyce Carol Oates. Hardback is OOP. HarperTeen, 2003. $8.99. 288p. ISBN10: 0064473473. ISBN13: 9780064473477. HarperCollins, 2002. $25.00. ISBN10: 0060089695. ISBN13: 9780060089696. (unabridged audiotape) Topeka, 2003. $16.45. 272p. ISBN10: 0613627253. ISBN13: 9780613627252. (library binding) Realistic fiction. Reading Level: MS. Interest Level: MS, YHS. English, Psychology, Sociology, Creative Writing, Government.

SUBJECT AREAS

school; peer pressure; friendship; justice; legal system; writing; self-knowledge; gossip; sports; censorship; legal system; betrayal; revenge; depression; animals; anger; fear; secrets; art; ethics; family relationships; self-destruction; problem parents; lying and deceit; guilt; suicide; therapy.

CHARACTERS

Matt Donaghy: he's always been a bigmouth, and now it's gotten him into major trouble

Russ Mercer, Skeet/Frank Curlew: Matt's friends who are working with him on a Drama Club project

Stacy Flynn: pretty, popular, and smart, she's also working on Matt's Drama Club project

Mr. Weinberg: he teaches English and sponsors the Drama Club

Ursula Riggs: she calls herself Ugly Girl; she's tall, has extreme moods, and is one of the best athletes in school

Ms. Schultz: she's the girls' gym teacher

Lisa Riggs: Ursula's younger sister, who's into ballet

Mrs. Riggs/Mom: Ursula's mother, who wishes her daughter was more girly

Mrs. Hall: school guidance counselor

Ms. Zwilich: she teaches biology and is one of Ursula's favorite teachers

Bonnie LeMayne: a basketball player who's sort of one of Ursula's friends

Clayton Riggs/Dad: CEO of an international company; he seldom misses Lisa's ballets and seldom attends Ursula's games

Mr. Harold Parrish: the high school principal

Trevor Cassity: a senior football player who's popular and aggressive

Mr. Rainey: the school psychologist

Mrs. Donaghy/Mom: Matt's mother, who's worried that the accusations are true

Mr. Leacock: Matt's lawyer

Uncle Jax: he wanted to teach Matt how to shoot a rifle

Mr. Drewe: the boys' track coach

Mr. Jenkins: he teaches calculus

Alex Donaghy: Matt's younger brother

Mr. Donaghy/Dad: Matt's father, who questions his son carefully

Eveann McDawd: a friend of Ursula's who also heard what Matt said

Mrs. Carlisle: Ursula's homeroom teacher

Mr. Steiner: faculty advisor of the school paper

Mr. Bernhardt: the junior class advisor

Murial and Miriam Brewer: mean senior twins who harassed Ursula because she defended Matt

Courtney Lavas: a senior on the girls' basketball team

Dr. Harpie: renowned Park Avenue psychiatrist who Matt's parents take him to

BOOKTALK

It was an ordinary January afternoon, a Thursday, when they came for Matt Donaghy. He was in Mr. Weinberg's study hall, working on a Drama Club project with three friends, when two unsmiling police detectives took him out of class and into the principal's office, and told him he'd been heard threatening to bomb the school and kill hundreds of people.

"We take bomb threats very seriously. What are you planning to do? Who are your co-conspirators? We have witnesses of your threats."

But Matt wasn't guilty of anything, and he told them so, over and over. They recorded what he said, they asked him the same questions, and they didn't notify his parents until he got to the police station.

Ugly Girl had been in a girls' basketball game when Matt left school, but she heard about it as soon as she left the gym. "He brought a bomb to school." "He said he wanted to kill hundreds of people." "He brought a gun to school." "A machine gun!" "He was pissed about something he wrote getting turned down by the school paper." The longer the gossip went on, the wilder it became. Suddenly, Ugly Girl couldn't keep quiet. "That's ridiculous. That never happened. I was there and I know what happened."

Matt wasn't guilty of anything other than acting juvenile and being a Big Mouth. But Ursula Riggs was the only person who believed that and the only person who was willing to say so. She'd been there. She knew the truth.

But even though Matt was exonerated, the taint of "terrorist" still clung to him. The scenes in the study hall and the principal's office had changed Matt, and the town he'd grown up in, forever.

MAJOR THEMES AND IDEAS

- Once you know who you are, things that used to bother you when you were younger aren't so important any longer.
- Girls' sports get less respect than boys', even when the girls are better players.
- Boring facts don't involve you or your life. Crucial facts not only involve you, they frequently hurt.
- We live and relive the moments of our worst humiliations.
- People frequently pay attention to how we look on the outside, rather than who we are on the inside.
- Having a talent for making people laugh by acting dumb or juvenile can get you into trouble.
- A joke or a sarcastic remark can be taken very seriously by people who don't know you.
- Almost everyone wants other people to like them, to be their friend, and making people laugh, being a comic, is a good way to do that.
- If you're a stand-up comic with a microphone, everyone knows it's a joke. But what if there's just you, without a microphone—is it still a joke, or something that can seem very, very serious?
- Name-calling hurts, whether it's you talking to yourself or someone talking about you.
- Acting dumb or showing off doesn't mean you can't also be very serious about some things.
- Being in police custody, suspected or accused of a crime, can make people confused or act crazy, even if they're innocent and the accusations are based on a misunderstanding.
- When someone is falsely accused and you know the truth, it's important to tell it and to stand up for them.
- You can't take away the mistrust and suspicion people feel about you even though you have been declared innocent. People still see you through lenses tinged by the past, and suddenly you are all alone.

- When you are totally disgusted with your world, it's best to keep to yourself and not infect other people.
- Information, especially gossip, is slippery. It escapes easily and spreads quickly.
- A good offense is the best defense.
- Sometimes parents can't protect their children. Other times, they just won't.
- There are reasons for events, even if we don't know what they are. Life is purposeful.
- A hero can be a fool, but he's still a hero.
- Lawsuits aren't always just about money.
- Many times the easy way isn't the best way.
- The hard part of humanity is history, the record of what we've done to each other over the years.
- There's no point in dwelling on the past, replaying old tapes of hurt, humiliation, and pain.
- Hard times will show you who your friends are. They're the ones who stand by you, no matter what.

BOOK REPORT IDEAS

1. Did Mr. Parrish overreact to Matt's joke? If the Brewer twins had such a poor reputation, why did he call the police and let them question Matt without a parent present?
2. Was it appropriate for the police to investigate Matt so carefully, given his position and involvement in school?
3. Analyze the scenes when Matt was being questioned as if you were one of the policemen. Look at Matt's statements, reactions, and body language to predict his guilt or innocence.
4. Explain why Mr. Parrish paid attention to Ursula and Eveann's statements when he hadn't given equal attention to Matt's friends.
5. After Ursula spoke to Mr. Parrish and Matt was cleared, why did she avoid him?
6. Discuss the role of the parents of the other high schoolers and how they contributed to the situation. If the parents had not taken such an active role from the beginning, do you think things would have gone as far as they did?
7. Discuss the idea of mass hysteria and "groupthink" and the role they played in the novel. What could have been done to reduce their impact?
8. Discuss what Matt's life will be like in the future. How comfortable will he be with his old friends?
9. Were Matt's friends *really* friends? Why or why not? Should he forgive and forget, or not? What would you do if you were Matt?
10. Speculate about what Matt and Ursula will be like in the future. Five years? Ten years?

11. There are many descriptions of friendship in the book. Compare and discuss them, and decide which ones agree with your idea or definition of friendship.

BOOKTALK IDEAS

1. Have Big Mouth and Ugly Girl introduce themselves and the situation that involves them both.
2. Write your talk from either Ursula's or Matt's point of view.
3. Use the newspaper headlines in your talk, or write it as if it was a newspaper story. Remember that one newspaper recognized that the claims about Matt could be hysterical, and include both points of view.
4. Introduce Matt and the kind of person he was by interviewing several of his friends and what they think about the bomb scare.

RISKS

- Parents make little effort to understand or support thin, unattractive daughter while focusing on their beautiful one
- Includes obscenities
- Teen and his family are ostracized even after his innocence has been proven
- School authorities overreact to joke
- Teen's parents reject him because they are threatened by the town's attitude toward them
- Teens beat up on fellow student because his parents are suing the school
- Persecuted teen seriously considers suicide
- Right-wing religious extremists are portrayed negatively and are the source of all the conflict in the novel
- The author has written other adult novels that are considered controversial
- Parents blame teen for starting all this, rather than the real culprits, who got him into trouble
- Dog is kidnapped and terrorized for revenge

STRENGTHS

- Alternating perspectives gives the reader a more complete view of people and events
- Realistic dialogue
- Graphic depiction of how damaging self-hatred can be
- Girl is a gifted athlete
- Shows how quickly rumors can grow, spread, and become "facts"
- Provides many topics for discussion
- Shows how lonely and isolated teens can be
- Gives insight into how painful adolescence can be
- Teen steps outside her comfort zone to help suicidal acquaintance

- Characters grow, gain insight, and are able to step away from their negative self images and destructive thoughts

AWARDS
ALA Best Books for Young Adults, 2003
ALA Popular Paperbacks, 2005

REVIEWS
"Oates delivers some realistic perceptions of the unforgiving adolescent world." C. J. Bott, *VOYA*, 8/02

"Readers will relate to the pressures these two [characters] experience, both at school and from their parents, and be gratified by their ability to emerge the wiser." *Publishers Weekly*, 5/03

"Distinguished novelist Oates's first young adult novel is a thought-provoking, character-driven drama about the climate of hysteria created by school violence in America, and how two teenagers find the courage to fight it and to find themselves in the process." Michael Cart, *Booklist*, 5/02

"Oates has a good ear for the speech, the family relations, the e-mail messaging, the rumor mills, and the easy cruelties waiting just beneath the veneer of civility. Matt's character and especially the heroic Ursula's are depicted with a raw honesty. Readers will be propelled through these pages by an intense curiosity to learn how events will play out. Oates has written a fast-moving, timely, compelling story." Miriam Lang Budin, Chappaqua Public Library, NY, *School Library Journal*, 5/02

📖📖📖

BOOT CAMP. Todd Strasser. Simon and Schuster, 2007. $15.99. 256p. ISBN10: 141690848X. ISBN13: 9781416908487. Simon Pulse, 2008. $6.99. 256p. ISBN10: 1416959424. ISBN13: 9781416959427. Realistic fiction. Reading Level: MS. Interest Level: YHS, OHS. English, Ethics, Sociology, Psychology, Government.

SUBJECT AREAS
problem parents; family relationships; physical abuse; crime and criminals; sexual relations; friendship; self-knowledge; school; anger; survival; bullying; violence; torture; lying and deceit; secrets; revenge; peer pressure; fear; gangs; prison life; intimidation; manipulation.

CHARACTERS

Garrett Durrell: an exceptionally intelligent fifteen-year-old who quietly but deter-
minedly refuses to obey his parents
Harry and Rebecca: enforcers who kidnap Garrett and take him to Harmony Lake, a
teen boot camp
Mr. Z: the director of Lake Harmony
Joe: the "father" of Garrett's "family" of boys
Mr. Sparks: one of the staff members, who is more sympathetic than the others
Mr. Gold: a cruel staff member who reminds Garrett of a troll
Lizard Teeth Adam: one of the "family" and the leader of a group of bullies; he has it
in for Garrett from the first time he sees him
Sabrina: Garrett's math teacher who's eight years older than Garrett and who is hav-
ing an affair with him
Pauly: a pale, delicate boy who everyone picks on
Sarah: she's been at Lake Harmony for almost three years and is still defiant
Chubby Rachel: a member Garrett's therapy circle; she's quick to pick on the others
David, Zitface, and Unibrow Robert: bullies in Adam's gang
Ron and Jon: teen guards who ignore Adam and his gang and take turns beating Gar-
rett when he's in isolation
Stu: a Level Three inmate who works hard to obey the rules
Ted: the nurse at Harmony Lake, who looks like a hippie biker
Baby Faced Miles: one of Adam's gang members
Mr. and Mrs. Durrell: busy, wealthy people who are embarrassed and angry because
their son refuses to fit in

BOOKTALK

My name's Garrett, and I'm fifteen. I taught myself to read when I was about two and
a half. At four, I scored off the charts on the entrance exam for the city's top kindergarten. At six, I was figuring out square roots and adding radicals. For the first seven
years of my life, all I heard about was how brilliant I was. But when I was eight, I
forged a note from my mom, excusing me from gym for severe asthma. Sports were
dumb, and I wasn't good at them. I got away with it for almost six months. After I
got caught, I wasn't brilliant any more—I was too smart for my own good, which is
why I ended up at Harmony Lake seven years later.

I have to admit that if I'd tried harder to fit in, it would've made my life easier.
But school was boring, and if I could maintain a 3.8 GPA and max out the PSATs
going only two or three days a week, why not? I'm six foot four and have to shave
every day—no one ever thinks I'm fifteen, more like seventeen or eighteen, and no
one ever asked why I wasn't in school.

The final straw was when I started seeing Sabrina, the new math teacher who
was only eight years older than me, and a math geek who was into manga and
anime, just like I was. For the first time in my life, I had someone I really con-

nected with, who liked me just the way I was. We fit together in a way that was just *right*.

But when my folks found out about it, they freaked and said Sabrina had to go. No matter how rationally I explained things, no matter how logical my arguments were, all they could see was how embarrassing it would be if their high-society friends found out.

That's how I ended up at Lake Harmony, a boot camp for teens who won't obey their parents, who are out of control, and who need to be taught a lesson. My parents had signed a form that said the staff could use any form of physical torture or restraint they wanted to in order to make me the respectful and obedient son they wanted, to learn my lesson.

And I learned, all right. I learned just how much mental and physical abuse my mind and body could take before I broke. I learned which kids were snitches and which ones I could trust. I learned just how much it hurts to lie facedown on a bare concrete floor, 24/7, for weeks. But I didn't learn how to give in to bullies. I didn't learn how to get with the program. And finally, when three of us tried to escape, I didn't learn that sometimes good deeds don't go unpunished.

MAJOR THEMES AND IDEAS
- Parents are not always right.
- No good deed goes unpunished.
- The way to succeed is to go with the program.
- Power corrupts. Absolute power corrupts absolutely.
- Being extremely intelligent can be a hindrance to conformity.
- Consistent torture will break everyone, eventually.
- The weakest member of a group is the one most likely to attract a predator.
- Power doesn't always have to do with physical size, but with psychological power, anger, and intimidation.
- If you want something badly enough, no punishment is too painful, if it gets you closer to your goal.
- Brainwashing is about power and domination and fear.
- No one can take your power from you. You must give it up in order to lose it.
- Doing the opposite of what someone expects of you can be a way to regain power.
- Sometimes, showing logic and rationality will only irritate someone who is showing neither.
- Staying calm and in control is a form of power.
- Knowledge is a dangerous thing. It gives people ideas, and ideas give them power.
- The best traps, physical or mental, are the ones you don't notice til it's too late.
- Resisting oppression takes an unshakable core of inner strength.

- Bullies are usually all bluff without someone to back them up.
- Be true to yourself. Don't let anyone else tell you what's right or wrong for you.

BOOK REPORT IDEAS

1. What will Garrett's life be like after boot camp?
2. How has Garrett changed and what has he learned? Compare Garrett in the first chapter and in the last chapter of the book.
3. Discuss some of the other measures Garrett's parents might have used instead of boot camp.
4. Garrett's parents and the staff at Lake Harmony accused him of being disrespectful. Give examples of this and discuss whether or not you think they were correct. If he wasn't disrespectful, what emotion was he showing?
5. Was Garrett's boot camp experience successful? Why or why not?
6. Describe the differences and similarities among the camp staff and discuss why you think they chose to work at Lake Harmony.
7. If Garrett's case goes to trial, how do you think he, Sarah, and Pauly will react on the witness stand when confronted by their torturers?
8. Which is smarter, showing your uniqueness or fitting in?
9. Both inmates and staff participated in the abuse of weaker inmates. Which group was better at it and why?
10. Speculate on how you might react if you were in Garrett's place. How would you respond and how would that response change you?
11. Speculate on whether Garrett and Sabrina will meet again and what the relationship between them might be. Can they ever recapture what they had?
12. Are boot camps and the parents who keep them in business criminal or merely immoral?

BOOKTALK IDEAS

1. Write a talk from Pauly's point of view, showing how he realizes Garrett is the key to his and Sarah's escape plan.
2. Write a talk in first person from Garrett's point of view, showing how he ended up in a teen boot camp.
3. Introduce your talk with some statistics about actual teen boot camps.
4. Write your talk as if it was a news story on Garrett, but be careful not to give too much away.

RISKS

- Irresponsible and neglectful parents
- Teens are beaten and tortured
- Psychological abuse and manipulation

- Cruel and manipulative adults
- Even sympathetic adults don't support teens
- Adults are self-serving
- Teacher has affair with student
- Sexually active teens
- Adults manipulate teens into bullying each other verbally and physically
- Horrifying punishments

STRENGTHS

- Characters grow, change, and show insight
- Storyline draws in reader immediately
- Lead character's background revealed gradually
- Demonstrates the power of being true to yourself
- Shows power of friendship
- Exposes a phenomenon that needs to be made more public
- Realistic language
- Ambiguous ending allows reader to speculate on story's final resolution
- Characters show an inner core of strength that allows them to survive
- Realistic, three-dimensional characters teens will identify with
- Storyline retains some hope
- Stark writing style is suited to story

AWARDS

ALA Quick Picks for Reluctant Young Adult Readers, 2007
New York Public Library Books for the Teen Age, 2007

REVIEWS

"Strasser comes out swinging against teenager boot camps, citing in an afterword information about real-life camps in which teenagers are detained for faulty reasoning and mistreated until they turn eighteen. . . . Readers should be on Garrett's side, and indeed they will share his frustration as his letters home are scrutinized for signs that he is coming around to the camp's way of thinking, or when he must confront the questionable ethics and motivations of Joe and company in trying to beat him down." Matthew Weaver, *VOYA*, 12/07

"While most teens will undoubtedly identify with the protagonist's sense of being misunderstood by his parents, many will be outraged by the manipulation, torture, and hopelessness experienced by the residents at Lake Harmony. However, all of them will certainly find themselves engrossed in this fast-paced and revealing story about the hidden side of teenage incarceration." Lynn Rashid, Marriots Ridge High School, Marriotsville, MD, *School Library Journal*, 4/07

"Strasser paints his protagonist as heroic, sympathetic, and rational. . . , and when he is ultimately broken—bodily and spiritually—the tragedy is all the more profound. Strasser offers no easy answers, and nimbly navigates a host of moral gray areas." *Publishers Weekly*, 5/07

"Teens, especially boys, will be riveted by Garrett's appalling experiences and by his suspenseful escape, even if the ending might not be what they hope or expect. The novel is a real eye-opener, and the helplessness of teens incarcerated in these boot camps, as exemplified by Garrett, is truly shocking." Paula Rohrlick, *KLIATT*, 5/07

📖📖📖

BOTTLED UP. Jaye Murray. Puffin, 2004. $6.99. 224p. ISBN10: 0142402400. ISBN13: 9780142402405. Tandem Library, 2004. $15.80. 224p. ISBN10: 1417626895. ISBN13: 9781417626892. Realistic fiction. Reading Level: MS, YHS. Interest Level: YHS, OHS. English, Health, P.E., Psychology.

SUBJECT AREAS
drugs; addiction; problem parents; dysfunctional family; school; therapy; family relationships; love; anger; violence; intimidation; secrets; friendship; abuse, physical; bullying; crime and delinquency; depression; manipulation; fear; rites of passage.

CHARACTERS
Pip/Phillip Downs: he drinks and gets high to keep from thinking about his life
Ms. Fleming: she's tired of watching Pip sleep through English every day
Jenna: she's a good girl with a gorgeous smile
Tony: he works at the deli across from the school
Coach Fredricks: he teaches P.E.
Mr. Giraldi: the principal who lays down the law for Pip
Dad/Michael Downs: Pip's violent and alcoholic father
Michael Downs Jr./ Mikey/Bugs: Pip's six-year-old little brother, who has a question
    for everything
Eddie Farrot: a friend of Mikey's
Frankie/Slayer: a friend of Pip's who also likes to drink and get high
Johnny: a friend of Pip's who knows what his father's like
Mo: a drug dealer in the Bronx that Johnny goes to
Mom/Eve Downs: she either tries to placate her angry husband or yells at him in-
    stead
Claire Butler: Pip's counselor
Mr. Kirkland: Ms. Fleming's substitute teacher

Paco, Darius, Mark, Anthony: members of Pip's therapy group
Officer Ross: he picks up Pip twice when he's drunk and gives him a second chance

BOOKTALK

I thought I had a deal with my teachers. I'd chill out in class, take a nap, not make any trouble, and they'd ignore me. It worked for me. But Ms. Fleming didn't see it that way, and I ended up in the principal's office again. I figured it would be another lecture and a week of detention, but it seemed like Giraldi had run outta patience too. He said he was expelling me and picked up the phone and called my dad. But when I heard my father's name, I reached over the desk and broke the connection. "You can't expel me. If you do, you'll see me on the front page of the paper—'Father Kills Teen Son.'" I guess he could hear the terror in my voice, so he said he'd give me one more chance. But I'd have to go to all my classes and not sleep through them, and see a family counselor every week. If I missed class or missed counseling, I was out of school and on the front page. I went to the rest of my classes. By the time school was over, I was dying for a joint. So I dropped off my little brother Mikey at a friend's house and took off for the Site, where Johnny, Slayer, and I go to chill out. Man, did that buzz feel good. *Too* good—I forgot to pick up Mikey and didn't get home til after five.

Everyone was at the table when I came in. Dad was in full Grinch mode, yelling at me for being late, then ragging on Mom about supper. Then back to me about cleaning the garage. He said I couldn't eat til the garage was clean. That started the fight with Mom all over again. I went out to the garage and Mikey followed me. He takes all the family-fun fighting a lot more seriously than I did when I was six.

He was running around, playing Superman, and knocked over a stack of boxes. He started to pick things up, and then came over to me with a handful of bottle caps. "What's all this?" I couldn't believe it. He'd found my collection of bottle caps that I thought I'd thrown out about a hundred years ago. I told him he could have them if he picked up all the stuff. I looked at some of them before I put them back in the box. I remembered every one, and how hard some of them had been to find. And after Mikey ran out of the garage with the box of caps, I looked down at the one in my hand, the one I didn't want Mikey to have. It was a Budweiser cap. It was from the top of my first beer. The one my father gave me. I was nine.

MAJOR THEMES AND IDEAS
- What you do, and what you don't do, have repercussions.
- When all you can see in your life is negative, it's easy to forget how to laugh.
- Sometimes teachers and principals know a lot more about their students than students give them credit for.
- Some bad habits are passed from one generation to another, like addiction, and anger, and going out of control in an instant.
- Truths for a character in a book can also be truths for you.

- Complaining doesn't change things. Actions do.
- You are responsible for your own choices.
- Life doesn't come with do-overs.
- The evil that exists inside us is only a small part of what we are, no matter how big and ugly it may seem to be.
- Sometimes fear can be your friend, and help you do what you should do, not what you want to do.
- Getting high might help dull the pain, but it doesn't do anything about actually making it stop. You have to be straight for that.
- When you stop feeling the need to go through life all on your own, without sharing your problems, life will get a lot easier.
- Keeping your anger and frustration inside means an explosion when you finally lose control.
- When someone breaks promises to you over and over, eventually you stop expecting them to be kept.
- Chances are something you don't take when you're lost.
- You are in control of you—nobody else.
- Who you are going to be, and what kind of a life you're going to have, is up to you and you alone.
- Change is never easy. It's hard, really hard, but it's also worth it.
- Changing from who you think you have to be into who you're meant to be is one of the biggest challenges you'll ever face.
- Change starts small, so you never notice it; then out of nowhere it slaps you in the face and makes you pay attention.
- You can't change anybody else, but you can change yourself.

BOOK REPORT IDEAS

1. Compare Pip and Mikey at the beginning and at the end of the book. How have they changed?
2. Pip wonders frequently what Mikey will be like when he is sixteen. Speculate on what the two brothers might be like at sixteen and twenty-six.
3. Discuss how addictions and habits can get handed down in a family. Look at both positive and negative things; for instance, Pip's father hands down his substance abuse to Pip. In a more functional family it could be a love of sports, art, music, or reading.
4. Officer Ross went out of his way several times to help Pip. Explain what he saw in Pip that made him do this.
5. The book gives no indication that Pip's parents will give up their substance abuse or violent fights. Give some ideas of things that Pip and Mikey might do to help them cope with this dysfunctional situation.
6. Jenna and Pip have a lot in common. Will this lead to a relationship between them? How might they be able to help each other, either as friends or as a couple?

7. Pip wishes he had a big brother. There are several men in the book who might fit that role. Which one do you think would fit best? How might he be able to help Pip?

BOOKTALK IDEAS
1. Use a Budweiser bottle cap as a prop.
2. Have Pip and Mikey introduce each other and talk about their family.
3. Have Ms. Fleming and Mr. Kirkland describe Pip, "introducing" him.
4. Use the idea of bottling up your emotions until they explode as a focus for your talk.
5. Write your talk in first person as Pip, talking about the pressure cooker his life has become.

RISKS
- Father is an alcoholic
- Teen drinks and smokes cigarettes and marijuana
- Adults smoke marijuana
- Vulgar and obscene language
- Father is violent with his children and his wife
- Teen's mother is a prostitute
- Teen sells marijuana and drugs
- Teen is addicted to marijuana
- Mother doesn't protect her sons from their father
- Mother relies on prescription drugs to function "normally"
- Family ignores and covers up violent episodes

STRENGTHS
- Written by psychotherapist
- Genuine voices of teens
- Powerful portrait of dysfunctional family
- Realistic dialogue
- Shows how parents' problems and ways of coping in a dysfunctional way get passed down to their children
- Older brother protects younger one as much as he can
- Example of a positive therapeutic process, with individuals and in a group
- Ending is not neat and tidy, leaving room for speculation and discussion
- Clear glimpse into a teen's mind
- Clear message about how each of us can change ourselves, but can't make others change
- Powerful statement about choices

AWARD
ALA Best Books for Young Adults, 2004

REVIEWS
"Pip's inner rage and desperation are poignantly portrayed and should provide some hope to teens facing addicted parents." Joel Shoemaker, Southeast Junior High School, Iowa City, IA, *School Library Journal*, 6/03

"First-time novelist Murray gives a grimly accurate view of a dysfunctional family as seen through the eyes of a sixteen-year-old. . . . The author's expectations of her characters are realistic and the limits she sets lend strength to the message of hope that she ultimately conveys." *Publishers Weekly*, 12/04

"Painfully believable scenes reveal his father's drinking and violence, his mother's addiction to Valium, and Pip's own escape from his miserable home life through marijuana and alcohol. No easy ending ensues, but Pip's emerging strength, realistically portrayed, bodes well for his future." *Kirkus Reviews*, 6/03.

📖📖📖

BOY MEETS BOY. David Levithan. Knopf, 2003. $15.75. 192p. ISBN10: 0375824006. ISBN13: 9780375824005. Knopf, 2005. $8.95. 192p. ISBN10: 0375832998. ISBN13: 9780375832994. Knopf, 2003. $17.99. 192p. ISBN10: 0375924000. ISBN13: 9780375924002. (library binding) Full Cast Audio, 2005. $45.00. ISBN10: 1933322330. ISBN13: 9781933322339. (audio recording) Realistic fiction/Fantasy. Reading Level: YHS. Interest Level: YHS, OHS. English, Psychology, P.E., Sex Education.

SUBJECT AREAS
romance; friendship; homosexuality; sex and sexuality; school; dating and social life; self-knowledge; religion; problem parents; love.

CHARACTERS
Paul: a sophomore in high school who falls for Noah at first sight
Joni: Paul's best friend
Tony: he's in the closet because his parents are very religious
Noah: the new kid in town, who meets Paul in a bookstore
Zeke: a Gaystafarian friend of Paul's
Ted: he and Joni go together and break up, over and over and over

Mrs. Benchly: Paul's kindergarten teacher, who told him he was gay
Cody: Paul's first boyfriend
Laura: a lesbian who helped form the elementary school's first gay-straight alliance
Infinite Darlene: star quarterback *and* Homecoming Queen
Coach Ginsburg: high school football coach
Kyle Kimball: Paul's ex, who won't go away
Trilby Pope: a drag queen who used to be friends with Infinite Darlene
Chuck: he fell for Infinite Darlene, but she rejected him
Jay: Paul's brother, who's a senior
Mara: Jay's doubles tennis partner
Lyssa Ling: chair of the school's committee on appointing committees
Claudia: Noah's younger sister
Spiff: he runs the local video rental store
Rip: the school bookie
Amber: a girl on Paul's Dowager Dance committee

BOOKTALK
Love isn't always easy the way it is in romance novels. It's confusing, difficult, and painful. Doing the right thing is impossible when you don't have any idea what it is. But when Paul meets Noah, they both know they have something special, that somehow they fit together. But other things don't fit so well. No sooner have Paul and Noah connected than Kyle, Paul's ex, shows up and wants to get back together; and Paul's best friend Joni is suddenly chasing after a football player that they've always thought was a lower form of life. Tony's parents, who are super-religious, find out that Paul's gay and tell Tony he can't see Paul or Joni ever again, in spite of the fact that they've been good friends for years.

MAJOR THEMES AND IDEAS
- We all need a place to be, to belong.
- There's a thin line between peer pressure and bravery.
- It doesn't matter whether you're gay or straight. Who you are is more than who you have sex with.
- What you feel is right for you.
- Falling in love is usually complicated and difficult.
- Falling in love means you're simultaneously happy and scared.
- Serendipity is real.
- The beginning of a new romance is always magical.
- It's important to take care of your friends.
- Sometimes it's good to leave feelings unspoken, especially when they're new.
- Hurt is essentially a first-hand emotion. It's difficult to really share it.
- Doing something for the first time can make you lose your sense of proportion.

- Sometimes you tell someone a story; other times you give it to them.
- New love is about hope and anticipation and proximity.
- It's hard to know who you're supposed to be.
- Sometimes all you need is to say the truth and have it heard.
- When you love someone it's important to tell them that you do.
- Love makes you do stupid things.
- Sometimes the space between knowing what to do and actually doing it is very small. Other times, it can seem impossibly vast.
- When you think you're at the bottom and things can't get any worse, they do.
- It isn't easy knowing who you are and what you want, because you have no excuse for not trying to get it.
- Love is letting a person be who they want to be.
- If there's no fear, there's no need for courage. They work together.
- If you want to be loved, be lovable.
- Writing someone a letter is like sharing a part of your life with them.
- When you're with the right person, it feels natural to be a couple.

BOOK REPORT IDEAS

1. Could a town like Paul's ever exist? Why or why not?
2. This book promotes the idea that gay love and straight love are not all that different. Do you agree or disagree with that idea? Why or why not?
3. Consider Tony, his parents, and their church. In your opinion, will his parents and their friends ever come to terms with his being gay?
4. What was the most significant scene in the book for you, and why did you choose it?
5. Discuss how the parents in the book interacted with their children and their friends. Which ones were the most supportive? The most difficult? If you could choose one couple to be your parents, which would you choose? Why?
6. The author chose to make important points using a humorous tone. Discuss how effective you think this was as a writing technique.
7. Which situations and characters did you most identify with?
8. When Paul was showing Noah he loved him, he did some really outrageous things. How real did that seem to you? Should it be realistic?

BOOKTALK IDEAS

1. Let Paul tell his own story, as he did in the book.
2. Have several students talk about Paul, Noah, and Kyle, perhaps including something about the bets on whether Paul would end up with one of them or alone.
3. Take a brief tour of the high school and introduce Paul and his friends, including Infinite Darlene, Lyssa Ling, Ted, Joni, Chuck, and others.

4. Focus your talk on romance and the various couples (and former couples) in the book.
5. Focus your talk on the idea of friendship and what you'd do for your friends.

RISKS
- Homosexuality is accepted and approved of
- Football star is a cross-dresser
- Negative portrayal of religious parents with a gay son
- Satirizes many high school traditions

STRENGTHS
- Positive portrayal of homosexuality
- Genuine, three-dimensional characters
- Humorous tone used to convey serious message
- Makes important points about tolerance and acceptance
- Accurate portrayal of the dance that is high school relationships and romances with their constant ups and downs
- Parents accept their son's homosexuality
- No graphic sexual scenes or sexual content beyond hugs and kisses
- Satisfying ending, but not all plot lines are neatly tied up
- Shows the courage and strength needed to come out to very religious parents
- Teens have solid friendships and support each other

AWARDS
ALA Best Books for Young Adults, 2004
ALA Quick Picks for Reluctant Young Adult Readers, 2004
Lambda Literary Award Recipient, 2003

REVIEWS
"Hilarious, romantic, and optimistic, the story provides another view of what life could be like if the world were more accepting, showing how youth solidarity can overcome the fears of the most homophobic parents. This title is a keeper for public and secondary school libraries." Cynthia Winfield, *VOYA*, 10/03

"In its blithe acceptance and celebration of human differences, this is arguably the most important gay novel since Nancy Garden's *Annie on My Mind*; it certainly seems to represent a revolution in the publishing of gay-themed books for adolescents." Michael Cart, *Booklist*, 8/03

"Levithan's prophecy of a hate-free world in which everyone loves without persecution makes this a provocative and important read for all young adults, gay or straight." Johanna Lewis, New York Public Library, *School Library Journal*, 9/03

📖📖📖

BOY TOY. Barry Lyga. Houghton Mifflin, 2007. $16.95. 416p. ISBN10: 0618723935. ISBN13: 9780618723935. Graphia, 2009. $8.99. 416p. ISBN10: 0547076347. ISBN13: 9780547076348. Realistic fiction. Reading Level: YHS. Interest Level: YHS, OHS. English, Sex Education, Psychology, Ethics.

SUBJECT AREAS
sexual abuse; rites of passage; self-knowledge; secrets; school; sports; family relationships; love; guilt; legal system; therapy; anger; betrayal; bullying; sex and sexuality; rape; child abuse; crime and delinquency; dating and social life; fear; prejudice; peer pressure; lying and deceit; justice; manipulation; gossip.

CHARACTERS
Josh Mendel: about to graduate from high school, he's still learning to cope with what happened to him when he was twelve
Bill Mendel: Josh's dad, who's in marketing
Jenna Mendel: Josh's mom, who's a research assistant at the local college
Rachel Madison: Josh thought he lost her long ago
Zik Lorenz: Josh's best friend, who's never asked about what happened
Coach Kaltenback: Josh's baseball coach, who has a big mouth and a mean streak
Roland A. Sperling: the high school assistant principal
Dr. Pierce: the school psychologist
Dr. Gene Kennedy: Josh's regular psychologist
Mike Lorenz: Zik's older brother, a major jock
Michelle Jurgens: Zik's girlfriend
Eve/Evelyn Sherman: she sexually molested and manipulated Josh when he was twelve
Mr. Tunney: one of Josh's middle school teachers
Mrs. Cameron: the middle school principal
George Sherman: Eve's husband, who's a video games tester
Mr. and Mrs. Lorenz: Zik's parents, whom neither Zik nor his friends like very much
Gil Purdy: the prosecutor who finally breaks Josh's silence and makes him confess
"The Judge": he presided over Eve's trial
Ms. Cresswell: Eve's defense attorney
The Heat: superstar pitcher

BOOKTALK

When Josh Mendel was twelve years old, he learned a lot of things. He learned how witches were killed in Salem. He learned how to calculate the area of a circle. He learned how to divide fractions. And he learned how to please a woman: one woman, Eve Sherman, his seventh grade history teacher.

She was beautiful and sexy, and she asked him to work on a graduate study project with her. That meant going to her apartment every day after school. He filled out tests and answered interview questions, and afterwards she let him play some of the Xbox games her husband had. Until one afternoon, when she showed him something better than Xbox.

No one found out until Rachel's thirteenth birthday party, and then *everyone* found out. Eve was arrested, there was a trial, and she went to prison. Josh's name was never in any of the newspaper stories, but everyone knew. Eve's confession even ended up on the internet.

No one knew what to do about Josh. He saw therapists, he picked fights until everyone avoided him, everyone but Zik, his best friend, and Michelle, Zik's girlfriend. They used to be the Four Musketeers, but after what had happened at her party, what Josh had done to her, he couldn't be around Rachel, so Zik and Michelle were with Rachel *or* they were with Josh. Always three, never four.

And that's how it was for five years, until Josh was about to get out of high school, until Eve Sherman was released from prison, until Josh's guilt released him from prison, until Josh's guilt got way too big to keep it inside him.

MAJOR THEMES AND IDEAS
- Even with therapy, some experiences are too terrible to recover from.
- Memories are powerful and, when they are unresolved and unforgotten, can change the way you think and act right now.
- Sometimes people just need to be punished.
- No matter how many times you hear something, it's not true til you believe it and accept it inside.
- Ripping off a Band-Aid covering an open wound and allowing the infection to escape so healing can begin is too painful and difficult. Ignoring it, letting the infection worsen and spread, is easier, at least in the short term.
- Ignoring a problem doesn't make it go away, and works for only a limited amount of time.
- The person being abused is the victim and isn't to blame for the abuse.
- You always have the right be angry with anyone who hurts you. But acting on that anger is sometimes unproductive.
- A best friend is someone who puts up with your shit and pretends it doesn't bother him.
- It's easier to feel safe when you know your predator is behind bars and unable to get to you or to appear unexpectedly.

- Your best friend really understands what's important to you—he just plain *gets* it.
- There isn't a better way to tell someone to fuck off than by ignoring everything they've tried to teach you, and win by doing it your own way.
- Not even a competent therapist can understand everything that's going on in the patient's mind.
- Recovering from sexual abuse isn't quick or easy. It's a long, hard road, but it isn't impossible.
- In a sexual abuse situation, the victim isn't the only one who's hurt—family and friends are too.
- It can be easier to simply avoid someone than to talk about the difficult issues that lie between you.
- Dreams can reveal what you may be unwilling to face when you're awake.
- It's easy to believe what you want to hear.
- An adult wanting to seduce a child has all the weapons on their side.
- When an adult is taking advantage of a child, it's hard to know what's really an accident and what is actually calculated to move the relationship toward consummation.
- Hearing parents during private moments can be unsettling and frightening to a child without the background to understand what's really going on.
- Teens and preteens appreciate it when adults respect them and treat them more like adults.
- Intelligence almost always makes an adolescent appear older and more mature. Intelligence can allow them to understand human interactions at a different level.
- Life takes strange and unexpected turns, and all we can do is hang on for the ride and hope we can figure out how to cope with them.
- Forgiveness isn't an event, it's a process. It happens in the back of your mind, until one day, you suddenly realize you don't hate someone anymore. The anger is gone, and forgiveness has happened.
- When everyone in town knows your secret, sometimes the only way to survive is to pretend they don't exist.
- In high school, athletic prowess can take you from pariah to superstar without a hitch.
- If there's one thing authority figures can't stand, it's being called on their own bullshit.
- You don't go to college to play ball—not if you have a mathematical genius brain. You go to *learn*.
- Tomboys do turn into beautiful women, and they can still be your friends when they do.
- Sooner or later, you grow up and realize you're just like everyone else. True or false?
- Not everything is the end of the world—even when it feels like it. Step back; get some perspective. Life doesn't always work well in a close-up view.

- You can't ever *really* escape your DNA.
- Sometimes with love, you have to go with instinct, not reason. Love doesn't always *have* a reason.
- Evidence doesn't necessarily make anyone believe it—not when their mind believes something else.
- Friends are there for you even in the hardest times, sometimes to support and defend you, sometimes just to distract you when things get too overwhelming.
- No matter how strong and determined a child is, sooner or later adults can break through his defenses and get *his* version of the truth. Not the whole truth, but what the child sees as the truth.
- As long as there's a chance, don't give up your dreams.
- Is that how it works—you make one mistake and it haunts you for life?
- Don't *ever* give up your dream.
- Everything's a risk. Life has no guarantees.
- You can run away from people and places, but you can't run away from your past.
- A teenager can love without compromise or distraction—pure, undiluted love.
- The past is past. History is just history. You just push it aside and get on with life.
- The batter may be a lone man against the world, but in order to hit a home run, someone else has to pitch the ball.

BOOK REPORT IDEAS

1. Eve set out to seduce Josh, drawing him deeper and deeper under her control. Why did she do it, and what did she get out of their affair?
2. Discuss Josh's flickers—what were they and what did they mean?
3. Josh believes Dr. Kennedy doesn't really understand what's going on with him. Explain why he feels that way and what he refuses to reveal.
4. Josh withdrew from everyone after his abuse was revealed, and he was the subject of lots of gossip. How might things have changed if he'd acted differently?
5. How did the relationship between his parents affect Josh?
6. How completely was Josh's personality destroyed by his abuse? Discuss how his guilt over his role affected him and changed his behavior.
7. Josh's parents were completely unconcerned when he started staying at Eve's later and later. Discuss this unconcern. What was its basis, its source? How does it reflect their relationships as a family? In your opinion, is this how the parents you know, including your own, would react? How would their reactions be similar or different?
8. How are Eve and Jenna alike? Consider how that may have added to Eve's attractiveness and Josh's fear.
9. Josh goes through several turning points in the book. List them chronologically and explain what each of them means and why each is important.

10. Discuss Josh's guilt, and how he feels responsible for what he and Eve are doing and the self-loathing he experiences as a result.
11. In your opinion, who was the pursuer in Josh and Eve's relationship? Explain how and why you decided this.
12. It takes Josh a long time to realize how Rachel feels about him. Discuss why he doesn't catch on sooner.
13. Discuss Josh's idea of forgiveness: it happens gradually without your knowing, until the day you suddenly know it's happened.
14. Josh thinks his peers treat him differently, in spite of his being a sexual abuse victim, because of his success in baseball. Discuss whether or not you think this is true, and compare it to how you think Josh might be treated at your high school, if everyone in town knew his secret.
15. Discuss Roland's relationship with Josh and whether or not Josh's opinions about his actions are true.
16. Josh has never liked people his age—with the exception of his friends. Discuss why you think he doesn't.
17. Imagine how you would feel and act if you were Josh and had to put up with regular, even daily, scornful and demeaning comments on your past, not only from teachers but also from your peers.
18. Speculate on where Josh will be in five years, ten years. What will he be doing and what will his life be like?
19. Josh assumes everyone in high school and in town has read everything about him on the web. How realistic is that and why?
20. At the prom, Rachel asks Josh if he ever knew how to have fun like the other kids at the party are doing. Did he? Will he ever know how to have fun again?
21. Rachel tells Josh that, sooner or later, all child geniuses grow up and learn they're just like everyone else. Discuss why he's unable to believe it.
22. Consider whether or not Josh will ever get used to being in a spotlight when he has spent so many years trying to be invisible. Will a new environment help, or is he locked into his own world?
23. Discuss how you think Josh felt when he heard his mother say about Eve, "This woman destroyed my child!" If she had reacted differently, how would the impact on Josh have differed?
24. Discuss Josh's police interrogation and how he must have felt, considering the evidence that confirmed what he and Eve were doing.
25. Discuss how parents express their relationship with each other—fights, anger, separation, or give-and-take discussions and open affection—affect and change their children. How are children of a loving couple different from those of an antagonistic, unhappy couple?
26. Josh refused to testify against Eve at the trial. Explain how you might have acted in the same situation.
27. Discuss what happened after Eve changed her plea, and how it affected Josh psychologically and emotionally. How would it have been different if he had testified against Eve?

28. After the trial, describe what it must have been like for Josh being under such close surveillance 24/7. How would that make you feel?
29. When he went back to school after the trial, Josh went out of control when a kid bumped into him in the hall. Discuss where that rage came from and the effect it had on the high school student body.
30. After the trial, none of his friends' parents would let Josh play with their children. Discuss their reasons and how the exile Josh was forced to endure affected him.
31. Examine Josh and Rachel's relationship and how she is able to understand him, even when he doesn't give her many clues.
32. Discuss how Josh's life would have been different if he'd trusted Dr. Kennedy more and shared his overwhelming guilt with him.

BOOKTALK IDEAS
1. Use a baseball cap or a bat as a prop.
2. Have Zik, Michelle, and Rachel describe Josh, what it was like growing up with him and what he's like now.
3. Write your talk in first person, letting Josh tell his own story.
4. Use the newspaper stories and headlines in your talk.
5. Write your talk as if it were a news story.
6. Include some of Josh's baseball stats and mathematical calculations.

RISKS
- Vulgar language
- Sexual abuse of a minor
- Sex scenes are graphic and sensuous
- Teens are sexually active
- Adult trains boy to please her sexually
- Teen's sexual abuse becomes public knowledge
- Teen is violent with adults
- Coach taunts teen maliciously and cruelly
- Parents are unable to protect their child or deal with his pain
- Teen has flashbacks to the time of his abuse
- When his molester is released from prison, teen has panic attacks about seeing her again
- Parents argue constantly, unaware their son can hear them or of his reaction to their animosity
- Boy has sexual fantasies about teacher
- Early sexual abuse interferes with boy's attempts to become sexually active as a teen
- Sexual predator creates a relationship with her victim's mother in order to gain her trust and allow her son more freedom

- Mother has five-year affair
- Woman plotted her seduction of a twelve-year-old boy
- Boy hides shame and guilt with anger and fighting

STRENGTHS
- Shows the longevity of the psychological impact of sexual abuse
- Characters are realistic, three-dimensional, easy to identify with
- Language is realistic and includes obscenities
- Shows positive therapeutic relationship
- The reader sees the events from inside the narrator's head, making the emotions more intense and visceral
- Portrays strong friendships that outlast the most traumatic events
- While sexual abuse destroys boy's self-confidence, his sports prowess helps him regain it
- Powerfully written, immediately involves the reader
- Graphic portrait of how a sexual abuse victim can blame himself for the abuse
- Reveals the details of the abuse gradually
- Teen finally accepts that he was the victim, not the instigator, and is able to get on with his life and begin to heal

AWARDS
ALA Best Books for Young Adults, 2008
Capitol Choices List, 2008 (Washington, D.C.)

REVIEWS
"Using several narrative voices—first person, transcribed therapy sessions, flash-backs—Lyga tackles this incredibly sensitive story with boldness and confidence. He does not shy away from graphic descriptions of Josh's past. . . . [Josh] works hard at healing himself and moving into healthy adulthood, and by the end of this well-written, challenging novel, the reader has high hopes that he will make it." Geri Diorio, *VOYA,* 10/07

"Blending present events with extensive flashbacks, Lyga creates a tightly paced narrative that explores psychological turmoil without resorting to either clinical ter-minology or oversimplification. . . . Deftly weaving together a painful confession and ambiguous ending, Lyga's dynamic writing style creates an emotionally wrenching and haunting tale." *Kirkus Reviews,* 9/07

"Lyga's skillful writing subtly reveals Eve's cleverly calculated abuse of Josh in a way that older teens will find fascinating, distressing, and worthy of their attention." Ginny Gustin, Sonoma County Library System, Santa Rosa, CA, *School Library Journal,* 10/07

⊞⊞⊞

BREAKING POINT. Alex Flinn. HarperTeen, 2003. $7.99. 256p. ISBN10: 0064473716. ISBN13: 9780064473712. Realistic fiction. Reading Level: MS. Interest Level: MS, YHS. English, Psychology, Sociology.

SUBJECT AREAS
school; manipulation; violence; vandalism; friendship; bullying; divorce and separation; depression; anger; guilt; problem parents; computers; suicide; crime and delinquency; ethics; peer pressure; secrets; death and dying.

CHARACTERS
Paul Richmond: homeschooled since second grade, he isn't prepared for the politics of a wealthy private high school
Mrs. Richmond/Mom: she works at Gate and is having a hard time with being divorced
Charlie Good: he's a jock *and* a star student, making him the top gun on campus
Binky Lapez-Nande: she befriends Paul on his first day at Gate
Randy Meade/Meat: he looks like a WWF wrestler and is one of Charlie's serfs
Gray St. John: a friend of Meat's, who's even taller than Paul
Lt. Colonel Glenn Richmond/Dad: he divorced his wife, leaving her and his son when his girlfriend got pregnant
Mrs. Ivins: Paul's Algebra II teacher
Old Carlos: the janitor at Gate
David Blanco: his mom is a lunch lady and his father's the janitor at Gate
Mr. and Mrs. Good: Charlie's parents; she's a lawyer and he's a businessman who's a tennis fanatic
Mrs. Zaller: she teaches biology and gave Charlie a D
Mrs. Booth: the librarian
Mr. Meeks: the principal of Gate
Miss Bundy: an English teacher at Gate
Amanda Colbert: Gray St. John's ex-girlfriend, who's beautiful and genuine
Kirby, Emily, Pierre, Ryan: they're part of Charlie's group
Mrs. Vega: she works in the office with Paul's mother
Mr. Rossi: Paul's lawyer

BOOKTALK
The breaking point—it's there in every possible situation, in every part of your life. The point when everything in that situation changes. But what does being at the breaking point really mean? It sounds like you'd know when you saw it coming, so

you'd have a choice about going past it or drawing back and pulling away from it. But what if it just zoomed by you before you had a choice? What if all the things you'd been doing just to make it through every day, little things, stuff that didn't really matter, what if all that stuff just blew up in your face, and the fire alarm at school that you pulled because you thought it would be a good joke turned out to be real? What if someone else decided when your breaking point would be? What if you didn't have a choice or a chance to pull away from that breaking point? What would you do then?

MAJOR THEMES AND IDEAS

- Bullies instinctively know who is weak and vulnerable.
- Homeschooling, when you don't have any contact with any kids, can leave you ignorant of the rules and nuances of teen culture.
- Happy teen years are overrated—and probably a myth.
- If you peak in high school, the rest of your life is all downhill.
- Pretty apples are all too often the poisonous ones. People too.
- Be careful what you wish for. It might come true.
- Revenge can backfire. Before you start, make sure those you love are protected, because they could be in danger.
- When you are part of a group, it's easy to get caught up in something you'd never consider doing by yourself.
- Sometimes it seems like some people can get away with anything.
- When someone tells you to do what you know is wrong, think carefully before you agree. What is their motive and what will happen to you if you're caught?
- Be careful before you make a bully angry. He *will* retaliate.
- In some divorces, only the parents divorce. In others, the person wanting out rejects the whole family.
- Being the person everyone expects you to be, rather than yourself, is incredibly difficult.
- Sometimes hurting someone who's been hurting you can feel really good.
- Anything's okay as long as you don't get caught. But if you get caught, you're on your own.
- True friends like you for who you are, not because the leader of their clique told them to like you.
- Life's on the barter system—we all use one another. You just have to make sure you get what you want.
- If you aren't like anyone, you'll always be alone.
- It's easy to wish the ones with perfect lives could feel just a little of the pain and isolation you feel.
- Sooner or later, everyone reaches their breaking point.
- It feels good to damage what you hate, even when you know it's wrong.
- A prank is one thing. Hurting people, maybe killing them, is another.

- No one makes you do something wrong. You are responsible for your actions, and you can always say no.
- Life doesn't have do-overs. You just have to keep going and figure out how to survive.

BOOK REPORT IDEAS

1. Discuss why Binky was so ready to make friends with Paul. How did she benefit from their friendship?
2. Discuss how Paul's mother manipulates him and how it is one of the reasons for his behavior at school.
3. Paul says he hates who he is around his mother. What does he mean by that?
4. Explain why Paul's father refused to contact him.
5. Explain why Binky said Charlie was trouble. Why didn't she tell Paul more about why she said that?
6. Discuss the dog's death and who the killer was.
7. Discuss David's comparison of Gate with the Holocaust and the Nazis, and explain how accurate you think the comparison is.
8. In their first conversation, Charlie tells Paul many things about himself. Paul feels like Charlie is reading his mind. What was Charlie's purpose in this? How did he use it?
9. Explain Paul's feelings as he breaks his first mailboxes. What does this night mean to him?
10. What hold does Charlie have over Meat, St. John, and Paul? Why does he persuade them to do delinquent and criminal acts while he watches? What is his payoff?
11. Discuss Charlie's relationship with his father and how it influences the rest of his life. Why is pleasing his father so important?
12. How would events in Paul's life have unfolded had his father not rejected him so harshly?
13. Discuss the stories Charlie tells, why he tells them, and whether or not they are true.
14. Speculate on what Paul and Charlie's lives will be like in the future. Will Charlie ever be caught? Will Paul be able to make some kind of success of his life?

BOOKTALK IDEAS

1. Use a baseball bat as a prop.
2. Center your talk on Paul's loser status at school and how it changed when he became a member of the Mailbox Club.
3. Focus your talk on bullies and how Paul and David were bullied.
4. Have the central characters introduce themselves in a couple of sentences each.
5. Let Paul introduce himself and his story in first person.

RISKS

- Depressed mother ignores son's problems and needs
- Bullying
- Vandalism
- Father takes everything in the divorce settlement
- Dog is brutally killed and decapitated
- Parents have impossible expectations of their children
- Teens steal liquor from their parents
- Teen manipulates his peers into criminal activity
- Father cruelly rejects his son and cuts off any contact
- Mother knows son is an evil manipulator but refuses to make him take responsibility for his actions

STRENGTHS

- Authentic characters readers can identify with
- Vivid, graphic depiction of bullies, their victims, and the effect of being bullied
- Shows how easy manipulation can be if you pick your targets carefully
- Unrelenting sequence of events leads to climax and ultimate betrayal, drawing reader into the book
- Realistic and authentic dialogue that includes few obscenities
- Examines the way bullied students are isolated and persecuted
- Opens the door for discussions on a wide variety of topics based on what happens in middle and high schools on a daily basis

AWARDS

ALA Quick Picks for Reluctant Young Adult Readers, 2003
New York Public Library Books for the Teen Age, 2003

REVIEWS

"Not since Cormier's *The Chocolate War* have characters been drawn to be so brilliantly twisted. Flinn's flair for creating disturbing characters in completely realistic situations is uncanny and leaves the reader thinking of Columbine and other school violence incidents whose perpetrators could have been quite similar to Charlie and Paul. This timely, engaging book is certain to grab the interest of teens." Kimberly L. Paone, *VOYA*, 6/02

"In this intense story of peer pressure and the need to be accepted, the characters are realistically drawn and reflect the nature of high school relationships." Janet Hilbun, formerly at Sam Houston Middle School, Garland, TX, *School Library Journal*, 5/02

"Alex Flinn, whose *Breathing Underwater* earned high praise, does tribute to the great Robert Cormier in this dark and brilliant novel about the high price of acquiescence to evil." Patty Campbell, Amazon.com Review

📖📖📖

CAN'T GET THERE FROM HERE. Todd Strasser. Simon and Schuster, 2004. $16.95. 208p. ISBN10: 0689841698. ISBN13: 9780689841699. Simon Pulse, 2005. $5.99. 208p. ISBN10: 0689841701. ISBN13: 9780689841705. Realistic fiction. Reading Level: MS. Interest Level: MS, YHS. English, Psychology, Ethics, Sociology, Government.

SUBJECT AREAS
homelessness; poverty, substance abuse; sexual abuse; friendship; death and dying; prejudice; problem parents; lies; physical abuse; anger; animals; suicide; survival; self-destruction; self-knowledge; secrets; depression; drugs; ethics; fear; grief and mourning; runaways; HIV/AIDS.

CHARACTERS
Maybe: she's the daughter of a carnie; she's lived all over til her mom kicked her out, now she's on the street, easy to recognize because of her spotted skin

Maggot/Stuart: he lives on the streets and is the reason the group sticks together

Rainbow/Mary Ellen Golding: she's blonde and pretty and cuts herself, and tries to keep going

Moro/Angel Perez: she's fifteen, lives on the street, and works hard to look dangerous with piercings and tattoos

Country Club/Alexander Mittelson: he lived on the street for five years before he died of alcohol poisoning

O.G.: he and Country Club had been together for a long time

Tears/Nikki Frimer: the newest and youngest member of the group; she's only twelve

Officer Johnson: a local cop who's usually mean

Officer Ryan: she's Johnson's partner, and new to the force

Jewel: he has purple hair and wears a leather coat and eyeliner

Last: he has an orange Mohawk and sells roofies

Anthony: a librarian at a nearby library, he has patchy brown-and-white skin like Maybe

Jack: a man who bought doctored cokes for Maybe and Tears

Bobby: cruel library custodian who harasses homeless kids in the library
Detective Charles: he's in charge of the youth program and tries to get kids off the
    streets
Laura: she works at the Youth Housing Project
Spyder: a girl that Maybe meets at the Youth Housing Project, who has multicolored
    hair, piercings, and tattoos
Grammy Emma: Tears's grandmother
Grandpa David: Tears's grandfather

BOOKTALK

There aren't a lot of chances for a kid on the street, but for a while, I thought we could
make it if we just stuck together. We didn't have families, but together we could make
one. We could help each other, look out for each other, and survive together. And one
day, maybe we'd even make it off the street.

But that was how I felt a long time ago, so long ago I can hardly remember it.
That was before I'd seen the death, the meanness, the cruelty, and the despair that
I've seen now. That was when we'd created a sort of home for ourselves in an old
building, when we didn't have to sleep in doorways or under bridges. That was before
life began picking us off one by one, as if it were a rifle, firing at us over and over
with horribly deadly aim.

You kids with beds to sleep in, food to eat, families and friends around you.
You kids who whine and cry when the most minor things go wrong with your lives.
And even you kids who don't have it so good, who only feel safe part of the time,
who struggle every day to keep your lives together. Do any of you ever think about
running away? Do you think how cool it would be to be on your own, to be free and
independent, and able to make your own rules?

Let me tell you what the streets are *really* like, the rules you'll have to obey when
you live there, and the things you'll have to do to survive. I've lived on those streets,
obeyed those rules, and done things I couldn't imagine doing, and I'll tell you about
all of them. My name on the street is Maybe, as in maybe I can change your mind
about how hard you have it now.

MAJOR THEMES AND IDEAS

- Going home isn't always an option for kids on the street. Home might be the very
  thing they're running from.
- When you're on the street, it's a lot more dangerous at night than it is during the
  day.
- Some people *can* get off the street—not many, but some.
- Sometimes being cold and hungry and even homeless is better than living by
  someone else's rules.
- Some adults are always ready to take advantage of homeless kids who have no
  one to protect them.

- Some people don't let anyone tell them anything. They just make up their minds, tell you what they think, and that's that. Nothing you say can change their mind.
- Some people use kids to get what they want and then throw them away—why not? There's nothing a kid can do about it.
- Some adults should never be parents. Their children are just things to take out their anger on.
- When you're hungry and cold and homeless, that's all you can think about. Survival takes all your time and energy. You don't have time to think about the world away from the street.
- A bath, a meal, and a comfortable bed can have a price that's higher than a street kid is willing to pay.
- It's easy to fear someone who doesn't look like you or live like you do.
- Living on the street can make you feel like a no one with nothing, not even a name.
- Sometimes survival is so difficult and life is so hopeless that it's just easier to give up and let go.
- Living on the street is what happens when you run out of choices. It's not fun or glamorous or cool. It's about cold and hunger and illness and death.
- Time is one of the most important things in the world. No one should throw it away.
- Even if your family doesn't care about you, you can still care about yourself.
- If you care about yourself, you will attract people who care about you, too.
- Maybe, if you try hard enough and don't give up, you can get somewhere, even if you started from nowhere.

BOOK REPORT IDEAS

1. On Maslow's scale of the hierarchy of needs, street kids are at the bottom. What would have to happen to allow them to move up the scale?
2. Why does Jewel create his elaborate fantasy of wealth? Is any part of it true? What does he get from believing in it?
3. Why do the kids in Maybe's tribe refuse help when it's offered to them? What has street life taught them?
4. What do kids gain from living on the street?
5. Compare the different backgrounds of the members of the tribe and discuss how they ended up homeless, and what could have happened that might have made a difference in their lives.
6. How has the system both helped and hindered these kids?
7. Discuss Maggot, what he said, the role he played in the tribe, and how he left it. Was he really a postcard punk? If so, does that make you see his previous actions differently? Why or why not?
8. Speculate on what happened to the surviving characters in the book—Maggot, O.G., Jewel, and the others. What might their lives be like in five years? Ten years?
9. Which of the tribe had the most compelling reason for running? Which had the least, and which never told their story?
10. What was the most important information you got from this book and why?

BOOKTALK IDEAS

1. Illustrate your talk with photographs of homeless kids you've taken yourself or found in research.
2. Have each member of the tribe introduce himself or herself, giving a glimpse of what you think is most important to them.
3. Play the role of a member of the tribe to tell their story.
4. Use excerpts from the obituaries as part of your talk, but don't include the street names.
5. Write your talk as if you were a newspaper reporter who'd interviewed some of the book's characters about their lives.
6. Do some research on the number of homeless teens in your area or from your area, and use the information you found as a setting for the talk.

RISKS

- Teens live on the street
- Teens smoke, drink, and panhandle
- Sexual abuse
- Parents reject their children, forcing them to run away
- Teens die on the street, killed because of the life they live
- The depiction of street life is hopeless, grim, and bleak
- Throwaway kids, left to survive alone
- Exposes most adults as uncaring and uninvolved

STRENGTHS

- Deglamorizes the lure of life on the streets
- Clearly developed characters
- Shows dangers and hopelessness of street life
- Shows the fear and distrust street kids have for adults and authority and where those emotions came from
- Ending has some hope, but still leaves room for speculation
- Shows that death is frequently what happens to street kids
- Taut, stark writing style
- Street kids bond together for safety, comfort, and company
- Allows reader to have an inside glimpse of the life of a homeless teen
- Dialogue sounds genuine; uses street slang effectively but without obscenities

AWARDS

ALA Best Books for Young Adults, 2005
ALA Quick Picks for Reluctant Young Adult Readers, 2005

REVIEWS

"This novel about runaway teens on the streets of New York, a group ignored by society, does not hold anything back. . . . The book is gritty and harsh, and urban teens will love it, being drawn into the story from early on when a cop warns members of the tribe, '[Y]ou don't have a chance.'" Rollie Welch, *VOYA*, 6/04

"Strasser's vibrant prose plunges young readers into Maybe's hard life, all without the use of profanity. A very welcome addition to the slice-of-life genre in YA literature that may help to change some real lives." *Kirkus Reviews*, 2/04

"Without sentimentality or exploitation, Maybe's disturbing first-person narrative lets readers know exactly what it's like to live without shelter, huddling in nests of rags, newspapers, and plastic bags. . . . A story about people that we pretend don't exist; Strasser makes us know them." Hazel Rochman, *Booklist*, 3/04

⏛⏛⏛

CHASING TAIL LIGHTS. Patrick Jones. Walker Books, 2007. $16.95. 304p. ISBN10: 0802796281. ISBN13: 9780802796288. Walker, 2008. $7.99. 320p. ISBN10: 0802797628. ISBN13: 9780802797629. Realistic fiction. Reading Level: YHS. Interest Level: YHS, OHS. English, Psychology.

SUBJECT AREAS

stereotypes; survival; violence; rites of passage; prison life; betrayal; dysfunctional family; self-destruction; substance abuse; problem parents; family relationships; working; friendship; drug abuse; school; sex and sexuality; sports; secrets; lying and deceit; fear; anger; love; cruelty; crime and delinquency; incest; justice; legal system; rape; abuse, sexual; child abuse; dating and social life; revenge; intimidation; manipulation; self-knowledge; poverty.

CHARACTERS

Christy Mallory: she's a senior in high school who can't wait to be on her own
Anne Williams: Christy's best friend, who lives in the wealthy part of town
Robert Mallory: Christy's oldest half-brother, who's in prison
Ryan Mallory: Christy's older half-brother, who lives at home
Mitchell Mallory: Christy's brother, who's sixteen
Bree Mallory: Robert's daughter, who lives with the family
Ms. Chapman: Christy's sophomore English teacher

Aunt Dee: Christy's father's sister
Tommy: Aunt Dee's son, who's nineteen and just out of juvie hall
Glen Thompson: he's smart, gorgeous, in Christy's class in school, and she has a huge
  crush on him
Seth Lewis: he thinks he's hot stuff
Mama/Mrs. Mallory: Christy's alcoholic mother
Chris MacDonald: student teacher in theatre
Rani Patel: she's a theatre diva with perfect everything
Terrell: another shelver at the library with Christy
Derrick: a boy Christy meets and dances with at a teen dance club
Tristan: one of Glen's friends, who's a straight-edge type
Dr. Williams: Anne's father, who disapproves of Christy
Mrs. Grayson: a social worker at the hospital
Officer Kay: she interviews Christy in the hospital

BOOKTALK

When I look back at my senior year, and all the things that changed in those nine
months, it's hard to believe that so much good and so much bad could be crammed
into such a short time. It seems like one minute I was smoking dope and chasing tail
lights on the bridge over I-69 with my best friend Anne, and the next I was walking
across the stage when my name was called.

But there actually was a lot of living between those two events. Sleepovers at
Anne's house, but not at mine, 'cause I never want anyone to know how I lived. Best
friend for years or not, Anne has never been inside my house. Seeing the outside is
enough. Think "poor white trash" and then double it a couple of times.

We figured school would be about the same, and we'd spend time cruising
around town, chasing tail lights and getting stoned. Ms. Chapman would try to persuade me to join the track team; I'd try to get near Glen, my long-time crush, who
only wanted to be friends; and we'd get enough studying done to make decent grades.
Anne was going to Northwestern and then med school, and I wanted to go anywhere
that wasn't Flint, Michigan.

But Anne's father had decided she had too much free time, so he got her a
job with one of his friends, and I got a job shelving books at the library. Anne
hadn't been working very long when her boss—and her dad's friend—started
making passes at her and more. She hated it, but she was sure her dad wouldn't believe her, so she didn't do anything. I liked my job and met Terrell there. Soon Glen
had competition for my dreams. And around Thanksgiving, Anne came by to pick me
up, and met my cousin Tommy. They had serious chemistry from the first look.

But while Terrell and Tommy did create some changes in our lives, it turned out
that the secrets we kept and the secrets we shared were responsible for a lot more
changes. Come on and hang out with Anne and me, and we'll make sure you know
all the secrets, the ones we kept and the ones we didn't.

MAJOR THEMES AND IDEAS

- Wanting things you'll never have is the worst feeling in the world.
- Can you ever really pay anyone back for what they've done to you? It's done by that time.
- You can't set someone free if they've been chained up all their life. You have to take small steps and learn the dangers to look out for.
- A non-box is a person who doesn't fit in anywhere—a triangle in a world of circles and squares.
- Loneliness is a weakness—you want to be left alone, but hate feeling lonely.
- There can't be a white knight without a black one.
- Even in the ugliest parts of our lives, there's a reason to believe.
- If you want or expect nothing, you'll never fail or feel like a screw-up.
- There's something comforting in the pain you know rather than the pain you don't.
- Liars frequently know when someone is lying to them.
- If you've been chained up for too long, when you get a chance to feel free you don't think about it, you grab it.
- I know the truth of who I was and who I am now, so someone else's labels don't hurt.
- It's easier to notice the stereotype of a social class than it is to notice the individuals who rise above it.
- Going to prison can be the best thing to happen to someone. It gives them a chance to slow down, to think, to plan, to decide.
- Quit thinking about what you want. Think about what you need.
- In some families, love skips a generation.
- Few people look past the surface to the person inside.
- In some ways, it's a blessing when unreachable dreams disappear.
- Some people are like icebergs—most of them is hidden.
- Don't diss yourself—too many other people are willing to do that for you.
- A suicide attempt is really a cry for help.
- Remembering the past is to relive it, but by forgiving yourself and others, you are set free.
- You can't kill someone who's already dead.
- Dreaming about something that's impossible is safe—you'll always want, but you'll never fail.
- When you get used to having no power in your life, the idea of change, of options, is taken away.
- The truth will set you free.
- Running away is the easy part, staying away is the hardest.
- When you hang with trash, you end up stinking yourself.
- Chasing tail lights sometimes takes you home again.
- Running away sounds like a good idea, until you realize that there's no place to go.

- You can't really run away from anything, because when you run, you take it with you.
- Hard times make you tough.
- A bully's power is your fear of him. And if you can give it to him, you can certainly take it back.
- When someone attacks you, whatever the reason, you're not to blame.
- When all you see is bars, you can't even imagine escaping.
- Love is a chain. It pulls you places you know you shouldn't go.
- Revenge is a dish best served cold.
- Forgiveness isn't the only way to get rid of the pain and hurt someone has filled your life with.

BOOK REPORT IDEAS

1. Explain why Anne and Christy are such good friends. What does their friendship give each of them?
2. Discuss why Christy hates the nights when Bree stays with Aunt Dee.
3. What does Christy mean when she says she can't chase tail lights any longer because she has to be one.
4. Discuss how Melinda in *Speak* and Christy are alike and different.
5. Compare and contrast Dr. Williams and Mrs. Mallory and their relationships with their daughters.
6. List and explain some of the changes Christy went through between the first and last pages of this book.
7. What gave Christy the power to fight back at Seth?
8. Compare the couples in the two love stories—how are they similar and different?
9. Discuss the most powerful lesson in this book and explain why you chose it.
10. Speculate on what will happen to the main characters in the future. Will they succeed or fail to accomplish what seem to be their goals at the end of the book?
11. Christy decided not to tell about what happened to Bree. Do you agree or disagree with that decision? Explain why.
12. After Christy talks to Officer Kay, she says she has one more lie to tell and one person to protect. What is the lie, and who is the person?
13. Explain when you think Christy decided on what her revenge would be.
14. There is a "conspiracy of silence" in this book. Who is a part of it, and what do they get from it?

BOOKTALK IDEAS

1. Use copies of the books Christy reads as props, and explain their meaning.
2. Write your talk as snippets of the conversations between Christy and Anne.
3. Use the flashbacks as part, or all, of your talks.

4. Have Christy describe herself and then what several other characters would say about her.
5. Focus your talk on the title. What does chasing tail lights mean, and who does it?

RISKS
- Drunk and uninvolved mother
- Abusive brother
- Teen deals marijuana
- Teens smoke marijuana
- Teens drink alcohol
- Daughter must visit her father in prison—he got life without parole sentence when she was about seven
- Criminal behavior of various kinds
- Mother spends money on gambling, not her kids
- Sexual abuse, rape, incest
- Calculated revenge
- Mother refuses to protect her daughter or to confront her son about raping her daughter
- Father refuses to believe daughter when she tells him about being sexually molested
- Characters are violent and angry
- Adult characters make negative assumptions about teens based on their situations and social class

STRENGTHS
- Shows the various levels of social class
- Teen works hard to be true to herself
- Accurate and authentic tone and voice
- Depicts the results of economic breakdown
- Realistic picture of falling in love with the right person at the wrong time
- Gritty, graphic scenes show the horror that daily life can become
- Includes people who have failed and given up, as well as those who have overcome their situation
- Using *Speak* early in the book gives a clue about Christy's problems
- Strong, supportive women characters
- Characters do not give up on each other when things get tough
- Shows reader that poverty and abuse can be overcome and that rapists can be caught, convicted, and punished
- Suspense builds through the novel, not releasing the reader even after the last word is read
- Many opportunities for discussions on a variety of topics

AWARDS
No awards.

REVIEWS
"Not shying from the complexities of life with 'plenty to run from, but . . . nothing and nowhere to run to,' this novel incorporates sexual abuse, suicide, neglect, drug use, alcoholism, depression, and homosexuality in this believable portrait of life on the 'other side' of the highway. Well paced, with fluent dialogue. . . . Readers looking for inspiration might find some in this story of developing resilience." Kim Carter, *VOYA*, 8/07

"Gritty and authentic, Jones's novel is a challenging portrait of a teen trying to come to terms with shocking brutality and the ultimate family betrayals." Frances Bradburn, *Booklist*, 9/07

"Teens. . . will love the oceans of angst and the many dire situations Christy and her friends and family face and eventually survive." *Kirkus Reviews*, 7/07

📖📖📖

THE CHOSEN ONE. Carol Lynch Williams. St. Martin's Griffin, 2009. $16.95. 224p. ISBN10: 0312555113. ISBN13: 9780312555115. Macmillan Young Listeners, 2009. $24.99. ISBN10: 1427207062. ISBN13: 978142720767. (unabridged audio CD) Realistic fiction. Reading Level: MS. Interest Level: MS, YHS. English, Psychology, Sex Education, Ethics.

SUBJECT AREAS
family relationships; problem parents; manipulation; intimidation; self-knowledge; child abuse; physical abuse; sex and sexuality; punishment; anger; bullying; reading; betrayal; secrets; death and dying; rites of passage; rape; gossip; love; lying and deceit; polygamy; obsession; customs; cultural identity; dysfunctional family; ethics; fear; friendship; runaways; religion.

CHARACTERS
Kyra Leigh Carlson: she's almost fourteen and lives in an isolated compound with her father, his three wives, and her twenty brothers and sisters
Mother Claire: she's the first wife, the mean one
Mother Sarah: Kyra's mother, whose pregnancy is making her ill; she's Father's third wife and Claire's younger sister

Laura: the sister Kyra is closest to, and only a year younger than she is

Adam, seventeen; Finn, sixteen; Emily, fifteen; Nathaniel, fifteen; Jackson, thirteen; Robert, thirteen; Thomas, eleven; Margaret, ten; Candice, ten; Abe, nine; April, eight; Christian, six; Meadow, five; Marie and Ruth, four; Carolina, three; Trevor, two; Foster, one; Mariah, eight months: Kyra's other brothers and sisters

Mother Victoria: the second wife, who tries to make peace

Richard Carlson/Father: he loves his wives and his children but struggles with some of the rules of the church

Hyrum Carlson: Father's sixty-year-old brother, who is a powerful church member with six wives

Prophet Childs: God's Chosen One, leader of the community and the church

Sister Georgia: she is Kyra's piano teacher

Brother Fields and Brother Stephens: two of the Apostles who come with the Prophet to bring the news of Kyra's wedding

Sister Janie Abbott: one of her newborn twins died and the Prophet took the other away to be killed because he wasn't perfect

Brother Abbott: he dug his twins' graves

Joshua Johnson: the boy Kyra loves and hopes to marry someday

Patrick: the bookmobile librarian who checks book out to Kyra

Brother Felix: the community's sheriff and a member of the God Squad

Randall Allred: another boy who ran away with Joshua

Brother Lamarie, Brother Nelson: members of the Prophet's God Squad

Officer O'Neill: she's one of the officers who helps rescue Kyra and arrest the Prophet and the God Squad

Samantha Oberg: she runs a safe house for kids who escape the cult

Madison Oberg: Samantha's second daughter

BOOKTALK

Kyra is thirteen. She has twenty brothers and sisters, and her father has three wives—Claire, Victoria, and Sarah. Sarah is Kyra's mother. Kyra has just one month to get ready for her wedding. She is going to be her Uncle Hyrum's seventh wife. Hyrum is sixty years old, her father's brother, and Kyra would rather die than marry him. And she might die, if she doesn't stop defying the Prophet.

Kyra is one of the Chosen Ones, a polygamous cult who live in an isolated desert compound. They grow their own food, have no TVs or radios, and are forbidden to read any books but the Bible. Women wear long-sleeved dresses that cover them from neck to ankles and are forbidden to cut their hair. They are permitted only to serve their husband and help raise huge families of children. The Prophet Childs, who is their ruler, decides who and when a girl will marry, almost always at thirteen or fourteen. He had a vision that Kyra and Hyrum should marry, even if he is her uncle.

But Kyra has fallen in love with Jacob, another boy in the cult, and sneaked out at night to see him, and talk, and sometimes even kiss. She has gone to the bookmobile that drives past the compound once a week and has read books and newspapers that tell her of a very different world outside the compound. She has refused to obey the Prophet, and she has sinned. Punishments are swift and harsh and cruel. What will Kyra's punishment be, and who else will be punished because of her actions?

MAJOR THEMES AND IDEAS
Rules of the Chosen Ones
- Rules of the church must be obeyed without question.
- It is a sin to question the Prophet and his Apostles.
- Only the Prophet and his Apostles are allowed to be wealthy.
- Those who are not whole must be condemned.
- The Prophet decides who must marry and when.
- The older men of the community are the only ones taking wives.
- It's a sin to even think about a boy you haven't been Chosen for.
- Disobedient children must be punished severely, even infants.
- The word of the Prophet must be obeyed, even if seems sick or wrong.
- Women must yield to their husbands in every way.
- Rape does not exist between a husband and wife.
- Marriages must be consummated immediately, no matter how young the bride is, or how unwilling.
- Children are a blessing from God, so women should have as many as possible.
- A man must have three wives to get into heaven.
- Women cannot get into heaven if they don't have babies.
- Members of the community may not leave without the blessing of the Prophet.
- Members of the community may not read anything except the Bible; doing so is a sin.
- Girls who run away are hunted, brought back, and forced to marry.
- Boys who run away are left to wander in the desert.

Other
- Reading and books change minds and lives.
- Sometimes, love will find a way.
- When you are ordered to do something wrong, refusing to obey is the right thing to do.
- Falling in love isn't a sin.
- Adults are not always right or strong.
- Parents can't always protect their children.
- Parents' kindness and leniency with children is seen as weakness.
- If you get too close to the edge of the cliff and peer too far over the edge, you might fall, and lose everything you have.
- Love does not always equal protection.
- Sometimes life changes you so much, you can see it in your face and eyes.
- Doing what you *must* do can hurt and damage those whom you love most.

- Power corrupts, and absolute power corrupts absolutely.
- Even when doing what is right is also dangerous, it's still important to try to do it.
- It's impossible to predict the future when you are not free to live the life you choose to live.
- Freedom is worth what you have to do to achieve it, no matter how hard it is.

BOOK REPORT IDEAS

1. Examine the Biblical quotes and references. Were they used appropriately and in context, or not?
2. Explain why the Prophet chose Kyra to marry Hyrum.
3. What characteristics of the Chosen Ones make it a cult, instead of a church?
4. What were the signs of power in the community, and who was able to gain power? Power that was equated with what?
5. What was the purpose behind all the young girls marrying only the old men?
6. Describe what it must be like to live in a group with such harsh rules and such limited chances for individuality and curiosity.
7. Speculate on what happens after the book ends. Does the Chosen Ones group continue to exist without the Prophet and many of his Apostles? Will Kyra be able to find Joshua? Will she ever see her family again, or will the family be destroyed as well?
8. Discuss the relationship between Patrick and Kyra. He knew she was breaking the rules, yet still encouraged her to come back. Do you think he considered how harsh a punishment she might face?
9. What would you have done if you were Kyra? Would you have been compliant or defiant? Why?
10. Love and protection are not the same things. Why are those in the cult not able to protect those whom they love?

BOOKTALK IDEAS

1. Use a Bible and some of the books Kyra checked out of the bookmobile as props for your talk, showing what she could or could not read.
2. Have Kyra tell her own story, in first person.
3. Focus your talk on the idea of the forbidden being attractive and why Kyra wanted to do what was forbidden.

RISKS

- Religious cult practices polygamy and forces teenage girls to marry old men
- Children, even infants, are cruelly and harshly punished
- Rape is acceptable and routinely practiced
- Church rules are enforced with punishment and violence
- No contact with the outside world is allowed

- Books and other printed material are forbidden
- Children who are "not perfect" are killed
- Friendship between boys and girls is forbidden
- Women must be subservient to men and are limited to keeping house and having and raising babies
- Women and girls may not cut their hair and must wear dresses that cover them from chin to ankles
- Incest is sanctioned
- Runaways are severely punished, even killed
- Runaways are hunted down like animals
- Girls are forced to marry old men and have babies

STRENGTHS
- Graphic portrayal of what it's like to grow up in a cult
- Main character struggles, gains insight, and escapes
- Shows the strength of family ties
- Portrays a situation seldom, if ever, seen in YA literature
- Intense writing style—suspense builds from the beginning
- Timeline covers only about three weeks, but plot reveals every detail of the action
- Characters' voices and emotions are clear and authentic
- The tragedies of the past intensify the situation in the present and show how things could go very wrong
- Shows the corruption of power and its effect on those allowed to have it
- Describes how much those who choose to stay in a cult must sacrifice on a daily basis
- Includes a courageous and heroic librarian
- Shows the differences between a benevolent and a cruel dictator
- Enforcing a harsh rule equally to all ages, infants through adults, shows an almost insane level of tunnel vision and lack of true love and understanding
- Immediate and unrelenting emotional impact on reader
- Unresolved ending leaves room for discussion and speculation

AWARDS
Title was published too recently to be eligible for awards.

REVIEWS
"This is a heart pounder, and readers will be held, especially as the danger escalates. Williams's portrayals of the family are sharp, but what's most interesting about this book is how the yearnings and fears of a character so far from what most YAs know will still seem familiar and close." Ilene Cooper, *Booklist*, 2/09

📖📖📖

CRACKBACK. John Coy. Scholastic, 2005. $16.99. 208p. ISBN10: 0439697336. ISBN13: 9780439697330. Scholastic, 2007. $6.99. 224p. ISBN10: 0439697344. ISBN13: 9780439697347. Realistic fiction. Reading Level: MS. Interest Level: YHS, OHS. English, P.E., Ethics.

SUBJECT AREAS

sports; school; ethics; peer pressure; self-knowledge; family relationships; secrets; drugs; addiction; anger; friendship; problem parents; bullying; homosexuality; intimidation; manipulation; lying and deceit; rites of passage.

CHARACTERS

Miles Manning: a junior in high school, he's a starting cornerback on the football team and wants to show his dad how good he is; he wants to do the right thing

Zack Turner: Miles's best friend, who's also a starting cornerback and who's willing to do anything to be the biggest and the best

Coach Stahl: he wants the team to play *his* way, not theirs; he is never satisfied, emphasizes the negative, and is especially hard on Miles

Coach Norlander: one of the assistant coaches

Tyson Ruden: the team's three-hundred-pound all-state tackle

Coach Sepolski: the head coach, who inspires rather than orders

Jonesy: one of the football starters and a superstar, til Tyson hits him too hard

Mom/Mrs. Manning: Miles's mother, who tries to keep the peace

Dad/Mr. Manning: Miles's father, who expects his son to be perfect, is big, and knows football

Martha Manning: Miles's eight-year-old little sister who loves musicals

Brooksy: one of the varsity football players; he's a linebacker

Lucia Lombrico: a new girl in Miles's history class

Megan Harkin: a tennis star, who's dating Brooksy

Sam Hunter: second-string football player who's also on the soccer team

Mr. Halbran: a history teacher who asks his students to research their own family history

Adams: football player

Kyra Richman: one of the cheerleaders; Miles is thinking about dating her

Stilwell: football player

Strangler: starting center for basketball

Kate Meyer: a gorgeous sophomore who likes to party

Drew: Miles's uncle on his mother's side; he's researched family history and lives with his partner Stephen

Toilet and Cooper: starters on the soccer team

Maggie Lombrico: Lucia's mother

BOOKTALK

What does loyalty mean? How far should you go to be loyal to your friends, your coach, and your team? To your family, your father? To yourself? How much of yourself do you want to give away, deny, or cover up to meet the expectations that surround you? Miles Manning is a football player, part of a team that has a good chance to win state, and he's going to have to find his own answers to all those questions during the football season he plays his junior year.

Miles may only be a junior and, at five foot ten and 155 pounds, isn't a big guy, but he loves to hit, to smash guys to the ground and take them out. That's why he's one of the first string, the starters, the stars. His father taught him how to play football almost as soon as he could walk, and expects only the best from his son. Miles is sure he can never be good enough for his dad. Zack, Miles's best friend, also a starter, is all about being the best, pumping more iron, building up more endurance, and he expects Miles to be the best as well. And on the night before their first game, he gives Miles two pills of Rip Blast. Just caffeine, he tells Miles, just like drinking a can of Red Bull, to give you a little extra edge. No big deal. Lots of seniors take them, including Tyson, their three-hundred-pound all-state tackle. Miles takes the pills, but he's not comfortable about taking them, so he sticks them in the pocket of his jeans and forgets about them.

The first game is a blowout. Miles intercepts the ball in the second play of the game and makes a thirty-one-yard touchdown. But even after a 45–3 win, Coach Stahl doesn't want them to relax. He just pushes for more. More practices, more plays, more wind sprints, and more weights, lots more weights. He wants everyone to be as bulked up as possible, as prepared as possible, as perfect as possible. For some reason, he picks Miles as his personal whipping boy. No matter what Miles does, no matter how hard he works, it's never enough. He doesn't like Miles's attitude or his performance, or the fact that he's not putting on muscle fast enough. Zack comes up with a solution—D-ball. Dianabol. It'll help Miles gain five pounds of muscle a week. Three a day, Zack says, giving Miles a package of pills. Doctor's orders. They're harmless—most of the older guys on the team take them. No big deal. Miles doesn't ask and Zack doesn't tell him where he got the pills. But after reading up on the dangers of steroids, he decides not to take them.

It's not long before he begins to see the consequences of his decision. He and Zack have a huge fight, and Zack starts hanging with Tyson and the other seniors. Coach demotes him to second string. Miles's dad is all over him to do whatever it takes to get back into the starting lineup. And Miles begins to wonder if maybe there should be something more in life than just football. Miles knows about a crackback play on the field and how to watch out for it. But this year, life is about to deliver a crackback play that he can't prepare for or bounce right back from.

MAJOR THEMES AND IDEAS

- Great players make great plays at crucial times.
- Never be satisfied until you crush your opponent. Hold him to zero points.

- Some people believe that no one needs to hear what they're doing right, just what they're doing wrong.
- Life can blindside you without warning.
- Football's a tough, physical game, but it doesn't have to be deadly.
- Who should you be loyal to—your friends, your team, or your family?
- Some men can't, or won't, share very much about themselves, especially how they feel about others.
- A good coach is one who tells the team, "Play hard. Play smart. Have fun."
- Which is braver—suicide or trying to survive as a slave?
- Slaves are the only immigrants who didn't choose to go to the New World.
- If the Atlantic Ocean were drained, there would be lines of bones indicating the major routes of the Middle Passage from Africa to America.
- Friendship is difficult when you don't agree on important choices.
- Sometimes it's almost impossible to forget your mistakes.
- Even in a team game, sometimes you're on your own: if you make a mistake, everyone sees it.
- Focusing on mistakes can make it more difficult to overcome them.
- Sometimes it's hard for parents to see how much high school's changed since they were teens. Teens today live in a culture far more different from their parents' than their parents' was from their own parents'.
- It's interesting to see where your mind takes you when you let it wander.
- Many people get angry to hide their fear and guilt.
- Letting a bully get away with bullying may help in the short term, but can result in more trouble over the long term.
- Life isn't always fair.
- Some people are just easy to be around. Being quiet together is just as important as talking.
- The longer a secret is kept, the harder it is to share.
- Doing what's right is frequently more important than doing what you're told.
- Sharing their secrets can help people understand each other.

BOOK REPORT IDEAS

1. Compare and contrast Coaches Stahl and Sepolski. Why do they coach? How do they feel about themselves, the football program, and the players?
2. After the final game Stahl tells Miles he'll never play again, this year or next. Consider all the different parts of the story and speculate on what might happen next year.
3. There is a lot of anger in this book. Do you see any characters trying to control it or get beyond it? Why or why not?
4. Discuss which takes more bravery, suicide or living in a desperate, difficult, and hopeless situation. Which would you choose and why?
5. Speculate on how the year might have gone had Stahl not been made head coach.

6. Examine what Miles's dad says after every game—how it was played and what Miles did during it. When did he support his son and why? When did he support the coach and why?
7. Several of the players used steroids openly. Discuss why none of the other players told any of the coaches. If they had, how would each of the coaches in the book have reacted?

BOOKTALK IDEAS

1. The picture book *Middle Passage* is mentioned in this book. Include in your talk Miles's history assignment and use it as a prop.
2. Focus your talk on what a crackback is, and some of the ones Miles had to deal with.
3. Focus your talk on the idea of loyalty, and one who deserves your first loyalty—your family, your friends, your team.
4. There are many secrets being kept in this book. Talk about some of them, and hint at other, more difficult ones to persuade someone to read the book.
5. Write your talk in first person as Miles or as his father.

RISKS

* Adults who hide their fear and guilt behind anger and take that anger out on others
* Homosexual characters are happy and successful
* Teens take steroids
* Adults tacitly condone steroid use
* High school athletic stars treated differently from other students
* Football coach encourages violence

STRENGTHS

* Realistic characters readers can identify with
* Characters grow and gain insight
* Ambiguous ending leaves room for reader to speculate on characters' futures
* Homosexual characters are strong, positive role models
* Dialogue is realistic but omits most vulgarities
* Football scenes are gripping, intense, and draw reader into the action
* Highlights contrast between a coach who coaches because he loves the game and the players, and one who cares about his image, his power, and winning the game
* History teaches about the horror and cruelty of the Middle Passage and the importance of knowing the history of your family

AWARD

ALA Quick Picks for Reluctant Young Adult Readers, 2006

REVIEWS

"Jumbled scenes pop into the story and then disappear, creating a slide-show effect, but the style works, and the storyline resembles a high school football season charged with sky-high emotions, devastating setbacks, and blazing moments of glory. Teen novels with truly realistic sports scenes are rare, but this one hits hard." Rollie Welch, *VOYA*, 12/05

"Coy connects the story's diverse elements—family secrets, his father's rage and homophobia, a burgeoning romance, football, and shifting friendships—in a loose jumble that, like Miles's strong first-person voice, is sharply authentic, open-ended, and filled with small details that signify larger truths." Gillian Engberg, *Booklist*, 9/05

"Boys will appreciate the well rounded characters and the plot that mixes sports with real life. It doesn't hurt that there is some great football action throughout." Julie Webb, Shelby County High School, Shelbyville, KY, *School Library Journal*, 12/05

📖📖📖

CRUISE CONTROL. Terry Trueman. HarperTeen, 2004. $15.99. 160p. ISBN10: 0066239605. ISBN13: 9780066239606. HarperTeen, 2005. $7.99. 160p. ISBN10: 0064473775. ISBN13: 9780064473774. HarperTeen, 2004. $16.89. 160p. ISBN10: 0066239613. ISBN13: 9780066239613. (library binding) Recorded Books, 2005. $30.75. ISBN10: 1419396072. ISBN13: 9781419396076. (unabridged audio CD) Recorded Books, 2005. $25.95. ISBN10: 1419331108. ISBN13: 9781419331107. (unabridged audiotape) Recorded Books, 2005. $30.75. ISBN10: 1419331094. ISBN13: 9781419331091. (unabridged audiotape, library version) Realistic fiction. Reading Level: MS, YHS. Interest Level: MS, YHS, OHS. English, Psychology, P.E.

SUBJECT AREAS

illness, physical; self-knowledge; handicaps; family relationships; anger; divorce and separation; school; sports.

CHARACTERS

Paul McDaniel: he's a jack-stud, a sports superstar with a secret he can never share and a hatred of his father that he can't control

Shawn McDaniel: he's fourteen, and his cerebral palsy keeps him from being able to communicate with anyone

Cindy McDaniel: Paul and Shawn's sister; she helps control Paul and take care of Shawn

Lindy McDaniel: she lives with her children and takes care of Shawn and puts up with Sydney's selfishness
Sydney McDaniel: he couldn't handle having a handicapped son, so he moved out long ago
Coach Davis: Paul's basketball coach
Hank Klimet/Hankster: the center on the basketball team, who's six foot nine and weighs 286 pounds
John-Boy Reich: another basketball team member
Tim Gunther/Tim-ho: Paul's best friend, who's an athlete and like a brother to him since ten years old
Eddie Farr: he's so out of it, he doesn't realize what a moron he looks like, but he's just about Shawn's only friend

BOOKTALK

My name's Paul, I'm sixteen and I'm about to graduate from high school in just a few months. I'm a triple-threat athlete—I've lettered in basketball, baseball, and football for three years. That ought to make me a major jock-stud, a shoo-in for an athletic free ride, right? Sometimes I agree with that, but sometimes my life feels totally whacked. Because while I've got this total groove going, my fourteen-year-old brother Shawn is a total veg. Yup, full fledged drooling idiot. He can't talk, and there's no way to know if he understands what's going on around him. He can't walk, feed himself, or go to the bathroom. He sits in his wheelchair and makes noises, and if they mean something, no one's been able to figure out what.

When I think about him, sometimes I wish he wasn't around, and then I feel guilty, 'cause I have so much and he has nothing. Mom and my sister Cindy take care of him, 'cause Dad bailed on us years ago. He couldn't stand being around Shawn. I can't stand even thinking about Dad. Yeah, I've got a bad temper—what they call "anger management issues." All I have to do is remember how he deserted us and then turned his poem about Shawn into a Pulitzer Prize and one TV broadcast pity party after another, and I'm ready to explode, just *looking* for a fight. The other day Tim-ho, my best friend, had to pull me off this guy twice my size, who'd almost hit a little girl and her dog in a pedestrian crosswalk. I was ready to stomp the guy's face when Tim-ho grabbed me from behind and held on til I calmed down.

That's why I like sports so much—they're a way to get out all that adrenaline and anger. Otherwise it would build up til it just overflowed, and God knows how much damage I'd do.

But now, ever since Dad was on this TV show, interviewing this man who killed his retarded son because he thought his son was in so much pain, I've watched Dad with Shawn and wondered just how far Dad would go. He's sure the noises Shawn makes when he tries to talk and the seizures that keep getting worse mean Shawn's in pain. But how can he be sure? No one can get into Shawn's brain and figure out if he loves or hates his life, or if he even knows we are his family.

When he left, Dad told me I would have to be the man of the house. But how can I? I don't know how I feel about Shawn, or about how my mother and sister have given up their lives for him. And what do I do with all the anger and the guilt and the confusion inside me? Sometimes I feel like I'm in a car, going 120 miles an hour with no way to see where I'm going, and no way to turn off the cruise control. And if I crash, what will happen to me? To my family?

MAJOR THEMES AND IDEAS

- Being the best can sometimes make you feel guilty about someone you love who isn't.
- It's hard to love someone when you don't know if they love you back and have no way of ever finding out.
- Parents can't always deal with having a child who is so severely handicapped that he can't communicate at all.
- If you can't confront the person you're mad at, it can be all too easy to take out that anger on someone else.
- Anger builds if you just sit and think about it. Getting active may be a way to defuse that energy that anger creates.
- It's hard to know how to please someone who can't give you any feedback at all.
- Everyone is entitled to life, no matter how limited it is.
- In a family with a member who has severe problems, no one but the family members and their close friends can understand what they must deal with on a daily basis.
- Ignorant sympathy means nothing.
- In some families, the children must be the strong ones.
- In the heat of the moment, it may be hard to distinguish among intense emotions, whether they are anger, fear, sadness, or guilt.
- Emotional explosions are, by nature, not logical.
- Sometimes you can get away with something stupid, with pushing the envelope and risking your life, surviving danger and death by the smallest margin. But sometimes you can't.
- You never know how it will turn out til it's over. And that may be too late.
- Even the mellowest people have limits when they're pushed too far for too long.
- Understanding yourself, even a little, can help bring you peace. Telling a secret, and apologizing, does too.
- Life will be easier for you if you just realize and remember that you get what you get and just have to learn to deal with it.
- The possibility of a miracle is always at your fingertips, if you believe it and feel the possibilities that are waiting for you.

BOOK REPORT IDEAS

1. Discuss where Paul's anger comes from and what it means.
2. Analyze Paul's feelings for Shawn and where they come from.
3. After Paul's anger is released, he feels numb and quiet. Is his normal state anger or calm? Which emotion does he show most frequently? What helps or causes him to go from angry to calm and vice versa?
4. Examine the actions of Paul's father, and look at how other people in the book see him: Paul, Lindy, Cindy, the Pulitzer Prize Committee, news reporters, the general public. Taking all these opinions into account, write an objective description of Sydney McDaniel.
5. After the *Alice Ponds Show*, Cindy and Paul begin to discuss whether or not Shawn is safe from his dad. What do you think? Could a parent kill his child, thinking it would end the child's suffering?
6. Discuss Paul's secret and what it means to him and to the others in his family.

BOOKTALK IDEAS

1. Talk about this book and its companion, *Stuck in Neutral*, in one booktalk, telling the story in first person while alternating between Shawn's and Paul's voices.
2. Have Tim-ho or Eddie tell part of the story, to give a view of Paul from outside his own head.
3. Give the talk in first person as Paul, using a letterman's jacket as a prop.
4. Include some brief information about cerebral palsy as a part of your talk.

RISKS

- Neglectful, distant father
- Alcoholic father
- Teen with out-of-control anger problems
- Realistic language
- Portrayal of completely disabled teen who cannot care for himself in any way
- Parent considers killing disabled son
- Teen beats up someone during an episode of rage

STRENGTHS

- Strong main character with clear, authentic voice
- Character questions himself, examines his emotions, and gains insight
- Clear, detailed description of what living with a profoundly disabled sibling could be like
- Portrayal of how powerful love can be
- Suggests positive ways to handle uncontrollable anger
- Shows the power of complete acceptance and long-standing friendship

AWARDS
Junior Library Guild Selection, 2005
International Reading Association Young Adult Choices, 2006

REVIEWS
"The conflict development throughout the book brilliantly portrays the emotional distress of a teenager who must cope with a handicapped sibling." James Blasingame, *VOYA*, 10/04

"Paul, like Shawn, is a victim of circumstance, and Trueman does a passionately convincing job portraying a boy who feels trapped and suffocated by responsibilities he never asked to shoulder. As he puts it, his life is "like a car roaring down the freeway in cruise control . . . and I can't even slow down." Michael Cart, *Booklist*, 3/05

"Paul's voice is convincing, and his suffering, his rage, and his conflicting emotions are portrayed well. This is a disturbing but ultimately hopeful tale about anger and love, and a must-read." Paula Rohrlick, *KLIATT*, 9/04

📖📖📖

CUT. Patricia McCormick. Front Street, an imprint of Boyds Mills Press, 2000. $16.95. 176p. ISBN10: 1886910618. ISBN13: 9781886910614. Push, 2002. $7.99. 160p. ISBN10: 0439324599. ISBN13: 9780439324595. Realistic fiction. Reading Level: MS. Interest Level: MS, YHS, OHS. Eng; Psych; P.E.

SUBJECT AREAS
mental illness; sports; therapy; friendship; self-knowledge; physical illness; problem parents; eating disorders; substance abuse; love; family relationships; rites of passage; self-destruction.

CHARACTERS
Callie: she cuts herself to help her deal with her life and has stopped talking
Sydney: Callie's roommate at Sea Pines, a residential treatment facility for troubled teens
Claire: the leader of Callie's therapy group
Tara, Becca, Debbie: food issues members of Callie's therapy group
Sydney, Tiffany: substance abuse members of Callie's therapy group
Cynthia: an attendant who supervises afternoon study hall

Ruth: a Level Three from another group, who is quiet and shy and takes Callie to her
    individual therapy sessions

"You": Callie's therapist, who's puzzled about what to do with her

Mrs. Bryant: the director of Sea Pines

Mom: Callie's mom, who comes to visit but doesn't know what to say to her daughter
    and worries about her son

Sam: Callie's eight-year-old little brother, who loves to draw and has severe
    asthma

Ruby: an attendant Callie trusts; she wears nurse's shoes that squeak on the floors

Rochelle: the bathroom attendant for Callie's group

Doreen: the person in charge of laundry exchange

Amanda/Manda: a new girl in Callie's group who cuts herself

Marie: the daytime bathroom attendant

BOOKTALK

I remember how it started. I can watch it like a video in my head. The cross-country
track meet, the empty house when I got home, the cluttered table, the Exacto knife,
the dark red drop of blood growing bigger and bigger, and the rush, the feeling of
satisfaction and relief, when it burst and ran over my skin.

I didn't tell anyone about it. I didn't cut deep enough to kill myself, just deep
enough to feel the pain, the rush, the release, just deep enough to make a scar. No one
said anything when I refused to wear anything without long sleeves. No one noticed
anything at all.

Life went on. My mother was still terrified of everything, my dad still worked
all the time and was hardly ever there, my little brother Sam still had to be careful
about everything he did so he didn't get another asthma attack and have to go to the
hospital. And me? Well, I cleaned house a lot, because of Sam, and I just kept cutting
and cutting and cutting.

And then one day at school, I had a really bad stomach ache, and went to the
nurse. She picked up my wrist to take my pulse, and then she saw them: the scars,
crisscrossing my arms, pale pink and white tattoos. That's how I ended up here at Sick
Minds with the rest of the crazies. It's really called Sea Pines, but there's no sea and
no pines, so our name really fits it more.

I decided right away that if I couldn't cut anymore, then I wouldn't talk either. I
hadn't been really hurting myself, and I really didn't want to change. If I didn't talk,
I couldn't change. After all, I knew I wasn't really crazy.

MAJOR THEMES AND IDEAS

* If you don't expect anything, you won't get disappointed.
* Sometimes it's easier to focus on the small things in life, rather than looking at
    the bigger issues you have to deal with, and figure out what you are going to do
    about them.

- In a situation where you don't have a lot of power and everything you do is controlled by someone else, you may choose to do or not do something just to give yourself the illusion of having some control or power over your behavior.
- Sometimes even talking takes too much energy.
- Cutting can be a way of dealing with overwhelmingly bad and frightening feelings. It isn't a good way, but it is a way.
- You are the only one with true control over your life and your actions.
- Other people's actions are not ever your fault. Each of us is responsible only for our own actions, not anyone else's.
- In a group or a family, one person's actions affect everyone else, because they are all connected by their membership in that group or family.
- Your scars tell a story about you, whether they are inside or outside. It might be a mistake to cover them up or erase them.
- There are all kinds of things in the world that you can use to hurt yourself. Only one person can keep you safe from all of them—you.
- No one can make you get better. You have to decide to do it yourself.

BOOK REPORT IDEAS
1. Discuss what Callie felt when she cut herself that made her keep doing it.
2. Why didn't the group really warm to Callie until she started talking? How does conversation change the relationships in a group?
3. There are two girls who cut themselves in this book. Discuss how they are different and how they are the same.
4. What do you think is the most important idea in the book and why did you choose it?
5. Explain why you think Callie ran. What happened that made getting away seem so important? And what made her decide to go back instead of going home?
6. Speculate on what will happen after the book is over—will any of the girls succeed in overcoming their problems? Why or why not?
7. Discuss why Callie called her father rather than her mother when she needed help.
8. The concepts of love and acceptance are central to this story. Discuss how each of the main characters showed their love for other people in the story.

RISKS
- Teens are anorexic, bulimic, substance abusers, and self-abusers
- Teens smoke
- Parents are ineffective or not present

STRENGTHS
- Teens work together in group therapy to gain insight
- Teens are able to improve and cope with their addictions more effectively

- Characters are three-dimensional and easy to identify with
- Characters gain insight and grow
- Members of the therapy group are a support system for each other
- Parents realize their role in their daughter's addiction to cutting
- Shows the power and emotional stranglehold of an addiction or habit
- Girls are able to see themselves through the eyes of others

AWARDS
ALA Best Books for Young Adults, 2002
ALA Quick Picks for Reluctant Young Adult Readers, 2001

REVIEWS
"This extraordinary novel explores the psychological phenomenon of self-mutilation known as cutting. . . . Realistic, sensitive, and heartfelt, this book explores the power of the human spirit as it struggles through mental illness." Mary Ann Capan, *VOYA*, 2/01

"McCormick's first novel is powerfully written. Not for the squeamish, the young women's stories avoid pathos and stereotypes. . . . *Cut* takes the issue one step further—to helping teens find solutions to problems." Gail Richmond, San Diego Unified Schools, CA, *School Library Journal*, 12/00

"*Cut* is another authentic-sounding novel in which elective mutism plays a part, this time with humor making the pain of adolescence gone awry more bearable. . . . This is an exceptional character study of a young woman and her hospital mates who struggle with demons so severe that only their bodies can confess." Frances Bradburn, *Booklist*, 1/01

📖📖📖

DAVID INSIDE OUT. Lee Bantle. Holt, 2009. $16.95. 192p. ISBN10: 0805081224. ISBN13: 9780805081220. Realistic fiction. Reading Level: MS. Interest Level: MS, YHS. English, Sex Education, Psychology.

SUBJECT AREAS
love; friendship; school; homosexuality; sex and sexuality; family relationships; self-knowledge; rites of passage; lying and deceit; secrets; anger; bullying; fear; GLBTQ; prejudice; sports; gossip; guilt; peer pressure.

CHARACTERS

David Dahlgren: he is on the cross-country team and worries about maybe being gay

Eddie: he's been David's best friend since they were in grade school

Kick/Katherine Shapiro: she's another good friend of David's, and would like to be more than a friend

Mrs. Dahlgren/Mom: David's mother, who's a college English teacher

Sean Iclandic: a junior like David; he's also on the cross-country team

Parker Grecian: he's on the team, a junior, and Sean's good friend

John Boehm: captain of the cross-country team

Mona, Kristy, and Alicia: they hang out a lot with Kick, Eddie, and David

Mrs. Timothy: David's next-door neighbor

Coach McIntyre: the cross-country coach

Mr. Detweiler: David's English teacher

Charlotte Grecian: she's a little strange

Jenny Melcher: she's Parker's girlfriend

Mark and Elaine: David's uncle and his wife

Willie: Eddie's baby brother

Grandma: David's grandmother

Rick Cutter and Brad Morte: they harass Eddie because he's gay

Mr. Shapiro/Dad: Kick's father

Harvey Gersh: David's lab partner for physics

BOOKTALK

David's a junior in high school, he runs cross country, gets along with his mom, has good friends, reads romance novels and writes to their authors, and worries about being gay. Kick's his best friend, but she's never turned him on the way Sean does, even if Kick comes on to him all the time and Sean doesn't really notice him all that much. David doesn't want to be gay, so he does all he can to change his own mind. He and Kick start dating and fooling around; he buys a *Playboy* to look at; he stays away from Eddie, who's just come out, even though they've been close friends since grade school; and he puts a rubber band around his wrist to snap whenever he has inappropriate thoughts. Nothing works. Then, he gets a note stuffed into his locker. "Want to get it on with a guy? I think you're cute. Wear your red jersey on Friday and wait on the steps outside after school. I'll meet you. DON'T TELL ANYONE!!! DON'T SHOW THIS NOTE TO ANYONE!!!! I am not messing with you." David doesn't know who wrote the note, or what would happen if he followed the note's instructions. Is the author really serious, and wants to hook up with him, or did one of the gay-hating jocks write it, and all he'd get out of it is a beating? David doesn't want his world to change, but it looks like it's going to, one way or another.

MAJOR THEMES AND IDEAS

- Being yourself works only if you're basically cool. Otherwise, it might make people reject you.
- How can you be yourself if you don't know who you are?
- Getting to know yourself better is the most important part of high school.
- Reading *Playboy* won't help a boy get over his thing for guys.
- Just because you feel like a misfit doesn't mean you are one.
- Things aren't always the way they look.
- Kissing a girl or having sex with her won't make you straight.
- Being gay won't stop you from falling in love.
- Accepting yourself as a gay man can be a difficult process.
- When someone you love breaks up with you, your friends are supposed to be there for you, to help you get over him.
- Gays threaten some boys' masculinity.
- Saying you're sorry isn't a cure-all.
- It hurts to hide the fact that you're gay.
- Not everyone is courageous enough to admit that they're gay.
- Friends accept you for who and what you are.
- First love changes you forever, even when it doesn't last.

BOOK REPORT IDEAS

1. Discuss Sean's decision to stay in the closet. Do you think he will ever come out?
2. David comes out at the high school dance. Explain what emotions he must have been feeling and how he dealt with them.
3. David and Eddie talk about how good it feels to stop keeping a big part of their lives secret. Explain why it is such a relief for them.
4. Coming out for both Eddie and David wasn't too traumatic. Discuss some things that could have happened that would have been dangerous for both of them.
5. If gay or lesbian students are harrassed or bullied at school, what should the school's response be? What is the school's most likely response?
6. David seems to agonize over admitting he's gay, snapping a rubber band on his wrist, looking at *Playboy*, trying to be attracted to Kick: what finally convinces him that he really is gay?
7. Explain what you thought the most important part of was book was, and why.
8. Discuss Kick's reaction to finding out that David was gay. Did she think she could make him change his mind?
9. Speculate on what will happen to the main characters in the future. Will Sean ever come out? Will Eddie, Kick, and David stay friends? Will they find their special someones? What else might happen to them?

BOOKTALK IDEAS
1. Have Kick, Eddie, and David introduce themselves or each other.
2. Include all the things that David does to "stop being gay."
3. Focus on the "red jersey" note that David got, and his reaction to it.
4. Build your talk around the idea of friendship and what it means to each of the main characters.

RISKS
- Promotes the idea that homosexuality is neither a choice nor a lifestyle
- Homosexual characters
- Teens are sexually active
- Teen tries to stop being gay
- Homophobic characters
- Gay teen is into hair and clothing styles—somewhat stereotypical
- Teen rejects longtime best friend when he comes out
- Masturbation scenes involving one or two gay males
- Mother forbids her son to associate with anyone she thinks is gay
- Mother sends son to psychiatrist to help him change from gay to straight
- Straight and gay sex scenes

STRENGTHS
- Strong, stable, and supportive friendships
- Positive view of homosexuality
- Includes gay athletes
- Boys read romance novels and write to authors
- Characters use reading as an appropriate escape mechanism
- Strong, caring relationship between teen and parent
- Shows how difficult it can sometimes be to admit that you're gay
- Shows the shame and guilt some teens feel when experimenting with gay sex
- Realistic dialogue including obscenities
- Genuine characters who speak and act realistically and believably
- Realistic relationships between and among teens
- Characters and situations that are easy for the reader to identify with
- Students start a Gay/Straight Alliance at school
- Teen calls gay hotline for information and support
- Teen comes out at high school dance
- Characters show a wide variety of responses when they realize they're gay
- Mother is supportive of her gay son
- Ending leaves room for speculation and discussion

AWARDS
Title was published too recently to be eligible for awards.

REVIEW
"The writing is meaty and full of well-conceived characterizations, believable plot devices and plenty of wisdom for teens trying to understand themselves. The relationships are obviously strong and fully formed—not just on paper." *Kirkus Reviews*, 4/15/09

DEADLINE. Chris Crutcher. HarperTeen, 2007. $16.99. 320p. ISBN10: 0060850892. ISBN13: 9780060850890. HarperTeen, 2009. $8.99. 336p. ISBN10: 0060850914. ISBN13: 9780060850913. HarperTeen, 2007. $17.89. 320p. ISBN10: 0060850906. ISBN13: 9780060850906. (library binding) Realistic fiction. Reading Level: YHS. Interest Level: YHS, OHS. English, Ethics, Psychology, Sociology, Health.

SUBJECT AREAS
anger; writing; sports; school; creativity; dating and social life; death and dying; ethics; family relationships; self-knowledge; friendship; grief and mourning; secrets; peer pressure; lying and deceit; love; illness, physical; religion; sex and sexuality; rape; guilt; unwed teen parents.

CHARACTERS
Ben Wolf: a senior in high school, who has just found out he has only a year to live
Doc Wagner: he gives Ben the bad news and agrees to tell no one else
Mom/Mrs. Wolf: she's a severe manic-depressive
Dad/Mr. Wolf: he is as even-tempered as his wife is moody
Cody Wolf: Ben's younger brother, who's also a senior and the team quarterback
Myrna Whitney: Doc's receptionist
Dr. Bachchau: a doctor in Denver who confirms Doc's diagnosis
Coach Lou Banks: the football coach, who loves what he does
Todd Langford: the assistant coach
Sooner Cowans: a football player with a bad attitude and an abusive father
Randy Dolven, Rick Glover: football players who are friends of Cody and Ben's
Coach Gildehaus: cross-country coach
Marla Dawson: Ben's therapist, a psychiatric social worker
Dallas Suzuki: the girl Ben's had a crush on for years, and the hottest girl at school

Mr. Lambeer: history, government, and current events teacher; Ben loves to debate with him

Rudy McCoy: the custodian for the car dealership where Ben works and the town drunk

Winona: the waitress at The Chief

Joe Henry: Dallas's little brother

BOOKTALK

When Ben Wolf gets a message from the family doctor a few days after a routine physical, he doesn't expect what he hears. His physical exam revealed that he has an aggressive blood disease, and even with treatment, he has only about a year to live.

Ben has always felt that he would die young, and Doc's news just confirmed it. After careful consideration, Ben decides not to get any kind of treatment and just live as long as he can. The length of his life isn't as important as its quality.

That's not all that unusual—many patients make the same decision. But Ben takes things one step further. He decides not to tell anyone he's dying and threatens legal action if his doctor says anything to anyone.

So what would you do if you had to cram your whole life into twelve months? Ben has some priorities: he wants to play football, even if he only weighs 123 pounds; he wants to make a play for Dallas Suzuki, the hottest girl in school; he wants to give his conservative civics teacher a daily migraine; and he wants to live life large as long as he can.

At first, things are going really well—the football team is winning just about every game, Dallas has asked him to the homecoming dance, and he's having a great time tormenting Mr. Lambeer. But then Ben realizes keeping everything a secret might not have been such a good idea. He's not the only person in town keeping secrets, and if people he cares about have trusted him with their secrets, how will they react when they find out he didn't trust them enough to share his secret?

Knowing you have only a few months to live is hard. Dying *isn't* for sissies!

MAJOR THEMES AND IDEAS

- Life isn't just about being alive, it's about living well.
- Football is just a game.
- Sports are about concentration and confidence, not just size. It's in the mind, not just the body.
- Energy never dies. There's something after death—we just don't know what it is.
- Think about the other guys on the team—harmony works better than its opposite.
- Worrying about how you'll be remembered is futile.
- Some people use comedy as a shield when they get too close to telling the real truth.

- Sometimes you just connect with someone the instant you meet them. It feels like you already really *know* them.
- When life gets hard, take it one day at a time, or one hour, or even one minute. One thing at a time.
- Concentrate on this week's game, not next week's or next month's.
- You can't fix everything. Some things just stay broken, no matter what you do.
- Life's short. Do what you love.
- When you know you're dying, you start looking for the most important things in life.
- Life's no fun without risk.
- Secrecy is okay with the general public, but not with people you care about. It can ruin everything.
- Love is unconditional acceptance.
- Being in love means my life is better with you in it, and vice versa. Love's intensity comes from how much better.
- Those in power get to write the history books.
- Help yourself before you try to help anyone else.
- Love turns to hate at the fringes of any belief system.
- If someone's different and it scares you and makes you mad, you need to stop and take a closer look at it. The fear or anger is about *you*, not the other person.
- Nothing dies. Things change.
- Sometimes we're privy to information that comes to us through senses other than our brains.
- Each of us has inside us everything the universe has within it. Everything that exists inside you also exists outside you.
- If you live life the best you can, you have the best chance of others seeing a piece of what you see.
- No one is ever exactly what you expect.
- The language in a book represents the time and culture in which it was written, not in which it is read.
- When there's no communication, people die.
- The only truly ruined people are the ones who believe they are.
- People who feel ruined can't tell the truth, so they keep it inside. When they can tell it, it means they own it instead of being owned by it.
- Things aren't always as they seem.
- The universe works in strange and mysterious ways.
- There's a lot in the universe that humans don't understand. But the truth doesn't need to be known or believed to be true.
- The thing that prevents the worst from happening is the truth.
- Free will is one of the best things about being human.
- Everything started as one, everything still is one, and everything will end up as one.
- Life is a game—a wonderful, beautiful, hard, scary game—that teaches you what you need to know to go on to what's next.

- Experience is the only teacher.
- Truth is the only universal.
- All bets are off when death is imminent.
- Living and dying isn't just about you. It's about you *and* all the other people your life touches.
- The more you act out of fear, the less you'll get done.
- Life doesn't come with do-overs.
- It's disrespectful to not let people deal with difficult things in a straightforward manner.
- Telling the truth brings freedom. At least you don't have to remember what lie you told.
- Connection is everything and life is risky.
- Do your best. You don't know how many lives will be touched or changed by what you leave behind.
- You put yourself out there in the truest way you can and hope that others will do the same. You'll connect, or you won't, but either way, you did everything you could.
- Almost every forward thinker in history was ridiculed, if not threatened or killed, for criticizing current and uninformed beliefs.
- Things happen because of faulty information, and the reason to get educated is to cut down on the amount of faulty information and make better decisions.
- None of us will ever be too old to die young.
- Dying isn't for sissies.
- Death is not an end. It is a change, and a beginning.

BOOK REPORT IDEAS

1. Ben spends a lot of time clarifying his personal philosophies. Choose two to three of them and discuss why you chose them and why they do or don't fit with your own philosophy.
2. Explain what you would do if you were faced with a situation like Ben's.
3. Discuss whether Ben was courageous or cowardly in not telling anyone about his disease.
4. Explain your understanding of "Live each day as if it were your last and as if you would live forever."
5. Speculate on what might have happened had Ben explained about his disease right away.
6. Speculate on what you think happens after the end of the book. How will people's lives have changed by Ben's life and death?
7. Discuss the information Ben gets from *Lies My Teacher Told Me*. Is it credible to you? How would you teach history?
8. Comment on Ben and Dallas's relationship. What did each of them get from it? How might it have developed had Ben lived longer?
9. Analyze what you think is the most important concept or idea in the book and why you chose it.

10. Discuss your belief or philosophy or ideas about death and what happens afterward.
11. Discuss why Crutcher wrote this book. What was he trying to tell his readers? What did he tell you?

BOOKTALK IDEAS
1. Focus your talk on the ideas of death and knowing when you will die.
2. Use quotes from Ben's conversations with "Hay-Soos" in your talk.
3. Have Ben tell his own story, but make sure you don't include information from the second half of the book.

RISKS
- Teen refuses treatment for fatal disease
- Teens are sexually active
- Various obscenities and slang words and phrases
- Teen is raped by family member
- Mother is bipolar and unable to be a parent to her sons
- Father is verbally and physically abusive
- Racist characters
- Child sexual abusers
- Conservative teacher wants students to accept his beliefs rather than form their own
- Suicide

STRENGTHS
- Authentic voice of narrator
- Opportunities for variety of discussions
- Realistic characters teens can identify with
- Accurate dialogue
- Strong marital relationship
- Discussion of life and death topics leads readers to examine their own beliefs, ethics, philosophies
- Very powerful ending that will impact most readers very dramatically and may require discussion or feedback of some sort to help readers understand it
- Suspense remains taut even though readers know how it will end
- Includes ideas and books teens may not have encountered before; for example, *Lies My Teacher Told Me*
- Author doesn't pull any punches or create a "deus ex machina" ending
- Gives readers a chance to examine their own ideas about life and death and afterwards
- Shows strong bond between brothers
- Football coach more interested in his players than in winning the game

AWARD
ALA Quick Picks for Reluctant Young Adult Readers, 2008

REVIEWS
"As usual, Crutcher does not hesitate to incorporate serious subject matter within an engaging first-person narrative. . . . Whether facing physical limitations, making a stand, or telling the truth, Ben is a teen hero for whom readers cannot help but cheer." Patti Sylvester Spencer, *VOYA*, 8/07

"Some discussion of sexual molestation and child abuse is present in the text, but is not graphic or overwhelming in its depiction. Crutcher uses dark humor and self-deprecation effectively to avoid maudlin situations, and teens will appreciate the respectful tone of the work." Chris Shoemaker, New York Public Library, *School Library Journal*, 9/07

"Crutcher writes vivid sports action scenes, and teens' interest will be held by the story's dramatic premise, Ben's unlikely turn as a football hero, love scenes with Dallas (including some mildly explicit sex), and Ben's high-gear pursuit of life's biggest questions." Gillian Engberg, *Booklist*, 9/07

⊞⊞⊞

DEVIL ON MY HEELS. Joyce MacDonald. Delacorte, 2004. $15.95. 272p. ISBN10: 0385731078. ISBN13: 9780385731072. Laurel Leaf, 2005. $6.50. 272p. ISBN10: 0440238293. ISBN13: 9780440238294. Delacorte, 2004. $17.95. 272p. ISBN10: 038590133X. ISBN13: 9780385901338. (library binding) Historical fiction. Reading Level: MS. Interest Level: MS, YHS. English, Social Studies, Ethics, American History, Government, Psychology, Sociology.

SUBJECT AREAS
racism; anger; cultural identity; ethnic groups; prejudice; poverty; justice; manipulation; fear; friendship; death and dying; gossip; school; love; secrets; censorship.

CHARACTERS
Dove Alderman: she discovers her safe and happy hometown is hiding some dark secrets
Miss Delpheena Poyer: Dove's English teacher who assigns controversial books
Chase Tully: the coolest boy in school; he has a silver-blue T-Bird convertible
Gator: he's a picker and has worked the Alderman groves for years

Jacob Tully: Chase's father, who owns over a thousand acres of orange groves
Dad/Lucas Alderman: Dove's father, who owns about seven hundred acres of
    groves
Silas Beaureve: he owns one of the smaller groves, about one hundred acres, the site
    of the fourth fire
Moss Henley: he's on the police force and his outhouse was the first of the fires
Travis Waite: he is crew boss for most of the pickers and his tool house was the
    second fire
Delia Washburn: she's the housekeeper for Dove and her father
Old Eli: he's worked in the Alderman groves since before Dove was born
Luellen: she runs the beauty shop in town
Mrs. Redfern: Judge Redfern's wife and a member of the school board
Nona Parker: she works for Luellen
Rosemary Howell: she's Luellen's cousin, and her parents are migrant workers
Rayanne Bucham: Dove's best friend
Willy Podd, Earl Hubbs: two troublemakers a year older than Dove and Rayanne
Teak, Jody: two migrant kids who work for the Aldermans
Julio Gonzalez: migrant worker with a new baby
Spudder Rhodes: police chief
Whidden Hadley: he's taking Rayanne to the senior prom
Jinny Culpepper: a friend of Dove and Rayanne
Cholly Blue: he owns a bar in the colored part of town and he saw Gus's death

BOOKTALK

I grew up in the Florida orange groves, living in a sleepy little town where nothing ever happened. But the year I was a sophomore, when I found out what most folks in town were covering up, all my expectations about myself, my life, and my town blew up in my face.

The first thing that happened was the fires. After four of them, people started talking about how someone was setting them. And that the someone, or someones, were pickers, migrant workers who came in to pick the oranges and the other crops.

That's why no one believed me when I said I saw the lightning strike that hit our old barn. By that time, everyone was believing the rumors, and when Willy said he'd seen a colored man running away from our place that night, no one questioned him.

But fires aside, the pickers were definitely not happy about the way they were being paid. Travis Waite, the crew boss, had taken advantage of them for years, but he'd set up a new scheme this year. He went down to Mexico and rounded up some folks to be on his crew. He said he'd pay good wages, but they'd have to pay him for the cost of the trip. Between that and having to buy everything on credit at Travis's camp store, Travis ended up keeping almost everything they made.

Then Delia, our housekeeper and the nearest thing I had to a mother, told me how her husband had died years ago. It was a hit and run, a car full of white men taking a shortcut through the colored part of town. And it wasn't an accident; it had been deliberate.

But when my boyfriend told me that he knew who'd done it and why it got covered up so fast, my neat and tidy world exploded. There are some things that just aren't right, and covering up a murder because of the color of a man's skin is one of them. Not taking care of your own workers to put more money into your own pocket is another. And finding your sleepy little town was run by the KKK was the final straw. I knew I had to act!

MAJOR THEMES AND IDEAS
- If you're colored, you need to remember your place and not get all big-headed.
- People are generally all too ready to believe a rumor, especially if they'd like it to be true.
- There are two kinds of justice in the world: one for colored people and one for white people.
- Everyone has a skeleton in their closet that they're trying to hide.
- Eventually, secrets aren't secret any longer.
- Finding out that someone you love has been covering up a crime for years makes them a lesser person in your eyes.
- It's impossible to unlearn or unknow something, no matter how much you'd like to.
- A white girl and a colored boy can't be friends or more than friends.
- Hate is powerful and hard to control.
- People generally do what's easiest and most expedient.
- The majority isn't always right, just because it's the majority.
- Covering up a mess or mistake doesn't make it go away.
- The truth changes everything. It also changes nothing.
- Sometimes it's more cruel to tell the truth than it is to perpetuate a lie.
- Doing the wrong thing for the right reason can be kinder than doing the right thing.
- Knowing the truth doesn't always make everything better.
- One person can make a difference.

BOOK REPORT IDEAS
1. Compare Dove and Rosemary. How are they alike? How have their lives made them different?
2. There is a great deal of anger in this book, some of it justified, some not. Discuss who was angry and why, and whether or not it was justified.
3. Compare Dove when we first met her with who she'd become by the end of the book.
4. Describe how the men in town rationalized Gus's murder.
5. Speculate on how Delia and Dove's relationship will evolve in the future.

6. Discuss how events might have changed if Dove hadn't found out about Gus's death. Would the conflict with the pickers still have gone so far out of control?
7. Compare the way minorities are treated in the book with the way they are treated today.

BOOKTALK IDEAS
1. Use a Valencia orange as a prop.
2. Let Dove tell her own story in first person.
3. Make Gator the focus of the talk, as Dove introduces him.
4. Focus your talk on the idea of secrets and what some of them were.

RISKS
- Set in a time period when racism was taken for granted
- Teens smoke
- Vulgar language
- Murder is covered up by police
- Blacks are harassed, beaten, and hunted
- Ku Klux Klan is active, and controls entire towns
- Minorities are cheated and taken advantage of
- Racist characters
- Father rejects son because he's not a racist

STRENGTHS
- Lead character fights for what she believes is right
- Accurate portrayal of a time period
- Realistic dialogue
- Shows the different ways blacks and whites lived
- Characters grow and gain insight
- Highlights the inhumanity of racism
- Strong, likable characters
- Fast-moving, suspenseful plot

AWARD
New York Public Library Books for the Teen Age, 2005

REVIEWS
"Some readers will be upset by the use of the offensive words by some of the Klansmen, but it is completely in context for the time and only accentuates their racism. The writing is excellent, and the story believable. This novel will provide

powerful supplementary reading for studies of racism." Leslie Carter, *VOYA*, 8/04

"This is certainly a page-turner and it will give readers insight into a difficult and shameful part of American history." Bruce Anne Shook, Mendenhall Middle School, Greensboro, NC, *School Library Journal*, 7/04

"McDonald uses realistic dialogue for the time period, . . . to deftly portray her well-developed characters in scenes that are equally vivid and sometimes violently graphic. Gripping historical storytelling." *Kirkus Reviews*, 4/04

ᘯᘯᘯ

THE DISREPUTABLE HISTORY OF FRANKIE LANDAU-BANKS. E. Lockhart. Hyperion, 2008. $16.99. 352p. ISBN10: 0786838183. ISBN13: 9780786838189. Hyperion, 2009. $8.99. 352p. ISBN10: 0786838191. ISBN13: 9780786838196. Brilliance Audio, 2008. $29.95. ISBN10: 1423366808. ISBN13: 9781423366805. (unabridged audio CD) Brilliance Audio, 2008. $74.25. ISBN10: 1423366794. ISBN13: 9781423366799. (unabridged audiotape, library version) Hyperion, 2009. $19.65. 352p. ISBN10: 1417832940. ISBN13: 978141832941. (library binding) Thorndike Press, 2009. $23.95. 502p. ISBN10: 1410414396. ISBN13: 9781410414397. (large print) Playaway, 2008. $64.99. ISBN10: 1606408909. ISBN13: 9781606408902. (unabridged audiobook) Brilliance Audio, 2008. $39.25. ISBN10: 1423366832. ISBN13: 9781423366836. (unabridged audio MP3-CD, library version) Realistic fiction. Reading Level: MS. Interest Level: MS, YHS. English, Sociology.

SUBJECT AREAS
secrets; dating and social life; school; self-knowledge; friendship; crime and delinquency; humor; ethics; guilt; anger; adventure; betrayal; creativity; fear; family relationships; rites of passage; peer pressure.

CHARACTERS
Frankie Landau-Banks: a student at Alabaster Preparatory Academy; she's quite possibly a criminal mastermind and responsible for the misdeeds of the Loyal Order of the Basset Hounds
Zada Landau-Banks: Frankie's older sister, who also went to Alabaster Prep
Ruth Landau: Frankie and Zada's mother
Uncle Ben: one of Ruth's brothers
Uncle Paul: Ruth's other brother

Franklin/Senior Banks: Frankie and Zada's father
Matthew Livingston: the boy Frankie has a crush on, who's one of the popular crowd and a big man on campus
Trish: Frankie's roommate, who's into hockey, lacrosse, and baking
Artie: Trish's boyfriend, who has keys to most of the buildings on campus
Porter Welsch: he met Frankie at the Geek Conglomerate party
Bess Montgomery: the girl who took Porter away from Frankie
Alpha Tesorieri: a senior who's always been alpha dog in any group he's in
Dean: one of Alpha's friends, who is always trying to make himself feel important
Callum: he, Matthew, Alpha, and Dean are in charge of sending out the little blue envelopes to certain students
Ms. Jessom: she's new to Alabaster and teaches Cities, Art, and Protest
Star: she's a sophomore in Frankie's class who is dating Dean
Claudia: she's a friend of Star's, who's tall, redheaded, and a soccer star
Elizabeth Haywood: she dates Alpha, and so she's called the "she-wolf"
Steve and Tristan: two more guys who hang out with Alpha and Matthew
The Loyal Order of the Basset Hounds: a secret, males-only society that's existed for years at Alabaster

BOOKTALK

The letter made it clear just who was responsible for the antics that went on that fall at Alabaster Prep. It said:

> I, Frankie Landau-Banks, hereby confess that I was the sole mastermind behind the actions of the Loyal Order of the Basset Hounds. I take full responsibility for the disruptions caused by the Order, including the Library Lady, the Doggies in the Window, the Night of a Thousand Dogs, the Canned Beet Rebellion, and the Abduction of the Guppy.
>
> Of course, the members of the Order are human beings, and could have refused to follow my directives, if they had chosen to do so. You have asked me to tell you their names. I respectfully decline.
>
> I do understand your unhappiness over the incidents. I see that my behavior disrupted the smooth running of your patriarchal establishment. But I would like to suggest that you view each of the Loyal Order's projects as the creative civil disobedience of students who are politically aware and artistically expressive, and view my behavior specifically from within the context of my and the Loyal Order's actions.

People have called Frankie many things, chief among them "criminal mastermind." This is the story of how she earned those titles.

MAJOR THEMES AND IDEAS

- Boys and girls have different rules for just about everything.
- High school is a chance to create a network of friends that will last a lifetime.

- Is an alpha dog still an alpha dog if you move him away from his pack? In the new pack, does he remain an alpha dog, or does he start at the bottom of the pack and work his way back to alpha dog?
- For some people, rules exist to be broken.
- The world is one giant panopticon, and someone, somewhere, somehow, is always watching you.
- If you think someone is watching you, you follow the rules, no matter what.
- Secrets are more powerful if people know you've got them. Show them just a glimpse, and keep the rest hidden.
- Too many girls let themselves be defined by the boy they're dating.
- Selective memory may not be stupidity or poor recollection; it can be a power play, intended to make someone perceived as a threat feel uncomfortable or challenged.
- Enlightened twenty-first-century males are happy to let women into their inner circles, once the female has proved her worth by joining them in their hunts, games, and adventures, and demonstrated that females can do anything males can do. Or the males at least like to think that's what they would do.
- If you don't like food, you probably don't like sex either.
- At boarding school, when the usual obstacles of transportation and suspicious parents are removed, relationships can progress very quickly.
- Some boys invite the girls they date into their lives, but the boy never enters the girl's world at all. She becomes a part of his life, but he isn't interested in becoming a part of hers.
- Money and popularity can make life very easy. When you've always been very wealthy, you don't need to impress anyone; you aren't always required to obey the rules, so you are free to be silly or careless, because you're secure. This quality can be very attractive, but it can also be very off-putting.
- Being a man's arm candy isn't always fun, and may be unpleasant part of the time.
- Comparing the gender relationships of animals to the gender relationships of humans can result in a lot of incorrect assumptions.
- There's more to people than what meets the eye—everyone has layers and layers underneath the surface, just like an onion.
- A strategist always considers her options before she speaks, which is almost always a good thing.
- The institutions of male supremacy have power over you only when you buy into their ideas and beliefs.
- Sometimes breaking rules, rebelling, can feel good, can feel free. But choose your rebellions carefully—make sure they are about something significant.
- Some people don't just want to be right, they need to be right, and will do anything to prove that they are.
- Calling a person harmless can backfire and make them want to prove that they are indeed capable of harming someone or something. It's a put-down that must be responded to.

- Schadenfreude—the enjoyment of another's pain or discomfort.
- Many boys and men put more emphasis on how girls and women look than how they think.
- He'll love you when you need help, when he can set the boundaries and make the rules, when you are a smaller, younger person than he is with no social power. He'll adore you for your youth and charm and protect you from the larger concerns of life. But what about when you are strong and smart and determined and make your own rules and boundaries—will he love you then?
- Some people want to be liked. Others just want to be notorious.
- There are people who follow the rules and don't walk on the grass, and then there are people who are off-roaders, who make their own paths, who ignore the rules. Those are the people who have a chance to change the world.
- It's better to be alone than to be with someone who can't see who you are. It's better to lead than to follow, to speak up rather than keep silent. It is better to open doors than to shut them on people.

BOOK REPORT IDEAS

1. Michel Foucault proposes that the world is like a giant panopticon, and someone is watching us all the time. Discuss this concept and how it is or isn't true in our culture today.
2. Living in a panopticon produces systemic paranoia. Explain first what that term means, and then discuss how paranoia is developed and encouraged.
3. Explain how Alabaster is like a panopticon.
4. How do we become ourselves, the people we are right now? Point out several milestones or turning points in your life and how they affected the person you are today.
5. Discuss the Old Boy concept, and explain how one becomes an Old Boy. Are there female Old Boys or Old Girls? Why or why not?
6. Discuss the Suicide Club and its two goals of urban exploration and public ridiculousness. What did they accomplish with their escapades? What might it be like to be a member of a group like this?
7. Frankie admires her own ability with words and her courage. Explain how these qualities help get her into trouble.
8. Discuss the mating and gender relationships of animals, and compare them to the mating and gender relationships of humans. How much do our actions echo theirs?
9. Was Frankie really the cause of the tension between Alpha and Matthew? Examine their relationship for other causes of tension or anger between them.
10. Discuss Frankie's fascination with negative or neglected positives. Can you think of any that are not in the book?
11. Discuss how Frankie felt when Alpha began to hijack her pranks.
12. How did Frankie benefit from her pranks? What did she get from them?

13. Explain why you think Frankie worked so hard to be a member of a group that would never want her or accept her. What did their rejection mean to her?

BOOKTALK IDEAS

1. Use a stuffed dog or a small figurine of a basset hound as a prop for your talk.
2. Use a quote from Wodehouse in your talk.
3. Use the copy from the dust jacket in your booktalk.
4. Use the text of the Basset oath in your talk.
5. Focus your talk on the scene where Frankie and Elizabeth debate the gender roles of men and women.
6. Let Frankie tell her own story, and introduce the other major characters.

RISKS

- Teens drink and smoke
- Delinquent behavior
- Obscenities
- Vandalism
- Girl demands to be thought of and treated as boys are

STRENGTHS

- Powerful discussion of gender roles in our society
- Characters' personalities are revealed slowly, creating suspense
- Pranks are funny and creative
- Ending is ambivalent and leaves room for discussion
- Omniscient narrator presents an intriguing perspective
- Characters interact with each other in a realistic way
- Main character is a smart, strong, empowered teen woman

AWARDS

ALA Best Books for Young Adults, 2009
Michael L. Printz Honor, 2009
Booklist Editor's Choice, 2008
SLJ Best Books for Children, 2008

REVIEWS

"Lockhart fashions a thoroughly enjoyable tale of a good girl who aches to be bad . . . The prose flows smoothly, and readers will remain engaged to see what new dastardly deed the heroine has planned. Fans will applaud at the conclusion as Frankie strides into the sunset, her head metaphorically bloody but unbowed." Angelica Delgado, *VOYA*, 12/07

"Lockhart has created a layered and engrossing story that is as smart and quick as Frankie, combining the thrilling prospect of how she will get caught with her earnest attempts to understand what it means to be an outsider, an underdog, and in love. An empowered female hero like Frankie is a rare and refreshing find. She is the ultimate feminist role model for teens: a girl with guts and imagination who's brave enough to take on the 'old boys' club.'" Emily Anne Valente, New York Public Library, *School Library Journal*, 3/08

"Lockhart creates a unique, indelible character in Frankie, whose oddities only make her more realistic, and teens will be galvanized by her brazen action and her passionate, immediate questions about gender and power, individuals and institutions, and how to fall in love without losing herself." Gillian Engberg, *Booklist*, 1/08

"Lockhart has transcended the chick-lit genre with this adroit, insightful examination of the eternal adolescent push-pull between meekly fitting in and being liked or speaking out and risking disdain." *Kirkus Reviews*, 2/08

ᘓᘓᘓ

DOUBLE HELIX. Nancy Werlin. Dial, 2004. 244p. $15.99. ISBN: 0803726066. ISBN13: 9780803726062. Puffin, 2005. $6.99. 256p. ISBN10: 014240327X. ISBN13: 9780142403273. Tandem Library, 2005. $15.80. 244p. ISBN10: 1417693967. ISBN13: 9781417693962. (library binding) Recorded Books, 2004. $77.75. ISBN10: 1419318306. ISBN13: 9781419318306. (unabridged audio CD) Recorded Books, 2004. $61.75. ISBN10: 140258377X. ISBN13: 9781402583773. (unabridged audiotape) Recorded Books, 2004. Recorded Books, 2004. $56.75. ISBN13: 9781428168060. (unabridged audiobook) Reading Level: MS. Interest Level: MS, YHS, OHS. English, Biology, Ethics, Psychology.

SUBJECT AREAS
ethics; family relationships; illness, physical; death and dying; secrets; friendship; working; self-knowledge; sex and sexuality; love; trust; taking responsibility; anger; computers; dysfunctional families; fear; justice; lying and deceit; problem parents; rites of passage.

CHARACTERS
Eli Samuels: he's almost seven feet tall, a gifted athlete, a straight-A student, and may carry a gene that will destroy his life
Vivian Fadiman: Eli's girlfriend, who loves and trusts him but doesn't understand why he hides so much of his life from her

Jonathan Samuels: Eli's father, who has been keeping too many secrets for far too long

Ana Samuels: Eli's mother, who is dying of an incurable genetic disease she may have passed on to her son

Dr. Quincy Wyatt: a brilliant and legendary geneticist who knew Eli's parents before Eli was born, and seems to know more about Eli than he is willing to tell

Kayla Matheson: a year older than Eli; she is staying with Dr. Wyatt for the summer and is Eli's equal in both brains and athletic ability

Judith Ryan: head of Human Resources for Dr. Wyatt's company, Wyatt Transgenics

Larry Donohue: Eli's boss at WT; he relates comic book characters to the genetic work the company is doing

Mary Alice Gregorian: she is in charge of the lab where Eli works and runs it on a daily basis

Mrs. Fadiman: Viv's mother, who treats Eli like her son

Foo-Foo 14: she's one of the rabbits that Eli takes care of and is the source of the incident that makes him start asking questions about what's really happening at WT

BOOKTALK

The email was a drunken impulse, impossible to recall once I'd hit the send button. Forget about drinking and driving; it's drinking and email that can really mess up your life and change it in ways you'd never even dreamed of.

But even though that email changed everything, it wasn't the thing that started it. The letter I'd found several weeks before had been the beginning. It was pushed to the back of the drawer in our hall table, dated ten years ago, telling my dad that he was negative for Huntington's disease, the obscene disease that was killing my mother and had a fifty-fifty chance of killing me one of these days. And my dad had never told me he was at risk too, never said a thing. He just kept nagging me about getting tested. But I didn't want to be tested. If I had it, I had it. It was fatal, untreatable, incurable. I'd lose control of my muscles, my emotions, my memory. For all practical purposes, I'd go insane, just like my mother had. And there was no way to know when it would happen—thirty, thirty-five, forty-five, fifty. If my DNA carried the same genetic flaw that my mother's did, sooner or later, the time bomb would explode. Fact. Absolute. No exceptions.

I was angry with Dad for keeping that secret, for trying to rule my life, refusing to let me do what I *knew* was right for myself. So I poured myself into a bottle of booze and wrote to Dr. Quincy Wyatt, who'd arranged for my father to be tested. I had no idea what their connection was—my father was a psychologist, and Wyatt was a genius, a legend in genetics. But I'd decided to put off college for a year and think about what I really wanted out of life, in spite of my father's opposition, and so I needed a job. I thought maybe Wyatt would be willing to give me one. Working for Wyatt Transgenics would be incredible!

I was sorry just seconds after I hit the send button for that email to Wyatt, but there was nothing to do about it but hope it would be read and deleted before it actually got to him. I never expected to get an interview with Wyatt himself.

And soon, a *lot* of things were happening that I'd never expected. I got a job at WT, one reserved for college, not high school, graduates. When I told my father, he went ballistic and forbade me to take the job, but refused to tell me why. That didn't seem like a good enough reason to turn down the biggest chance of my life, and so I didn't. Dad and I had been fighting for a while about my mother and about my refusal to get tested, but now anytime Wyatt's name came up, I could feel the anger rolling off Dad in waves. I met Kayla, who was staying with Wyatt for the summer and felt a strange, almost mesmerizing attraction for her. In fact, the day I met her I stood up my girlfriend Viv for a celebration dinner we'd been planning for ages. That night Viv met my father and found out about my mother, and my carefully compartmentalized life began to fall apart. The next day Foo-Foo 14 got out of her cage, and I found that hidden, private elevator behind what looked like a regular door and realized that there were mysteries and secrets at WT that involved me, even though I knew nothing about them.

Why hide an elevator? And why did the control panel have five levels of basements when all the others had only four? What was going on at Wyatt Transgenics, and why did I feel so sure that I was involved in a very major way?

MAJOR THEMES AND IDEAS

- Sooner or later, parents must understand that their teenagers will be making their own decisions about what is best for them.
- Secrets kept from those you love can tear both families and relationships apart. They must be revealed before healing can begin.
- Trust is a prerequisite for true intimacy and must be given equally by both people.
- Love means letting someone else see all of you, even the parts you don't like to share.
- Genetic manipulation can have positive, negative, and most of all, unforeseen results.
- Anger can destroy both its source and its target.
- Absolute power can corrupt absolutely, but also stealthily, and with malice aforethought.
- Things happen for a reason. Trust the universe.
- There is no way for us to know how many lives we touch without realizing it or how the world has changed because we have been a part of it.
- It's impossible to protect your children forever, and as they grow up, trying to do so might even cause them harm.
- If you want to know something, you have to ask about it and talk about it. No one is going to know you are searching for information unless you speak up.

- Secrets can eat away at the person who keeps them, helping to destroy them from the inside out.

BOOK REPORT IDEAS

1. Both Kayla and Eli are gifted athletes, extremely intelligent, and unusually attractive. Discuss some of the reasons why they might share these characteristics.
2. Compare and contrast Dr. Wyatt's and Dr. Fukuyama's philosophies about genetic engineering, explaining which perspective makes more sense to you.
3. After spending time with Wyatt and Kayla, Eli is unable to reconnect with Viv. Explain your perception of his state of mind at that point and why he reacted in the way that he did.
4. Kayla grew up with knowledge about herself that Eli's parents kept from him. Discuss how you think having that knowledge impacted her life and her relationships with Wyatt and Eli.
5. Discuss how Eli's life might have been different had he grown up with the knowledge about himself and Wyatt that Kayla did.
6. Viv and Eli disagree about the place that trust and openness play in a relationship. Explain both perspectives and discuss which is more likely to enhance an intimate relationship and why.
7. Compare and contrast Quincy Wyatt and Jonathan Samuels, discussing their philosophies of life, their ethics, and their relationships with Eli.
8. The people in this book all believe that at one time or another, their actions are moral and ethical. Choose the persons you think were the most and least morally and ethically correct or appropriate, and explain why you chose them.
9. Several people go to a great deal of effort to keep secrets from each other. Discuss how lives would have been changed had some of those secrets not been kept.
10. Share your philosophy about the ethics of creating human life in a laboratory environment. Will humans ever become their own creations?
11. Examine the relationship between Eli and his father, and discuss how it changed at crucial turning points; for instance, when Eli found the letter, when he decided to work for WT, when Jonathan met Vivian, and several other situations.
12. Genetic manipulation can take place in many ways, for many reasons. Discuss your own opinion about what is ethical and not ethical about this process, whether it is done with animals or humans.
13. Viv, Eli, and Wyatt all discuss their concepts of what a human soul might be. Summarize and compare their ideas with your own, including why you do or do not agree with any of their ideas.
14. Viv tells Eli several times to "Trust the universe. Everything happens for a reason." Explain what that means to you and whether you see life as purposeful and directed or random. Do you see life as ordered and sequential or chaotic?

15. Speculate what the future will be like for Eli, Viv, and Kayla. Based on who they are at the end of the book, what will they be like and what will they be doing in five years? Ten years? Twenty?
16. Choose the idea or ideas in the book that you are most interested in, that resonate with you the most; discuss them and explain why you chose them.
17. This is a book that might be used in middle or high school classrooms for class discussions. In your opinion, why would it be appropriate or inappropriate in such a setting? What parts would be interesting or involving to discuss or debate? What parts would not?
18. Explain why you changed and how you are different as a result of your reading this book. If you have not changed your ideas or opinions, explain why not.

BOOKTALK IDEAS

1. Use a picture of a strand of DNA as a prop for your talk or report.
2. Write your talk as a memoir, as Eli looks back on this transitional part of his life. Be careful, however, not to give away too much and ruin the book for the listener.
3. Write your talk alternately from Eli's and Viv's perspectives, as they think about their differences or problems in communication, for instance, Eli's need for privacy and Viv's need for openness.
4. Structure your talk as if it were a newspaper story on Wyatt Transgenics.
5. Use the crumpled-up letter from the hall table drawer as a prop.

RISKS

- Teens are sexually active
- Parents are distant and uninvolved in their children's lives
- Parents keep secrets from their children, even when they are over eighteen and considered to be adults
- Parents lie to children
- Realistic language reflects the way teens today talk
- Cold and hostile relationship between father and son
- Discusses the ethics of genetic manipulation without discussing the religious implications or giving absolute answers

STRENGTHS

- Characters are three-dimensional and realistic
- Twists in the plot are revealed gradually
- Ending is ambiguous and does not give pat answers
- Ending leaves the door open for a sequel
- Characters grow and gain insight about themselves and others as they deal with difficult situations

- Discusses the morality of genetic engineering and the dangers it presents
- Presents an issue today's teens will be likely to confront as adults
- Encourages discussion of a major "hot-button" issue

AWARDS
SLJ Best Books for Children, 2004
Booklist Editor's Choice, 2004
ALA Best Books for Young Adults, 2005
ALA Popular Paperbacks, 2006
New York Public Library Books for the Teen Age, 2005

REVIEWS
"The story is well told . . . and explores the ethical questions surrounding genetic engineering, an issue with which the next generation will undoubtedly wrestle." Kevin Beach, *VOYA*, 4/04

"Readers will be as intrigued as Eli, who discovers more than he ever bargained for. A solidly crafted, thoughtful novel featuring a clever, obsessed kid who finds truths, small and large, about life, family, and, of course, himself." Stephanie Zvirin, *Booklist*, 2/04

"Werlin clearly and dramatically raises fundamental bioethical issues for teens to ponder. She also creates a riveting story with sharply etched characters and complex relationships that will stick with readers long after the book is closed. An essential purchase for YA collections." Jack Forman, Mesa College Library, San Diego, *School Library Journal*, 2/04

ᚋᚋᚋ

DUNK. David Lubar. Clarion Books, 2002. $15.00. 256p. ISBN10: 061819455X. ISBN13: 9780618194551. Graphia, an imprint of Houghton Mifflin, 2004. $7.99. 272p. ISBN10: 0618439099. ISBN13: 9780618439096. Fullcast Audio, 2003. $34.00. ISBN10: 1932076239. ISBN13: 9781932076233. (unabridged audio CD) Playaway, 2007. $44.99. ISNB10: 1602524998. ISBN13: 9781598959994. (unabridged audiobook) Fullcast Audio, 2003. $25.95. ISBN10: 1932076077. ISBN13: 9781932076073. (unabridged audiotape) Fullcast Audio, 2003. $29.00. ISBN10: 1932076085. ISBN13: 9781932076080. (unabridged audiotape, library version) Fullcast Audio, 2003. $45.00. ISBN10: 193332208X. ISBN13: 9781933322087.

(unabridged audio CD, library version) Reading Level: YHS. Interest Level: YHS, OHS. Humor, English, Psychology, Sociology.

SUBJECT AREAS

working; humor; friendship; love; divorce and separation; rites of passage; problem parents; drugs, substance abuse; death and dying; physical illness; self-knowledge; family relationships; anger; fear; depression; lying and deceit; poverty; secrets; sports; writing.

CHARACTERS

Chad Turner: he wants to be the Bozo in the Dunk Tank, who screams at and hooks the marks

Ms. Hargrove: Chad's history teacher from last year

Jason: Chad's best friend, who's an awesome volleyball player

Annie Turner/Mom: Chad's mother, who works as a waitress and takes classes to be a legal secretary

Doc: he owns the best arcade on the boardwalk

Anthony Glover: a year older than Chad, he's a troublemaker

Officer Manetti, Officer Costas: they think Chad is a thief

Gwen O'Sullivan: She's from Montana and works in one of the arcade booths

Mike, Corey: some of Chad and Jason's friends

Malcolm Vale: the Bozo in the Dunk Tank and the Turners' new upstairs tenant

Waldo: the other Bozo, who isn't very good at it

Ellie: a friend of Chad's, who works as a lifeguard

Bob/Boss: the barker at the Dunk Tank

Stinger: he's just graduated and is a school hero for his pitching ability

Franco: one of the guys Jason practices with

Jason's mom and dad: he's a roofer and she's an accountant

BOOKTALK

His voice ripped the air like a chainsaw. The sound cut deep, but the words cut deeper. He shredded any fool who wandered near the cage. He drove people crazy, he drove them wild. And he drove them to blow wads of cash for the chance to drop his sorry butt in a slimy tank of water. It was the coolest thing I'd ever seen. And I hadn't watched for very long, when I knew I had to try it. I wanted to make my targets dance like puppets on a string, crazy to get revenge for my insults. I wanted to shout and scream at the world from the safety of a cage. I wanted to be the Bozo in the Dunk Tank.

Chad expects to have a summer about like all the others, hanging with his best friend Jason, running errands for the people who ran the games and arcades at the

New Jersey boardwalk for a little spare change, maybe dating the gorgeous redhead from Montana who worked at the Catapult booth last summer, who told him she'd be back this year.

But that was before he saw the Bozo, before the Bozo became his mother's new upstairs tenant, before Jason ended up in the hospital instead of winning the volleyball tournament, before his life shattered into too many pieces to put back together.

Think it's easy to make people hate you? Step into the tank and up to the mike and find out.

MAJOR THEMES AND IDEAS
- Some people are just magnets for trouble.
- Sometimes work can get in the way of life.
- All the world's a stage.
- Almost any kind of work is harder than it looks.
- Revenge can be quite sweet.
- Sometimes it seems like your own dreams never come true, and it's always someone else who gets to live his dream.
- In a way, we're all actors, acting differently when we're with different people.
- It's the little things you remember.
- Resigning from the world and giving in to depression won't make anything any better.
- Even when life sucks, you can still fight back.
- Everything looks easy from the outside.
- Practice makes perfect—no one can be good without it.
- You don't get good at something you aren't willing to work at.
- Being someone's friend isn't always easy. And when it's the hardest, it's also probably the most important thing you can do.
- Shit happens. Deal with it.
- Every group has a leader. He's the one with the most to lose if the group laughs. That makes him the perfect target.
- A world without pain is also a world without possibilities.
- Whatever doesn't kill you makes you stronger.
- Parents don't always know what's best for their kids.
- Sometimes people who give you advice are talking to themselves as much as you.
- Laughter can heal, but it can also hurt.
- Make a choice. You don't necessarily have to live your whole life with it.
- Anything is possible, so everything is possible.
- You'll never get anywhere if you don't take the first step.
- Reach for the gold ring on the carousel—you just might grab it.

BOOK REPORT IDEAS
1.   Compare and contrast the Bozo's humor with the humor Chad shares with Jason in the hospital.
2.   Speculate on what might happen to Chad in the future.
3.   In what ways is Chad different at the end of the summer from the person he was at the beginning?
4.   Create a Bozo routine for yourself.
5.   Discuss the idea that doing almost anything well requires practice and Malcolm's comment, "It only looks easy from the outside."

BOOKTALK IDEAS
1.   Use some of Malcolm's routines as part of your talk.
2.   Focus your talk on the conflict between Chad and Malcolm, after Chad realizes he's the Bozo.
3.   Let Chad tell his own story in first person.
4.   Focus your talk on some of the changes Chad faces over the summer.

RISKS
*   Realistic language, including vulgarities
*   Boardwalk clown insults people
*   Teen drug and alcohol use
*   Cops unfairly judge a teen based on no evidence

STRENGTHS
*   Shows healing power of laughter and friendship
*   Unique and intriguing characters
*   Reader is drawn into the book from the first sentence
*   Shows the value of hard work and practice to achieve a skill

AWARDS
ALA Popular Paperbacks, 2006
New York Public Library, Books for the Teen Age, 2003
Parent's Guide to Children's Media, honor list

REVIEWS
"Dunk confirms Lubar's growing stature as an author of distinctive, intriguing, and highly original young adult fiction." Walter Hogan, *VOYA*, 10/02

"A solid novel about the anger and aggression that often fuels humor—and the compassion that can enhance it." *Horn Book*, 11/02

"The author creates immediacy through the protagonist's very typical problems; he wants to find romance, to thwart a troublemaker, and to help his friend. Similar to heroes in stories by Chris Crutcher, Chad learns valuable life lessons in a thoroughly enjoyable and convincing way." Susan Cooley, Tower Hill School, Wilmington, DE, *School Library Journal*, 8/02

"Lubar ably charts a watershed summer between boyhood and manhood, just one of the attractions of [his] engrossing novel." *Publishers Weekly*, 9/02

📖📖📖

ENDGAME. Nancy Garden. Harcourt, 2006. $17.00. 287p. ISBN10: 0152054162. ISBN13: 978152054168. Realistic fiction. Reading Level: YHS. Interest Level: YHS, OHS. English, Psychology, Sociology, Ethics, P.E.

SUBJECT AREAS
bullying; manipulation; friendship; family relationships; fear; school; mental abuse; physical abuse; problem parents; dysfunctional families; self-knowledge; anger; violence; crime and delinquency; ethics; gossip; intimidation; legal system; secrets; revenge; peer pressure.

CHARACTERS
Gray Wilton: a fourteen-year-old who hopes he won't be bullied at his new school
Lindsay Maller: she lives next door to the Wiltons
Peter Wilton: Gray's seventeen-year-old brother
Joni Maller: Lindsay's seven-year-old sister
Dad/Harry Wilton: he's hard on Gray, and prefers Peter
Mom/Samantha Wilton: she tries to keep the peace
Jemmy: Gray's best friend in Massachusetts
Sam Falco: Gray's lawyer
Hannah Roget: Lindsay's best friend
Kathy Roget: Hannah's little sister, who's a freshman like Gray
Ross Terrell: Gray's best friend at his new school
Mrs. Saunders: she works in the high school office
Fitz: a guy who knows Ross

Morris: another friend of Ross's
Ms. Blanchard: Gray's homeroom teacher
Daisy: a girl in Gray's homeroom
Zorro: a jock who's captain of the football team and a school hero
Bruce Tolliver and Hank Angelo: bullies at Gray's old school, who liked to hassle
   Gray
Mr. Vee: P.E. teacher and varsity football coach
Mrs. Terrell: Ross's mother
Johnson: a friend of Zorro's, who torments Gray and Ross
Dick Cathrell: president of the church youth group
Mr. Wallace: Gray's math teacher
Mr. Halifan: music teacher and band leader
Ms. Throckmorton: the guidance counselor
Mr. Gomez: the Spanish teacher
Dr. Bowen: a psychologist who talks to Gray while he's in detention
Ms. Felby: the English teacher in charge of the school plays
Cal Johnson: the little brother of the jock who beats up on Gray and Ross

BOOKTALK

Gray told himself over and over that it would be different at his new school. No more
bullies picking on him. He'd have his drums and his archery, and he'd avoid getting
picked on. No more getting shoved around and called a fag. No more trying to fight back.
No more suspensions. He'd just keep his head down and try not to attract attention.

But by the end of the first week of school Gray and his new friend Ross were targeted by the jocks on the varsity football team. Gray couldn't figure out why—none
of the other freshman misfits were singled out, just him and Ross. They were slammed
into lockers, roughed up, and called names. Reporting them did no good—they had
their own set of rules because they were jocks. The teachers just ignored them.

Things weren't any better at home. Gray's dad resented having to move and
change jobs after Gray was suspended twice, and was harder than ever on his younger
son. It was like he'd assigned Gray's brother to be "the good son" and Gray to be "the
bad son." And no matter how much Gray tried to either please him or stay invisible,
it was never enough. No way could Gray tell him about what was going on at school.
He even kept Gray from playing his drums because he thought the neighbors might
complain.

After Zorro and Johnson gave Gray a black eye, he realized he was trapped. He
made up a story for his parents and teachers, but Zorro didn't like it. "Next time, I'll
make up the story." That's when Gray realized he was going to get beaten up again.
There was no way they were ever going to leave him alone, even if he got up the
courage to report them.

Gray was trapped and desperate, and in that situation, he could see only one way
out. Destroy his tormentors before they destroyed him.

MAJOR THEMES AND IDEAS
- It's hard to do the right thing when someone is just waiting for you to make a mistake.
- Sometimes if a bully knows you'll fight back, you're safe.
- It's all too easy for teachers to ignore and overlook bullies.
- Names can hurt you. "Sticks and stones will break your bones, but names will never hurt you" is a lie.
- Sometimes even when you're determined to make things better, they only get worse.
- Standing out from the crowd, looking or acting different, can get you noticed, and that can be dangerous.
- Policies against bullying and fighting don't work when they aren't applied to everyone, including the bullies themselves.
- Everyone, sooner or later, when they are pushed too hard, fights back.
- Standing up to bullies can be effective, but sometimes it can also be dangerous.
- If you don't tell people what is being done to you, they won't be able to help you.
- When you feel completely trapped and without choices, it's hard to see more than one way out.
- Expecting too much is a sure way to get disappointed.
- News stories don't always tell the whole truth.
- Depression isolates you from everyone, even those who are trying to help.
- Ultimately, your actions are your own responsibility and can't be blamed on anyone else.
- A trapped animal will chew off its limb to get out of a trap. A human will too—destroying himself to stop the pain.
- Mental anguish is even more painful than physical anguish.

BOOK REPORT IDEAS
1. Write your report as if you were interviewing Gray.
2. Discuss the various ways different people tried to help Gray and explain why he refused to let them.
3. Explain why you think Gray and Ross were bullied when other outsiders weren't.
4. Several people, including Lindsay, knew what was happening to Gray. Discuss why you think they didn't go to the principal on their own and whether or not it would have made a difference.
5. List some other options Gray might have seen if he had not felt so trapped.
6. Examine how Gray's father's actions and opinions exacerbated Gray's isolation and depression.
7. If you had seen what was happening to Gray and Ross, what would you have done? Why?

8. Speculate about what might change, if anything, about the high school as a result of the shooting.
9. Speculate what Gray will be like in five years. In ten.
10. List ways that bullies can be controlled and stopped.
11. Speculate about what might have happened to Gray if he had told someone in power what was really going on.
12. What would you have done if you had been in Gray's place?
13. Discuss what might have happened if Ross had shared Gray's plans of violence with Ms. Throckmorton.
14. Once the bullying had begun, was there any chance to make it stop?

BOOKTALK IDEAS
1. Write your talk in first person, as Gray.
2. Write your talk in first person, as Ross, describing Gray.
3. Write your talk as if it were a news story.
4. Use drumsticks or handwritten sheet music as props for your talk.
5. Write the initials Z, R, D, H, L, G on the board and talk about each person, describing them as Gray saw them, but don't reveal that they are his victims.

RISKS
- Parents are oblivious to son's being bullied
- Father blames younger son when he is tormented by bullies
- Father blatantly prefers and pays attention to older son while being cold, harsh, and judgmental of younger son
- Younger son is hit and physically abused by father
- Ineffectual mother doesn't protect younger son
- Bullies terrorize younger boys in and out of school
- Teachers ignore repeated reports of bullying
- Guns in the home are accessible to children
- Realistic language, including obscenities
- Teen becomes a school shooter
- Fourteen-year-old tried as an adult
- Jocks sexually abuse younger boys

STRENGTHS
- Graphic portrayal of the impact of bullying
- Characters teens can identify with
- Uses both narrative and interview sections
- Ending leaves room for speculation
- Shows the necessity of teachers being aware of possible bullying

- Shows importance of enforcing the same rules for everyone, including high-status students
- Graphic description of the negative effect of isolating a teen from everything valuable to him
- Many opportunities for discussion on a variety of issues
- Can give parents of teens who are outsiders or at-risk a picture of what their children may be experiencing

AWARD
SLJ Best Books for Children, 2006

REVIEWS
"Garden presents readers with a well-written, thought-provoking novel that parallels reality all too closely." C. J. Bott, *VOYA*, 4/06

"The ending provides an emotional punch that is difficult to forget. This is a hard-hitting and eloquent look at the impact of bullying, and the resulting destruction of lives touched by the violence." Jennifer Ralston, Harford County Public Library, Belcamp, MD, *School Library Journal*, 5/06

"Engrossing and solemn, *Endgame* powerfully delves into the mind of a boy who became a killer. He is never depicted as blameless, but readers are left with the notion that he could have been saved, and his victims could have been saved." Deanna Spears, *Bulletin (Center for Children's Books)*, 6/06

📖📖📖

FADE TO BLACK. Alex Flinn. HarperTeen, an imprint of HarperCollins, 2005. $16.99. 192p. ISBN10: 0060568399. ISBN13: 9780060568399. HarperTeen, 2006. $7.99. 208p. ISBN10: 0060568429. ISBN13: 9780060568429. HarperTeen, 2005. $17.89. 192p. ISBN10: 0060568410. ISBN13: 9780060568412. (library binding). Realistic fiction. Reading Level: YHS. Interest Level: YHS, OHS. English, Psychology, Ethics.

SUBJECT AREAS
HIV/AIDS; mental illness; crime and delinquency; secrets; school; prejudice; violence; lying and deceit; racism; anger; divorce and separation; homosexuality; gossip; bullying; family relationships; poetry; rites of passage; legal system; substance abuse; problem parents.

CHARACTERS

Alex Crusan: a junior in high school who is HIV positive and whose car windshield was smashed with a baseball bat

Clinton Cole: known for harassing Alex at school, he was seen leaving the scene of the crime

Daria Bicknell: she's a special ed student who never lies and says she saw Clinton do it

Principal Runnel: principal of Pinedale High School

Miss Valez: Mr. Runnel's secretary

Alyssa Black: a beautiful girl in Clinton's English class

Mom/Adele Cole: Clinton and Melody's mother, who has a liberal perspective

Melody Cole: Clinton's little sister, who's friends with Carolina Crusan

Carolina Crusan: Alex's nine-year-old sister

Officer Bauer and Officer Reed: they were the first to question Clinton about the crime

Mr. Crusan: Alex and Carolina's father

Rosario Crusan: Alex and Carolina's overprotective mother

Mrs. Gibson: she teaches government and didn't move Clinton's seat away from Alex

Mr. David: he teaches trig, and he did move Alex's seat

Joyce Taub: she's the special ed counselor

Jennifer Atkinson: she's a candy striper at the hospital where Alex is

Aunt Maria: Alex and Carolina's aunt, who lives in Miami

Mr. Kahn: he runs the Dunkin' Donuts shop where Alex gets donuts every Monday morning

Andy, Brett, Mo: friends of Clinton who think he's crossed the line by attacking Alex

Bernard Eutsey: Clinton's lawyer

Austin and Danny: Alex's friends from Miami

Leigh: a college student who meets Alex after a frat party, when he's sixteen

BOOKTALK

Monday, October 27, 6:00 A.M. Alex Crusan is on his way to Dunkin' Donuts, just like he is every Monday. He sees Daria, a teenager with Down's Syndrome he's seen at school. And then he sees someone in a football jacket, carrying a baseball bat. And suddenly the windshield explodes, and glass shatters all over him, cutting his face and eyes.

Alex is HIV positive, and his father's just been transferred from Miami to a small rural Florida town. Everyone knows he has HIV because the school had an assembly before they got there and told everyone. He has no friends and one major enemy, a football player named Clinton Cole. Clint wants Alex gone and doesn't hesitate to let him know it.

So when Daria says it was Clint who attacked Alex, everyone believes her. She's never lied before, her mother says, why would she lie now? But Clint swears he didn't do it—ragging on a guy is one thing, whaling on him with a bat is over the line. It's just wrong. He's innocent—at least of swinging a bat.

What's the truth? Alex is in the hospital, that's true, but who put him there? Suddenly, with the whole town believing he's guilty, Clint is as alone as Alex has been.

What really happened on Monday, October 2 at 6:00 A.M.?

MAJOR THEMES AND IDEAS
- Not everyone with HIV is homosexual.
- HIV is spread only by blood and sexual contact.
- You are treated differently when you are HIV positive. People are afraid to get close to you.
- Being identified as a disease instead a person is painful and isolating.
- At night, when it's dark and quiet, all the thoughts you didn't *let* yourself have during the day float to the surface so you can't sleep.
- Logic doesn't work very well on emotion.
- If you look different, kids may not want to be friends with you.
- When you are really sick, and scared about it, you can't tell your parents because it would worry them more.
- When you have HIV, people make themselves feel good by being nice to you, but they aren't your friends; they don't hang out with you, or touch you, or hug you.
- Once you really *look* at someone in the eye, and really see who they are inside, you can't go back to not seeing them.
- You never think it could happen to you. But it can.

BOOK REPORT IDEAS
1. Compare and contrast how Daria and Alex are treated by the other high school students, before and after the attack and after the truth came out.
2. Speculate on what might happen to Alex, Daria, and Clint after the end of the book.
3. Discuss the scene at 3:01 on Tuesday at the hospital between Alex and Jennifer. What was he trying to tell her?
4. When Clinton goes to school Tuesday, everyone thinks he's guilty and doesn't believe him when he says he didn't do it. Describe how he felt when his friends who had known him all his life turned against him so quickly.
5. Discuss the friendships that are described in the book. How many are close and supportive and how many aren't?
6. At the end of the book, who has genuinely changed and who has not? Why?
7. Discuss the role that gossip played in the novel, both before and after the attack.

BOOKTALK IDEAS
1. Use a bat as a prop.
2. Tell the story from the point of view of all three main characters, using quotes from the book.
3. Make the timeline of the book at the first of each chapter a part of your talk, showing how quickly things happened.
4. Write your talk as if you were a student, sharing the latest school scandal with your friends.

RISKS
- Teen with HIV
- Bullying
- Vandalism
- Homophobia
- HIV teen ostracized
- Curse words, including homophobic epithets
- Unsafe sex
- Teens drink

STRENGTHS
- Multiple points of view allow reader to experience the points of view of the three main characters
- Involves the reader from the first page
- Allows for discussion of HIV, AIDS, homophobia, and isolating anyone infected with HIV
- Shows Down's Syndrome teen and an HIV positive teen are ostracized in similar ways
- Parents stand up for their children
- Characters grow and gain insight
- Presents characters who are seldom heard from in young adult literature

AWARD
ALA Quick Picks for Reluctant Young Adult Readers, 2008

REVIEWS
"As in her previous novels, Flinn focuses on a contemporary issue and explores it with unexpected plot twists and multi-dimensional characters. Her approach and readable style will again have high appeal for junior and senior high students." Lucy Schall, VOYA, 4/05

"Flinn draws perceptive pictures of family relationships and of the emotions of a teenager scared about his future but determined to make the most of the present in this readable exploration of ethical issues." *Kirkus Reviews,* 3/05

"Teens will enjoy ferreting out the reality from the conflicting narratives and arguing about the sensitive issues raised along the way." Cindy Dobrez, *Booklist,* 4/05

ᗡᗡᗡ

FAULT LINE. Janet Tashjian. Henry Holt, 2003. $16.95. 248p. ISBN10: 0805072004. ISBN13: 9780805072006. Henry Holt, 2006. $7.95. 256p. ISBN10: 0805080635. ISBN13: 9780805080636. BT Bound, 2006. $16.95. 248p. ISBN10: 1417761083. ISBN13: 9781417761081. (library binding) Listening Library, 2004. $25.00. ISBN10: 0807220817. ISBN13: 9780807220818. (unabridged audiotape) Realistic fiction. Reading Level: YHS, OHS. Interest Level: YHS, OHS. English, Music, Sex Education, Creative Writing, Film, Psychology, Drama.

SUBJECT AREAS
music; humor; sexual abuse; dating and social life; friendship; school; working; physical abuse; bullying; intimidation; anger; love; family relationships; manipulation; lying and deceit; obsession; self-knowledge; secrets; sex and sexuality.

CHARACTERS
Becky Martin: smart, funny, ambitious, she wants to be a stand-up comic
Abby: Becky's best friend, who shares her love of comedy and old movies
Christopher: Becky's six-year-old brother, who's in a serious Captain Underpants stage
Delilah: tall, black, athletic drag queen and Becky's mom's assistant
Mom/Mrs. Martin: a lawyer, she supports Becky's quest to be a comic
Dad/Bennett Martin: he's a waiter at San Francisco's Ritz-Carlton Dining Room and loves to cook
Rick: manager of the Comedy Stop, who encourages Becky and Abby
Charlie: Becky's lab partner
Peter: Becky's old boyfriend
Mr. Perez: he runs a bus tour company that features famous movie spots in San Francisco
Kip Costello: another budding comic who falls for Becky
Alex Costello: Kip's mother, who owns an antique shop
Harold: Becky's boss at the Goodwill store

Mike Leone: a comic at the Comedy Store in LA
Tom: he owns the new comedy club
Zach and Susan: Kip's older brother and sister-in-law
Hannah: Kip's niece
Mr. Bowen: an old man with an unusual collection

BOOKTALK

Statistics say that one in every five teen girls is involved in an abusive relationship. Professionals who work with abused girls say that number isn't high enough. I should know—I'm one of those statistics.

My name's Becky, and ever since I was a kid, I've wanted to be a comic. But this isn't a comedy set. What happened to me could never be funny, even though it starts in a comedy club in San Francisco. The first time I saw Kip, he was working on new jokes, scribbling on a roll of paper towels. My best friend Abby and I had finished our sets and were watching the other performers. When Abby yelled at him, he came over and introduced himself. He was tall and thin with blue eyes and curly dark hair. We hit it off right away.

Even from the first, I couldn't believe a guy like Kip could be interested in me. Abby was the gorgeous one; boys just tended to overlook me. I have long messy red hair and I'm kind of a klutz—but Kip liked those things about me, and everything else too. And we both loved performing, and old movies, and music—it was like we were made for each other, soul mates. Our love was special, different, more pure than anyone else's. I'd never had someone so perfect for me before. I'd dreamed and hoped, of course, but I'd never expected it to really happen.

Living in San Francisco, I'm used to earthquakes, but I think of fault lines as being in the earth, not in people. Maybe that's why it took me so long to see the fault lines in the relationship I had with Kip. Maybe that's why it took an emotional earthquake to make me see reality.

MAJOR THEMES AND IDEAS

- Laughter is one of the only things in life that helps you deal with absolutely anything.
- Laughing in the midst of tears is a good thing.
- Humor can change everything in an instant.
- If life gives it to you, use it.
- Wherever you go, there you are.
- Life is what you're stuck with while you're waiting to have one.
- Having someone really pay attention to you, and notice the details about you, is intoxicating.
- Don't drop your friends when you fall in love and start a relationship with someone.

- Letting someone monopolize your time, even in the name of love, isn't a good thing.
- Being in a relationship is the most complicated thing in the world.
- People who don't respect the boundaries you set don't respect *you*.
- Relationships change gradually, and sometimes it's easy to miss the danger signs, even if they're obvious to everyone else.
- When someone you love tells you the problems in your relationship are all *your* fault, it's not true and it's not healthy.
- When your boyfriend tells you not to spend time with your best friend so you can be with him, he's asking for too much.
- There are no easy answers.
- Spending all your time with just one person and ignoring your other relationships isn't love; it's obsession.
- Those who really love you accept you as you are, and don't try to make you into someone else.
- Love is more than sexual tension and adrenaline.
- A roller coaster relationship, full of highs and lows, can also be full of pressure and danger.
- When you love someone, you don't put them down just so you can feel better about yourself.
- If you have to hide big parts of your life from the person you love, maybe the relationship isn't as positive or strong as you might think it is.
- A relationship's like a hot bath. The more you get used to it, the more you realize it's not so hot.
- Trust your instincts. When they say a situation is dangerous, they're probably right.
- When something happens to one person in a family, it happens to everyone.

BOOK REPORT IDEAS

1. Discuss Kip's growing need to control Becky. What are some of the first signs of this?
2. Explain why Becky ignores what her mother and Abby are saying about Kip. What makes her so vulnerable to him?
3. Discuss Becky's reaction when she realized she was being abused. Why did she keep everything to herself? How had the relationship changed her?
4. When and how did Becky's rant at the hecklers go off course? What and who was she really yelling at?
5. Explain the significance of the stuffed animals that Becky keeps hidden.
6. Discuss the cycle of abuse and how Kip became involved in it.
7. Explain the situations that set off Kip's need to abuse Becky.
8. Examine the movies mentioned in the book. How many of them involved difficult or abusive relationships?

9. Speculate on what happens to Becky, Abby, Mike, and Kip after the book is over. What will they be like in five years? In ten?
10. Control is a big issue in this book. Compare several situations when one person wanted to control another.

BOOKTALK IDEAS

1. Write your talk from both Becky's and Kip's points of view, using Becky's journal and Kip's roll of paper towels as props.
2. Write your talk as one of Becky's comedy routines.
3. Write your talk from Abby's perspective as she worries about her best friend.
4. Use some current statistics about teen abusive relationships in your talk.

RISKS

- Homosexual characters
- Teens smoke and drink
- Teens perform in night clubs, starting as young as fifteen
- Teens are sexually active
- Stalking behavior, invading privacy
- Abusive relationship
- Physical violence
- Some vulgar language
- Shows verbal, emotional, and physical abuse

STRENGTHS

- Alternating points of view give different perspectives of the characters and their actions
- Humor
- Authentic, realistic characters
- Hard-working, stable parents
- Power of friendship
- Teens learn from their mistakes
- Teens are responsible
- Drag queen is loud, dramatic, and accepted
- Formatting of Becky and Kip's notes to themselves makes them stand out
- Teens use safe sex practices
- Parents actively support daughter's career
- Excellent portrayal of an abusive relationship and how easy it is to become trapped in one
- Shows the recovery process after ending an abusive relationship
- Both abuser and victim are well-rounded, not black-and-white characters
- Characters are true to life
- Characters grow and gain insight

- Doesn't demonize the abuser
- Shows the recovery process for *both* the abuser and victim
- Impact of abuse on the whole family
- Teens and parents are able to communicate

AWARDS
IRA Young Adult Choices, 2003
New York Public Library Books for the Teen Age, 2003

REVIEWS
"The violence builds slowly and realistically, allowing readers to understand how Becky could get into such a situation and have trouble getting back out. . . . Becky and Kip do make love, but there is almost no strong language and the violence is deftly handled, making this book highly recommended for school and public libraries." Snow Wildsmith, *VOYA*, 10/03

"Tashjian allows readers to feel Becky's overpowering happiness and blindness to Kip's faults as they empathize with his overwhelming fear of losing control." Susan Riley, Mount Kisco Public Library, NY, *School Library Journal*, 10/03

"This should find a place in all libraries that serve teens, many of whom will recognize aspects of their own relationships in Becky and Kip's." *Kirkus Reviews*, 8/03

📖📖📖

FEED. M. T. Anderson. Candlewick, 2002. $16.99. 240p. ISBN10: 0763617261. ISBN13: 9780763617264. Candlewick, 2004. $7.99. 320p. ISBN10: 0763622591. ISBN13: 9780763622596. Listening Library, 2008. $30.00. ISBN10: 0739356208. ISBN13: 9780739356203. (unabridged audio CD) Science fiction. Reading Level: YHS. Interest Level: YHS, OHS. English, Psychology, Science.

SUBJECT AREAS
friendship; love; dating and social life; death and dying; self-knowledge; grief and mourning; computers; environmental issues; family relationships; peer pressure; obsession.

CHARACTERS
Titus: he and his friends decided to spend spring break on the moon
Link and Marty: the guys Titus went to the moon with

Calista, Quendy, and Loga: the girls who went to the moon, too
Violet: she's beautiful, unique, and a little old fashioned
The old man in a bow tie: a hacker with the Coalition of Pity who messed up people's feeds
Mom: Titus's mother
Dad/Steve: Titus's father
Smell Factor: Titus's little brother
Mr. Durn: Violet's father and a specialist in dead languages
Chas: one of the guys playing Spin the Bottle at Link's party
Nina: a FeedTech representative

BOOKTALK

We thought we'd go to the moon for spring break, but the moon turned out to really suck. Link is real tall, and seriously rich—so rich it's kinda like radar, and people can just look at him and they know he's rich. Marty can get into anything, so he fits right in, and I just stand there and look cool, so we figured when we got to the moon, we could crash some of the college parties. But no way, so we went to the Ricochet Lounge, this lo grav club that was very hip a year ago but now just looked kinda sad and worn. It was all about slamming into each other in these huge padded suits, which was kinda fun. And after, I saw the most amazing girl in the snack bar. She still had her suit on, but she was holding her helmet, and her face was just beautiful. She had short blonde hair, and I couldn't quit looking at her. Quendy and Loga went off to the restroom, and Link and I just stared at her playing with her juice. When the girls came back, Quendy was like all "Ohmygod, why didn't any of you tell me that my lesion is totally spreading?" She was completely freaked out, and didn't pay any attention to us telling her she looked fine. Finally Link turned to the girl who was watching us, and asked her about Quendy's lesion. And her answer just totally rocked. She talked about Quendy's face and how the lesion framed it, and drew attention to her face. By the time she finished, we were all serious youch on her, and she and the other girls spent a bunch of time fixing Quendy's hair to go with her lesion.

By that time, we were pretty tired and ready to go to bed, but this was the moon, and no one slept on the moon. So we decided to go to the Rumble Spot, a place we'd heard about on the feed, and we asked the blonde girl to come with us. Her name was Violet, and she stayed near me, which was mega cool with me. Then we saw this weird old guy on the dance floor. He was like a hundred years old, with long white hair and a bow tie. He was pretty creepy looking. And then we started touching people's heads, and everyone started saying over and over, "We are entering a time of calamity. We are entering a time of calamity," and we couldn't stop. Finally, the police came, and we still couldn't stop chanting, so the cops just turned us off. And there was nothing but black.

Yeah, there's no two ways about it—spring break on the moon can really suck.

MAJOR THEMES AND IDEAS
- Space is old and empty. You need the noise of your friends in space.
- It's essential to keep up with all the latest trends and fashions.
- Everything comes through your feed—education, news, styles, and feedcasts. The feed is all you need.
- The feed knows everything you want and need, sometimes even before you know you want it.
- Friends are worth their weight in gold.
- If you want to appeal to everyone, you have to make everything simple and basic.
- When you have a feed, you are brought up not to think about things that aren't a part of it.
- People are more important than the environment.
- People are taught immediate gratification through the feed, and are driven to buy things they may not even like or want.
- Self-control, anticipation, and delayed gratification may mean that when you get what you've been wanting, it means more to you.
- Knowing when your good times are going to end makes you appreciate and enjoy them more.
- Knowing you're going to die makes you want to cram as much as possible into your last days.
- When someone you love is dying you want both to be there and to get away from them.
- Cool isn't something you buy, it's something you are.
- Love matters more than anything else.

BOOK REPORT IDEAS
1. Discuss how Titus and his friends feel when the feed is shut off, and when it is turned back on. Describe their emotions and reactions at both of these times.
2. What does Violet do to her feed by asking about and wanting all kinds of strange things?
3. How is Violet different because she had to use her imagination when she was a child?
4. Discuss why the doctors have such a hard time fixing Violet's feed.
5. What did Violet mean during her outburst at the party, when she said, "You don't have the feed, you are the feed. You're being eaten. You're food. You're raised for food."
6. Discuss how much we have in common with people on the feed. Which of their characteristics or qualities do we share?
7. Compare Violet's list of things she wants to do with your own list of things you want to do before you die.
8. Compare our society today with Titus's society, and show how they are similar and different.

9. The worse Violet gets, the more Titus withdraws from her. Discuss why he decides to do that and why.

10. Violet is worried about the environment; Titus doesn't seem to care. Is the feed totally responsible for that?

11. What does the author's dedication mean—"To those who resist the feed"?

12. Explain why you do, or don't, want a feed and how it might change your life.

BOOKTALK IDEAS

1. Record the feed excerpts and use them as a soundtrack for your talk, just as if you had a feed yourself.

2. Focus your talk on Titus and Violet and their relationship.

3. Have Titus introduce his friends and what they like to do.

4. Write your talk in the same style as the book itself.

RISKS

- Graphic language
- Society obsessed with buying and having
- Individuality is suppressed
- Minor characters are not three-dimensional, but flat
- Environmental concerns and signs of danger are ignored

STRENGTHS

- Written in flowing free-form style
- Shows the power of the urge to buy and to have
- Two main characters are three-dimensional, realistic, and easy for readers to identify with
- Provides the opportunity for discussion on many levels
- Speculative, sarcastic picture of what our future might be like

AWARDS

ALA Best Books for Young Adults, 2003
National Book Award Finalist (Young People's Literature), 2002

REVIEWS

"Although set in the future, Anderson's novel is a stunning indictment of contemporary America and its ever-increasing obsession with consumerism even in the face of impending environmental collapse. Narrated by Titus in a sometimes obscene, sometimes almost incoherent future slang designed to highlight the emptiness of his life, the novel is both intense and grim. It should, however, appeal strongly to mature and thoughtful readers who care about the future of their world." Michael Levy, *VOYA*, 12/02

"The crystalline realization of this wildly dystopic future carries in it obvious and enormous implications for today's readers—satire at its finest." *Kirkus Reviews*, 9/02

"A gripping, intriguing, and unique cautionary novel." Sharon Rawlins, Piscataway Public Library, NJ, *School Library Journal*, 9/02

⌖⌖⌖

THE FIRST PART LAST. Angela Johnson. Simon and Schuster, 2003. $15.95. 144p. ISBN10: 0689849222. ISBN13: 9780689849220. Simon Pulse, 2004. $5.99. 192p. ISBN10: 0689849230. ISBN13: 9780689849237. Thorndike Press, 2004. $22.95. 147p. ISBN10: 0786265108. ISBN13: 9780786265107. (large print) Recorded Books, 2004. $19.99. ISBN10: 1400090652. ISBN13: 9781400090655. (unabridged audio CD) Realistic fiction. Reading Level: MS. Interest Level: MS, YHS, OHS. English, Health, Psychology.

SUBJECT AREAS
teen parents; unwed parents; self-knowledge; rites of passage; love; family relationships; school; dating and social life; friendship; death and dying; grief and mourning.

CHARACTERS
Bobby: a sixteen-year-old boy who's about to become a father
Nia: Bobby's girlfriend
Feather: Bobby's daughter
KBoy and J. L.: Bobby's best friends since they were in preschool together
Fred: Bobby's dad
Mary: Bobby's mom
Mr. and Mrs. Wilkins: Nia's parents
Dr. Victor: Feather's doctor
Coco Fernandez: Bobby and Mary's downstairs neighbor
Mr. Philips: Bobby's British Literature teacher
Jackie: Feather's babysitter
Paul: Bobby's older brother
Nick and Nora: Paul's kids

BOOKTALK

Then it was me and Nia, and all I knew was I wanted to be with her more than anything else in the world. We were sixteen, about to graduate, go to college, and then conquer the world.

Now it's me and Feather, and I *am* her world. She has big, clear eyes and tiny baby hands. I feel her breath on my chest and she sleeps. She is eleven days old and I am her father.

When Nia told me she was pregnant, we wanted to do the right thing. We just didn't know what that was, and we waited too long to decide. We were still kids, too young to be having one ourselves.

But Feather's here now, she belongs to me and I belong to her. It's not the way I wanted it to be, or even hoped it would be, but it's the way it is now. And it's up to me to make things right for her.

MAJOR THEMES AND IDEAS

- Love makes everything different.
- Having someone depend on you for everything is scary.
- No one can write you a note to excuse you from taking care of your baby.
- The only way to change something is to pay attention to the signs.
- Even not making a decision is making a decision.
- Not wanting a baby doesn't make it go away.
- You can't run away from your responsibility.
- Once you're a parent, it all changes.
- When you have a child, you can't *be* a child anymore.
- Sometimes you just have to suck it up and make it work.
- Actions have consequences.
- Friends are always there for you.
- Doing what's right for your child is the best thing to do.

BOOK REPORT IDEAS

1. Discuss how Bobby's life changed when he found out he was going to be a father and then changed again when he decided to keep Feather. What are some of the things he didn't expect?
2. If you were in Bobby's place, what would you have done? Why?
3. Discuss what Bobby's life in Heaven might be like.
4. Discuss why the author chose to tell the story from the past and present at the same time.
5. In this book, Bobby and Paul are the primary parents for their children. Discuss why this is or isn't a good thing. Can a man be as good a parent as a woman?
6. Discuss the ethics of putting someone in a coma in a nursing home, kept alive by machines, rather than letting them die naturally.

7. Bobby says we should live life backward, and do the first part last. What do you think he means by that?

BOOKTALK IDEAS
1. Tell the story from both Bobby's and Nia's points of view.
2. Use something a baby might need as a prop.
3. Write your talk in first person, as Bobby.
4. Alternate between "then" and "now" as the author did.

RISKS
- Teens are sexually active
- Teens ignore available birth control
- Realistic language
- Even smart kids make stupid decisions
- Delinquent behavior

STRENGTHS
- Shows the power of parental love
- Teens take responsibility for their actions
- Vivid picture of how much a baby changes a parent's life
- Characters the reader can identify with
- Characters gain insight and maturity
- Parents are supportive of their children, even when they make mistakes
- Divorced parents treat each other with respect
- Authentic voice of teen
- Ambivalent ending allows for speculation and discussion
- Shows the strength and support of close friends

AWARDS
ALA Popular Paperbacks, 2008
Coretta Scott King Author Award, 2004
Michael L. Printz Award, 2004

REVIEWS
"Told through Bobby's eyes in spare, eloquent prose . . . Realistic characters, an honest look at teen pregnancy, and Bobby's thoughts and dreams combine in a wonderful novel sure to appeal to most young adult readers." Rachelle Bilz, *VOYA*, 6/03

"As the past and present threads join in the final chapter, readers will only clamor for more about this memorable father-daughter duo—and an author who so skillfully relates the hope in the midst of pain." *Publishers Weekly*, 6/03

"Brief, poetic, and absolutely riveting, this gem of a novel tells the story of a young father struggling to raise an infant." Miranda Doyle, San Francisco Public Library, CA, *School Library Journal*, 6/03

"While this [story] isn't bereft of humor . . . , what resonates are the sacrifices Bobby makes for Feather's sake." *Horn Book*, 7/03

📖📖📖

FORTUNES OF INDIGO SKYE. Deb Caletti. Simon and Schuster, 2008. $15.99. 304p. ISBN10: 1416910077. ISBN13: 9781416910077. Simon Pulse, 2009. $9.99. 320p. ISBN10: 1416910085. ISBN13: 9781416910084. Thorndike Press, 2008. $23.95. 441p. ISBN10: 1410409465. ISBN13: 9781410409461. (large print) Realistic fiction. Reading level: MS. Interest level: MS, YHS. English, Economics, Ethics, Psychology, Sociology.

SUBJECT AREAS
family relationships; dating and social life; love; ethics; gossip; peer pressure; secrets; self-knowledge; friendship; animals; working; philosophy; rites of passage.

CHARACTERS
The Carrera's Team
Indigo Skye: a part-time waitress who marches to a different drummer, loves her job and her customers, and one day, gets a really big tip
Jane: Indigo's boss and the owner of Carrera's
Harold Zaminski: he makes all the baked goods for Carrera's and loves practical jokes
Luigi: the cook at Carrera's, who loves to sing
Alex: he washes dishes at Carrera's
Zach: he works the afternoon shift at Carrera's

The Carrera's Irregulars
Nick Harrison: his life has been destroyed by a long-lasting rumor that he murdered his wife

Leroy Richie: he has so many tattoos — that's all anyone ever notices about him, especially when he applies for jobs

Joe Awful Coffee: an ex-boxer, who eats like he's still in the ring

Funny Coyote: she's a poet with a "chemical imbalance" and flips between depressed and manic

Trina: she drives a red and white '53 Thunderbird and dates losers who lie to her

Richard Howards/Vespa Guy: he comes into Carrera's for coffee

Trevor: Indigo's boyfriend, who has endless get-rich-quick schemes

Mom/Naomi Skye: Indigo's mother, who has a complicated relationship with her old Datsun and is a wonderful cook

Bex Skye: Indigo's little sister, who wants to help poor and needy all over the world

Dad/Will Skye: Indigo's father, who lives in Hawaii and runs a surf shop with his wife, Jennifer

Bomba: Indigo's grandmother

Lindsay: she's in Bex's grade at school

Severin Skye: Indigo's brother, who doesn't march to a different drummer; he hangs with the rich kids and has a rich girlfriend

Melanie Gregory: Indigo's best friend, whose dad does PR for rock bands

Chico: the Skye's obnoxious parrot who loves to lure people to his cage and bite them and lives to torture Freud

Freud: the Skye's cat, who has psychological issues and is a merciless hunter who brings home his trophies

Bill and Marty: two guys who work with Nick at the hardware store and harass him constantly about killing his wife

Mrs. Denholm: the Skyes' nosey neighbor

Lisa Gregory: Melanie's mother, the modern equivalent of a fifties mom

Allen Gregory: Melanie's father, who does PR for several very popular bands

Kayleigh Moore: the girl Severin asks to the Prom, whose family is mega-rich

Neal, Zach, Eric: the men who work for Will in Hawaii

BOOKTALK

They tell you that money fixes everything, but I'm here to tell you that money broke a lot of things in my life, and didn't fix one of them. I'm a waitress at Carrera's, on the morning shift. I can tell a lot about a customer just by what they eat for breakfast. There are full breakfast folks, who need something to get them started on their day; and cereal only ones, who are thinking about making sure they get enough fiber. But what does a cup of coffee say? A cup of coffee you can get anywhere and not have to go into a restaurant, sit down, have someone bring your coffee, and then wait to get a refill — why would someone who's never been here before walk in and order *only* a cup of coffee?

All the morning regulars know each other, and when Vespa Guy walked in, no one knew him — he was a stranger to all of us. But it was obvious from the way he was dressed that he was worth a lot of money. Even his jeans had a "creative-but-wealthy" look to them, and his soft leather shoes, which were too simple and elegant to *not* be expensive, were Italian. And all he ordered was coffee. He stayed awhile, didn't talk to anyone, and drank his coffee. The tip he left me was more than the cost of the coffee. He was the topic of speculation as soon as he got on his orange Vespa, and putt-putt-ed off. That's one of Carrera's specialities, along with Luigi's pies: gossip and speculation. He's been in a few times, and he orders coffee and stares out the window while he drinks it. He never gets anything else, turns down all my suggestions, and stays mysterious and intriguing. Until the morning when it's a little warmer than it's been, and he takes off his jacket and hangs it on the chair next to him. I go over to give him a refill, and that's when I saw it, a pack of cigarettes. It's really hard for me to be around people who smoke without reminding them how dangerous it is, not to mention how smelly and ugly it makes them. I poured his coffee, debating inside whether I should say something or not, and by the time the cup was full, I'd decided. "I wouldn't be saying this if I didn't care about your health and well-being," I said, "but did you know that those cigarettes have over four thousand toxic chemicals in them? I wouldn't say anything, except that I'm concerned about you." We talk for a couple of minutes, and he leaves with the pack of cigarettes lying on the table.

Did I know that was the conversation that was going to change my life completely? I'd chatted with customers lots of times, even had some fairly serious conversations, but none of them had the impact that five minute or so exchange had on my life. I wasn't there the next time he came in, so he just left a sealed envelope with my name on it. Inside were a letter and a check, a check with more zeros on it than I'd ever seen. A check made out to me, Indigo Skye. Remember that Nicolas Cage movie about the cop who wins the lottery and splits the money with a waitress? It was sort of like that, only it was real, and Vespa Guy didn't split lottery ticket winnings with me. He was tired of being rich, the letter said, so he'd given me all his money—all two and a half million dollars of it!

How much difference can money make in your life? Read on, and find out!

MAJOR THEMES AND IDEAS

- Waitressing isn't just a job, it's a talent: a talent for giving nourishment, for creating relationships.
- You can destroy a man with a suspicious glance.
- Who you are on the outside isn't necessarily who you are on the inside.
- Most people wish they could escape from their boring lives and have the exciting kind of lives that you see on the movies and TV.
- Like it or not, mothers and daughters know the truth about each other.
- People like to have a choice about things, even if it's something minor; it gives them the illusion of control.
- People are creatures of habit. There's so much in life we have no control over, and changes constantly, that it's important to make sure that what we can control stays the same.
- The only privacy some people get is in their own thoughts.

- An absence of wanting equals happiness.
- Most of the time, facing facts sucks.
- Not knowing what you want to be when you grow up can be scary.
- Among the nouveau riche, nobody seems to think for themselves. They walk the tightrope of acceptability, afraid that they will lose what they have if they make a misstep.
- For some, money makes everything decided and possible. Just walk the straight and narrow. No side paths allowed.
- People have an odd need to sort people into groups and keep them there, whether or not it's really the right group for them.
- There is a severe sadness about injustice.
- Some people spend hundreds of thousands of dollars on trivial things, when somewhere else people have no food and no shelter. This would seem to indicate that there is something terribly wrong with our society.
- Unless you're very careful, money changes everything. And nothing.
- Anticipation can be just as delicious as having.
- Your expectation about a surprise is based on what past surprises have been—positive or negative.
- Consuming something can help fill the empty spaces inside, even if it's only temporary.
- Money means a person can rely on what he has, not who he is.
- Doing the right thing is harder than it sounds, especially when it's not your first choice.
- Happiness, like forgiveness, isn't a final destination. You don't go there and get to stay. It ebbs and flows like the tide moving in and out.
- Things you thought would set you free can eventually imprison you.
- Freedom doesn't just happen, you have to choose it, and choose to let it make you bigger, not smaller.
- You never know when or how you will really connect with another human being.
- Money makes you see things differently, see yourself differently, and changes what other people expect from you.
- Money can make you expect certain things, as if you are owed things because of the money just by having it, not by earning it.
- Hope isn't something that someone bestows upon you; it's a decision you make.
- There are some words you can't take back, even if you want to. You just have to deal with what you didn't really mean to say.
- Conflict is about power, about who has it and who hasn't, who gets to play and who doesn't, who's up and who's down. And money is the shortcut to power.
- Money gives you the power to say *fuck you* to anyone you want to. But that doesn't mean that the person who has it will do the right thing by it.
- The loneliness you feel when you're with the wrong person is the worst of all.

- Those you love help you be you. Being with loved ones lets you all complete each other.
- In the end, we're all just people, all as real or as false as we choose to be.
- Believing in the person on the magazine cover is probably putting your faith in a lie, or at the least a façade.
- Each of us has the right to change our minds, to stop doing something when we know it isn't right, to insist on good and real things for ourselves and those we care about.
- Insist on yourself. Be true to yourself and to what is right and good for you.
- We are influenced too much by what people have, and not who they are.
- Stopping to think about who you are and what you are doing is hard work, especially when you have to face some things in yourself that you don't want to look at.
- Do what makes your world grow bigger, not smaller.

BOOK REPORT IDEAS

1. Discuss the positive and negative changes that money made in Indigo's life.
2. Explain how you define happiness. When are you most and least happy, and why?
3. Examine the changes in Indigo's life after Richard gave her the money. Compare those changes to the ways your life might change if you were given that much money.
4. In what ways are the Skyes' eccentricities reflected in their pets' personalities?
5. Discuss the idea that anticipating is as good as knowing.
6. Compare Indigo and Melanie, and discuss why Indigo's money changed their relationship so drastically.
7. Indigo realizes when she tells the Irregulars about the money that she is on the edge of change, life-shifting change. Discuss how you might react to changes in your own life that might be that major and long-lasting.
8. Discuss the changes Indigo has made in herself and in her life by the end of the book.
9. How was Indigo true to herself? How would you be true to yourself?
10. What is the most interesting or important idea you learned from the book, and why did you choose it?

BOOKTALK IDEAS

1. Have each of the main characters introduce himself or herself in first person.
2. Use a manila envelope with "Indigo Skye" written on it as a prop.
3. Write your talk in first person, as if you were Richard Howards.
4. Focus your talk on the idea of changes, from small ones to those that impact your life at every level.

5. Focus your talk on the two scenes when Indigo told her family and her coworkers about the money.

RISKS
- Includes obscenities
- Homosexual characters
- Uninvolved parents
- Money creates problems, rather than solving them

STRENGTHS
- Realistic language
- Caring parents
- Close-knit family
- Characters grow and gain insight
- Philosophical content and ideas the reader can consider and/or adopt
- Three-dimensional characters reader can identify with
- Ambiguous ending allows reader to speculate on the final outcome
- Shows how large amounts of money can make life more difficult, rather than less

AWARD
ALA Best Books for Young Adults, 2009

REVIEWS
"Caletti's coming-of-age story with an infinitely likeable heroine and richly limned supporting characters makes a fine counterpoint to the ubiquitous rich-girl series books." Bina Williams, *Booklist*, 4/08

"Filled with rich characters and hilarious interactions mixed with Indigo's astute perceptions of conformity and frivolous wealth, this book encourages thought and examination of what is truly important in life." Jessie Spalding, Queen Creek Branch Library, AZ, *School Library Journal*, 4/08

"Although the lesson of this rags-to-riches tale is evident from the beginning, Caletti (*Honey, Baby, Sweetheart*) builds characters with so much depth that readers will be invested in her story. Indigo's ability to recognize and appreciate what makes other people tick makes her an unusually compelling narrator, even when her values get blown off course." *Publishers Weekly*, 2/08

◫◫◫

FRICTION. E .R. Frank. Atheneum, an imprint of Simon and Schuster, 2003. $16.95. 208p. ISBN: 068985384X. ISBN13: 9780689853845. Simon Pulse, 2004. $6.99. 208p. ISBN10: 0689853858. ISBN13: 9780689853852. Listening Library, 2003. $25.00. ISBN10: 080721647X. ISBN13: 9780807216477. (unabridged audiotape) Tandem Library, 2004. $15.80. 208p. ISNB10: 141779885. ISBN13: 9781417719884. (library binding) Realistic fiction. Reading Level: MS. Interest Level: MS. English, P.E., Ethics, Psychology.

SUBJECT AREAS
school; sports; lying and deceit; friendship; gossip; handicaps; secrets; manipulation; abuse, sexual.

CHARACTERS
Alex: she's chosen to show Stacy around
Tim: Alex's best friend
Simon: he's teaching Alex's class for the next two years
Stacy: she's the new kid at Forest Alternative School, is a year older than everyone else, and seems really cool
Viv: he's East Indian and wears a turban
Sebastian: he has braces on his legs and his arms end at his elbows, and he hates being pitied
Teddy: he's a genius and he's really fat
Danny: he has blue hair and hates math
Marie: another girl in Alex's class
Ann: Alex's mother, who's an oncologist
Jack: Alex's dad, who's a psychiatrist
Maggie: the principal at Forest Alternative School
Sophie: Maggie's daughter
Paul: Teddy's dad, who goes on the campout with Simon's class
Reade: Stacy's father

BOOKTALK
Sometimes things are just too confusing to talk about. Like the way Stacy keeps saying Simon likes me, as in *likes me* likes me. That's just so lame—Simon's our teacher, and I'm just an eighth-grade girl. But the more she says it, the more I start to wonder—does he pay more attention to me? Does he look at me all the time? When he gives me a hug, or ruffles my hair, does it mean he's being friendly, or something more?

And how come everyone else in the class believes her? Not at first so much, but after our camping trip, they changed their minds. And no matter how many times I tell them nothing happened, they all believe what they saw.

How can I make Stacy stop? Doesn't she know what she's doing? She's going to ruin everything if she doesn't stop!

MAJOR THEMES AND IDEAS

- Sometimes it can be hard to not think about something you hear, even when it's not true.
- Gossip can be like a poison, making innocent actions seem wrong or guilty.
- Two people can see the same event and interpret it completely differently.
- If you say something enough times, people will begin to believe it, even if it's not true.
- Sometimes it's difficult to know what's the right thing to do.
- There aren't always right answers.
- Once you figure out one problem in life, you move onto the next; it's called growth. You can't just sit still, even if you'd like to.
- People lie for all kinds of reasons, and understanding the reason for the lie is as important as knowing what the truth is.
- It's important to look at situations and people from all sides if you want to understand them.
- The truth isn't only just the facts. It's also how you feel about the facts.
- There's a germ of truth behind every lie.
- Life happens. There aren't any do-overs and no way to go back.
- The reason for a lie can give us a clue about where the truth is.
- You can't force someone to tell you what's wrong.
- Sometimes the harder it is to share a secret, the more important it is to tell.
- We can't reverse what's been done to us. We just have to figure out how to go on.
- You outgrow people and places just like you outgrow clothes and shoes.

BOOK REPORT IDEAS

1. Discuss what it means to tell the whole truth, the facts, and the meaning behind them. Can emotion change the way facts are perceived?
2. Explore why Stacy lied. What did she gain from it?
3. Once you have finished the book, go back and reread the scenes about Stacy's first day at Forest Alternative. What things about her do you see differently from the way you did when you first read it?
4. Discuss how gossip can change a whole group's perception of someone.
5. What are some things Alex could have done to stop Stacy's lies?
6. Discuss what Alex's mother meant when she said Simon taught the way people did thirty years ago.
7. Speculate what will happen to Alex, Tim, and Simon during the next year.
8. Examine the idea that you outgrow people and places so they don't fit you anymore.

9. Was there a "tipping point" when nothing could be done about stopping the process from an inevitable end?
10. Simon said he had made some bad choices. Explain what he did and why you think it was a bad choice.

BOOKTALK IDEAS
1. Write your talk as a dialogue between Stacy and Alex or between Alex and Tim.
2. Use a soccer ball or a small green pine-scented candle as a prop.
3. Write your talk as if you were gossiping about Simon.

RISKS
*   Teen boys and girls sleep in the same bedroom or tent
*   Male teacher is physically affectionate with female student
*   Realistic language, including vulgarities
*   Parent glosses over child's attempts to discuss her problems/fears
*   Girl lies about teacher molesting her and convinces his class that he's a pervert
*   Father sexually abuses daughter

STRENGTHS
*   Portrays a strong, healthy family relationship
*   Matter-of-fact treatment of characters' differences or handicaps
*   Shows the strength of a long friendship
*   Shows the destructive power of gossip, especially sexual gossip
*   Examines the differences between the facts and the emotions behind them
*   Character confusion about first sexual feelings is clearly portrayed
*   Realistic ending doesn't sugarcoat the damage to Simon and his class
*   Authentic voice
*   Characters reader can identify with
*   Provides many opportunities for discussions about gossip, lying, and sexuality

AWARDS
ALA Best Books for Young Adults, 2004
Kirkus Editor's Choice, 2003

REVIEWS
"Frank . . . doesn't shy away from difficult topics, and this novel is no exception. She conveys Alex's confusion convincingly, and in the end readers will sympathize with

everyone involved. An excellent way for teachers, counselors, and parents to open up discussions of what constitutes sexual abuse, and a gripping read for younger adolescent girls." Paula Rohrlick, *KLIATT*, 5/03

"The author invites readers to explore the large gray area between truth and falsehood." *Publishers Weekly*, 11/04

"Frank's focus on the highly combustible environment of a classroom full of pubescent children and the chaos one abused teen can bring to those around her is subtly done, and will be immediately recognizable to her readers." *Kirkus Reviews*, 5/03

ⅢⅢⅢ

GENTLEMEN. Michael Northrop. Scholastic, 2009. $16.99. 249p. ISBN10: 0545097495. ISBN13: 9780545097499. Mystery and suspense. Reading Level: YHS. Interest Level: YHS, OHS. English, Psychology.

SUBJECT AREAS
school; friendship; self-knowledge; crime and delinquency; manipulation; sex and sexuality; violence; secrets; mystery.

CHARACTERS
Micheal/Mike Benton: he likes 10R, and it's where all his friends are
Tommy: he's disruptive, loud, fidgety, and always up to something, but he's a good guy
Mixer: he steals things cause he likes to have cool stuff he can show off
Bones: most people are afraid of him, with good reasons—he's terminally angry
Mr. Dantley: he teaches remedial math at the Tits
Natalie: she's in 10R math, and Tommy has a crush on her
Trever: the assistant principal
Ms. Chaney: she teaches Spanish
Grayson: he teaches science and is one of the coolest teachers at Tits
Haberman: he teaches English, and likes to play mind games with his students
Lara, Max, Reedy: they're in the same English class as the "Gentlemen"
Joey: Mixer's older brother
Sherriff Throckmorton: he's the County Sheriff, and comes to the school to investigate Tommy's disappearance
Ms. Yanoff: Haberman's substitute teacher

BOOKTALK

It was just another school day til Tommy flipped his desk. It was math class, and Mr. Dantley and Tommy didn't get along at *all*. Mr. Dantley was walking up and down the aisles giving everyone a number, and you were supposed to give him the square root. When he got to Tommy, he said, "Nine." Now that was just cold on so many levels. It was so easy, it was insulting, and besides, he knew Tommy couldn't really answer it. He couldn't say *three*. It was something about the *th* and the *r* back to back. It came out too quick, too loud, and just plain wrong. And Dantley knew it.

I turned around to see what he would do, and he flipped his desk! He put his palms under the edge of it and threw it up in the air. All his stuff went flying, and the desk came crashing down. We all just sat there looking stunned, including Tommy, and then Dantley started yelling at him. He yelled til spit was coming out and faces began appearing in the little window of the door, kids and teachers wanting to see what all the noise was about. Finally Dantley ran down, told Tommy to pick up the desk and get his things and report to Trever, the assistant principal.

We figured we'd see him the next period, which was science, but he didn't show up. That's why we knew he was in serious trouble, maybe suspended. But he never showed up.

Then when we got to English, there was a weird setup in the front of the room. Haberman was standing in front of a big blue plastic barrel, watching us file in. He had a wooden bat in one hand. Turns out there's something in the barrel, and each of us was supposed to hit it and guess what it was. No one got the right answer, and Haberman started his lecture, and we all zoned out like usual.

When the bell rang, Bones, Mixer, and I were set on getting out the door as fast as possible, but Haberman called us back and told us to take the barrel out to his car. It was so heavy we could barely manage it. We got to the car and no way was that barrel going into the trunk of a sports car. So we sort of dumped what was inside into the trunk, and Haberman pushed at it til it all fit in. We still couldn't see what was inside—something wrapped in old blankets, with duct tape to keep it fastened. It looked like it had lumps or humps in it, but Haberman just slammed the trunk before any of us could get a good look. Just the same, the way it looked under the blankets, it didn't look like a *thing*, the way it moved when Haberman shoved it in, it looked like it had joints, like it was a body wrapped up in those blankets.

Why would Haberman put a blanket-wrapped body in his trunk? We knew he was strange and into serious head games, but this went way beyond strange.

MAJOR THEMES AND IDEAS

- Crime and punishment are ideas that are linked and universal. Crime creates an imbalance, punishments restore balance.
- Friendship is partly about the history you have with someone.
- Words represent ideas, and we all define those ideas differently.
- Murder is a complicated business. There is the act, and there is the aftermath.
- "God gives peace to the dead, the living still have to live." —Dostoyevsky

- A crime extends past the moment it was committed.
- The easiest thing to do when something's bothering you is to make fun of it.
- Each person has his or her own place in a group of friends, and when one's gone, it leaves a hole, and the group seems off balance, somehow.
- Separating what someone says from what he meant isn't always easy.
- It is sometimes difficult to know what is real and what is opinion, and to distinguish between them.
- Ideas can be very dangerous things.
- Your past influences your present and your future.
- Realizing that things are going to get violent real quickly can sometimes make you think very clearly.
- Just because you didn't do anything doesn't mean you aren't guilty.
- You can let a lot go, if a guy's your friend. But how much is too much?
- It's not hard for one person to keep a secret, but the more people that know, the harder it gets. If enough people know, it's not a secret any longer.
- At some point it stops being OK to lash out and hurt people who haven't hurt you. And it stops being OK to just let that happen.
- Friendships end. You have to move on.

BOOK REPORT IDEAS

1. Discuss what Mike means about fitting into the 10R group. What kind of kids are in remedial classes?
2. Explain why you think Tommy flipped his desk.
3. Discuss Haberman and his mind games. What kind of a person is he? How does he fit in with the rest of the school?
4. Explore the ideas of crime and punishment.
5. Explore the idea of murder and the impact it has on those around the victim, friends, family, the community as a whole
6. This story has a kind of inevitability about it. Could Mike and Mixer have changed anything? What could they have done?
7. Discuss how well they know Bones. Is the attack on Haberman entirely unexpected?
8. Explain Mike's thoughts while the attack is going on and why neither he nor Mixer did anything to stop Bones.
9. Mike and Mixer choose to do two different things at the trial. Explain what they each did and why they made their choices.
10. Compare and contrast the four boys in the first chapter and in the last chapter. Then speculate on what their future lives will be like.
11. Explain how the relationship among the four boys is similar to the one shared among you and your friends.
12. Explain what you think is the most important idea or event in the book, and why you chose it.
13. Discuss the role of imagination and suspicion in the book and how they make unbelievable things sound possible.

BOOKTALK IDEAS

1. Have Mike introduce the three other boys and focus your talk on their friendship.
2. Focus your talk on Tommy's disappearance.
3. Talk about imagination and suspicion and how they can create false impressions.
4. Use some of the information about *Crime and Punishment* in your talk.

RISKS

- Teens smoke, drink, and use drugs
- Teens are sexually active
- Detailed sex scene
- Scenes of graphic violence
- Teen beats teacher severely for no reason
- Teens make no effort to stop the beating
- Homosexuality/homosexual characters
- Rape
- Teens are in denial about their friend's increasing psychosis

STRENGTHS

- Well-rounded, authentic characters the reader can identify with
- Authentic dialogue, including slang and some obscenities
- Tension builds slowly
- Author makes the unbelievable sound possible, even likely
- Strong mother-son relationship
- Realistic ending, which leaves room for speculation and discussion
- Friends still accept teen after he comes out as gay
- Strong and loyal friendships

AWARDS

Title published too recently to be eligible for awards.

REVIEWS

"Michael's practiced, smart-yet-slacker voice is authentic . . . The boys' immediate, assured suspicion of Haberman's complicity in Tommy's disappearance is frightening and realistic." *Kirkus Reviews*

"Northrop's debut is one dark ride, as events spin out of control for three friends who haven't had many lucky breaks . . . The brutal narration, friendships put through the wringer and the sense of dread that permeates the novel will keep readers hooked through the violent climax and its aftermath." *Publishers Weekly*, 4/6/09

"This is a rare sort of book that may work just as well for reluctant readers as it will avid ones. . . .What are the boys going to do about it propels the action, and the well-rounded characters and their plausible obsessions provide buoyancy to the story. Laced throughout is a steely and intricate look at the permutations of adolescent friendship and the various roles that teens adopt or are assigned in both their social and academic worlds. A riveting thriller? Yep. A nuanced examination of morality? Yep again. What's amazing is that they never get in each other's way." *Booklist*, 5/1/09

GEOGRAPHY CLUB. Brent Hartinger. HarperTeen, an imprint of HarperCollins, 2003. $17.99. 240p. ISBN10: 0060012218. ISBN13: 9780060012212. HarperTeen, 2004. $7.99. 240p. ISBN10: 0060012234. ISBN13: 9780060012236. Realistic fiction. Reading Level: MS. Interest Level: MS, YHS. English, Psychology, Sociology.

SUBJECT AREAS
school; friendship; self-knowledge; stereotypes; secrets; bullying; family relationships; rites of passage; prejudice; intimidation; peer pressure; homosexuality; sex and sexuality; gossip; sports.

CHARACTERS
Russel Middlebrook: he's convinced he's the only gay kid at Goodkind High School
Kevin Laud: he's a jock, but he's also gay
Min: Russel's best friend, who's bisexual and one of the school brains
Gunnar: Russel's good friend, but he's a bit high strung
Brian Bund: the unquestioned outcast, the lowest of the low; he's teased mercilessly by the jocks while everyone else looks on
Teresa Buckman: she's a lesbian and Min's girlfriend
Ike: a friend of Teresa's who's gay
Trish Baskin: she has a crush on Russel
Kimberly Peterson: Gunnar wants her to be his girlfriend
Mr. Kephert: the Geography Club advisor and the most uninvolved teacher at school

BOOKTALK

They were all alone. That's why they started the Geography Club. They were all gay, or lesbian, or bisexual, and they were the only people who knew the truth about each other. Outside the classroom where they met on Tuesdays and Thursdays after school, they all wore masks. Russel and Min had been best friends for years, but they'd still kept some secrets—some very big secrets.

But all that changed when Russel met someone named GayTeen in a chat room, and found out they both went to the same high school, and they were both in the same class. Russel couldn't believe it when Kevin walked out of the shadows that night, after they'd agreed to meet. Kevin Land, baseball jock extraordinaire, was gay? They talked for hours that night, and both their lives changed in ways they'd never expected.

Russel found out Min was bisexual, and her girlfriend was a lesbian. He also found out that a jock could fall for a guy who was just ordinary, not popular, and not really part of a clique.

And all of them, Russel, Kevin, Min, Teresa, and Ike found out how good it felt to take off their masks and be real and honest with each other.

But while they could be honest with each other, they still couldn't be honest with anyone outside their group. Secrets can bind people together and tear them apart. What will they do to this group?

MAJOR THEMES AND IDEAS

- In one way or another, we're all alone, even when others don't see us that way.
- Pretending to be someone you aren't is difficult and stressful.
- Even if you can't share your secrets with everyone, it feels good to have at least a few people who know who you really are.
- Sometimes friendship needs privacy, not an audience.
- It's lots harder for a group to keep a secret than it is for one person.
- There's a difference between being alone and being lonely. You can be lonely even with friends.
- If you have a secret, you can't ever really relax, even around friends. If they knew the truth, they might not be your friends any more.
- Sometimes being popular just means pressure—pressure to be the person you're expected to be, not who you really are.
- No one knows how to hurt you like your best friend.
- People make mistakes. If there were no such thing as forgiveness, there wouldn't be any friendships left in the world.
- The ugliest place in the world is okay if you're there with friends.

BOOK REPORT IDEAS

1. Discuss the idea of bullying and how people at Goodkind were bullied. Could anyone have done anything to stop it? Who? How?

2. Compare and contrast Kevin and Russel. How are they both strong and weak?
3. Speculate on what happens with the GSLBA after the book ends.
4. Explore the character of Brian Bund and discuss how he copes with being the outcast.

BOOKTALK IDEAS
1. Russel is the narrator of the book. Let him tell his story.
2. Have each of the main characters introduce themselves and share a little of their part of the story.

RISKS
- Jocks pick on outcasts mercilessly, with no reprisals at all
- Gay teens meet online and then in person, alone, late at night
- Teens are gay, lesbian, and bisexual
- Realistic language, including homophobic slurs
- School is divided into cliques, with the jocks holding the most power
- Teachers demonstrate use of condom in a classroom
- Straight and homosexual teens are sexually active

STRENGTHS
- Authentic teen voice of narrator
- Accurate portrayal of the risks of coming out in high school
- Teen friendships based on honesty
- Characters grow and gain insight
- Ending is realistic and somewhat unresolved
- Three-dimensional, believable characters

AWARDS
ALA Popular Paperbacks, 2005
New York Public Library Books for the Teen Age, 2004
Lambda Literary Award Finalist, 2003

REVIEWS
"Hartinger grasps the melodrama and teen angst of high school well. Russel's narration rings true, as he walks through the social jungle that is high school." Mike Brown, *VOYA*, 4/03

"Characterization is excellent, with all of the teens emerging as likable but flawed individuals caught in a situation that few young adults could handle with maturity.

This author has something to say here, and his message is potent and effective in its delivery. Many teens, both gay and straight, should find this novel intriguing." Robert Gray, East Central Regional Library, Cambridge, MN, *School Library Journal*, 2/03

"With honest talk of love and cruelty, friendship and betrayal, it's Russel's realistic, funny, contemporary narrative that makes this first novel special. The dialogue is right on; so is the high-school cafeteria; so is the prejudice. Booktalk this." Hazel Rochman, *Booklist*, 4/03

⊞ ⊞ ⊞

GODLESS. Pete Hautman. Simon and Schuster, 2004. $15.95. 208p. ISBN10: 0689862784. ISBN13: 9780689862786. Simon Pulse, 2005. $8.99. 208p. ISBN10: 1416908161. ISBN13: 9781416908166. Thorndike Press, 2004. $20.95. 240p. ISBN10: 0786270705. ISBN13: 9780786270705. (large print) Realistic fiction. Reading Level: YHS. Interest Level: YHS, OHS. English, Ethics, Psychology, Religion.

SUBJECT AREAS
religion; friendship; family relationships; bullying; peer pressure; crime and delinquency; mental illness; obsession; anger; dysfunctional families; fear; self-knowledge; secrets; lying and deceit; art.

CHARACTERS
Jason Bock/Jay-Boy: fed up with his parents' boring religion, he invents his own
Peter Stephen Schinner/Shin: Jason's best friend, who collects snails and is a science geek
Henry Stagg: a juvenile delinquent type with no fondness for Jason or Shin and a history of violence
Mitch Casmo, Marsh Anderson, Bobby: Henry's friends and cohorts
Dr. Hellman: Jason's doctor
Mom/Maggie Bock: she's obsessed about diseases and imagines all kinds of illnesses in other people
Dad/Mr. Bock: he's obsessed about religion and drags his son and wife to Mass every week
Allen Anderson: head of TPO, Teen Power Outreach, that has weekly meetings so kids can talk about God, religion, and Catholicism
Magda Price: a member of TPO, she is pretty and petite and asks a lot of questions

Brianna: another TPO member who has definite opinions

Dan Grant: Jason's ordinary friend who is a preacher's kid, but who joins Jason's church of the Ten-Legged God

Gerry Kramer: an old, gray cop who doesn't like to get calls about Henry climbing the water tower

Jack Bock: Jason's dad's cousin, who's a jerk

Jack Bock Junior: a year older than Jason, he's heavily into sports and is very religious

BOOKTALK

It started the day that Henry Stagg slugged me in the face and laid me out under the water tower. Lying there, looking up at the dripping silver bottom of the water tower, I had a religious experience. The water tower was everything to the people of St. Andrews Valley. The water it held was piped to every home and business. It connected us all. It kept us all alive. Water was life, and the water tower was God, the Ten-Legged One.

It's not hard to start your own religion. You need a god, some members, a holy book, some sacraments, and some rules. That's about it. My best friend Shin joined immediately and was appointed Keeper of the Sacred Text and began to channel the Ten-Legged One to help him write it. Dan, my ordinary friend, became the First Acolyte, and Magda, who is way too little and pretty for a neckless hick like me, appointed herself High Priestess. I am the Founder and Great Kahuna of the Chutengodians. Our sacraments include Giving Thanks to the Tower, Drinking the Holy Water that drips from the tower, the Sacred Washing of Hands, the Flushing of the Toilet, and the Daily Immersion. We're working on coming up with some more.

Things were going along pretty well when I discovered Henry could climb the tower, even though the spiral staircase that went up the central column ended fifteen feet above the ground. Yeah, that same Henry that started all this, the same shrimpy, violent, psychotic cowboy that loved to give Shin and me grief. And he won't tell me how to climb the tower until I make him a Chutengodian, too.

That was my first mistake, taking him into my church without consulting the other members—especially Shin. Too bad it wasn't my last mistake as well. Starting a religion, finding a god to worship was easy. Staying in control of it turned out to be harder than I'd ever imagined.

MAJOR THEMES AND IDEAS

- You cannot prove that God exists or doesn't exist.
- Making up a religion isn't all that difficult.
- You don't have to be a believer to be religious or serious about your religion.
- You can't be responsible for what someone else does with his life.
- It's important to stand up for your friends.
- Sometimes a lie is kinder than the truth.

- People will surprise you—it's impossible to predict what anyone's going to do.
- An adventure can change to a disaster in an instant.
- There are some experiences you'll never forget, even if they were foolish and dangerous.
- If you know your friends will go along with what you say to do, are you responsible for their actions?
- You can be one person on the outside and another on the inside.
- It's difficult and sometimes impossible to keep someone from doing something he's determined to do.
- Religions are easier to create than control.
- Your friends listen to what you say.
- You can't really understand something you don't believe in.

BOOK REPORT IDEAS

1. Discuss Shin and speculate on why he became so quickly obsessed with Jason's religion.
2. This book is about control. Jason's dad tries to control his beliefs; Jason tries to control his followers. Discuss how both of them fail to control others.
3. Jason questions the validity of religion in general. How would you respond to him, either as a member of TPO or CTG?
4. Is Jason right when he says all your need to create a religion is a god, some rules, and a few converts? What is a religion? What is a god? What is a church?
5. Speculate on what will happen to the CTG members after the book ends. How will their experiences affect their lives?
6. Jason knows he is bigger than Henry, but he allows Henry to hit him twice and manipulate him in several ways. Why?
7. Discuss the meaning of obsession as it's seen in the book, in Shin's and in Jason's parents.
8. Examine the relationship between Henry and Magda—what was his attraction for her?

BOOKTALK IDEAS

1. Use a sketchbook like Shin's as a prop.
2. Write the talk in first person, as Shin, perhaps reading parts of the Sacred Text as a part of your talk.
3. Have each of the Chutengodians speak in the talk, explaining their own view of Jason and the CTG.
4. Use a picture of a water tower as a prop.
5. Focus your talk on the CTG and its beliefs.

RISKS
- Character creates his own god and religion
- Negative view of religion, and Catholicism in particular
- Teens exhibit life-threatening behavior just to get a thrill
- Obsessive characters
- Questions the validity of Christianity
- Abusive parent
- Religious families portrayed as dysfunctional

STRENGTHS
- Characters the reader can identify with
- Requires that the reader think about religion and religious beliefs
- Examines the issues of personal responsibility
- Demonstrates the power of peer pressure
- Ambiguous ending leaves room for speculation
- Characters change and gain insight

AWARDS
National Book Award for Young People's Literature, 2004
ALA Best Books for Young Adults, 2005
Booklist Editors' Choice, 2004
CCBC Choices (Cooperative Children's Book Council)
New York Public Library Books for the Teen Age, 2005
ALA Popular Paperbacks, 2007

REVIEWS
"Readers will find Jason's first-person narrative compelling and provocative. Although Hautman chooses an atypical subject for a young adult book, he succeeds in creating a flawlessly paced and painfully realistic tale of the power and influence of religion." Jamie S. Hansen, *VOYA*, 10/04

"Jason's explorations of faith, belief, and religion, told in a compelling and imaginative voice, will leave him a solitary, ostracized prophet. Thought-provoking and unique." *Kirkus Reviews*, 5/04

"Most scenes are honest and true to the bone . . . Anyone who has questioned his or her religion, especially as a teenager, will respond to Jason's struggles with belief. Many individuals, upon reading this, will consider their own questions once more." Ilene Cooper, *Booklist*, 6/04

⛤⛤⛤

GONE. Kathleen Jeffrie Johnson. Roaring Brook, 2007. $16.95. 176p. ISBN10: 1596431385. ISBN13: 9781596431386. Realistic fiction. Reading Level: MS. Interest Level: YHS, OHS. English, Sex Education, Psychology.

SUBJECT AREAS
sex and sexuality; friendship; addiction; rites of passage; problem parents; substance abuse; anger; dysfunctional family; school; self-knowledge; secrets; love; lying and deceit; manipulation; family relationships; fear; guilt.

CHARACTERS
Connor Donaghue: he's seventeen, just out of high school; up until six months ago, his social life consisted of taking care of his alcoholic mother
Corinna Timms: Connor's history teacher, whom Connor has a crush on
Zach: Connor's closest friend, who's a little hyper
Tom McDaniel: he had Connor for shop and thinks he has talent
Annie McDaniel: Tom's wife and Corrina's friend
Sylvia/Aunt Syl: Connor's great aunt, with whom he lives
Walter: Aunt Syl's boyfriend
Mr. Donoghue/Dad: Connor's father, who lives in a nursing home as a result of brain injuries from a drunk driving accident
Mom: Connor's mother, an alcoholic from whom he's estranged
Sean: assistant manager at Chow Line where Connor and Zach work
Mil: Aunt Syl's long-time neighbor and friend, who's black
Risa: Mil's granddaughter, who's sixteen
Darnell: Risa's younger brother
Jenny: she's hot, and also works at Chow Line
Mary Anne: Connor's mother's best friend and drinking buddy
Miss Toni: Mil's girlfriend, who's white
Mitch: Corrina's brother
Mr. Dumant: the "big boss" at Chow Line

BOOKTALK
She *saw* him. So few people did, but when she met his eyes, Miss Timms *saw* him. In a world where he felt invisible most of the time, knowing someone really saw him was incredible, special. But there was no way he could share his feelings with her, or with anyone else. Corinna Timms was Connor's history teacher, and she was off limits, even if his friend Zach said she was serious babe material.

That didn't keep Connor from thinking about her, even after he'd graduated and didn't see her every day. It didn't keep him from being jealous of the man she was with sometimes, until he found out Mitch was her brother. She was moving to New Mexico at the end of the summer. He'd never see her again. But he couldn't stop his hopes, his dreams, his desperate need to be with someone who saw who he was.

The she invited him and Zach on a picnic, and there was a private moment for a first kiss. And after his Aunt Syl's birthday party, there was time and space for more than that.

Connor thought he needed Corinna to fill the vast, dark emptiness, the nothing-ness that lived inside him. He didn't know no one could do that for him, and so he reached out to her, and found her reaching back.

MAJOR THEMES AND IDEAS

- When you can picture something in your mind, seeing every detail, you can create it.
- Woodworking takes time and patience, step after step, beginning to end.
- Things like wood always retain their essence, no matter what you do to them.
- A good time never hurts.
- Thinking too much can get you into trouble.
- Being an outsider is partly how others treat you, but it's also how you act and see yourself. To be an outsider, both you and others must define you that way.
- Sometimes loneliness can take you down a dangerous path.
- No one can fill the emptiness inside you. You have to do it yourself.
- Sometimes family members aren't connected by blood, but by love. Who's to say they aren't a "real" family?
- Blood may be thicker than water, but it's not stronger than love.
- When you feel unlovable, it's hard to believe someone really likes you and wants to be with you.
- Loving yourself makes it easier for others to love you.
- Sometimes lies are necessary and unavoidable.
- When life slaps you in the face, you just have to cut your losses and move on.
- Lying to your best friend just makes you look like an idiot.
- When you use your fist to settle a dispute, especially if you hit a woman, you're headed down the wrong road.
- If you don't deal with the past, the past deals with you.
- You can't escape your past. You have to face it, accept it, and accept yourself, and move on.
- Unless you accept your past as being part of you, you cannot truly accept yourself.
- If pain is what you knew as a child, it can feel familiar and comfortable when you are older and lead you to gravitate towards people who can provide it. An addict's child may fall in love with an addict.

- A broken person can't help anyone else.
- Home is where the people who love you are.

BOOK REPORT IDEAS

1. Discuss and define "the black heart of nothing" that Connor holds inside him. What does it mean and where did it come from? How is it connected with his feelings of invisibility?
2. Discuss the idea of falling for a person like your parent because the relationship feels familiar. Include how this can be a good thing, as well as a bad thing.
3. Explain what "family" means to you. How do you include and exclude people in your "family"?
4. Connor believes that Zach and Risa told Mil about him and Corinna. Do you think that's what happened, or could there be another reason for it?
5. Explain why you think Connor and Corinna were drawn together. Is there any situation in which their relationship could have become solid?
6. Compare and contrast the stable and long-lasting relationships/couples in this book with those who were neither. How are they different and how are they alike?
7. Discuss Connor's relationship with Mary Anne and how it affected him.
8. How would Connor's life have been different if his father had been injured in some way that didn't involve brain damage?
9. Connor feels he is losing everyone he loves. How is this true and how is it not true?
10. Speculate on what Connor's future might be like and how his relationships with his friends and family might evolve over time—a year, five years, ten, twenty. How will his childhood and adolescence affect his adult life?
11. This book centers around an adult, and authority figure, seducing a minor. Include reasons why an adult would choose this kind of a relationship and why a teenager might want to respond to such an offer.

BOOKTALK IDEAS

1. Use a sparkly old-fashioned pin with blue stones as a prop.
2. Tell the booktalk in first person as Connor.
3. Have Zach introduce Connor and hint at his relationship with Corinna.
4. Write your talk in alternating voices, as Connor and Corinna, as they describe each other.
5. Focus your talk on the idea of loss, and how much Connor has lost.

RISKS

- Alcoholic mother, brain-damaged father
- Interracial couples

- Son is forced to take care of his alcoholic mother
- Teacher has sex with former student, who is fourteen years younger
- Teen masturbates while fanatisizing about former teacher
- Teen is approached by his mother's drunk best friend
- Teacher uses drugs of various kinds

STRENGTHS

- Realistic, three-dimensional characters
- Great aunt helps provide a created family
- Characters mature and gain insight
- Examines the impact of loneliness on an individual's life
- Two older couples have solid relationships even if they aren't married
- Adults are supportive of teens who are family and friends
- Next-door neighbors form a created family with children and grandchildren
- Frank, realistic discussion of first sexual experiences

REVIEWS

"The focus of this novel is going to be on the relationship between the adult and the teen, but it is really a story of a damaged boy who is finding himself and his family." Mary Ann Harlan, *VOYA*, 4/07

"Johnson creates a feverish atmosphere—the humid summer, the blazing grill at the restaurant where Connor works—to underline the physical desire, and crushing emotions are beautifully drawn." Jennifer Mattson, *Booklist*, 3/07

"In addition to the scintillating premise of a teacher-student affair, this is a raw novel about a 17-year-old's search for a home. . . . Johnson imagines a well-drawn backdrop to this story, both in the steamy summer setting, and in the colorful, full-bodied characters." *Publishers Weekly*, 2/07

◫◫◫

THE GOSPEL ACCORDING TO LARRY. Janet Tashjian. Holt, 2001. $16.95. 192p. ISBN10: 0805063781. ISBN13: 9780805063783. Laurel Leaf, an imprint of Random House, 2003. $6.50. 256p. ISBN10: 0440237920. ISBN13: 9780440237921. Thorndike Press, 2005. $22.95. 235p. ISBN10: 078627543X. ISBN13: 9780786275434. (large print) Tandem, 2003. $15.25. 192p. ISBN10: 0613723333. ISBN13: 9780613723336. (library binding) Realistic fiction. Reading Level: MS. Interest Level: MS, YHS. Ethics, Psychology, Government.

SUBJECT AREAS
religion; philosophy; self-knowledge; writing; death and dying; family relationships; computers; internet; lying and deceitfulness; love; rites of passage; activism; cultural identity; gossip; environmental issues; ethics; manipulation; friendship; politics; runaways; secrets; step-parents.

CHARACTERS
Janet Tashjian: Josh gave her this manuscript, and she published his story
Josh Swenson: a loner, a thinker and a philosopher who decided to tell his story
Beth: Josh's best friend, who persuades him to start a Larry Club
Peter Swenson: Josh's stepfather, who runs an advertising firm
Katherine: Peter's girlfriend, who wants to marry him
Ms. Phillips: high school guidance counselor
Mrs. Swenson/Mom: Josh's mother who loved Bloomingdale's and died of ovarian cancer
Marlene: she's worked the makeup counter for over twenty years
Todd: Beth's current crush
Marlon, Eli, Jessica, Leah, Sharon, Barry: members of the Larry Club that Beth and Josh start
Betagold/Tracey Hawthorne: one of Larry's fans who wants to "out" him
Billie North: a University of Georgia student who tried to identify Larry through clues in his sermons
Bono: U2's lead singer

BOOKTALK
Everyone had their own idea of who Larry was. Some jerk trying for his fifteen minutes of fame. An anonymous coward. A hacker into culture-bashing. A televangelist trying to reach the teen market. A bored housewife.

But whoever he was, Larry had people's attention with his sermons against the advertising supergiants using people's bodies as their personal billboards, ranting about pollution, global warming, and how we are destroying our own home. He wanted to contribute, to make his life mean something, and he wanted everyone else to do the same thing.

The only thing Larry refused to share was his identity, and soon that's all some people cared about—who Larry was became more important than what he said. There were hundreds of posts to his website, demanding he reveal himself. And one poster was especially vicious.

I'M CLOSING IN ON YOU LARRY. I'M GOING TO TRACK YOU DOWN. LOTS OF PEOPLE THINK YOU'RE WONDERFUL, BUT I THINK SOMEONE WHO DOESN'T STAND BEHIND HIS OWN WORDS IS A COWARD. I'M GOING TO FIND YOU AND I'M GOING TO EXPOSE YOU, LARRY. GET READY—I'LL BE THERE SOON. –betagold.

Who is Larry and why do people react so strongly to the messages in his sermons?

MAJOR THEMES AND IDEAS

- Possessions can tie us down and distract us from who we're trying to become.
- We need people stirring up the way we think about things.
- Our lives are inundated with advertising, pressuring us to buy.
- Just because someone's dead doesn't mean you can't talk to them.
- The people we choose to spend our lives with are the ones who share our journey. Do they encourage us to reach higher and dig deeper, or do they hold us back?
- For some people, privacy is crucial, and fame is to be avoided.
- A prophet is without honor in his own country.
- There's something to be said about living simply and alone and at peace with yourself.
- The gap between the haves and the have-nots just keeps getting bigger and bigger.
- We are courting disaster by misusing and abusing our planet.
- Most everyone wants their fifteen minutes of fame—even if they do nothing productive with it.
- Who knows why some things catch the attention of the public and rise to cult status so quickly?
- Whoever dies with the most stuff is still dead.
- The United States is using way too much of the world's resources.
- Wearing clothes with designer labels is like using your body as a billboard. Why not advertise *yourself* instead?
- Being alone doesn't have to be lonely.
- For some people, being alone is peaceful. For others, being in a crowd is. For everyone, occasionally being where you are not at peace can be educational.
- When something gets so big it takes on a life of its own, it's no longer controlled by its creator.
- One person *can* make a difference—and *does*.
- Live your dream and make it come true.
- It's important to strive to be emotionally honest with those you love and who love you.
- We alternately worship and denigrate those who are famous.
- Being a celebrity isn't always what it's said to be. There is a downside, too.
- Be the hero of your own life.
- You have to fix yourself first.

BOOK REPORT IDEAS

1. Write your report as if you were Larry.
2. Discuss why Larry became so popular so quickly.

3. Examine the idea of opinions and ideas being seen differently when we know the person who's expressing them.
4. Write a response to one of Larry's sermons, either supporting it or criticizing it.
5. Identify themes that appear in Larry's sermons and discuss how they are reflected (or not) in today's society.
6. Comment on using the internet to promote anti-consumerism, when it functions because of ads.
7. Josh first enjoyed, then hated, his celebrity status. Imagine how you might react to the same situation and how you might feel about it.
8. Larry doesn't explain his logo. Discuss what you think it means.
9. Speculate on what Josh might have done after the book was published.
10. What is the most important thing you have learned from this book and why did you choose it?

BOOKTALK IDEAS
1. Base your talk on quotes from Larry's sermons.
2. Use some of Larry's possessions as props.
3. Write your talk in the style of Larry's sermons.
4. Illustrate your talk with anti-stuff stickers or Larry's logo.
5. Write your talk from Beth's point of view.

RISKS
- Anti-consumerism philosophy
- Teen perpetuates huge fraud
- Teen plans his own death
- Debunks fascination with the cult of celebrity
- Manipulation
- Encourages readers to think for themselves on controversial topics

STRENGTHS
- Unique format and premise
- Three-dimensional characters readers can identify with
- Authentic teen voices
- Presents several philosophic viewpoints
- Promotes discussion on many topics
- Realistic language
- Realistic family relationships
- Strong focus on the importance of being genuine

AWARDS
ALA Popular Paperbacks, 2005
ALA Best Books for Young Adults, 2002

REVIEWS

"This story will speak clearly to many teens looking to create their own place in the world—those who have not been able to make their mark as jocks or cheerleaders or even geeks in the rough world of high school cliques . . . Tashjian skillfully uses humor and provides one of the most honest voices in young adult literature." Lynn Evarts, *VOYA*, 12/01

"A terrific read with a credible and lovable main character." Francisca Goldsmith, Berkeley Public Library, CA, *School Library Journal*, 10/01

"Tashjian's inventive story is a thrilling read, fast-paced with much fast food for thought about our consumer-oriented pop culture. . . . The voice is clear, the ending satisfying. Teenagers will eat this one up." *Kirkus Reviews*, 10/01

📖📖📖

GYM CANDY. Carl Deuker. Houghton Mifflin, 2007. $16.00. 320p. ISBN10: 061877713X. ISBN13: 9780618777136. Graphia, 2008. $8.99. 320p. ISBN10: 0547076312. ISBN13: 9780547076317. Realistic fiction. Reading Level: YHS. Interest Level: YHS, OHS. P.E., Ethics, English, Psychology, Health.

SUBJECT AREAS

sports; manipulation; substance abuse; school; friendship; self-knowledge; family relationships; anger; bullying; gossip; lying and deceit; intimidation; peer pressure; rites of passage; problem parents; secrets; dysfunctional family; ethics; violence.

CHARACTERS

Mick Johnson: his dad started training him hard to play football when he was only four
Mike Johnson: Mick's dad, who was a football star in high school and college and demands that his son be the same
Patti Johnson: a former gymnast in college, she tries to persuade Mike to let up on his son
Ben Braun: host of "Ben in the AM" and Mike's boss
Mr. Pengilly: Mick's seventh-grade teacher, who made Mick really think about football for the first time
Mr. Knecht: he coached Mick in Pop Warner football
Mr. Rooney: he became coach when Mr. Knecht left, and he had it in for Mick
Drew Carney: he was Mick's friend, Rooney's favorite and the quarterback
DeShawn Free: he organized flag football games at Crown Hill Park

Mr. Trahane: a high school football coach scouting the Pop Warner teams for future players

Brad Middleton: a high school football player who plays flag football with Pop Warner boys

Lion Terry: Mike's new partner at the radio station

Coach Downs: head football coach at the high school, who drafted Mick, Drew, and DeShawn

Matt Drager: starting running back, and the guy Mick has to beat

Coach Carlson: he goes from head custodian to head coach when Downs leaves

Bert Bronson: he runs the gun range and showed Mick how to shoot

Peter Volz: Mick's trainer at Popeye's Gym

Mr. Chavez: the school vice principal

Kaylee Sullivan, Natalie, Vick, Heather Lee, Russ Diver, Nolan Brown: they go to Mick's school

Dave Kane: an eighth grader who wants Mick's starting position

Lee Skida: policeman who helped convict Peter

Jonas Riley: Mick's counselor at the drug rehab center

BOOKTALK

My name's Mick Johnson, and I've been playing football my whole life. Dad didn't let me go to kindergarten til I was six so I'd be bigger than the other kids I played with. I was a star til I got to high school. Then, suddenly, things were different. I wasn't as big or as strong as the other guys on the team or the ones we played against.

I couldn't deal with that. Dad couldn't deal with that. He'd been pushing me to play better as far back as I could remember. He'd been a champion player in high school and college, and was even a third-string draft pick for the NFL, before an injury put him on the sidelines for good. He'd always wanted me to go even further than he did, so nothing I did was ever good enough.

That summer before I started high school, I was determined to do whatever it took to be a first-string running back with a starting spot. I ran. I worked out. I lifted weights. I took vitamins and drank protein shakes. And when Dad got a membership to Popeye's Gym, so I didn't have to use the ratty old equipment at the high school, I was sure I'd get great results. But the bulk and the strength came slowly, so when school was just weeks away, I finally decided to listen to Peter, my trainer. He could get me pills that would make a huge difference in my progress, like stepping on an express train instead of walking. I'd be where I needed to be before school started.

So I handed him the money and I took the pills. Hey—don't freak out, it's no big deal. It's just gym candy. Sooner or later, everybody does it.

MAJOR THEMES AND IDEAS

- A little pressure is good for you, keeps you on your toes. But too much pressure can destroy you.

- Football isn't fun—it takes a lot of hard work to be good.
- In football, being physically tough isn't enough. You have to be mentally tough as well, to think through the game, think through pain, and keep on going.
- When someone reminisces about his past successes, he generally includes the failures he had as well.
- It's easy to tell a convenient lie to hide an embarrassing truth.
- Football is more than a game only when you make it or let it be.
- You get what you pay for—very little worthwhile is cheap.
- On a football team, friendship matters as much as great plays; it's the glue that holds the team together when the going gets rough.
- Lies don't protect you, they make you worse.
- Steroids can make you think and act like someone who isn't you.
- You have to take responsibility for your actions and admit that no one forced you to do anything. It was your own decision.
- What you want and what you get aren't always the same thing.
- Recovering from a mental addiction is more difficult than a physical one.
- Turning in a friend who is in trouble and needs help isn't always a betrayal. Sometimes it's the right thing, and the hardest thing, to do.

BOOK REPORT IDEAS

1. Discuss the relationship between Mick and his father. In what ways did it hurt Mick? In what ways did it help him?
2. How did Mick feel about football? How important was it to him? When do you think it stopped being a game? What was it then?
3. In what ways did the juice change Mick inside, just as it changed him on the outside?
4. At the end of the book, Mick says, "I don't know if I can stand being ordinary." Explain what you think he means, and what his future will be like. Do you think he will stay clean or not? What will he have to do, how will he have to change to stay clean?
5. What does friendship mean to Mick? Does his understanding of it change over the years? If it doesn't, how and why not?
6. How realistic is this book in its discussion of the wide use of steroids. Are there athletes at your school who might be taking them?
7. Discuss the ethics of steroid use in high school, college, and professional athletics. Should they be made legal? Why or why not?
8. Mick was under pressure from many sources, on and off the field. Explain why he gave in to taking steroids and the other players on his team didn't. Or did some of them also go on the juice?
9. Describe the most important idea or information you got from this book and why you chose it.
10. If you will encourage your friends to read this book, what will you tell them about it to make them want to read it?

BOOKTALK IDEAS

1. Use some kind of football equipment as a prop for your talk, like a football or a helmet.
2. Write your report from the point of view of Mick's friends on the team. Have several of them talk about what he's like and how he's changing.
3. Use facts and statistics on steroid use among high school athletes to introduce your talk, and then move into Mick's story to give a personal face to those facts and figures.
4. Write your talk as if you were Peter Volz, trying to talk Mick into trying steroids. Use their conversations about steroids as the basis.

RISKS

- Father is obsessed with football
- Father is willing to risk his son's health to make him and his team into winners
- Rather than praising his son's victories, father tells him he's got to improve
- Coaches and parents recommend steroid use
- Teen will do anything to succeed at football
- Teen takes steroids to keep his place on the team
- Steroids presented as having few, minor, side effects

STRENGTHS

- Exciting accounts of football games
- Realistic portrait of the pressures on high school athletes to improve and get bigger at any cost
- High school coaches are honorable, don't pressure teams too much
- Demonstrates the importance of real friendship
- Steroid use is treated as substance abuse
- Parents support their son
- Teen takes responsibility for his actions
- Trainer who sold steroids is arrested
- Realistic ending doesn't resolve any problems
- Shows the difficulty of staying clean from a mental addiction

REVIEWS

"This well-written work highlights the 'bigger, stronger, faster' competitive culture to which Americans have been conditioned to subscribe in sports. Steroids have become commonplace, but this persuasive story is able to disseminate the facts and heartbreak of their use by showing what can happen to a driven, everyday guy." Ava Ehde, *VOYA*, 10/07

"Deuker skillfully complements a sobering message with plenty of exciting on-field action and locker-room drama, while depicting Mick's emotional struggles with loneliness and insecurity as sensitively and realistically as his physical ones." Jennifer Hubert, *Booklist*, 9/07

"The story's tight focus is its real strength—subplots are few and are linked to football—mirroring Mick's single-minded focus on the sport. . . . Deuker doesn't wimp out with an everything-turns-out-peachy-keen ending. Instead, Mick lands in rehab, where he says all the right things to the counselors but still longs for the juice." *Horn Book Magazine*, 9/07

📖📖📖

HANGING ON TO MAX. Margaret Bechard. Roaring Brook Press, 2002. $16.95. 160p. ISBN10: 0761315799. ISBN13: 9780761315797. Simon Pulse, 2003. $6.99. 176p. ISBN10: 0689862687. ISBN13: 9780689862687. Topeka Bindery, 2003. $15.80. 208p. ISBN10: 0613708210. ISBN13: 9780613708210. Realistic Fiction. Reading Level: YHS. Interest Level: YHS, OHS. English, Sex Education, Ethics, Psychology, Sociology.

SUBJECT AREAS
unwed parents; teen parents; adoption; ethics; rites of passage; school; self-knowledge; family relationships; responsibility; fear; friendship; school; love; dating and social life; ethics.

CHARACTERS
Sam Pettigrew: a senior in an alternative high school and Max's father
Ms. Garcia: Sam's math teacher
Mrs. Harriman: Sam's school mentor
Andy Pederson: he used to be Sam's best friend before Max
Max Pettigrew: Sam's eleven-month-old son
Mitch Pettigrew/Dad: Sam's father, who's a widower
Aunt Jean: she moved in with Sam and his dad for several months so Sam could keep Max
Jenny: she dates Andy
Brittany Ames: Max's birth mother, who gave up custody of him
Brianna, Christy, Meredith, Tawna, Nicole: teen moms who leave their kids in the high school day care center with Max
Mrs. McPherson: she runs the day care center
Claire Bailey: a girl Sam likes, whose daughter Emily also goes to the day care center
Mrs. Perris: Sam's eighth-grade English teacher

Mr. Gatt: Sam and Claire's senior English teacher
Martine Vickers: she watches the babies when the SAT group meets
Natalie Bailey: Claire's mother, who adores Emily
Uncle Ted: Aunt Jean's husband
Theresa Bailey/Mom: Sam's mother, who died of cancer when he was in fourth
    grade

BOOKTALK

It's not the senior year Sam thought he'd have. He's not playing on the varsity football team, hanging out with his friends, and dating someone hot. He's not even at the same school, and he feels like he's a completely different person. He's not a kid any longer—he's a father. Max's father. Max, with big blue eyes and blond curls, who's just starting to walk. Instead of going to his old high school, Sam is spending his senior year at an alternative high school, as the only teen father in the midst of lots of teen mothers. When Brittany told Sam she was going to give up their two-week-old son, Sam said, "Give him to me." It was the right thing to do. But almost a year later, is it still the right thing? Shouldn't having a child be more than just figuring out how to make it work?

MAJOR THEMES AND IDEAS
- Having a baby changes your life forever.
- Some people treat teen mothers differently from teen fathers.
- It's easier to take care of a baby when you have someone to help you.
- Living with a baby isn't always the way you imagined it would be.
- Life doesn't give you do-overs. You just have to deal with reality.
- Sometimes you just have to let go of people.
- It's possible to outgrow your friends.
- Frequently, doing the right thing isn't easy.
- What is right for one person can be very wrong for another.
- Loving someone means doing what's right for them, no matter how much it hurts.
- Having a child is more than just trying to make it work.

BOOK REPORT IDEAS
1. Discuss whether people tend to have major turning points in their lives that arrive unexpectedly or many small changes that add up gradually.
2. Sam is treated differently than teen mothers in several different situations. Explain why you think this happened.
3. Can a boy or a man be just as good a parent as a girl or a woman? Why or why not?
4. Describe the different things that happened to Sam that led him to his decision to give up Max.

5. Speculate on what life would have been like for Sam if he had kept Max. Did he really do the right thing?
6. Speculate on what relationship Max will have with his father after they meet again.

BOOKTALK IDEAS
1. Use something Max might have liked as a prop.
2. Focus your talk around the scene when Sam decides to keep Max.
3. Have Sam introduce Max and talk about how hard it is to be a teen dad.

RISKS
- Teens are sexually active
- Teens don't use birth control
- Teen mother gives up her child
- Alternative high school accepts teens with children
- Distant and non-supportive father
- Teens drink alcohol

STRENGTHS
- Teens take responsibility for their actions
- Realistic portrait of the complications of being a teen parent
- Three-dimensional characters readers can identify with
- Demonstrates that sometimes it's right to keep your baby and sometimes it's not
- Depicts teen parenting from a different point of view
- Ending leaves some questions unanswered to facilitate speculation and discussion
- Shows that teen fathers are treated very differently from teen mothers
- Realistic language doesn't include obscenities

AWARDS
ALA Best Books for Young Adults, 2003
ALA Quick Picks for Reluctant Young Adult Readers, 2003
ALA Popular Paperbacks, 2005

REVIEWS
"This book is a quick, easy read that touches upon many real-life issues. . . . The story will make the reader think, 'What would I do?'" Kevin Beach, *VOYA*, 4/02

"The author should be commended for taking on a tricky topic, the demands, delights, and difficulties of being young, single, and a dad." *Kirkus Reviews*, 04/02

"Bechard has written a poignant winner of a book peopled with human beings all struggling to make their lives work. And she has created in Sam an unforgettable and realistic protagonist full of heart and guts." Jane Halsall, McHenry Public Library District, IL, *School Library Journal*, 05/02

⊞⊞⊞

HEAVY METAL AND YOU. Christopher Krovatin. Push/Scholastic, 2005. $16.95. 186p. ISBN10: 043973648X. ISBN13: 9780439736480. Push, 2006. $7.99. 186p. ISBN10: 0439743990. ISBN13: 9780439743990. Realistic fiction. Reading Level: YHS. Interest Level: YHS, OHS. English, Music, Psychology, Film, Drama.

SUBJECT AREAS
self-knowledge; rites of passage; friendship; love; dating and social life; music; bullying; substance abuse; anger; school; family relationships; depression; fear; manipulation; secrets; sex and sexuality.

CHARACTERS
Sam Markus/Conan the Barbarian: short, awkward, overweight; he loves horror movies, heavy metal, and Melissa
Melissa Andrews: she meets Sam at play practice and falls in love
Brent Bolman: one of Sam's best friends; he's tall, slick and preppy
John McKinney/Irish: Sam's other best friend, a redheaded punk in vintage clothes
Liam/Pudgy, Tyler/Tygirl, Mark, Jamie: the rest of Sam's crew, who go to the same private school he goes to
Kat: a friend of Melissa's
Erica Markus: Sam's annoying little sister
Mr. and Mrs. Markus: Sam's parents, who are fairly cool, for 'rents
Carver Markus: Sam's older brother, who's cool, crazy, and totally rocks
Dr. Bersner: Brent and Sam's English teacher
Shane: heavy metal fan Sam sees at concerts
Death Metal Dan: smart, cool, nice, funny metalhead
Mickey Brock: a sophomore with a big mouth and no respect for his elders
Richard and Tracy Andrews: Melissa's parents
Josh, Adrian, Kyle, Leslie: Melissa's very preppy friends
Ivy: one of Sam's ex-girlfriends, who's still a good friend

BOOKTALK

Sam Markus had it all. He had friends to hang out with, friends that he knew had his back 24/7. He had his music, heavy metal, black, scary, evil, Satanic, music that was like the soundtrack of the horror movies that he liked so much, that was like the soundtrack of his life. And now he had Melissa, the girl he adored, his goddess, who made him feel like a god, who was even interested in his music, and wanted to know more about it. Yeah, Sam really did have it all.

When he was with his friends, Sam was complete. Brent was a tall, handsome, slick preppy teenager in sunglasses. Irish was a ragged redheaded punk in vintage clothes. Sam was a short, antisocial, awkward, overweight kid wearing spiked leather and heavy metal shirts. They might not look like they belonged together, but they did. Together, they completed each other.

When Sam was with Melissa, he felt complete, just like he did with his friends. She loved him, was fascinated with him, wanted to belong to him. She wanted to know more about his music, so he made a mix of it for her. But when she found out that when he was with his friends, he liked to drink and party hard, she asked him to change, to be a straightedge like she was. No drinking, no smoking, no drugs. Sam loved her, so he said yes. It wasn't hard—he wanted to please her so she'd stay with him forever.

It took a while for Sam to notice he wasn't seeing his friends that much any more, other than at school. It was a while before he got a Dr. Jekyll and Mr. Hyde feeling about himself, like he was one person with Melissa and another person when she wasn't around. Sam was still thinking about that and what it meant when Melissa begged to go to a concert with him. Deicide was playing, and Sam had already decided to go—he'd never seen them and he was a big fan. He wasn't sure Melissa would like the dark, angry, energetic music or the Goth kids who would show up for the concert. They only looked scary, but Melissa didn't know that. Sam was sure he could take care of Melissa, even if she wasn't into heavy metal, so they went.

It was a disaster. Melissa hated it, the whole scene that Sam dug so much. And suddenly there was another decision to be made. Give up heavy metal or give up Melissa. Sam adores Melissa, but his music defines him; it's the bedrock and the soundtrack of his life. It soothes him and brings him peace when nothing else can, and its dark energy is as familiar as his horror movies. He has changed so much of himself for Melissa, but who will he be if he gives up the one thing that has defined him more than any other, that has freed him to be himself?

MAJOR THEMES AND IDEAS

- When you're into heavy metal, your music defines you to the point when you need it more than anything else in the world.
- For many people, life has a soundtrack of their favorite music.
- Friendship is sometimes a language of its own, and words or phrases don't mean to friends what they do to people outside the friendship.
- The music you listen to most helps define and shape you.

- Dark music can help you get out all the anger, angst, and rage that you carry inside.
- Being accepted for who you are is a powerful thing.
- Bros before hos. Girls are great, but your friends are what really count.
- With horror movies, you can create a monster; you can *be* the monster.
- What you look like doesn't always reflect who you are on the inside.
- Your friends are your friends, no matter what, and they will always be there for you, so there's no need for them to prove it somehow.
- Judging someone based on how they look and the music they like isn't cool.
- Watching people just being themselves is fascinating.
- Human nature is more often terrible than it is inspiring or admirable.
- When people aren't being watched, they are free to show their true natures.
- Everyone has different sides to them. We choose how to act based on the situation and the people in it.
- Changing what you do can also changes who you are.
- Real friends don't ask friends to change.
- Live how you want, feel like you feel, and get the phonies outta your way.
- Breaking up doesn't come out of nowhere. If you look for them, there are warning signs.
- The charming boyfriend/girlfriend routine is one of the keys to a happy social life.
- Sex changes everything in a relationship.
- Becoming someone you aren't to make a relationship work is never a good idea. Sooner or later, the real you comes out.
- Being true to yourself is essential.
- If someone you love can't accept you for who you are, they don't love you.

BOOK REPORT IDEAS

1. Compare Holden Caulfield and Sam. How are they alike and different?
2. Sam comments on how adults and parents might be afraid of the music he loves. Explain why Sam loves it and what it does for him.
3. Speculate on whether or not Melissa and Sam will be a couple in the future.
4. It's possible to see in teens glimpses of the adults they will become. Describe Sam at twenty-five or thirty. What's he like as a person, as a friend, as a family member?
5. Analyze the scene with Brent and Irish when Sam tells them he's breaking up with Melissa, and describe how realistic you think it is.
6. Explain how this book could help someone understand the appeal of heavy metal.
7. A number of people in this book are judgmental, even though they say they aren't. In your opinion, who are the most judgmental people and why?
8. The author uses flashbacks. How does this detract from or add to the story?
9. Sam has a strong support system. Who is in it and what roles do they play?

BOOKTALK IDEAS
1. Use one of Sam's mixes as a soundtrack for your talk.
2. Use some of Sam's favorite albums as props.
3. Write your talk as a heavy metal lyric.
4. Have Sam and Melissa introduce each other and their story.
5. Let Brent and Irish introduce Sam and how his relationship with Melissa is changing him.

RISKS
- Teens enjoy smoking
- Vulgar language
- Teens drink and smoke
- Teens smoke marijuana
- Teens get wasted regularly
- Mentions bands and albums that are violently anti-Christian
- Portrays death metal music as addicting, "wonderfully evil," "satanic death rock"
- Teens are sexually active

STRENGTHS
- Realistic language
- Power of friendship
- Shows heavy metal culture from the inside
- Writing has a rhythm, a beat
- Crisp, realistic dialogue
- Leading characters are outsiders
- Authentic teen voice
- Nonlinear storyline
- Talks about and analyzes actual death and heavy metal bands
- Includes some excerpts from lyrics
- Excellent explanation of why heavy metal can be so fascinating
- Shows the impact of violent childhood bullying
- Show how important it is to be genuine with yourself, your friends, and your girl/boyfriends
- Difficult relationships ends with maturity and friendship
- Shows how males don't express their feelings and how that can damage friendships
- Characters grow and mature and gain insight
- Positive portrait of a strong and functional nuclear family
- Demonstrates the necessity for common experiences to support an intimate relationship
- Portrays the absolute importance of being true to yourself

- Teen shows mature understanding of the impact of becoming sexually intimate in a relationship

AWARDS
ALA Best Books for Young Adults, 2006
ALA Quick Picks for Reluctant Young Adult Readers, 2006

REVIEWS
"The story is genuine and well told. It is refreshing to see more teen books about relationships told from the masculine point of view. It should be a popular book among older teens who enjoy . . . novels in the *Catcher in the Rye* tradition." Jan Chapman, *VOYA*, 10/05

"The plot moves quickly and jumps from past to present, with Sam interspersing his current situation with relevant scenes from his past. This rapid progression, as well as the realistic situations and language, keep teens' attention, making the book a good choice for reluctant readers." Heather E. Miller, Homewood Public Library, AL, *School Library Journal*, 10/05

"Teens don't have to like heavy metal to appreciate this novel, which is guaranteed to attract readers looking for a book to reach their death-metal souls." Cindy Dobrez, *Booklist*, 8/05

ᨒ ᨒ ᨒ

HOLDUP. Terri Fields. Roaring Brook Press, 2007. $16.95. 176p. ISBN10: 1596432195. ISBN13: 9781596432192. Square Fish, 2009. $8.99. 192p. ISBN10: 031256130X. ISBN13: 9780312561307. Realistic fiction. Reading Level: MS. Interest Level: YHS, OHS. English, Ethics, Psychology, Sociology, Vocational Education.

SUBJECT AREAS
working; friendship; crime and delinquency; prejudice; elderly; anger cooking; self-knowledge; secrets; school; child abuse; physical abuse; poverty; homeless; sexual harassment.

CHARACTERS
Jordan: a senior in high school with a heavy load of AP classes, a part-time job, and a starting spot on the girls' basketball team

Sara: she shoplifted a skirt and was sentenced to life at Burger Heaven
Phil: one of the Burger Heaven managers
Alex: he's a flirt and player who wants to make it big in Hollywood
Theresa: a vegetarian who's hung up on health and works in fast food
Manuel: he works the drive-up window and prides himself on his speed
Keith: a regular at Burger Heaven who is mentally handicapped
Mrs. Wilkins: a regular who's made friends with Manuel
Stephanie: she talked Jordan into being on the Mock Trial team
Maria: one of the Burger Heaven managers
Dylan: in spite of a near-genius IQ, he was kicked out of high school for bringing a gun to school
Joe: he never takes any chances til he learns everyone thinks of him as a white wall—colorless and unnoticed
Alicia: Joe's lab partner, who's new at school
Jesse: Joe's older cousin who owns a killer truck he had to save for for years
Greg: Dylan's partner in crime; they're the Ski Mask Bandits
Officer Rick Jeffries: a police officer who's had a busy night
Officer Marc Baume: he hears a call about a possible robbery
Berenice Martinez: Theresa's mother

BOOKTALK

We make over six hundred decisions a day. Most of them are so routine we don't even think about them. But what if one of those decisions, like turning right instead of turning left, meant our whole lives were changed? That one decision started a whole series of events that took our lives in a whole different direction.

When Maria calls her in a panic, Jordan decides to take the late shift at Burger Heaven, even though it's her day off.

Alex decides to take the same shift, even though he's already worked as long as he's supposed to, because they'll pay him cash and not put him on the schedule.

Theresa isn't supposed to work on the same shift with Alex, but decides to stay when Jordan explains how shorthanded they are.

Sara decides not to clean the gross-out restrooms, because Jordan's only the acting manager.

Mrs. Wilkins decides she is entitled to a hamburger on a Saturday night even if she is eighty-six and shouldn't be driving at night.

Manuel decides to take a break and talk to Mrs. Wilkins about college.

And, at 9:45 on that Saturday night in October, Dylan and Joe decide to walk through the door of the Burger Heaven, with ski masks on their faces and guns in their hands.

MAJOR THEMES AND IDEAS

- Believe in yourself and you can make almost anything happen.
- Getting older doesn't mean you don't have a life.

- A person who thinks too well of himself may find out that few people agree with him.
- For some people, saying "no" is difficult, which can complicate their lives.
- Criminals are never as smart as they think they are.
- Discovering what your peers think of you can be devastating.
- Making plans you can't cancel, based on what you don't have is never a good idea.
- In pleasing everyone else, you are unable to please yourself.
- No one can be strong all the time. Everyone has to have help sometimes.

BOOK REPORT IDEAS
1. Discuss the idea that small, routine decisions can change someone's life in dramatic ways.
2. Discuss some of the turning points, where things could have gone differently.
3. Explore the idea that nothing (or very little) in life is coincidental, using examples from the book.
4. How did the characters' lives change as a result of the holdup? What decisions or actions led them to where they were a year later?

BOOKTALK IDEAS
1. Write your talk as if you were a TV reporter on the scene.
2. Use a hat or some other part of a fast food uniform as a prop.
3. Let each character introduce himself and give clues to what's happening in the story.
4. Write your talk as the book is written: first the teens gripe about working at BH on a Saturday night, then Dylan and Joe plan, ending when the hold-up begins.

RISKS
- Teens commit armed robbery
- Teens carry out five successful holdups
- Sexual harassment
- Child abuse
- Physical abuse
- Unsympathetic characters

STRENGTHS
- Varying points of view let readers into the heads of each of the main characters
- Characters grow and gain insight
- Realistic dialogue
- Familiar setting readers can identify with
- Characters readers can identify with

- Final section shows long-term impact of the holdup on everyone involved in it
- Shows how characters' strengths and weaknesses evolve over time

AWARD
ALA Quick Pick for Reluctant Readers, 2008

REVIEWS
"The story is compelling, and the message is clear. Even the smallest of decisions can change lives." Victoria Vogel, *VOYA*, 4/07

"Perhaps most successful is the way Fields' collage of distinct personalities shows how an after-school job creates an unlikely, fleeting community among employees who wouldn't normally connect." Jennifer Mattson, *Booklist*, 5/07

"The story is compelling and the characters are well drawn, giving the book wide appeal for a general audience." Sharon Morrison, Southeastern Oklahoma State University, Durant, OK, *School Library Journal*, 4/07

📖📖📖

HOUSE OF THE SCORPION. Nancy Farmer. Atheneum, an imprint of Simon and Schuster, 2002. $17.95. 400p. ISBN10: 0689852223. ISBN13: 9780689852220. Simon Pulse, 2004. $9.99. 400p. ISBN10: 0689852231. ISBN13: 9780689852237. Simon and Schuster, 2008. $39.99. ISBN10: 0743572467. ISBN13: 9780743572460. (unabridged audio CD) Topeka, 2004. $19.85. 380p. ISBN10: 1417619007. ISBN13: 9781417619009. (library binding) Thorndike, 2003. $24.95. 515p. ISBN10: 0786250488. ISBN13: 9780786250486. (large print) Science fiction. Reading Level: MS. Interest Level: MS, YHS, OHS. English, Biology, Psychology, Ethics.

SUBJECT AREAS
Science; rites of passage; secrets; love; other countries; fear; self-knowledge; love; manipulation; intimidation; bullying; revenge; greed; anger; cultural identity; crime and delinquency; drugs; friendship; lies and deceit; prejudice; gossip; ethics; elderly; abuse, physical; death and dying; grief and mourning; poverty; survival; violence.

CHARACTERS
The Alacrán Family
Matt: Matteo Alacrán, the clone

El Patron: Matteo Alacrán, a 140-year-old drug lord, who says that Matt is the most important person in his life, because he is the old man's clone

El Viejo: El Patron's grandson and Mr. Alacrán's father, he is very old

Mr. Alacrán: El Patron's great-grandson, husband of Felicia, father of Benito and Steven

Felicia Alacrán: Mr. Alacrán's wife, mother of Steven, Benito, and Tom

Benito and Steven Alacrán: El Patron's great-great grandsons, eighteen and thirteen, who are very spoiled

Tom: Felicia and Angus MacGregor's son, spoiled and mean

Fani: Benito's wife, who's from Nigeria; she dislikes him, but couldn't refuse him when El Patron ordered them to marry

Others Associated with the Alacrán Family

Eduardo: one of the technicians who works on the clones for El Patron

Lisa: senior technician who works with Eduardo

Anna: Eduardo's wife

Senator Mendoza: he's a powerful politician in the United States, and he and his daughters visit El Patron often

Emilia Mendoza: she's thirteen and is very curious about Matt and why Rosa has him locked up in a sawdust filled room

Maria Mendoza: she's the senator's younger daughter, the same age as Matt, and she is the one who tells Celia where Matt is

Mr. MacGregor: a drug lord

Celia: she's the chief cook for El Patron, has taken care of Matt for years, and is the only mother he has

Tam Lin: Matt's bodyguard and friend

Daft Donald: El Patron's bodyguard

Rosa: she's El Patron's housekeeper, hates Matt, and kept him a prisoner in a filthy room for six months

Willum: he's the doctor for the Alacrán family and knows how Rosa is treating Matt, but does nothing about it

Mr. Ortega: Matt's music teacher

Esperanza Mendoza: she's Emilia and Maria's mother, who disappeared when Maria was five

Raul: one of the Keepers of the Lost Boys; in Aztlan (accent on last *a*)

Chacho: one of the Lost Boys who explained to Matt how things worked on the border

Fidelito: one of the youngest of the Lost Boys; he gets pushed around by the others

Carlos: the Head Keeper at the plankton factory in San Luis

Jorge: another of the Keepers at the plankton factory, who tries to force Matt to obey him

Ton-Ton: one of the boys who works at the plankton factory

Luna: he used to be a Lost Boy, but he's now a trainee in the infirmary

Flaco: a Lost Boy who stands up to the Keepers
Guapo and Consuela: an elderly couple who rescue Matt and the other boys with
   him

BOOKTALK

Until Matt was about six, he thought he was normal, just like everyone else. He lived
in a small cottage with Celia. She wasn't his mother, but she took care of him and
loved him. The only thing he couldn't do was go outside. When Celia left him to go
to the Big House to cook every day, he stayed inside and played with his toys, or
watched television, or looked at the huge fields of white poppies outside his window.
But he was lonely. The children he saw on television didn't have to stay inside. They
had friends that they played with, and places to go that weren't a tiny cottage. The
windows of their houses weren't nailed shut, and their mothers didn't lock them inside the houses every morning when they went to work. That's why when he heard
voices outside, children's voices, he ran to the window to look out, even though Celia
had told him to stay away from the windows. There were three children outside, a girl
about his age, and two who were older, a boy and a girl. They wanted him to come
out and play. There was only one way he could do that. He grabbed Celia's biggest
pot, and threw it through the window. Then he moved a chair over to the window,
climbed on it, and jumped out. But when he landed outside, he felt a horrible pain in
his feet, his hands, and his knees. He'd jumped onto the glass from the window and
was badly cut.

   That was the day he went to the Big House, that was the day he found out he
was different from everyone else, that was the day he traded his home with Celia for
a small narrow cell that he never left. That was the day he found out he was not a
person, not a human. He was something called a "dirty clone." It would be six months
before he left that cell where he was kept like a caged animal, because that's all that
clones were, animals.

   By the time Celia rescued him, he was thin, sick, and covered with rashes and
bruises. He refused to speak, too afraid of what might happen to him if he said anything. But that was the day his life changed yet again, when he met El Patron. Matt
was the last of the clones of the 140-year-old drug lord, who wasn't ready to die
yet, and needed clones for organ transplants when his own organs began to fail. El
Patron wanted Matt to stay strong and healthy until he was needed. But in spite of
everything that Matt now had—clean clothes, healthy meals, Celia to help take care
of him, and other children to play with—he was still just a clone. He'd be kept alive
only until El Patron needed him. Then he would be slaughtered the same way cows,
pigs, or chickens were. Only instead of becoming part of a meal for the household,
he would be slaughtered so his organs could be transferred into El Patron's body—a
perfect genetic match to keep the old man alive a little longer. What was Matt, the
last clone—a person or an animal?

MAJOR THEMES

- Too often, kids with too much money, who are spoiled by their parents, end up being selfish, self-centered, or mean.
- Your mother is the woman who takes care of you and loves you, whether or not you are related by blood.
- It's not hard to recognize an insult, even if you don't understand all the words.
- When pain is the only result of someone's attention, you learn to be quiet and still.
- When you have been held a prisoner for a long time, leaving your familiar surroundings can be terrifying.
- What goes around, comes around. Evil never gets home free.
- When you are young, you can choose the way to grow. If you are a kind and decent boy, you will grow up to be a kind and decent man.
- Childhood frequently predicts adulthood, in terms of the kind of person each of us turns out to be.
- It's easy to dislike or hate someone who is very different from you.
- You can tell how much someone loves you by the size of the present. The flow of the wealth should be from the outside in.
- The truth is always best, even when it's unpleasant or painful. Lying is the most personal act of cowardice there is.
- A little extra forgiveness never hurts.
- Act like you are in control, no matter how scared you are, and most of the time you'll get away with it, because most people are cowards and won't challenge someone who seems to be in charge and know what he's talking about.
- A dragon always knows when even one coin has been stolen from his hoard and takes immediate and vengeful action to eliminate the thief.
- Power can be like a drug, and once addicted to it, it's almost impossible to do without it.
- Work is freedom; freedom is work. It's hard but it's fair.
- Things go smoothly only when people work together toward a goal that they all agree on.
- It's best to walk carefully around people who take offense when you talk about what you believe is right.
- Choose easy targets to punish at first; it's a chance to frighten the enemies you don't want to confront quite yet.
- Nothing protects you from punishment, not even slavish obedience.
- Some people may think very slowly, but they are very thorough about it and they notice everything.
- A jailer has many things on his mind, but a prisoner has only one—escape.
- Friendship involves obligations that are difficult to escape from. You can't turn your back on your friend even if you want to or it would be easier for you if you did.
- Having a conscience can be just as much of a pain to deal with as friendship when it dictates what you should or shouldn't, will or won't, do.

- People's souls are like gardens—you can't turn your back on someone just because his garden is full of weeds. You have to help him get rid of the weeds and grow productive crops.
- Your mother and father don't have to be blood relatives—your parents are the people who love you and take care of you.
- Humans seldom give up and consent to death. They keep fighting even when everything seems hopeless, and sometimes, even if there is no chance of winning, somehow, they do.

BOOK REPORT IDEAS

1. Discuss the way Matt was treated before he met El Patron. How much of what he thought and did later in his life can be traced back to the first six years of his life?
2. Matt found El Patron interesting to be around and to look at because he is the old man at a younger age. Have you ever met anyone with whom you were comfortable instantly? Explain what happened and why you felt that way.
3. Maria tells Matt he is just an animal and doesn't have a soul. Discuss the idea of a soul—what it is, and who does or doesn't have one.
4. Analyze the character of El Patron. What was important to him? How did he control those around him, and how did he act when someone defied him? Discuss the forces in his life that caused him to become the person he is in the book.
5. There are several people in the book who could be considered evil. Identify them, describe how they are evil, and why they have chosen to be evil.
6. Discuss the ethics of creating clones for the purpose of either harvesting organs or creating docile workers. How is it right or acceptable, and how is it wrong and unacceptable?
7. Why did El Patron collect his "dragon hoard"? What was in it? What did it mean to him? Why was it so important?
8. Why did everyone hide information on the clones from Matt? If he had known the secrets of the clones and the eejits, how might he have acted differently?
9. Discuss what it takes to be seen as an aristocrat among the Lost Boys and the Keepers. Compare Matt's actions to those of the others.
10. Explain how the Keepers justified their lifestyle as compared to that of the Lost Boys.
11. What was Matt's greatest strength, and what was his primary weakness? Discuss where they came from and why.
12. Tam Lin and El Patron both told Matt he was only one of several clones who had been brought up as he was. Discuss whether or not this was the truth, and explain the reasons for your decision.
13. Speculate on what the future will be like for Matt. He is a clone of El Patron, and he is in a position of power. Will his reign be different from that of the man whose genes he carried? If so, how and why will it be different?

14. Speculate on what will happen to Matt and his friends during the next five or
ten years. What will change in Opium, and what will stay the same? Describe
the kind of men Matt, Chacho, Fidelito, and Ton-Ton will be by that time.

BOOKTALK IDEAS

1. Use a drawing of a red scorpion from the book to illustrate your talk.
2. Focus your talk on the part of Matt's life when he lived in the Big House, and
   was treated almost as a person. Use the very end of your talk to reveal that he is
   a clone and that his organs will be used to extend El Patron's life.
3. Celia has a great deal of information on Opium and the Alacrán family. Have her
   introduce herself, Matt, and the rest of the major players from the family.
4. Focus your talk on the idea of "eejits" and clones, and how they are thought of
   as animals, then introduce Matt as the exception, and explain why, how he lives,
   and how he will die.

RISKS

- Child is treated like an animal
- Child is held prisoner by an angry and cruel woman for six months
- Clones of the wealthy are created to be used for organ harvest
- A dog is almost drowned in a toilet
- Clones are mutilated to keep them docile
- Clones are not considered to be humans. They are subhumans, and treated as
  animals.
- The use of "fetal brain implants" to rejuvenate the very old
- Children are forced to work long hours at grueling jobs in order to be fed

STRENGTHS

- Presents one possible future for our society and world
- Strong characters the reader can identify with
- Science shown in the book is accurate
- Shows how power can corrupt those who believe they are better than those they
  rule
- Protagonist fights to maintain a sense of self in a world that treats him as nonhu-
  man
- Plot moves swiftly, with enough suspense to keep the reader involved
- Ending is ambiguous, leaving room for speculation and discussion
- Involves many ethical questions/dilemmas for readers to ponder
- Shows the rites of passage process of becoming an adult
- Examines the question of humanity—what makes someone human

AWARDS

ALA Best Books for Young Adults, 2003
ALA Notable Children's Books, 2003

John Newbery Honor Books, 2003
Michael L. Printz Honor, 2003
National Book Award for Young People's Literature, 2002

REVIEWS

"This novel . . . is. . . enormously powerful and may well win Farmer further award nominations." Michael Levy, *VOYA*, 10/02

"Farmer's . . . novel may be futuristic, but it hits close to home, raising questions of what it means to be human, what is the value of life, and what are the responsibilities of a society. Readers will be hooked from the first page . . . . The questions she raises will haunt readers long after the final page." *Publishers Weekly*, 7/02

"Farmer has a talent for creating exciting tales in beautifully realized, unusual worlds. With undertones of vampires, Frankenstein, dragons' hoards, and killing fields, Matt's story turns out to be an inspiring tale of friendship, survival, hope, and transcendence. A must-read for SF fans." *Kirkus Reviews*, 7/02

"This is a powerful, ultimately hopeful, story that builds on today's sociopolitical, ethical, and scientific issues and prognosticates a compelling picture of what the future could bring. All of these serious issues are held together by a remarkable coming-of-age story, in which a boy's self-image and right to life are at stake." Sally Estes, *Booklist*, 9/02

THE HUNGER GAMES. Suzanne Collins. Scholastic, 2008. $17.99. 371p. ISBN10: 0439023483. ISBN13: 978043902348-1. Science fiction. Reading Level: YHS. Interest Level: YHS, OHS. English, Government; Psychology, Sociology, Ethics.

SUBJECT AREAS

friendship; love; ethics; rites of passage; anger; manipulation; family relationships; responsibility; self-knowledge; violence; death and dying; survival.

CHARACTERS

Katniss Everdeen: her family's sole support; she volunteers for the Hunger Games when her little sister is chosen
Prim Everdeen: Katniss's twelve-year-old sister, who is sweet, pretty, and innocent
Gale: he's Katniss's best friend and hunting partner

Effie Trinket: she reads the names at the reaping for District 12
Madge Undersee: the mayor's daughter
Mayor Undersee: the mayor of District 12
Haymitch Abernathy: he survived the Games years ago and is now a drunk and a laughingstock
Peeta Mellark: one of the baker's sons, who's the boy tribute from District 12
Vinia, Flavius, Octavia: members of Katniss's prep team
Cinna: Katniss's stylist
Portia: Cinna's partner and Peeta's stylist
Atala: head trainer for all twenty-four tributes
Cato: he's the leader of the Careers and has had it in for Katniss from the beginning
Rue: a thin, small girl who is one of the tributes from District 11, who watches Katniss whenever she can
Thresh: the boy from District 11, who ignores Rue
Claudius Templesmith: the legendary announcer for the Hunger Games
Foxface: the girl from District 5 who turns out to be more of a survivor than Katniss expected her to be
Clove: the girl from District 2, who's a knife-throwing expert
President Snow: the president of Panem

BOOKTALK

It's the day of reaping, an annual ritual, an annual punishment, an annual reminder that rebelling against the Capitol is futile. This afternoon all the residents of Panem will gather in the town square of each of its twelve districts to watch the drawing. The names of all the children in every district between the ages of twelve and eighteen have been put into large bowls filled with slips of paper. One boy's name will be drawn, and one girl's. They will represent their district in the Hunger Games. All twenty-four will be trained for a week then herded into an arena, where they will be forced to fight to the death as the entire population watches on live television. The winner is the last person left alive.

Katniss is from District 12, the smallest and the most distant from the Capitol. She's sixteen and the sole support of her mother and younger sister. She hunts for food to feed them and to barter at the market for soap, or salt, or clothing. That afternoon, she doesn't hear her own name called, but her little sister's! Prim is only twelve; this is her first Hunger Games, and as gentle and fragile as she is, she won't live long. She wouldn't fight, even if she knew how. Katniss immediately fights her way through the crowd and volunteers to take Prim's place. She would be a part of this year's Hunger Games.

The boy's name is drawn, and Peeta, the baker's son, walks toward the stage, his face emotionless, stunned. He doesn't look like he's ever missed a meal, muscular and strong. Everyone in the town likes him, even Katniss. He helped her once, long ago, when she was alone and desperate. She's never forgotten, and from the looks he's giving her, he hasn't forgotten either.

In another world, they might have been friends, or more. But in this world, they must be enemies, prepared to kill each other. In the Hunger Games, there is only one winner.

MAJOR THEMES AND IDEAS

- You're more likely to be chosen for the Games if you're poor.
- It is possible to starve to death, even if the official reason is something else.
- The odds that something will or will not happen aren't always dependable.
- Killing people isn't hard if you think of them as just another animal.
- Kind people make it easy to lower your defenses, leaving you unprotected when their kindness turns out to be false.
- Once you have put up a wall to keep someone out, to keep them from hurting you, you can't go back to the relationship you had before.
- A broken trust may be difficult or impossible to mend.
- People can be likable and also deadly at the same time.
- Stopping to help someone; not stopping to help. There's no way to know which one you will regret years later.
- In a fight to the death, never underestimate your skills and strengths.
- When you begin to trust your enemy, it becomes a weakness, not a strength.
- It's not only the bad guys who can band together against others; the good guys can as well.
- Desperation makes you careless, and careless makes you dead.
- Watching a friend's senseless death changes you forever.
- Revenge is a dish best served cold.
- Deliberately killing another human being changes you forever.
- Killing a person and killing an animal are similar in execution, but completely different in the aftermath.
- It's the first gift that's the hardest to pay back.
- When you've always had plenty, it's harder for you to go without than it is for someone who's familiar with the way hunger feels.
- Sometimes, when you get an unexpected gift, it's wise to check to see if it comes with strings and conditions.
- No one can completely protect his or her family from harm.
- Victory indicates only that you have won, not the price you had to pay to get there.
- It's as dangerous to overestimate your enemies as it is to underestimate them.

BOOK REPORT IDEAS

1. Discuss the kind of society that would allow the Hunger Games to take place.
2. What similarities and differences exist between Panem and the United States?

3. Killing another tribute is encouraged and rewarded. But what happens to those that refuse to kill?

4. Consider how many cameras there must have been to capture the tributes' every move, and broadcast them to the rest of the world. What events in our society mirror that?

5. Examine Katniss's and Peeta's relationship before and after the Games. If they had not been selected for the Games, would they have ever gotten to know each other? What might their relationship have been like?

6. If you had been selected as a tribute, what kind of player would you have been?

7. Compare the way Katniss and Peeta felt about each other when the book began and when it ended. Speculate about what their relationship might be in the future.

8. Discuss the whole idea of the games—taking children from each of the districts and forcing them to kill over and over again, until the winner is the one who has killed the most. Describe what it might be like to be that person.

9. List the characters that Katniss and Peeta killed, and how it happened. Do these deaths have any commonalities? Could any of them have been avoided?

10. How is the Hunger Games like a war? How is it not?

11. Katniss is a survivor when she volunteers for the games, and is able to use her knowledge immediately. How long did it take Peeta to become a survivor? When did each of them decide to survive, and what happened to give them that certainty?

12. What kept the people of Panem from rebelling against the Capitol and ending the Hunger Games? How did that one annual event keep them under the control of the Capitol?

BOOKTALK IDEAS

1. Use a silver bow and arrow as props.
2. Write your booktalk in first person as either Katniss or Peeta.
3. Write your talk as if it was part of the TV coverage of the Hunger Games.
4. Write your talk in two sections, one Katniss's description of Peeta, and then Peeta's description of Katniss.

RISKS

- Teens forced to kill or be killed
- Mother neglects her daughters when her husband dies
- Eleven-year-old girl is the only source of support for her mother and sister
- Teens encouraged to gang up on each other to kill as many as possible
- The winner is the one who has killed the most
- Teens are forced to support their family from childhood

- Winners rewarded for murder and given whatever they want for the rest of their lives
- Love, caring, and other softer emotions are seen as weaknesses
- Government forces teens into acts of cruelty and injustice
- Killing, murdering is seen as entertainment
- Citizens accept the deaths of twenty-three children each year without question.
- Government forces everyone in the country to watch the live feed of what happens to each of the teens in the games, including their deaths
- Government creates genetic mutations of various breeds to use in the games and elsewhere

STRENGTHS
- Hard-hitting questions about the power of government
- Teen sacrifices herself to save her little sister
- Taut, gripping suspense from beginning to end
- Family is seen as more than biology
- Realistic, identifiable characters that readers can empathize with
- Author is able to manage large cast of characters, and to make the major ones seem three-dimensional
- Many aspects of the idea of war and death that can be discussed
- Book is first of a series
- Characters are not black-and-white—even the most negative ones have hints of goodness
- Shows the power of the will to live and to survive
- Strong family relationships

REVIEWS
"This is a grand-opening salvo in a new series by the author of the Underland Chronicles . . . . Populated by three-dimensional characters, this is a superb tale of physical adventure, political suspense, and romance." *Booklist*, 9/1/08

"Survivor meets 'The Lottery' as the author of the popular Underland Chronicles returns with what promises to be an even better series. . . . The plot is front and center here—the twists and turns are addictive, particularly when the romantic subplot ups the ante—yet the Capitol's oppression and exploitation of the districts always simmers just below the surface, waiting to be more fully explored in future volumes. Collins has written a compulsively readable blend of science fiction, survival story, unlikely romance, and social commentary." Hornbook, 9/1/08

"Brilliantly imagined dystopia . . . where the poor battle to the death for the amusement of the rich. Impressive world-building, breathtaking action and clear philosophical concerns make this volume, the beginning of a planned trilogy, as good as *The Giver* and more exciting." *Kirkus Reviews*, 9/1/08

"Collins's characters are completely realistic and sympathetic as they form alliances and friendships in the face of overwhelming odds; the plot is tense, dramatic, and engrossing. This book will definitely resonate with the generation raised on reality shows like 'Survivor' and 'American Gladiator.' Book one of a planned trilogy." Jane Henriksen Baird, Anchorage Public Library, AK, *School library Journal*, 9/1/08

📖📖📖

HURRICANE SONG. Paul Volponi. Viking Juvenile, 2008. $15.99. 144p. ISBN10: 0670061603. ISBN13: 9780670061600. Puffin, 2009. $6.99. 160p. ISBN10: 0142414182. ISBN13: 9780142414187. Brilliance Audio, 2009. $24.99. ISBN10: 142338220X. ISBN13: 9781423382201. (unabridged audio MP3-CD, library version) Realistic fiction. Reading Level: MS. Interest Level: MS, YHS, OHS. English, Music, Ethics, Government.

SUBJECT AREAS
family relationships; music; anger; violence; self-knowledge; ethnic groups; survival; love; crime and delinquency; death and dying; dysfunctional family; ethics; gangs; rites of passage; racism; prejudice; problem parents; politics; peer pressure; manipulation; lying and deceit; homelessness; mental illness.

CHARACTERS
Miles Shaw: he lives with his father, a jazz musician in New Orleans
"Doc" Show/Pop: Miles's father, who plays trumpet and is obsessed with jazz
Uncle Roy: he plays trombone with Doc
Mom: Miles's mother, who lives in Chicago
Dunham and Cain: seniors on the varsity football team who are taking advantage of everything they can
Cyrus Campbell: the dishwasher from the jazz club Miles and his father live over
Preacher Culver: a preacher who moved close to Cyrus and his family
Cyrus's daughter and granddaughter: they shared the section with the Shaws and the Culvers
Tess/Lonnie Easterly: a jazz clarinetist who's a good friend of Doc and Roy
Captain Hancock: one of the soldiers on duty in the Superdome; he has a bad attitude
Sergeant Scobie: he's easier to get along with than Hancock

BOOKTALK

It happened in New Orleans, in August, and the city would never be the same. It was a hurricane named Katrina, and among the people who sat it out in the horror that was the Superdome were Miles Shaw, a high school sophomore; his father "Doc," a jazz trumpet player; his Uncle Ray, who played jazz trombone; and Fess, a jazz clarinetist who'd played with them. This is their story, hour by hour, day by day, what they saw, what they did, how they survived, and what they found when they left.

This isn't a rewrite of what you saw on TV, carefully cropped and edited to make it palatable for the rest of the country. This is the reality—the noise, the gangs, the stench are all here. Miles and his family got to the Superdome the morning of Sunday, August 28. They left the afternoon of Tuesday, August 30. This is the story of those three days.

MAJOR THEMES AND IDEAS

- What you love gives back everything you put into it, whether it's football or music.
- Be respectful of people, but don't close your eyes on anyone.
- In an emergency, it's everyone for themselves.
- Race was a factor in the response to Katrina. Almost everyone in the Superdome was black.
- Weekend warriors, like the National Guard, aren't trained to be soldiers.
- In an emergency, people are stressed, tempers are short, and fights can begin over almost anything.
- Going along with the crowd isn't always the thing to do, especially if you don't agree with them.
- You do things to survive in an emergency that you would never do any other time.
- If you have to be someone you aren't to get your parents' approval, maybe it's not worth the effort.
- Going through the same experience can make strangers seem like family.
- What goes around, comes around. When you do evil or negative things, they will come back around and be done to you.
- Television reporters covering a tragedy—are they really doing something good, or are they just after the ratings?
- The more uncomfortable people are in a crowded setting, the shorter their tempers are.
- Once you choose the road to follow, you can't turn to go back.
- Looting is nothing but stealing.
- Most bullies aren't looking for a real fight.
- What happened at the Superdome during Katrina was too important to let go of, or to give a free pass to anyone who caused it.

BOOK REPORT IDEAS

1. Compare this novel to first-person news stories, magazines, and books written about what happened in the Superdome.
2. Discuss the title of the book, and how music is a central part of the story.
3. Discuss the quick erosion of civilization inside the Superdome, and then speculate what kind of event or individual might have made a difference.
4. From the moment Miles enters the Superdome to discover that almost all of the evacuees are black, race plays a huge role in the novel, just as it did in reality. Explain your understanding of the role and its importance.
5. The relationship between Miles and his father changed greatly during the book. Trace how it changed and explain why.
6. The two soldiers, Hancock and Scobie, had very different views of the evacuees. Explain what each of them expressed and why they each felt that way.

BOOKTALK IDEAS

1. Illustrate your talk with photos of the various locations in the book.
2. Use sound bites or news headlines to help you create your talk.
3. Use a jazz version of "When the Saints Go Marchin' In" as a soundtrack.
4. Read the introductory paragraph as part of your talk.

RISKS

- Graphic depiction of the Superdome during Hurricane Katrina
- Realistic language
- Gangs of bullies rob, rape, and kill
- Father neglects son to further his career
- Violence between various groups and gangs
- Describes revolting scenes accurately and in detail
- Father is obsessed with jazz and ignores son
- Brutal descriptions of violent deaths

STRENGTHS

- Realistic setting, dialogue, and characters
- Documents a cataclysmic event accurately and in detail
- Characters change and gain insight
- Shows the differences between those who want to survive tragedy and those who just want to take advantage of it
- Introductory section draws in reader immediately
- Shows how quickly civilization can be stripped away
- Many sections give opportunities for discussion
- Length and reading make it widely accessible
- Male narrator

- Father and son begin to see each other more accurately, leading to a better relationship
- Highlights the racism of the south
- Puts a very human face on a huge tragedy widely covered on TV

REVIEWS

"A brilliant blend of reality and fiction, this novel hits every chord just right. If it is not the best teen book of 2008, it is certainly one of the most important." Matthew Weaver, *VOYA*, 6/08

"Not for sissies—a riveting and readable exploration of the effects of race in today's world." *Kirkus Reviews*, 5/08

"Volponi effectively portrays how too many people in one space with too little food, supplies, and basic services quickly deteriorates from mere displacement to human suffering on a massive scale . . . A sprinkling of common vulgarities realistically punctuates the fast-paced story of unprecedented unease in the Big Easy." Joel Shoemaker, Southeast Junior High School, Iowa City, IA, *School Library Journal*, 8/08

"Volponi pulls no punches in his visceral depiction of the horrors that New Orleans' black residents experienced. . . . [His] passionate outrage is palpable, and his infectious indignation will surely invite much reflection and discussion." *Booklist*, 5/1/08.

⊞⊞⊞

IMPOSSIBLE. Nancy Werlin. Dial, 2008. $17.99. 384p. ISBN10: 0803730020. ISBN13: 9780803730021. Brilliance Audio, 2008. $24.99. ISBN10: 1423378628. ISBN13: 9781423378624. (unabridged audio MP3) Brilliance Audio, 2008. $39.97. ISBN10: 1423378636. ISBN13: 9781423378631. (unabridged audio MP3, library edition) Reading Level: YHS. Interest Level: YHS/OHS. English, Creative Writing, Psychology.

SUBJECT AREAS

foster parents; family relationships; problem parents; secrets; friendship; love; sports; school; dating and social life; mental illness; supernatural; rape; death and dying; suicide; writing; teen pregnancy; rites of passage; self-knowledge, homelessness.

CHARACTERS

Lucy Scarborough: her life is different because of the secrets about her mother

Miranda Scarborough: Lucy's haunted, and haunting, mother, a ghost who's actually
   very much alive
Soledad Markowitz: Lucy's loving foster mother, who's a full time midwife
Leo Markowitz: Lucy's foster father, who's a musician and teaches Lucy Miranda's
   song
Zach Greenfield: Lucy's oldest friend, who lived with the Markowitz's after his par-
   ents moved to Arizona
Sarah Herbert: Lucy's best friend, who believes falling in love is always painful
Gray Spencer: Lucy's date for the prom
Jeff Mundy: Sarah's in love with him, but he doesn't want to get serious
Padraig Seeley: a charismatic, magnetic social worker who joins Soledad's mid-
   wifery staff
Jacqueline Jackson: a friend of Soledad's at the hospital clinic where she works
Mrs. Angelkis: she lives across the street from the Markowitz's
Mr. and Mrs. Greenfield: Zach's parents
Mrs. Spenser: Gray's mother
Mr. Spenser: Gray's father

BOOKTALK
In many ways, seventeen-year-old Lucy Scarborough's life was 100 percent, completely normal. She had wonderful parents, made decent grades in school, ran track,
had two best friends, Zach and Sarah, and she was even going to the junior prom with
a really cute guy from the band, Gray Spencer.

But all that was on the surface. There were scary, ugly secrets she kept hidden
underneath, secrets that only Soledad and Leo, her foster parents, and Zach knew
about. If Zach hadn't spent his senior year living with them after his parents moved to
Arizona, he wouldn't have known. But he'd been there when Miranda came back, and
he'd seen the three weeks of hell Miranda had put them all through, three weeks during which he'd learned all the secrets about Lucy, and Soledad, and Leo, and most of
all, about Miranda, Lucy's mother. Lucy's crazy, broken, homeless, bag lady mother,
and the song she sang to torment them all.

> Are you going to Scarborough Fair? . . .
> Remember me to one who waits there, she must be a true love of mine.

But then Miranda disappeared, as she always did, and life got back to normal.
Zach graduated and left for college, and Lucy began her junior year in high school.
But it wasn't til the end of that year, just weeks before prom, that Miranda showed
up again, Zach came back for the summer, a new man was hired at the hospital where
Soledad worked, and the calm surface of Lucy's life shattered like fragile glass, splin-
tering into too many shards to ever be pieced together again.

Lucy discovered that she came from a long line of women who were cursed to give birth to a baby girl when they were eighteen and unmarried, and to then go mad, ending up broken, crazy, homeless women—just like Miranda.

Lucy has only one chance—she can do the three impossible tasks and break the curse, the tasks in the verses of Miranda's song:

> Tell her to make me a magical shirt. . . .
> Without no seams nor needlework. . . .
>
> Tell her to find me an acre of land. . . .
> Between the salt water and the sea strand. . . .
>
> Tell her to plow it with just a goat's horn. . . .
> And sow it all over with one grain of corn. . . .

Lucy has begun the battle of her life, against the evil the women in her family have been bound to for centuries. Does she have the courage, the cunning, the determination to win, when so many others have failed?

MAJOR THEMES AND IDEAS
- Continued pain is a signal that something isn't right.
- Falling in love means you care passionately about someone, and that leaves you vulnerable, easy to hurt.
- If love doesn't hurt sometimes, then maybe you don't truly care.
- Music links us, heart to heart, across time and space, life and death.
- Some people who are smart and attractive use it to get whatever they want.
- Smart and savvy people can be really blind when it comes to someone they're in love with.
- Live in the present. *Carpe diem!*
- Sometimes when it hurts too much to talk about something, it's a relief to have a friend who can say all those things for you.
- Healing takes time, whether your wounds are mental or physical. You can't rush through it, no matter how much you want to.
- A well-meaning but overprotective parent can stifle their child, even if it's unintended.
- You're in charge of your own life, no matter who pressures you to do anything. In the final analysis, it's *you* who gets to decide.
- When you have knowledge, no matter how hard it is to believe, your choices will be better.
- A best friend is someone who, even when they don't understand, still understands.
- There's a difference between the way a homeless eighteen-year-old sees her world and her choices and a loved and grounded seventeen-year-old with

supportive family and friends does. It's unlikely they will make the same decisions.

- The choices and influences you had as a child will govern your self-perception and choices as a teen and as an adult.
- It's impossible to help someone who doesn't choose to be helped.
- You can't always be the one who gives to others. Sometimes you have to sit back and let them give back to you, even if it does take some getting used to at first.
- Manipulation isn't always obvious. Sometimes it's hard to tell if someone is controlling you with what they say and do, changing your thoughts and actions to fit what they want.
- Sometimes we hear and see only what we want and expect to hear and see.
- Holding things inside doesn't really work. Sooner or later they leak out, or explode out, and you have to face them, talk about them, and figure out what to do.
- When you have something different and important to do, it's good to have a close friend there with you, to do what they can, and to just be there, even if there's nothing to do.
- Love doesn't always burst upon us. Sometimes it happens slowly, and as it builds, we gradually realize what it is and how we've been changed.
- Even if the problem is bizarre, the way to approach it is through logic, knowledge, and common sense.
- It only takes a moment for a life to change and head off on a whole new course. Of course, dealing with these changes can take a lifetime.
- Sometimes we can know people forever, and yet never know them at all.
- In life, sometimes a chain of weird events can lead to a perfect ending.
- When life gets tough, we all have the right to whine for a while before we get back to work.
- You don't just have to learn to accept what others want to give you or do for you; you have to learn to accept with grace, valuing both the gift and the giver.
- Sometimes we forget how wise our friends can be until they say or do something that makes us remember just how well they know us.
- It's a blessing to have people praying for and with you, even if you don't believe.
- There are reasons for the events of our lives, even if we don't know what they are.
- To accept yourself and your life today, you must also accept the past and the events that made you who you are today.
- There are many paths in life; each of us can choose only one. And once that choice has been made, there is no way to go back and choose again.
- You cannot reject your past and embrace your present. Your past created your present, and if you want to accept one, you must accept both.
- There's gotta be a happy ending sometimes. There's just gotta.

BOOK REPORT IDEAS

1. Compare the novel's version of "Scarborough Fair" with the traditional lyrics. How are they similar, and what are the significant changes in the song as it's found here? (There are several versions on Wikipedia, and there are videos on YouTube. Just search for the title.)
2. Discuss and explain Padraig Seeley's charismatic effect on people around him. Who was affected? Who was not? Why?
3. There are many strong friendships and relationships in this novel. Discuss how they were, or might have been, formed, and what was the basis for their strength and power?
4. Padraig was very careful to always call Lucy by her full name—Lucinda. What is the power of a person's real name, and where did these beliefs come from?
5. Miranda told Lucy she should be an ugly girl and expect less from life. What do you think she meant by that? How would Lucy be different if she were unattractive and expected little? Would that affect the fate Miranda expected for her?
6. Pierre seemed to dislike Padraig from the very beginning. What clues did that give you about his motives and plans? Are dogs able to sense things that people can't?
7. What were the clues in the book that let the reader know Zach no longer saw Lucy as just a friend or family member? What were the clues about how Lucy felt about Zach?
8. On prom night, Padraig did many things, some of them onstage, at the Markowitz home, which were described for the reader, and other things offstage, that the reader knows about only because of the results. Discuss both kinds of actions and describe their effects. Include his influence on Gray before, during, and after the prom.
9. Discuss how you would have approached the three tasks Lucy had to do, and whether or not you would have been able to complete them.
10. Put yourself in Lucy's and Zach's place, as they faced an acre of land that had to be plowed and sown in freezing sleet. How impossible does the task seem? Make this more real by marking out the borders of an acre plot and calculating the weight of the wheelbarrow Lucy has to push.

BOOKTALK IDEAS

1. Use the song as a soundtrack for your talk.
2. Include the book trailer from the author's website.
3. Let Lucy tell her own story in first person.
4. Have Lucy and Zach introduce themselves or each other.
5. Use something from the song as a prop, such as the goat's horn.
6. Focus your talk on the song and the tasks that Lucy must complete.

RISKS
- Homeless, mentally ill mother stalks her daughter
- Teens drink and are sexually active
- Rape
- Teen marriage
- Suicide
- Supernatural themes and creatures

STRENGTHS
- Supportive and loving foster parents
- Strong friendships
- Strong and individualistic heroine
- Haunting storyline reveals secrets slowly
- Prologue pulls reader into story
- Characters readers can identify with
- Solid relationship between Lucy and Zach gradually evolves from friendship to love
- Padraig enters on a minor chord—he's trouble but the reader doesn't know why
- Great foreshadowing
- Lucy has love and support for tasks: she's not alone
- Great girl-girl friendship and support and love and acceptance: "Even when I don't understand, I understand."
- Characters grow and gain insight and wisdom
- Teens act responsibly
- Rites of passage are successfully passed
- Tragedy and trauma draw married couples together instead of dividing them
- Parents are supportive of their children's choices even when they don't agree
- Almost all of the controversial content having to do with sex and sexuality takes place offstage

AWARDS
ALA Best Books for Young Adults, 2009
Booklist Editor's Choice, 2008
SLJ Best Books for Children, 2008

REVIEWS
"Werlin's book seamlessly weaves fable and fairy tale with Lucy's modern life. Lucy herself is a treasure of a character; she is spunky and unique and fiercely independent. Lucy's rape and subsequent teenage pregnancy are treated compassionately but are discussed in vague terms . . . . The story is original and makes for a fast-paced, compelling read. With its fantasy, mystery, and romantic aspects, the story will appeal to many readers." Courtney Wika, *VOYA*, 8/08

"Werlin addresses tough topics. Rape, teen pregnancy, and family madness set the story in motion, but the strength of Lucy's character and the love of her family and friends allow her to deal with such difficult matters and take on the impossible. Teens, especially young women, will enjoy this romantic fairy tale with modern trappings." Jennifer D. Montgomery, Western Kentucky University, Bowling Green, *School Library Journal*, 9/08

"The conclusion is startlingly wholesome, comfortable and complete for the usually dark Werlin, and the melding of magic and practicality produces a lovely whole." *Kirkus Reviews*, 8/08

ⅢⅢⅢ

INEXCUSABLE. Chris Lynch. Atheneum, an imprint of Simon and Schuster, 2005. $16.95. 176p. ISBN10: 0689847890. ISBN13: 9780689847899. Simon Pulse, 2007. $6.99. 176p. ISBN10: 1416939725. ISBN13: 9781416939726. Bt Bound, 2007. $15.80. 176p. ISBN10: 141777780X. ISBN13: 9781417777808. (library binding) Thorndike Press, 2006. $22.95. 192p. ISBN10: 0786288124. ISBN13: 9780786288120. (large print) Realistic fiction. Reading Level: YHS. Interest Level: YHS, OHS. English, Ethics, Sociology, Sex Education, P.E.

SUBJECT AREAS
dating and social life; sexual abuse; lying and deceit; secrets; intimidation; self-knowledge; anger; ethics; fear; rites of passage; peer pressure; bullying; dysfunctional families; family relationships; rape; problem parents; school; sports; substance abuse; betrayal; violence; guilt; anger; irresponsibility.

CHARACTERS
Keir Sarafian: he's a good guy, a loyal straight shooter, and good guys don't do bad things
Gigi Boudakian: Keir's lifelong love, who says he raped her
Carl: Gigi calls him for help
Mary and Fran Sarafian: Keir's brainy and insightful older sisters, who take no nonsense from anyone
Ray Sarafian: Keir's father and best friend; he's a long-time widower
Quarterback Ken: he gave Keir his nickname, "Killer"
Rollo: Ray's cousin who owns a totally tricked-out stretch limo
Cory, Brian, James, Arthur, Phil, Jon-Jon: members of the football team
Grace: Mary and Fran's roommate

BOOKTALK

"Gigi, you don't get it. I would *never* hurt you. I love you."

"You can't love me. You raped me."

"I *couldn't* rape you, I *wouldn't*. I'd kill anyone who raped you. I would!"

"I said no—I *did!*"

He said, she said, but who is right? Was it sex or was it rape? Is he telling the truth? Is she lying?

The only way to know is to watch and listen as he tells the story of their senior year and how it changed him, and her.

MAJOR THEMES AND IDEAS

- Good guys don't do bad things.
- Sometimes things are *exactly* what they look like. Sometimes they aren't.
- People involved in the same situation can tell *very* different stories about what happened.
- Sometimes, it's all too easy to fool yourself.
- Do as you're told. Do as you were taught. Follow the letter and the spirit of the law.
- Doing something good, and doing it perfectly, can sometimes have tragic results.
- Everyone needs someone to give them a little grief every so often.
- Nicknames say something about how others see you, not how you see yourself.
- Just be yourself, and don't let circumstances change who you are.
- When people you love scream at you, it goes right through you like a knife, like nothing else can.
- Excuses change nothing. What happened, happened. Trying to interpret it a certain way to allay blame doesn't change the facts of the matter at all.
- In a dangerous situation, it's easy to get hurt if you don't pay attention to what you're doing.
- No always means no.
- Even when you do something perfectly, the results can be far from perfect.
- Be who you are, not what other people say you are.
- A man needs not to be afraid of himself. A man needs to be sure of himself.
- When things go wrong, sometimes it's not an issue of intent, but one of intensity.
- Things done in the heat of the moment can look very different the next day.
- It can be easy to let yourself live up to a nickname, even if it was uncomfortable at first.
- You can't not choose. Even doing nothing is a decision.
- Sooner or later, you run out of excuses.
- Memories don't always reflect reality. They can be created to reflect what you wish had happened instead.

- Decisions made when you're drunk or high aren't always good or wise ones.
- The more excuses you make for yourself, the easier it becomes.
- It always hurts when people you love let you down.
- Sometimes it's easier to get in trouble when you are part of a crowd.
- Even if you're a good guy, you can still be wrong.
- At some point, you have to stop being a kid, grow up, and face the facts.
- If the girl who said no says it was rape, it was.
- Good guys aren't rapists.

BOOK REPORT IDEAS

1. At what point in the book did you realize that Keir is actually guilty? Why?
2. Keir excuses himself from blame when the "accident" on the football field happened. Did he deserve any of the blame? Some of it? All of it?
3. What lessons should Keir have learned from the football incident?
4. Would Keir have been nicknamed "Killer" if he had no blame for crippling the boy he tackled? What does the nickname really mean? Why do you think Keir accepted the nickname?
5. Discuss why Keir didn't do "involvement" very well. How did others in his high school really see him?
6. Discuss the relationship between Ray and his children. How successful is he at parenting?
7. Keir was a very black-and-white, all or nothing, person. Describe some of the situations where he exhibited this characteristic.
8. What does Keir think is inexcusable? Why?
9. Examine the scenes of Keir and Gigi together. Are they being honest with each other, or are they hiding parts of themselves?
10. Keir says he changed before he graduated—point out the signs of those changes, and their results.
11. When Keir says he doesn't know when part of him will show up, as he begins his graduation limo ride, what does he mean?
12. Discuss why Gigi went out to Rollo's limo and took Keir into the party.
13. Keir says over and over how much he loves Gigi. Do you believe him? Why or why not?
14. What does Keir mean when he tells Gigi he has two hearts? What is he trying to tell her about himself?
15. Was Keir a good guy? Why or why not?
16. Speculate on what happened after the book ended. Will Keir's revelation change him or not? How will his sisters react? What will Gigi do? Predict where you think Keir will be in five years, or in ten.
17. What did the unending game of Risk symbolize? What did it mean for Keir and Ray?

BOOKTALK IDEAS
1. Use a refrain as part of your talk, like "It's inexcusable" or "It's not my fault."
2. Shape your talk like the book, including several of the incidents Keir claims no responsibility for.
3. Focus your talk on the excuses Keir makes for himself so he can tell himself he isn't at fault.
4. Contrast the bad guy and the good guy sides of Keir. Let each half tell part of the talk.
5. Focus your talk on the idea of date rape, citing news stories and statistics.

RISKS
- Teen rapist
- Teen refuses to take responsibility for his own actions, including rape
- Obscenities
- Vandalism
- Bullying
- Substance abuse
- Father buys beer for minor son
- Father overlooks signs his son is out of control
- Delinquent and criminal behavior goes unpunished
- Adults leave teens without supervision and with permission to party
- Teens are sexually active

STRENGTHS
- Narrator finally realizes what he has done
- Powerful storyline
- Graphic depiction of how completely a person can blind himself to the truth
- Realistic characters the reader can identify with
- Demonstrates how a "good guy" can do things that are terribly wrong
- Demonstrates the idea that when a girl or woman is unwilling, no matter what the situation, it is rape
- Reader realizes quickly that Keir has done something wrong more than once
- Unresolved ending leaves room for speculation and discussion
- Shows how disconnected family members can be
- Focuses on situation that's all too real, all too frequent
- Author doesn't pull any punches and faces the problem of date rape unflinchingly

AWARDS
Kirkus Reviews Editor's Choice, 2005
SLJ Best Books for Children, 2005

ALA Best Books for Young Adults, 2006
Booklist Editor's Choice, 2005
National Book Award Finalist (Young People's Literature), 2005

REVIEWS
"Looking through the eyes of a rapist is uncomfortable, but this book is about more than date rape. Lynch's masterful exploration of the difference between perception and reality is fascinating. Teens will reread this short but complex story debating the issues of violence and responsibility." Cindy Dobrez, *VOYA*, 12/05

"Throughout this unforgettable novel, Lynch raises fierce, painful questions about athletic culture, family denial, violence, and rape, and readers will want to think and talk about them all. Where does personal responsibility begin? What defines a 'good guy'? Are we all capable of monstrous things?" Gillian Engberg, *Booklist*, 9/05

"This finely crafted and thought-provoking page-turner carefully conveys that it is simply inexcusable to whitewash wrongs, and that those responsible should (and hopefully will) pay the price." Diane P. Tuccillo, City of Mesa Library, AZ, *School Library Journal*, 11/05

ㅁㅁㅁ

INSIDE OUT. Terry Trueman. HarperTeen, an imprint of HarperCollins, 2003. $15.99. 128p. ISBN10: 0066239621. ISBN13: 9780066239620. HarperTeen, 2004. $7.99. 128p. ISBN10: 0064473767. ISBN13: 9780064473767. HarperTeen, 2003. $16.89. 128p. ISBN10: 006623963X. ISBN13: 9780066239637. (library binding) Realistic fiction. Reading Level: MS. Interest Level: MS, YHS. English, Ethics, Psychology, Sociology, Government.

SUBJECT AREAS
mental illness; crime and delinquency; suicide; fear; anger; family relationships; love; legal system; justice; death and dying; self-knowledge.

CHARACTERS
Zach Wahhsted: a sixteen-year-old with schizophrenia who's in the wrong place at the wrong time
Dr. Curt/Dr. Cal Curtis: Zach's psychiatrist
Frosty/Alan Mender and Stormy/Joey Mender: two teenaged boys who decide to rob a coffee shop

Fat Suit, Thin Suit, Mean Old Lady, Nice Old Lady, Pretty Mom, Katy/Cute Little Girl, Coffee Shop Girl, Coffee Shop Guy: coffee shop customers
Dirtbag and Rat: mean voices in Zach's head
Mom/Louise Mender: Alan and Joey's mother
Mom/Emily Wahhsted: Zach's mother

BOOKTALK
It was supposed to be so simple, right? Me and my little brother were just going to walk into this coffee shop with our guns, scare everyone, take the money and walk out again. No harm, no foul. But that's not the way it went down, because this kid Zach was there. He looked pretty normal, but man, was he weird. Turns out his brain's all messed up—inside out and upside down, and he wasn't ever gonna get any better. It was really strange, talking to him, because he wasn't afraid. Everyone else in the place was scared to death of us and our guns, but not Zach. He was just as cool, as calm, as he could be, and when either Joey or I said something, he answered us. Even when we didn't want an answer.

Even after the cops showed up, and we ended up with nine hostages jammed together in a back room while we tried to figure out how to get outta there, Zach was still cool, still calm, and still saying these off the wall things. And believe it or not, that wasn't the worst part. Things were about to get a whole lot stranger and a whole lot more desperate.

MAJOR THEMES AND IDEAS
- It hurts when people call you names, whether they are real or are only in your head.
- Sometimes mental illness makes someone act in strange ways.
- If you feel no emotion, you can't feel fear, but you can't feel happiness either.
- Guns are dangerous and most people are immediately afraid of them.
- Difficult situations can get out of control very quickly.
- Is it wrong to commit a crime if your goal is saving the life of someone you love?
- Sometimes something is so painful, the desire to end it is overwhelming.
- Help and solutions can come from the least likely sources.
- Knowing you're mentally ill can't always help you overcome it.
- The police are willing to compromise to end a hostage situation safely.
- Saying something to make someone feel better can be a good thing.
- Even if you know the people telling you that you're worthless are only in your head, after a while, you begin to believe them.

BOOK REPORT IDEAS
1. Describe what might have happened in the coffee shop if Zach hadn't been there.

2. Discuss Zach's role as the catalyst in the situation—the one element that changed everything.
3. Analyze Alan and describe how his perceptions changed during the afternoon.
4. Discuss the ethics of committing a crime to get money for medicine.
5. Discuss how Zach's illness was treated with both therapy and medication, based on comments from Dr. Curt and from Zach himself.
6. Discuss Zach and how he saw himself. Did he know how sick he was? What makes you think that?

BOOKTALK IDEAS
1. Have Zach describe what happens in the coffee shop.
2. Write your booktalk as a newspaper story reporting the crime or a TV reporter covering the story outside the restaurant.
3. Write your talk as if you were one of the two kids working at the coffee shop.
4. This book is very brief, so be sure not to reveal too much or tell the ending.

RISKS
- Mentally ill teen is mocked and made fun of by both teens and adults
- Dialogue includes obscenities
- Teens have access to guns
- Teens commit crimes

STRENGTHS
- Brief and intense story
- Realistic language
- Allows the reader to understand the thought processes of a schizophrenic teen
- Provides a point of view and perspective not seen before in young adult literature
- Characters grow and gain insight
- Tragic and unexpected ending
- Tension and suspense never let up
- Clues to the proper treatment of schizophrenia

AWARDS
ALA Best Books for Young Adults, 2004
ALA Quick Picks for Reluctant Young Adult Readers, 2004

REVIEWS
"Certainly Trueman is an excellent writer. This book is highly recommended for school and public libraries as both pleasure reading or to start discussions." Amy Alessio, *VOYA*, 10/03

"Despite the suspenseful storyline, this is ultimately a book about understanding and empathy; the climax is surprising, logical and moving. Fans of Cormier will likely enjoy this psychological and gripping tale." *Publisher's Weekly*, 8/03

"Give Trueman credit for attempting to provide some empathy for the 'others' of our world who are too easily dismissed and ridiculed—in a plot line that grabs and doesn't let go." *Kirkus Reviews*, 7/03

"Trueman . . . captures moments of heartbreaking truth, and his swift, suspenseful plot will have particular appeal to reluctant readers." Gillian Engberg, *Booklist*, 9/03

ꀀꀀꀀ

INVENTING ELLIOT. Graham Gardner. Dial, 2004. $16.99. 192p. ISBN10: 0803729642. ISBN13: 9780803729643. Penguin, 2005. $5.99. 192p. ISBN10: 014240344X. ISBN13: 9780142403440. Listening Library, 2004. $26.00. ISBN10: 0807223190. ISBN13: 9780807223192. (unabridged audiotape) Sagebrush, 2005. $14.65. 181p. ISBN10: 1417681314. ISBN13: 9781417681310. (library binding) Realistic fiction. Reading Level: MS. Interest Level: MS, YHS. English, Ethics, Psychology, Sociology, P.E.

SUBJECT AREAS
school; bullying; self-knowledge; peer pressure; intimidation; rites of passage; friendship; gangs; mental illness; problem parents; family relationships; secrets; sports; violence; lying and deceit; gossip; anger; fear; dysfunctional family.

CHARACTERS
Elliot Sutton: a fourteen-year-old freshman hoping to escape being bullied at school
Mrs. Sutton/Mom: she works hard to pretend everything is all right
Mr. Sutton/Dad: he sits and stares all day, silent and depressed
Kevin Cunning, Steven Watson, John Sanders: bullies who enjoyed tormenting Elliot at his old school
Oliver: the first student to talk to Elliot at Holminster High
Mr. Phillips: the gym teacher
Stewart Masters: a jock, a bully, and a school hero
Baker: Stewart's favorite target
Richard, Cameron, Gareth: the Guardians, a group that runs Holminster High and notices Elliot
Ben: one of the victims; he likes to swim and is into photography

The Principal: he notices Elliot and asks him the one question Elliot does not want to answer

Louise: a girl in Elliot's English class whom he is attracted to

Mrs. Davidson: Elliot's English teacher

Sean Askmore: Elliot's chosen punisher

Simon Kilworth: Elliot's chosen victim

BOOKTALK

It was a new town, a new house, a new school. It was a chance for Elliot to reinvent himself, to stop being a victim, to fit in. He made sure his school uniform didn't look too new, got a spiky, bleached haircut, and practiced an expression of calm indifference. He hid his terror behind that expression when he discovered that the bullies at this school were just as bad as the ones as his old school. To escape their notice, he had to stop thinking like a victim, flinching whenever someone looked at him, expecting someone to pounce on him. So, when he didn't feel confident, he acted like he was, making sure his face was calm and his body relaxed. And he was stunned to discover that it worked! He wasn't seen as a victim, but just himself—Elliot, the new freshman who's on the swim team.

Then he found out about the Guardians, a secret group of students who ruled the school, who decided who was to be punished, and how. If they noticed someone, he was dead. And one day, they noticed Elliot, and summoned him to meet with them. He'd lied to a teacher, in front of the whole gym class, and protected a bully. That, along with his indifferent attitude, made him interesting. They investigated further, tested him, and made their decision. The three of them were juniors and needed successors, boys they could train to be Guardians when they were gone, boys like Elliot, the new Elliot, the invented Elliot. He'd just wanted to escape the bullies—and he had. But now they have invited him to join them! Can he treat other kids the way he was treated for so long? Create fear in kids like the Elliot he used to be? Be the one doing the punishing, instead of the one who endures it?

Who is the real Elliot, the old one or the new?

MAJOR THEMES AND IDEAS

- If you're serious about a thing, and you put your mind to it, you get it done.
- In a place where no one knows your past, you can create a new you, looking differently, acting differently.
- Very few things are impossible, if you're willing to work for them.
- Once bullies have noticed you, you can't become invisible or slip under their radar. Trying too hard not to be noticed may make you even more obvious.
- Bullies can sense fear, pick it out in a crowd.
- If you're going to be noticed, make sure you're noticed in the right way, standing out just enough to fit in.
- Stand out for the wrong reason, and you're dead.

- Bullies have long memories.
- Some kids get noticed, not because they're asking for trouble, but because they're waiting for it, because they make no attempt to act like they aren't victims.
- If you see yourself as a victim, you'll never be safe.
- If you are present when bullying is going on, you are a part of it, even if you do nothing.
- Bullying involves three different roles: the victims, the bullies, and the observers.
- Some teachers don't really want to know the truth, because then they'd have to *do* something about it.
- Once you lie, you cross the line, and there's no going back.
- Thinking and acting in a new way, rather than like a victim, can be scary, but that doesn't mean you should stop doing it.
- You may be tougher than you think you are. Toughness only shows when it's needed.
- Those who watch want to have control, and want those they watch to know it.
- Power isn't a means to an end—it *is* the end. The point of having power is *power*.
- One person's clinical depression affects and is inflicted upon everyone close to him.
- Power is seduction—it sucks you in, it feels good.
- It's possible to hide fear and terror with a calm expression and relaxed stance. It's difficult but possible.
- You generally see in others what you expect to see, because that's what you're looking for.
- Delaying gratification increases it.
- Once you learn to accept things as they are, it's so much easier. Or is it?
- Choosing to live and act as the person you genuinely are makes you free.

BOOK REPORT IDEAS

1. There are several bullies in the book. Discuss their similarities and differences.
2. How did Elliot change after he met the Guardians?
3. Elliot describes some kids as "waiting for trouble." What do these kids look like? Act like?
4. Describe the difference between not being noticed and being noticed enough to fit it in.
5. Speculate on what you think will happen after the end of the book. What will Elliot's life be like?
6. Do you agree or disagree with Elliot's final decision? In his place, what would you have done?
7. How are the worlds of *1984* and Holminster High alike and different?

8. Richard tells Elliot to rule the crowd, to remember that, as one of the Guardians, no one is above him. Explain Elliot's reaction to that statement. Why is it so seductive?

9. Elliot says he has several "new Elliots." What does he mean, and how are each of them different or unique? Describe each one and why they each exist.

10. How does Elliot change his thinking after he becomes a Guardian, and how does he express this shift?

11. What does Louise mean when she says the hero in *1984* became free by losing?

12. Why did Elliot's world turn gray? What did that symbolize?

13. What is the most important idea in this book, in your opinion? Why is it most important?

BOOKTALK IDEAS
1. Use a copy of *1984* like Louise's as a prop.
2. Write the talk in first person, as Elliot.
3. Write the talk as a dialogue between the new Elliot and the old one. Be careful not to give too much away.
4. Have Richard introduce Elliot, as he gradually learns more and more about the new kid.

RISKS
- Teachers ignore jocks' bullying
- Depressed and neglectful father
- Graphic descriptions of bullying behavior
- Teachers participate in bullying
- Dark, depressing, hapless tone
- Weaker kids are victimized
- School administration tacitly approves of bullying behavior
- Exploitive, manipulative teens control others' behavior
- School gang
- Bullies are portrayed sympathetically

STRENGTHS
- Characters teens can identify with
- Strong statement against bullying
- Shows the seductiveness of power
- Details a victim's behavior and how to change it
- Main character grows and gains insight
- Abrupt ending leaves room for discussion and speculation
- Writing style draws in reader immediately
- Powerful depiction of a person trying to resist evil

- Intense contrast between good and evil
- Use of *1984* may encourage the reader to read or re-read it
- Characters shown to be both good and evil

AWARD
New York Public Library Books for the Teen Age, 2005

REVIEWS
"This book should appeal to a broad range of readers—almost everyone knows what it is like to be bullied. . . . The locker-room bullying scenes are harrowing and all too real, but most students should find hope in Elliot's transformations and final decisions." Rebecca Vnuk, *VOYA*, 4/04

"Elliot's character changes as the story develops, giving readers the needed clues, amid nail-biting suspense, to the culminating event in the final chapter. References throughout to Orwell's *1984* add depth and keep readers thinking of the principles at stake when those with power abuse it." *Kirkus Reviews*, 2/04

"A chilling and heartbreaking study of bullying and adolescent terror." GraceAnne DeCandido, *Booklist*, 5/04

📖📖📖

INVISIBLE. Pete Hautman. Simon and Schuster, 2005. $16.99. 160p. ISBN10: 0689868006. ISBN13: 9780689868009. Simon Pulse, 2006. $7.99. 160p. ISBN10: 0689869037. ISBN13: 9780689869037. Bt Bound, 2006. $16.95. 160p. ISBN10: 1417764260. ISBN13: 9781417764266. (library binding) Thorndike Press, 2005. $20.95. 184p. ISBN10: 0786279095. ISBN13: 9780786279098. (large print) Recorded Books, 2006. $46.75. ISBN10: 1419384562. ISBN13: 9781419384561. (unabridged audio CD) Recorded Books, 2006. $25.95. ISBN10: 141938452X. ISBN13: 9781419384523. (unabridged audiotape) Recorded Books, 2006. $30.75. ISBN10: 1419384511. ISBN13: 9781419384516. (unabridged audiotape, library version) Realistic fiction. Reading Level: MS. Interest Level: MS, YHS. English, Psychology, Art, Shop, Communication.

SUBJECT AREAS
friendship; mental illness; sports; theatre; school; therapy; obsession; problem parents; anger; bullying; lying and deceit; secrets; guilt; creativity; self-destruction.

CHARACTERS
Dougie Hanson: he's shy, quiet, obsessed with trains
Andy Morrow: he's popular, and into football and theatre
Mrs. Felko: Dougie's art teacher
Henry Clay Hanson: Dougie's father and an economics professor
Andrea Hanson: Dougie's mother, who worries about her son, and thinks he is troubled and disturbing
Dr. Eleanor Ahlstrom: Dougie's psychiatrist
Melissa Hoverman: she's in school plays with Andy and thinks Dougie is a disgusting troll
Mr. Kesselbaum: Dougie's calculus teacher
Mr. Haughton: Dougie's language arts teacher, who finds him frustrating
George Fuller: a man who's been staying with the Morrows
Mr. Haverman: Melissa's father, who thinks Dougie is spying on his daughter
Freddie Perdue, Ty Bridger, Aron Metz: football players who beat up Dougie
Mr. Janssen: the high school principal
Ms. Neidermeyer: the school counselor
Officer John Hughes: a cop who believes Dougie is a troublemaker
Dr. Monahan: he's the director of a private school, St. Stephen's Academy

BOOKTALK
When you're best friends with someone, you know what not to talk about. Andy and I are best friends, but we never talk about the Tuttle place. We've been friends forever, even though we aren't even a little bit alike. Andy's handsome, an athlete, and really popular. He's the quarterback of our football team. I'm really smart, but I'm not good at small talk, so a lot of people think I'm strange. Andy doesn't, though. He likes me, and we can talk about anything. Except the Tuttle place, of course.

Andy and my parents are the only ones who know about the bridge I'm building in our basement. It's a suspension bridge, like the Golden Gate. It connects East Madham and West Madham, and it's eleven feet long. Bridges are good things—they connect people. Andy and I are connected by a lot of things, and my bridge is one of them. Of course, we're also connected by the Tuttle place and what happened there, but we don't like to talk about that. Talking about it makes me remember, and remembering hurts.

MAJOR THEMES AND IDEAS
- It doesn't matter if people live in different worlds, they can still be best friends.
- An obsessive hobby can be a mask for great pain.
- Focus is important. If you take your time and do the job right, it can last forever.
- Focusing on one thing allows you to block out the things you don't want to think about.

- Even a highly intelligent person can do dumb things.
- One of the secrets of keeping best friends is knowing what *not* to talk about.
- It's hard to argue with logic.
- Doing a thing over and over can be very satisfying.
- Denying you did something does not necessarily convince others of your innocence.
- Some people can be oblivious to something right in front of them.
- Medication may cover up the signs of mental illness, but it doesn't cure it.
- Parents don't always know what's best for their child.
- Ignoring a behavior doesn't make it go away.

BOOK REPORT IDEAS

1. What do trains symbolize in this story?
2. Discuss Dougie's parents' attitude toward their son. They realize he's troubled, but seem completely unaware of his obsession with Andy. When his mother hears him talking to Andy, she doesn't confront him, but tells her husband instead.
3. Explain the title of the book. Who or what is invisible? Who isn't seeing what's right in front of their eyes?
4. What is the reason for Dougie's obsession with his train, town, and bridge?
5. Dougie's "sigil" changes as the story progresses. Explain what those changes mean to him and why he is making them.
6. Discuss why Dougie is bullied at school.
7. How much of Dougie and Andy's friendship was in Dougie's head? Were they ever really best friends?
8. Dougie says bridges are important because they connect things. What connection does his bridge make?
9. There are three destructive fires in this book, and the knife plays a role in each of them. Compare them, their causes, their results.
10. Speculate on the rest of Dougie's life. Will he ever be normal? Why or why not?
11. How does Dougie express his anger? His guilt?
12. When the book ends, where is Dougie? When does this scene take place? Is the smoke real?

BOOKTALK IDEAS

1. Use matches or a picture of the Golden Gate as props for your talk.
2. Write your talk as if you were Andy describing Dougie.
3. Focus your talk on the idea of invisibility and how Dougie's problems were invisible to other people.

4. Use enlarged pictures of the sigil to illustrate your talk, showing how it changed. Let Dougie explain the changes and why he made them.
5. Write your talk as if you were Dougie.

RISKS
*   Athletes harass troubled teen
*   Teen spies on others
*   Ineffectual parents
*   Psychiatrist prescribes drugs but doesn't connect with or help disturbed teen
*   Obsessive behavior is ignored

STRENGTHS
*   The discovery of truth comes as a complete surprise
*   Frighteningly real portrait of mental illness
*   Genuine voice of a teen
*   Realistic, believable characters
*   Unresolved ending, leaves room for discussion
*   Demonstrates how disturbed an individual can be while seeming to be normal

AWARDS
ALA Best Books For Young Adults, 2006
ALA Notable Children's Book Nominee, 2006
ALA Quick Picks Nominee, 2006
Kirkus Editor's Choice, 2005
YALSA Teens Top Ten (TTT) Nominee, 2006

REVIEWS
"With excruciating care, Hautman builds an unbearable tension toward disaster. . . . Hautman takes the reader into the very core of the victim and the dynamics of heartless targeting, and forces all to accept responsibility for stopping the cycle of violence." Beth E. Andersen, *VOYA*, 8/05

"The mentally ill Dougie, who evokes echoes of Faulkner with his unreliable narration, is confronted with truths he can't bear. The deceptively simple prose doesn't keep secrets from its readers, but Dougie's harrowing mysteries are no less tragic for their visibility." *Kirkus Reviews*, 5/05

"With its excellent plot development and unforgettable, heartbreaking protagonist, this is a compelling novel of mental illness." Susan Riley, Mount Kisco Public Library, NY, *School Library Journal*, 6/05

ㅁㅁㅁ

JUST LISTEN. Sarah Dessen. Viking Juvenile, 2006. $17.99. 384p. ISBN10: 0670061050. ISBN13: 9780670061051. Puffin, 2008. $8.99. 400p. ISBN10: 0142410977. ISBN13: 9780142410974. Realistic fiction. Reading Level: YHS. Interest Level: YHS, OHS. English, Psychology.

SUBJECT AREAS
eating disorders; self-knowledge; family relationships; friendship; secrets; school; working; depression; anger; manipulation; obsession; dating and social life; rape; legal system; love; sexual abuse; betrayal; bullying; cooking; fear; gossip; guilt; justice; music; revenge; peer pressure.

CHARACTERS
Annabel Greene: she tries to avoid confrontations, but they seem to catch up with her anyway
Sophie Rawlins: she and Annabel were best friends until one night changed everything
Clarke Reynolds: she used to be one of Annabel's best friends
Whitney Greene: Annabel's older sister, who's a loser
Kirsten Greene: Annabel's oldest sister, who's a drama queen
Molly Clayton: Kirsten's best friend
Chris Pennington: the most gorgeous guy in the neighborhood
Emily Schuster: she used to be Annabel's friend, but now she's Sophie's friend instead
Owen Armstrong: angriest boy in school; he's determined to tell the truth, no matter what
Ronnie Waterman: a complete jerk and the most annoying boy in school
Will Cash: Sophie's boyfriend and part of the reason that Sophie and Annabel aren't speaking
Lindy: Annabel's agent for modeling jobs
Mom/Grace Green: Annabel's mother, who wants everyone to be nice and polite
Dad/Andrew Greene: he works hard and lets Grace handle the girlie things
Greg Nichols: an obnoxious junior
Hillary Prescott: she works for the same agency as Annabel and is a huge gossip
Dr. Hammond: Whitney's therapist

Mallory Armstrong: Owen's little sister, who is into fashion and is one of Annabel's biggest fans
Teresa Armstrong: Owen's and Mallory's mother
Ted and Dexter: they play in a band and are friends of Owen's
Remy: she travels with the band

BOOKTALK

I can't tell. I just can't. You'll hate me, I know you will. You'll leave me alone, you'll disappear. Everyone does. You glare at me, already angry, and even if I told you, that anger would still be there.

Maybe if I'd had more courage and tried to explain sooner. But I didn't, and as the days and weeks and months went by, the chasm between us grew so deep and so wide that it seems like no one could ever cross it.

I'm so alone. Everyone at school believes your story, and they avoid me, drawing back, as if my touch were poison. At home, everyone's problems are louder, more extreme, more important than mine, and I keep my story, my secret, hidden deep inside where no one can see it.

But the pressure of keeping my secret begins to grow, making it harder and harder to keep it inside. It's unfair of me to meet your honesty and openness with evasions and silence. I take a deep breath, and say, "Don't think. Don't judge. Just listen."

MAJOR THEMES AND IDEAS

- Being nice isn't easy, especially when the rest of the world can be so mean.
- Families are not always what they appear to be from the outside.
- The unknown isn't always the greatest thing to fear. People you know can be riskier because the words they say can be not only scary, but true as well.
- It's hard to trust someone who's been deliberately mean to you, because there's always the chance that it will happen again.
- People who don't like themselves may find fault with those around them to make themselves feel better.
- Sometimes, sorry isn't good enough.
- After a disagreement, the chasm it caused between two friends gets bigger and bigger as more time passes, and less and less likely that it can be crossed.
- You are not responsible for what other people do.
- The truth hurts, but so do lies.
- Being honest is difficult and sometimes painful, but pretending everything is fine has a higher chance of making it all worse.
- Confronting a problem at least opens the door for a change. Pretending the problem doesn't exist closes that door.
- Even white lies are dishonest.

- Holding in what you really want to say can be stressful and can make you angry.
- It's important to talk about what you think and feel inside. Keeping it inside too long may mean there's an explosion when it finally comes out.
- Anger isn't bad, it's human. And most of the time people get over their anger.
- If someone is really close to you, a disagreement doesn't change that. You deal with it and go on.
- Sometimes silence can be deafening.
- Anger is inevitable, so it's essential to find a productive way to handle it.
- If you can't trust yourself, who can you trust?
- You may omit telling the whole truth to someone else, but always tell yourself the whole truth.
- Wait for the perfect moment.
- People involved in the same situation all have different memories and emotions about it, each just a piece of the whole.
- Life has some moments that are so real, so personal, even if they look false from the outside, if you take a second look, you can tell.
- What if you told the truth and nobody listened?
- Some memories don't fade with time, they just grow more clear and distinct.
- To make a difference, you have to tell your side of the story, not suck it up and hold it in, so that all anyone knows is the *other* side of the story.
- Changing who you are, even when you end up in a better place, is always difficult and uncomfortable.
- When you try to run from the past, it overtakes you, blotting out everything, so the only path you can take is through it.
- You can't always get the perfect moment to say or do something. Sometimes you just have to do the best you can under the circumstances.
- Even though you feel on the outside and alone, you may only be an arm's length away. All you have to do is ask, and you'll be brought back inside.
- There are no such things as absolutes, in life or in people.
- Just take life day by day. You'll make it.
- Sharing long-held and painful secrets sets you free.

BOOK REPORT IDEAS

1. Examine the roles in the Greene family. Which role does each member play?
2. Discuss how Annabel feels caught in the middle, both at home and at school. How does she change because of the rift between Kirsten and Whitney?
3. Discuss which is more difficult, telling your story or deciding whom you tell it to.
4. Annabel spent most of the year alone, but what do you think would have happened if she'd reached out to someone else?
5. Explain why keeping a secret can be more difficult and painful than sharing it.

6. Discuss the idea of broken promises and the impact that they have on various people.
7. Evaluate Owen's policy of always telling the truth as an anger management strategy. How well or how poorly do you think it would work for you?
8. Remy believes that sometimes violence draws people together. It's true in the book, but how true is it in real life?
9. What were some of the milestones Annabel encountered in the book? What did they mean and how did she change with each?
10. Explain how Annabel's assumptions worked against her.
11. Speculate on what happens after the book ends. What might be happening in five years? In ten?
12. Examine the idea of fighting *for* a relationship, rather than simply abandoning it the first time there's conflict.

BOOKTALK IDEAS
1. Have two or three characters introduce themselves and Annabel.
2. Let Annabel tell her own story.
3. Focus your talk on the idea of secrets.
4. Make a soundtrack for your talk based on what either Owen or Annabel likes.

RISKS
- Realistic language including slang and obscenities
- Eating disorders
- Uninvolved parents
- Teens are sexually active
- Several teen girls are raped
- Several characters are cruel to each other

STRENGTHS
- Author doesn't reveal the reasons Sophie and Annabel aren't friends
- Characters are easy to identify with
- Shows the price of keeping a secret
- Demonstrates what weak and strong really mean—someone who is seen as strong is actually broken, and vice versa
- Shows the good results of telling a long-kept secret
- Demonstrates how we use our assumptions to limit our lives
- Shows that some secrets need to be told
- Anorexic character improves
- Characters learn how to stand up for themselves
- Rapist is convicted and sent to prison
- Character learns keeping secrets is more difficult than sharing them

- Opportunities for discussions on many topics
- Estranged friends are able to reconnect

AWARD
ALA Best Books for Young Adults, 2007

REVIEWS
"Dessen's books are engrossing, each one better than its predecessor, and her prose is smooth. Teens will relate to this story about a girl feeling isolated from family and friends. The characters are real—some quirky, some manipulative, some weak, some strong. . . . Dessen weaves a sometimes funny, mostly emotional, and very satisfying story." Ed Goldberg, *VOYA*, 4/06

"Dessen explores the interior and exterior lives of her characters and shows their flaws, humanity, struggles, and incremental successes. This is young adult fiction at its best, delving into the minds of complex, believable teens, bringing them to life, and making readers want to know more about them with each turn of the page." Roxanne Myers Spencer, Western Kentucky University, Bowling Green, *School Library Journal*, 5/06

"In delicate, unassuming prose, naturally flowing dialogue, and a complex, credible plot, Dessen portrays Annabel's socially endorsed self-repression with depth and intensity. The romance with Owen, which forms the core of the story, is everything a romance should be—challenging, heartfelt, and most of all organic. In the end, families are healed, friendships are resurrected, and love—in all its unexpected incarnations—triumphs." *Horn Book Magazine*, 5/06

📖📖📖

THE KNIFE OF NEVER LETTING GO. (Chaos Walking, Book 1) Patrick Ness. Candlewick, 2008. $18.99. 496p. ISNB: 9780763639310. Science fiction. Reading Level: YHS. Interest Level: YHS, OHS. English, Ethics, Psychology.

SUBJECT AREAS
family relationships; self-knowledge; cultural identity; rites of passage; animals; friendship; secrets; anger; travel; violence; lying and deceit; revenge; mystery; death and dying; animals; love; fear; courage; gossip; betrayal; ethics; crime and delinquency; religion; manipulation; survival.

CHARACTERS

Todd Hewitt: he's the only boy in a town of men, men with a terrible secret

Manchee: Todd's dog, whose thoughts he can hear in his mind

Benison Moore/Ben: he and Cillian raised Todd after his parents died; he and Todd get along very well

Mr. Phelps: he runs the town store

Cillian Boyd: he bought Manchee for Todd's birthday, even though Todd didn't want a dog and doesn't get along with him at all

Aaron: he's the town preacher, and quite crazy

Mayor David Prentiss: he governs the town of Prentisstown and believes order can be brought to the Noise and that it can be harnessed and put to use

Mr. Hammer: he aims his noise right at you, and it's ugly Noise, angry Noise

Dr. Baldwin: he's the town doctor

Davy Prentiss, Jr.: he's the sheriff and locks up in his jail anyone his daddy tells him to

Mr. Turner: he didn't turn over enough of his corn crop to the mayor, so he got thrown in jail

Viola Eade: the girl Todd finds in the swamp, who carries a strange silence with her

Matilda/Hildy: an old woman whose bridge they burned down, and who takes them to Farbranch

Tam: Hildy's husband, who's a Noisy Man

Matthew Lyle: he tries to keep Todd out of Farbranch

Francia: deputy mayor of Farbranch and Hildy's sister

Ivan: he puts Todd to work in the barn at Farbranch

Wilf: he gives them a ride into Bar Vista

Jane: she's traveling with Wilf

Doctor Snow: the doctor in Carbonel Downs who treats Todd

Jacob: Dr. Snow's four-year-old son

BOOKTALK

I'm the youngest person in Prentisstown. I'm a month away from my thirteenth birthday, when I'll become a man. There aren't any women any more—the Noise germ killed them all. There were just men and boys left, and I'm the last boy. It's not a bad place to live, but it would be better without the Noise. Being able to hear what everyone is thinking and feeling all the time, and not being able to turn it off or down, is a real pain. And there's nowhere to go where you can't hear it—'cause you can even hear the thoughts of all the animals around you—and there's nothing else in the world but Prentisstown and the swamp. That's why it was so strange to find a big bubble of Quiet out in the swamp. A hole in the Noise, a hole where there can't be a hole. A Quiet where there can't be a Quiet. And it seems to pull me to it, and suddenly I feel like I'm going to lose the most important thing in my life, and then I'm running, running, running, to get away from it.

And then I'm home and I'm telling Ben and Cillian about the Quiet, and suddenly Ben says, "You have to get away from here. You have to get away *now*!!" And he gets a bag and starts putting food into it, and a medical kit, while Cillian is in the other room, pulling up floorboards to expose a packed knapsack. I tell them I don't want to leave, but it makes no difference. Then when my bag is almost full, the sheriff knocks on the door. He wants to ask me about the Quiet in the swamp. Cillian went outside to distract him, and Ben hustled me out the back door and toward the swamp. I sure did want to know what was going on and how they knew to have all my things packed and hidden away. But I never expected to know that Ben and Cillian had had a plan for me to escape, and I never expected Ben to share with me what really happened when a boy turned thirteen. It was terrifying and horrible and I could hardly believe it. But Ben didn't lie, so I had to believe it. He showed me a map, hidden in the book he put into my knapsack, with directions to the next town. And just about that time, there was a huge BOOM from the direction of our farm, and Ben grabbed me and said, "Follow the map, and go as fast as you can. Don't turn back. Keep your promise—follow the map. I'll find you if I can. Now go!" And that was it. I knew looking into his eyes and listening to his Noise, that I'd never see him or Cillian again. This was goodbye, unwanted, unexpected, but goodbye just the same. I was on my own.

Hours later, when I got to the place where the Quiet had been, I saw it, something I'd never seen before in real life, just in pictures. It was a girl. A real girl. A girl who didn't speak, and who was terrified of Manchee, my dog, who was barking at her frantically. Where had she come from, and what did she have to do with the silence that surrounded her?

MAJOR THEMES AND IDEAS
- It's important to remember who you are, because sometimes it gets lost in all the Noise.
- Men lie, and they lie to themselves most of all.
- Roads aren't always the best way to get somewhere fast.
- The Noise isn't the truth—it's what men *want* to be true.
- On your thirteenth birthday, you become a man.
- The Noise is a man unfiltered, and without a filter, a man is just chaos walking.
- In a country where everyone can hear your thoughts, knowledge is a dangerous thing.
- In the Noise, everything that ever happened to you keeps right on talking, forever and ever.
- Sometimes, the only place you belong is the place you can never go back to.
- When you can't say everything, it's better if you say nothing.
- A girl is completely different from a boy.
- A knife isn't just a thing, it's a choice, something you *do*. A knife says yes or no, cut or don't, die or not.
- When luck ain't with you, it's against you.

- Some men are just too mean to die.
- Time goes on, even when you aren't thinking about it.
- History is less important when you are spending all your time trying to survive.
- People are scared of what they don't know. But once they get to know you, the fear goes away.
- It's better to make your own decisions than letting someone else make them for you.
- Sometimes good news has bad news coming along behind it.
- There's only forward, only outward and up.
- Knowing a man's mind isn't knowing the man.
- Sometimes there are things you know you have to do, no matter how difficult, so you just do them.
- Life doesn't go backwards. You have to live with what you've done and find a way to deal with it.
- When it's two against an army, there's no question about what to do—you just run as fast as you can.
- Some choices are between losing and losing, not losing and winning. Sometimes there is no good choice.
- Guessing about something isn't the same as knowing about it.
- All you can do is your best at the time. Everyone makes mistakes that they have to live with.
- There's hope waiting for you at the end of the road.
- You can accomplish great things if you have hope.
- It's important to tell the truth, but the truth has many sides—which part of the truth is the right one to tell?
- Too much information can drive men mad when there's no way to get away from it, and it never stops.
- War is a monster. It starts and grows and grows, and it makes men into monsters as well.
- Doing what's right should be easy, but it almost never is.
- Life ain't fair, and there's not a thing to do about it.
- God works through men, but so does evil.

BOOK REPORT IDEAS

1. Discuss the relationship between Todd and Viola, and how it changes during the course of the book.
2. Explain why the men of Prentisstown are chasing Todd. Why is he so important to them?
3. Aaron is a man who is purely evil. How did he move from the man of God Todd's mother sees him as to the person he is in the book?
4. What could have been done to prevent the Prentisstown men from going on a killing spree? Who or what could have changed their minds?

5. Discuss what happened to the people of Farbranch and the other towns Todd and Viola went through. Were they slaughtered, or were they able to survive?
6. Speculate what is going to happen in the second book of this series. If Viola dies, Todd will have to fight on alone. Do you think he will be able to do that? Why or why not?
7. Many people have wondered what it would be like to know what their friends or family are thinking. Having read this book, how realistic do you think that is?
8. Compare the Noise in each of the towns Todd and Viola visited, starting with Prentisstown.
9. Speculate why Haven surrendered so easily and quickly, when it was supposed to be such a large and well-defended city.
10. Had Todd not felt the silence around Viola and had not met her, what do you think would have happened in a month when he went through the ritual of becoming a man?
11. What is the major theme of the book? The major lesson?

BOOKTALK IDEAS
1. Focus your talk on the idea of the Noise and never being alone.
2. Have Todd and Viola tell their story in alternating voices.
3. Use a picture of a knife similar to Todd's as a prop for the talk.
4. Focus your talk on the ritual of becoming a man and what it meant to Todd.

RISKS
- Homosexual characters
- Violence
- Prejudice
- Murder
- Obscenities
- Non-grammatical language and spelling
- Dog is brutally murdered
- Man of God is actually pure evil, demonstrating how a man can be completely corrupted
- Ending is also the end of hope
- Many brutal murders

STRENGTHS
- Suspense builds without let-up throughout the book
- Characters are three-dimensional and easy to identify with
- Narrator's voice is genuine and authentic
- Concept of the Noise draws reader into the book
- Shows that we all need a quiet place away from other people

- Shows the need for hope
- Powerful portrayal of the bonds between parents and children and between friends
- Realistic dialogue, including alternative spellings that characters might have used
- Demonstrates the importance of knowing how to read
- Combines a quest with a mystery
- Majority of the novel is very dark and compelling, especially the ending
- Excellent sense of place, including the new planet itself and each of the towns on it

REVIEWS

"Crack dramatic and comic timing . . . featuring one of the finest talking-dog characters anywhere, this troubling, unforgettable opener to the Chaos Walking trilogy is a penetrating look at the ways in which we reveal ourselves to one another, and what it takes to be a man in a society gone horribly wrong. The cliffhanger ending is as effective as a shot to the gut." Ian Chipman, *Booklist*, 9/08

"Ness's first contribution to young adult literature is mesmerizing . . . . His skillfully structured narrative creates an elegant mixture of action, dialogue, and dark, dystopian pathos. Steer this one to mature fans of Patrick Carman's House of Power series who want something darker and better written." Angelica Delgado, *VOYA*, 10/08

"This riveting SF thriller is action-packed, with edge-of-your-seat chase scenes, a monstrous villain who just won't die, and moments of both anguish and triumph. Todd must deal with learning the surprising truth about his world while wrestling with moral dilemmas: is he capable of killing? Emotionally intense, violent at times, this haunting page-turner may be awkwardly named, but it's a great read." Paula Rohrlick, *Kliatt*, 9/08

"Todd, who narrates in a vulnerable and stylized voice, is a sympathetic character who nevertheless makes a few wrenching mistakes. Tension, suspense, and the regular bombardment of Noise are palpable throughout, mitigated by occasional moments of welcome humor. The cliff-hanger ending is unexpected and unsatisfying, but the book is still a pleasure for sophisticated readers comfortable with the length and the bleak, literary tone." Megan Honig, New York Public Library *School Library Journal*, 11/08

ᘌ ᘌ ᘌ

LAST CHANCE TEXACO. Brent Hartinger. HarperTeen/HarperCollins, 2004. $15.99. 240p. ISBN10: 0060509120. ISBN13: 9780060509125. HarperTeen, 2005.

$7.99. 240p. ISBN10: 0060509147. ISBN13: 9780060509149. HarperTeen, 2004.
$16.89. 240p. ISBN10: 0060509139. ISBN13: 9780060509132. (library binding)
Realistic fiction. Reading Level: MS. Interest Level: MS, YHS. English, Psychology,
Sociology, Ethics.

SUBJECT AREAS
school; survival; therapy; violence; self-knowledge; self-destruction; rites of passage;
secrets; love; lying and deceit; mystery/suspense; peer pressure; friendship; fear;
anger; family relationships; grief and mourning; depression; dysfunctional family;
bullying; adoption.

CHARACTERS
Lucy Pitt: after being in foster care for eight years, Kindle Home is her last chance
   to turn herself around

Kindle Home Staff
Leon Dogman: he survived the foster care system when he was a teen
Ben and Gina: a married couple that runs Kindle Home and are the live-in counsel-
   ors
Mrs. Morgan: she's old and tough, and doesn't put up with any nonsense
Emil: the Kindle Home therapist
Megan/God: the program supervisor

Kindle Home Residents
Yolanda: Lucy's roommate; the girls all pick on her
Joy: she's trouble and likes to be at the top of the pecking order
Melanie: Joy's stooge; she has a crush on Eddy
Damon: the Mole; he has information on everyone
Eddy: the Cute One
Juan: the Big Lug
Roberto: the Cocky One and the Hothead
Alicia: she's rich, snobby, and hates "the groupies"
Nate Brandon: he's rich, a jock, and makes rude comments to Lucy
Margaret and Frank Kindle: they are contesting their father's will to get the house
   back from the social services system

BOOKTALK
When I arrived at Last Chance Texaco, aka Kindle Group Home, I was sure what
would be happening to me. After eight years in The System, moving from one group
home to another, I knew the drill. This one was the next-to-the-last stop for me. I was
pretty sure that within just a few days, I'd be outta here and off to Eat-Their-Young

Island, a prison for kids who couldn't make it anywhere else. They had locks on the doors and surveillance cameras and restraints on the beds. The only way anyone ever got out was by turning eighteen. I figured that since I was fifteen, I'd be on the island for three years. It was a lot longer than I'd been anywhere else since my family was killed in a car accident when I was seven.

But just because you think something's gonna happen doesn't make it so. And Kindle Home wasn't like the other group homes I'd been in and out of for years. It was unique, and so were the people who lived there.

MAJOR THEMES AND IDEAS

- A group home is a storage shed for broken teenagers, because you can't fix them, but you can't throw them away.
- When everything you own fits in one bag, you learn to keep a grip on it.
- Group homes have a pecking order, just like chickens. It's important not to be on the bottom.
- Put seven or eight broken teens in one room and sooner or later it'll get a little wild.
- Doing something different makes people look at you more carefully.
- High school isn't about anything real. It's not about who you are. It's a really major hoop you have to jump through—that's all.
- You only have to hear the truth once to know it's the truth.
- There's no good way to reply to a threat, except silence.
- If you let someone think they're the boss, they usually are.
- Never squeal to a counselor about what another kid did. Kids' punishment will be lots worse than anything a counselor will do.
- Kids have rules of their own, and they respect them a lot, even if they don't respect adult rules.
- If you're smart, you can always get another kid in trouble and not break any rules doing it.
- Kids almost always know when an adult is being straight with them, especially if it doesn't happen very often.
- Some adults take kids at face value, others prejudge them. It takes only an instant to make an enemy.
- In a group home, someone always says what's on everybody's mind. In many families, everyone ignores the problem instead.
- People who have been rejected over and over try to push people away and never get close to anyone, so they won't be rejected again.
- If it's politics, fair has nothing to do with it.
- Sometimes the only way to stop an out-of-control fire is with another one—a controlled burn, to take away the fire's fuel.
- Fires can be destructive, but they can also have strength and passion when they're controlled.
- Sometimes, you just gotta have a happy ending!

BOOK REPORT IDEAS

1. Compare and contrast Lucy when she arrived at Kindle Home and when the book ended.
2. Speculate about why Emil continued to do a job that obviously made him and others unhappy.
3. Lucy says several times that Kindle Home is unique. Discuss how and why it's different from other group homes she's been in.
4. Speculate on what Lucy's life will be like after Kindle Home. Will she be able to overcome her fear of rejection and let people love her?
5. Compare and contrast the counselors in the book. How were they different and alike?
6. Discuss the relationship between Nate and Lucy. How realistic was it? What made it either realistic or unrealistic?
7. There were several clues about the arsonist before it was revealed at the end of the book. What were they and did you figure them out as you were reading?

BOOKTALK IDEAS

1. Have some of the kids at Kindle Home introduce themselves and talk about Last Chance Texaco.
2. Let Lucy introduce several of the characters in the book.
3. Focus your talk on the mystery of the burning cars.
4. Center your talk around dinnertime on Lucy's first day.

RISKS

- Troubled teens act out violently
- Vicious and vindictive therapist
- Some stereotypical characters
- Portrays social service system in poor light
- Group home residents are bullied by other students and principal

STRENGTHS

- Teen learns self-control and gains insight
- Shows strong, concerned counselors
- Authentic picture of group home life
- Suspense is maintained
- Shows the response of teens who have been rejected over and over
- Authentic dialogue and action

AWARD

ALA Quick Picks for Reluctant Young Adult Readers, 2005

REVIEWS

"Hartinger does an excellent job of addressing the 'lost cause' feelings of a teen trapped in the foster care system. Readers will root for Lucy as she fights for her new life." Ruth E. Cox, *VOYA*, 2/04

"Hartinger clearly knows the culture, and Lucy speaks movingly . . . about her anger and grief as well as about the other troubled kids." Hazel Rochman, *Booklist*, 1/04

"Hartinger excels at giving readers an insider's view of the subculture, with its myriad unspoken rules created by the kids, not the system. There is a touch of romance and mystery, and . . . the memorable aspect of the novel is the way it takes readers inside a system most of them have never experienced." Faith Brautigam, Gail Borden Public Library, Elgin, IL, *School Library Journal*, 3/04

📖📖📖

THE LAST DOMINO. Adam Meyer. Putnam Juvenile, 2005. $16.99. 272p. ISBN10: 0399243321. ISBN13: 9780399243325. Realistic fiction. Reading Level: YHS. Interest Level: YHS, OHS. English, P.E., Psychology.

SUBJECT AREAS

school; violence; death and dying; friendship; manipulation; working; secrets; crime and delinquency; problem parents; lying and deceit; guns; anger; bullying; dysfunctional family; gossip; intimidation; justice; peer pressure; revenge; sports.

CHARACTERS

Travis Ellroy: a junior in high school whose brother committed suicide
PJ Riley: an athlete who loves to hassle Travis and Sheriff Riley's son
Jordan Beaumont: an athlete with a blown-out knee; he works at Coffee Time with Travis
Amy Hasselman: she dates Jordan and dislikes Travis
Lee Kartinski, Missy Relling, Sean Delany, Tiffany Ersted: kids in Travis's class
Karyn Walker: prettiest girl in school, who's nice to Travis
Daniel Pulver: the new kid, who makes friends with Travis
Detective Upshaw: New York State policeman
Moira and Ross Lansbury: twins who have been friends of Travis's for years
Toby Danzig: she works at Coffee Time
Gus Benedict: he's the manager of Coffee Time
Taffy: PJ's girlfriend who's always been one of the popular kids
Principal Lyle McCarthy: the high school principal

Beth Kittinger: she's the new school guidance counselor and has known Travis for years

Laurel Zito: a friend of Karyn's

Dr. Hawke: therapist Travis's mother goes to

Eleanor and Thomas Ellroy: Travis's parents, who fight constantly and compare him to his older brother Richie, who committed suicide five years ago

Mrs. Saxon: it's the third year she's been Travis's English teacher

Ted Burnitz, Gil Schlom: football players

Dana La Bret: a cheerleader who dates Gil

Madeline Pulver: Daniel's mother

Max Monroe: a high school student who's into heavy metal

Craig Pulver: Daniel's father

Mrs. Barker: Daniel's next door neighbor, who has a little dog named Alfie

Mrs. Burrows: the principal's secretary

Sheriff Eugene Riley: he thinks Travis is a troublemaker and a broken kid

Sebastian Toye: Travis's lawyer

BOOKTALK

The first day of school my junior year, and I was late. When I finally got to class, the new kid, Daniel, had taken my seat. I didn't know it then, but that was when the countdown started. Sixteen days to go.

Daniel was skinny, like me, and we started being friends right away. But he didn't put up with all the stuff that I just tried to endure—he pushed back, and he made me want to push back, too. And the angry voice inside my head told me that he had the right idea. So I pushed back with words, with my fists, with a tire iron, and sixteen days from that first day of school, the day I met Daniel, I fought back with a gun.

How did I go from a loser nerd to a school shooter in just over two weeks? Daniel was a good teacher, and I had a lot to learn.

MAJOR THEMES AND IDEAS

- Sometimes you can't wait for things to come to you. You have to go after them, especially things you really want.
- Shooting a gun can make you feel powerful.
- Once a line of dominoes starts falling, they can't be stopped.
- Picking on someone just because he won't fight back isn't a good idea. Sooner or later, he'll decide to stand his ground.
- Friends are the people who have your back—always.
- Parents frequently don't know what their children think or do, and see only what they choose to see.
- If someone encourages you to do things that hurt you, he isn't your friend.
- Sometimes, evil wins.

- Persuading someone to believe the lies you tell them is easy, if they are willing to listen.
- A gun is a deadly thing, especially in the hands of a hurt and angry teenager.
- Once you hit the tipping point, there's no turning back.

BOOK REPORT IDEAS

1. Comment on Ross's statement about dominoes. What were the dominoes in Travis's life?
2. Travis hears an angry voice in his head—who is it? What does it represent?
3. Speculate on what might have happened if Daniel hadn't moved to town. Would Travis have found a way to cope with his anger, or was he already too far gone?
4. At the end of the book, Daniel is revealed as a sociopathic personality. Looking back on his two-week relationship with Travis, at what points did he give glimpses of what he was really like beneath the surface.
5. Speculate on what the students who were in school with Travis learned from those sixteen days. Will they be different, or will another Travis be treated just as he was?
6. We don't know if PJ lived or died. If he lived, do you think he and his father ever recognized their roles in Travis's revenge?
7. Discuss how realistic this story is. Do you know kids like Travis? PJ? Moira? Ross? Daniel?
8. Examine the roles of adults and especially parents, in this story, what they see and don't see, what they believe or ignore.
9. What did the rock-throwing incident really mean to Travis? What did it say about him?

BOOKTALK IDEAS

1. Write your talk as if you were Detective Upshaw, trying to piece together what happened and why.
2. Use excerpts from the interviews to create a picture of Travis.
3. Center your talk around the timeline of the book.

RISKS

- Parents idolize dead son and don't see the problems their other son is having
- Teen shoplifts
- Bullying
- Realistic language
- Teen shoots parents, classmates, and teachers
- Teen manipulates another boy to acts of violence
- Torturing and killing a dog

- Parents are manipulated by their children
- Manipulative teen exemplifies pure evil
- Bullied, manipulated teen gets revenge
- Dysfunctional parents
- Physically abusive parents

STRENGTHS
- Powerful depiction of how easily a vulnerable teen can be manipulated
- Shows how little parents can understand their children
- Dangers of bullying
- Three-dimensional characters with strengths and flaws
- Taut, suspenseful storyline draws reader in immediately
- Brilliant, chilling portrait of psychopath/sociopath
- Realistic language

AWARD
ALA Quick Picks for Reluctant Young Adult Readers, 2006

REVIEWS
"This story reveals the first-person downslide of a mentally and emotionally needy teenager while integrating the points of view of others via interviews. It is an unnerving depiction beyond common definitions of 'peer pressure.' The psychological undermining of Travis and the book's chilling conclusion are heartbreaking, just like the all too frequent real events in the news." Diane Tuccillo, *VOYA*, 8/05

"Meyer clearly communicates that insane crimes have reasons, and that the only sad certainty is that they can happen anywhere." Joel Shoemaker, Southeast Junior High School, Iowa City, IA, *School Library Journal*, 11/05

"Obviously, the subject matter isn't for every teen reader, but the social psychology is compelling, making the book a good springboard for discussion with mature teens, who will be able to see how the details of Travis' bloody spree bring relationships into sharp focus." Francisca Goldsmith, *Booklist*, 9/05

⊞ ⊞ ⊞

THE LAST MALL RAT. Erik E. Esckilson. Houghton Mifflin, 2003. $15.00. 192p. ISBN10: 0618234179. ISBN13: 9780618234172. Houghton Mifflin, 2005. $5.95.

192p. ISBN10: 0618608966. ISBN13: 9780618608966. Realistic fiction. Reading Level: MS. Interest Level: MS, YHS. English, Ethics, Journalism, Government.

SUBJECT AREAS
crime and delinquency; friendship; working; racism; substance abuse; problem parents; child abuse; gangs; school; homelessness; anger; intimidation; secrets; self-knowledge; runaways; peer pressure; rites of passage; lying and deceit; gossip; dysfunctional families; divorce and separation.

CHARACTERS
Mitch Grant: a sophomore in high school; he was just looking for a way to make some money

The Chair: the best salesman in the mall; he can get someone from "just looking" to trying on shoes faster than anyone else

Mom/Sal Grant: Mitch's mother

Mr. La Gasse: Mitch's history teacher

Dad/Reg Grant: Mitch's dad, who is separated from Sal

Page: an athlete and a friend of Mitch's

Keith Sullivan: a senior and a basketball star who works at the mall

Jimmy Biggins: a troublemaker who's Mitch's oldest friend

Stu: security guard at the mall

Lance Hungerford: mall security chief

Maggie St. Germaine: she runs Hattie's Attic

Marcus Walker: one of the three black kids at school and one of Mitch's best friends

Armand: a mall security guard

Andy Briggs, Brian Bigelow, Mavis Carter, Brenda Allen, Sheila Burke, Louise Carruccio: they all work at the mall

Captain Freynne: he hears Mitch, Page, and Marcus confess what they did

BOOKTALK
It was a good deal from the first. After my dad lost his job and moved out, my mom and I had a hard time. No allowance. No extras. So when the Chair offered me an Alexander Hamilton to pay back a woman who's been a major pain-in-the-neck customer, I went for it. I'd watched the way she's treated the Chair, like he was dirt under her feet, and she deserved some payback.

And, after all, I really didn't *do* anything to her. I just followed her to her car and got in her face, saying "Caveat emptor" over and over in my creepiest voice. She freaked and ran to get in her car. It felt good.

I let my best friends in on it too, and pretty soon all the kids who worked at the mall were just throwing money at us to deal with customers that were just plain mean to them. And just like that, we were cool, the heroes of the school, the Mall Mafia.

But you know what they say about what goes up, must go down? It wasn't long until folks started coming down on us, and we had to figure out how to handle a situation that was suddenly *way* out of control.

MAJOR THEMES AND IDEAS
- Some people seem to get off on being mean to someone they consider their inferior.
- Let the buyer beware.
- It pays to be in the right place at the right time.
- When someone who was rude to you gets taken down a peg or two, it feels good.
- Insult or be insulted.
- In life, you don't get what you deserve. You get what you negotiate for.
- It feels good to fight back at your oppressor.
- If doing something just feels wrong, even just thinking about it, it probably is wrong.
- News stories are not always completely accurate, if implications and innuendos can make the story seem bigger and more important.
- Sometimes it doesn't take much for a situation to spin out of control.
- People make mistakes. It's what we do.
- Payback can be a real pain sometimes.
- Frequently it's best to confess what you did, pay the price, and get on with your life.
- A lesson is what you get when you don't get what you want.
- A teen with violent, abusive parents is probably also violent and abusive.

BOOK REPORT IDEAS
1. Discuss Jimmy and what his life was like. How did his home life affect how he saw himself? Speculate about the kind of man he might become, given his experiences during the first fourteen years of his life.
2. Discuss how quickly Marcus, Page, and Mitch become "cool" at school. Will they maintain that status in the future? Why or why not?
3. Discuss the way the situation went out of control, when it happened, why, and how.
4. None of the four original "Mall Mafia" got away with what they did, but none of the mall employees were punished. Discuss the ethics and appropriateness of this. Should Mitch and his friends have revealed the names of the people who paid them, especially the Chair?
5. In one sense, the rude people at the mall were getting what they deserve. Does that make frightening them less wrong?
6. If you had been a student at that high school, what would you have done when the news about the mall came out?

7. It is clear that the local paper slants the news it reports. Compare the truth to what appears in the paper, and comment on the editor's ethical choices.

BOOKTALK IDEAS

1. Use a ten-dollar bill, or several of them, as a prop for your talk.
2. Have each of the four main characters introduce themselves and justify what they did at the mall.
3. Write your talk as if it were a news story.

RISKS

- Teens harass and verbally attack strangers for money
- Alcoholic parents abuse sons
- Racists and racism
- Teen makes deals with the police
- Teens form gangs to harass shoppers
- Police ignore abusive situation
- Unethical mall employees pay for payback to rude customers

STRENGTHS

- Shows power of friendship
- Teens take responsibility for their own actions
- Authentic teen voices
- Shows how quickly situations can escalate out of control
- Shows power of group thinking, being a part of a mob
- Separated parents treat other with respect and work together to help their son
- At-risk teen is given a second chance

AWARD

International Reading Association Notable Book, 2003

REVIEWS

"Young people will identify with why the money-making venture of Mitch and his friends has so much appeal. . . . They will find a book that is well written." Elaine J. O'Quinn, *VOYA*, 6/03

"This clever, believable first novel captures teen boredom and frustration, while never evading the moral issues. . . . Realistic dialogue and a keen sense of what matters to teens will draw them to this quick read." Debbie Carton, *Booklist*, 4/03

"This is a thoughtful exploration of the mistakes even ordinary teens can make and—in sometimes frightening fashion—the ways in which one's actions can lead to serious and unintended consequences." Coop Renner, Blackshear Elementary School, Austin, TX, *School library Journal*, 6/03

📖📖📖

LITTLE BROTHER. Cory Doctorow. Tor, 2008. $17.95. 384p. ISBN: 9780765319852. Science fiction. Reading Level: YHS. Interest Level:YHS, OHS. English, Ethics, History, Government, Sociology, Psychology.

SUBJECT AREAS
government; politics; terrorism; fear; computers; friendship; school; betrayal; love; intimidation; lying and deceit; family relationships; sex and sexuality; rites of passage; self-knowledge; secrets; violence; peer pressure; activism; bullying; gossip; justice; legal system; manipulation; ethnic groups; prejudice; war.

CHARACTERS
Marcus Yallow/w1n5t0n: a high school senior who's at the wrong place at the wrong time

Fred Benson: a vice principal at Cesar Chavez High School in San Francisco, who's fairly clueless

Ms. Galvez: Marcus's social studies teacher

Darryl Glover: Marcus's best friend and team member, whom Marcus gets in and out of trouble regularly

Vanessa Pak: she's on Marcus's Harajuku team

Charles Walker: he's a bully and the biggest snitch in school

Jose-Luis/Jolu Torrez: he's also on Marcus's team

"Severe Haircut Lady"/Carrie Johnstone: member of the Department of Homeland Security, who questions and tortures Marcus

Drew Yallow/Dad: Marcus's father, who's a librarian

Lillian Yallow/Mom: Marcus's mother, who is British

The Turk: Marcus gets coffee from his shop everyday on his way to school

Booger and Zit: two cops who follow Marcus because he has a non-average travel profile

Major General Graeme Sutherland: Regional Commander of Department of Homeland Security, Northern California

Kurt Rooney: the president's chief strategist

Ange Carvelli: a friend of Jolu's who comes to the key exchange party and goes to the same school Van goes to

Mrs. Anderson: the teacher who replaces Ms. Galvez

Mrs. Carvelli: Ange's mother

Tina Carvelli: Ange's little sister, who'd do anything for her big sister
Zeb: a homeless guy Marcus runs into who is a lot more together than he looks
Ron Glover: Darryl's father, who thinks his son is dead
Barbara Stratford: an investigative reporter for the *Bay Guardian*
Nate and Liam: two Xnetters who are thrilled about the chance to help Marcus

BOOKTALK
It wasn't an attempt to overthrow the government. They weren't terrorists. They weren't members of any kind of conspiracy. They were kids, ditching school to play a computer game on the streets of San Francisco. Harajuku Fun Madness was an Alternate Reality Game that required you to find places and things in real life. Marcus, Darryl, Van, and Jolu were about to figure out a clue when they were caught on camera by a rival team. Seconds later, they heard a huge explosion and the ground trembled as if there'd been an earthquake. And then the civil defense sirens started, so loud no one could think, and they could see a black cloud of smoke forming over the bay. Suddenly, announcements spoke over the noise of the sirens: REPORT TO SHELTER IMMEDIATELY! REPORT TO SHELTER IMMEDIATELY! Marcus and the others headed to the BART station, thinking it would be safer than being on the streets. They were caught in the stampeding crowd for only a few minutes before they realized that they were in far greater danger than they were on the street. Getting out of the station and up the stairs to the street was a nightmare, but they finally made it. But almost immediately, Darryl collapsed. He'd been stabbed by someone in the crowd, and was bleeding out rapidly. Marcus tried to stop ambulances and police cars as they hurtled past the group on the bench by the BART station, but none of them even slowed down. He decided that he would just jump in front of the next car and not move, so they'd have to stop. It was a good idea, and it worked. But Marcus hadn't stopped a police car or an ambulance, he'd stopped a Hummer full of members of the Department of Homeland Security, and everyone was immediately taken into custody. Now, what had seemed like a nightmare turned into one. When Marcus refused to give his interrogators the password to his phone, or to anything else that he had in his backpack, they decided that he was a terrorist and had helped to bomb the Bay Bridge, the source of the black cloud they'd all seen. He was not allowed a phone call, he was not allowed a lawyer, he was not allowed to know what had happened to his friends, he was not allowed even to go to the bathroom. He was questioned, and when he refused to reveal anything he considered private, he was locked in a cell, his arms handcuffed behind him and his ankles shackled, and left there. He had no way to tell time, and he had only his imagination for company. Finally, after days of threats and torture, he broke, and gave his interrogators everything they wanted to know. Then they set him free, warning him that they would be watching him, and that if he told anyone, even his parents, what had happened to him, they would take steps that would make the previous four days seem like child's play.

Unfortunately, they had underestimated Marcus's intelligence, his skill with a computer, and finally, his anger. By the time they realized that they'd made a terrible mistake, it was much too late. Marcus had begun his retaliation.

MAJOR THEMES AND IDEAS

- Almost every computer can be outwitted.
- Terrorists can look like anyone, including your next door neighbor.
- Being in the wrong place at the wrong time can be very dangerous.
- Almost any behavior can appear suspicious, no matter how innocent it actually is.
- The mere possession of information doesn't imply guilt.
- Even honest people can have something to hide.
- You have a right to keep information private or secret, especially personal information.
- Most people have everything and nothing to hide.
- Free speech is not a crime. Neither is having, possessing, information.
- If you watch someone closely enough and long enough, he or she will do something that appears suspicious.
- There should be parts of your life that no one can get to see but you. That's not about doing something wrong or shameful. It's about the right to be private, to keep some things secret.
- Terrorists enjoy scaring people.
- There is nothing that adults can come up with that technologically savvy children and teens cannot evade or invalidate.
- Never underestimate the determination of a kid who is time-rich and cash-poor.
- If you use it right, technology can give you privacy and power.
- If you really want to be in charge of your computer, you have to learn to write code.
- Adults forget what it's like being a teen, under suspicion 24/7.
- Don't trust anyone over twenty-five.
- Anyone can design a security system he can't break into. But it's safe only as long as someone smarter doesn't break into it.
- Only bad security depends on secrecy. Good security works even if all the details about it are public.
- We win freedom by having the courage and conviction to win every day freely and to act as a free society, no matter how great the threats on the horizon.
- Enough people, enough determination, and you can change the world.
- When the cops have to decide whether or not to treat a mob like the ordinary people they are or like terrorists, they frequently choose the terrorist option.
- Sometimes your brain gives you solutions as well as problems.
- There's no way to control a mob, even with the best of intentions.
- Freedom is something you have to take for yourself.

- When you're upset, angry, betrayed, take action—but choose your action wisely. Carefully considered plans give the best results, the maximum impact.
- Revenge is a dish best served cold.

BOOK REPORT IDEAS

1. Choose one of the projects or technologies Marcus discusses and investigate it. Has the author used what is real, rather than something that doesn't exist?
2. Compare Marcus at the beginning of the book with the person he was at the end of it, and discuss the ways he has changed, and changed his world.
3. Discuss the DHS and the privileges that it holds. How much of this novel could be true?
4. Compare the activists from the 1970s and today, and discuss how much they had in common.
5. Examine the role of the media in the book and how a huge story is created from just a few facts.
6. Marcus says that Darryl isn't the only one who was broken by the DHS. Explain what he means by that.
7. Speculate on what will happen after the end of the book, to the characters, to the Bay Area, and to the country.
8. Investigate whether any LARPs were actually played in San Francisco hotels. Do the same for ARGs. How accurately did the author describe them?
9. Critics have called this novel didactic, something that teaches lessons. What lessons have you learned from it, and what do you intend to do because of those lessons?
10. Examine the idea of patriotism as it is depicted in the book. Who is patriotic, who isn't, and how each of the major characters, including DHS members, defines it.
11. If you had been one of Marcus's group, what would you have done—stick by him, or back away? Explain why you made that choice.
12. Create a timeline from the dates mentioned in the book, and show what our society has learned and not learned from our history.
13. Discuss the reactions of Marcus's parents to his return and then to the actions of the DHS.
14. Define your understanding of some of the terms in the book, and show how reading it changed or didn't change your understanding of them: for instance, truth, reality, freedom, choice, terrorist, patriot.
15. Explain why this book could come true or couldn't come true.

BOOKTALK IDEAS

1. Use some of the technology from the book as props or to help you deliver the talk.
2. Write Marcus's story as if it was one of the games he liked to play.

3. Use some of the newspaper and television stories in the book as part of your talk.
4. Focus your talk around the idea of secrets and how they can separate people.
5. Let each of the Harajuku players in Marcus's game introduce themselves, some of them before they were captured, and some afterwards.
6. Feature some or all of the passwords from the book in your talk.

RISKS
- Characters rebel against a federal agency
- Negative portrayal of government and its employees
- Characters are considered guilty without the benefit of a lawyer, a trial, or a jury
- Teens are sexually active
- Police and paramilitary personnel use violent methods to break up mobs
- Characters are jailed for no cause
- Characters, including teens and minorities, are tortured in a variety of ways
- Explains what to do to rebel against government surveillance
- Teens hide their activities from their parents
- Makes heroes out of hackers
- Teens figure out how to outwit security systems of all kinds
- Encourages teens to think suspiciously and negatively about their government's measures to protect them and keep them secure
- Media overreacts to situations with little threat to them the same way it does in a genuine disaster

STRENGTHS
- Characters are realistic and three-dimensional, allowing readers to identify with them
- Clear and seemingly accurate information about how to use technology against the government
- Dialogue is realistic, including slang and obscenities
- Premise of the book hooks readers from the first page
- Suspense doesn't falter and is maintained until the last page
- Powerful depiction of the freedoms we have lost since 9/11
- People begin to change their minds about what the government is doing when they discover the whole truth
- Almost all sexual activity happens offstage
- Many ideas about our society and its government to consider and ponder
- Many opportunities for discussion resulting in changes in thinking
- Hero of the book is not one of the popular crowd, but a self-proclaimed geek
- Intelligence, especially computer-related intelligence, is seen as good and valuable

- Hero is attracted to heroine by her intelligence, courage, and determination, not just her appearance
- Novel is didactic, but powerfully written, engaging the reader's emotions as well as intellect

AWARDS
ALA Best Books for Young Adults, 2009
Booklist Editor's Choice, 2008
SLJ Best Books for Children, 2008

REVIEWS
"Through the voice of his young protagonist, the author manages to explain naturally the necessary technical tools and scientific concepts in this fast-paced and well-written story. . . .The reader is privy to Marcus's gut-wrenching angst, frustration, and terror, thankfully offset by his self-awareness and humorous observations. As with 'Big Brother' in George Orwell's 1984, this book will motivate the reader to contemplate free speech, due process, and political activism with new insights." Lynne Farrell Stover, *VOYA*, 4/1/08

"Filled with sharp dialogue and detailed descriptions of how to counteract gait-recognition cameras, arphids (radio frequency ID tags), wireless Internet tracers and other surveillance devices, this work makes its admittedly didactic point within a tautly crafted fictional framework." *Publishers Weekly*, 4/14/08

"Doctorow's novel blurs the lines between current and potential technologies, and readers will delight in the details of how Markus attempts to stage a techno revolution. Obvious parallels to Orwellian warnings and post-9/11 policies, such as the Patriot Act, will provide opportunity for classroom discussion and raise questions about our enthusiasm for technology, who monitors our school library collections, and how we contribute to our own lack of privacy. An extensive Web and print bibliography will build knowledge and make adults nervous." *Booklist*, 4/1/08

"Unapologetically didactic tribute to *1984*. . . . Long passages of beloved tech-guru Doctorow's novel are unabashedly educational, detailing the history of computing, how to use anti-surveillance software and anarchist philosophies. Yet in the midst of all this overt indoctrination, Marcus exists as a fully formed character, whose adolescent loves and political intrigues are compelling for more than just propagandistic reasons. Terrifying glimpse of the future—or the present." *Kirkus Reviews*, 4/1/08

"One afterword by a noted cryptologist and another from an infamous hacker further reflect Doctorow's principles, and a bibliography has resources for teens interested in intellectual freedom, information access, and technology enhancements. Curious readers will also be able to visit BoingBoing, an eclectic group blog that Doctorow coedits. Raising pertinent questions and fostering discussion, this techno-thriller is an outstanding first purchase." Chris Shoemaker, New York Public Library *School Library Journal*, 5/1/08

📖📖📖

LIVING DEAD GIRL. Elizabeth Scott. Simon Pulse, 2008. $16.99. 176p. ISBN10: 1416960597. ISBN13: 9781416960591. Simon Pulse, 2009. $8.99. 176p. ISBN10: 1416960600. ISBN13: 9781416960607. Realistic fiction. Reading Level: MS. Interest Level: YHS, OHS. English, Psychology, Sex Education.

SUBJECT AREAS
violence; survival; sex and sexuality; intimidation; lying and deceit; manipulation; obsession; rape; secrets; fear; crime and delinquency; child abuse; betrayal; anger; abuse, physical and sexual; suicide.

CHARACTERS
Alice: she was kidnapped five years ago, when she was ten
Ray: the man who kidnapped and imprisoned Alice
Lucy/Annabel: a little girl in the park
Jake: Lucy's brother
Barbara: a cop who patrols the park Alice goes to

BOOKTALK
Once upon a time, I did not live in Shady Pines Apartments. Once upon a time, my name was not Alice. Once upon a time, I didn't know how lucky I was. Once upon a time, when I was ten, a man at the aquarium said he'd show me to the movie theatre, where the rest of my class was. Once upon a time, that was the moment when my world and my life ended.

Now I am fifteen, and my name is Alice, and for five years I have lived with Ray. He makes sure I don't eat too much, so I stay very thin, less than a hundred pounds. He likes little girls, and I have to struggle to look like one, because I am getting old for him. The girl who was Alice before me was killed when she was fifteen. But before he kills me, he needs my help to find a new Alice. Then I will help him train her, and hold her down so she will get all his love, so there will be none left for me. I cannot save myself and I do not want to save her.

When he has his new little girl, he will not need me, and I will die. I don't know how he will do it, and he doesn't know how much I yearn for it—the peace, the silence, the solitude. I won't have to force my body to look like a little girl's, or remember to lie still, eyes on the ceiling, when he gets on top of me. And in the house on Daisy Lane, where I lived once upon a time, everyone will be safe at last. When I am gone, Ray won't ever need to hurt them, the way he has threatened to for all these years. Is it wrong for me to yearn for death? I hope not, because anything will be better than the life I have now.

MAJOR THEMES AND IDEAS
- People see what they want to see and don't probe beneath the surface for the truth.
- An adult's threats of retribution can force obedience from a child.
- Monsters masquerade as the man next door, normal and non-threatening.
- You can get used to anything if you have enough time, and no other choice.
- People blame the kidnapped girls for not running or not asking for help. And the girls, now women, still broken, are still ready to accept the blame.
- Some people are missing something inside. They look like people, but if you look closer, you can see they're rotted out inside.
- That's the thing about your body: it doesn't want to die—hearts keep beating, lungs keep breathing, even when your brain is ready to let go.
- Three life lessons: No one will see you. No one will say anything. No one will save you. And one more: Now you have to pay.
- Most people, children or adults, are willing to hurt someone else if it reduces their own pain.
- Broken girls will do anything. They are empty inside and nothing will fill them.
- Even if someone is charming, with a wide smile and a sunny happy expression, they can still be rotten underneath, dead inside.
- Everyone says they want to help, but no one ever does. Instead, they just turn away and go on with their lives.

BOOK REPORT IDEAS
1. Discuss what kept Alice from running when Ray left her alone.
2. Explain why you think this book is important and why teens should read it and libraries own it.
3. Speculate on what Ray would have done had Alice run from him as a fifteen-year-old. Would he actually have burned down her family's house? Or would he have just written her off and relocated.
4. How did Ray have power over Alice? How did she have power over him?
5. What can be done to stop men like Ray from abducting little girls?
6. What happened in the end? What is the meaning of the last sentence, and why do you believe that?
7. Explain why you think Ray was never caught, in spite of being only four hours from Alice's home.

8. The police now issue Amber Alerts when children are reported missing. How might that have made a difference in this situation? (Remember, she'd been alone for a while when Ray found her.) Include information on what Amber Alerts are and why they were created.

9. Discuss some of the things a child about six to ten years old could do to prevent their being abducted.

10. Speculate on what happened after the end of the book. Was Alice dead, or did she survive? What was her life like if she did survive? What were Lucy's and Jake's lives like? How did meeting Alice change them? How did it change Barbara? The people from the apartment complex?

BOOKTALK IDEAS

1. Write your talk as if it were a news article on Alice's disappearance.
2. Include some actual statistics on missing children from your state or region.
3. Write part of your talk as Alice when she was ten or eleven, and part when she was fifteen. (Remember she's almost become another person by the time we meet her.)
4. Use a picture of a very thin girl, Alice, to illustrate your talk.
5. Figure out what Alice was allowed to eat in one day, and take a picture of it to use as a prop. To make a bigger contrast, take a picture of what an average teen eats in one day.

RISKS

- Serial pedophile kidnaps and repeatedly rapes little girls
- Girls are forbidden to eat so they stay thin and have their pubic hair removed to appear prepubescent
- Threats to hurt their families make terrified girls compliant and obedient
- Kidnapped girl is willing to help kidnap her replacement, if it means her rapes stop
- Horrifying and repugnant subject matter

STRENGTHS

- A perspective not represented previously
- First-person narration draws in reader immediately
- Graphic details give depth and realism
- Horrific story may mean more wary children and fewer abductions
- Unresolved ending provides opportunity for discussion about what happened and if anyone was killed
- Understated and flat emotional tone makes the crime/situation even more horrific

AWARDS
ALA Best Books for Young Adults, 2009
ALA Quick Picks for Reluctant Young Adult Readers, 2009
Bulletin Blue Ribbons, 2008

REVIEWS
"Scott does a tremendous job of showing the pervasive sexual and physical abuse Alice suffers without being graphic. If anything the subtlety of the descriptions is even more haunting than a detailed description would have been. This book is one of those rare novels that is difficult to read but impossible to put down and should not be missed." Vikki Terrile, *VOYA*, 2/09

"Scott's prose is spare and damning, relying on suggestive details and their impact on Alice to convey the unimaginable violence she repeatedly experiences. Disturbing but fascinating, the book exerts an inescapable grip on readers—like Alice, they have virtually no choice but to continue until the conclusion sets them free." *Publishers Weekly*, 9/08

"I was knocked over by *Living Dead Girl*. Most authors want to hear 'I couldn't put it down' from their fans. *Living Dead Girl* is a book you have to put down; then you have to pick it right back up. The beauty of this story is that, though none of its readers will have had this experience, all will feel connected to it. It is told in the rarest of air, yet speaks horrifically to all our imaginations." Chris Crutcher, author of *Staying Fat for Sarah Byrnes* and *Deadline*

"Alice tells her story in a flat, curt voice that reflects her emptiness and despair, and the lurid details of Ray's sexual and physical abuse are suggested obliquely in a matter-of-fact style that is more horrifying than actual graphic description . . . A thoroughly unpleasant but magnetic read, Scott's novel is repellent in exact proportion to the brilliance of its execution." *Horn Book Magazine*, 11/08

THE LONG NIGHT OF LEO AND BREE. Ellen Wittlinger. Simon and Schuster, 2002. $15.00. 128p. ISBN10: 0689835647. ISBN13: 9780689835643. Simon Pulse, 2003. $6.99. 128p. ISBN10: 0689863357. ISBN13: 9780689863356. Tandem Library, 2003. $15.80. 128p. ISBN10: 0613734335. ISBN13: 9780613734332. (library binding) Realistic fiction. Reading Level: MS. Interest Level: MS, YHS. English, Ethics, Psychology.

SUBJECT AREAS

death and dying; grief and mourning; problem parents; self-knowledge; family relationships; mental illness; anger; crime and delinquency; physical abuse; addiction.

CHARACTERS

Leo: his mother freaks out, so he does too
Ma: Leo's mother hasn't gotten over the murder of her daughter four years ago
Gramma: Leo's grandmother, who lives with Leo and his mother
Aunt Suzanne: Leo's aunt, who just had another baby
Michelle: Leo's sister, who was murdered four years ago
Bree: she's tired of being pulled in too many directions and just wants to be free and
 herself
Jesse: Bree's boyfriend for the last two years, who is very possessive and critical
Bree's mother: she wants only the best for Bree and is willing to do anything to
 ensure it
Bree's father: a workaholic who spends little time or energy on his family
Novack: the man who killed Leo's sister Michelle

BOOKTALK

Leo:
It was March 19, four years after my sister died, and Ma was really off her rocker, worse than ever before. I promised Gramma I'd stay in the storage area in the basement, but listening to Ma scream about wanting me to be with her was more than I could take. Maybe if there'd been a couple of floors between us so I couldn't really hear her all that well, it would have been okay. But with her on the next floor, I could hear everything. I couldn't take it. I went upstairs, grabbed my keys, and got out the door as soon as I could. My mother is a total lunatic and couldn't care less what she's doing to me and Gramma because of it.
Bree:
 I hated my life sometimes. I mean, my mother wanted to totally control me, my boyfriend sometimes acted like he hated me unless I did *exactly* what he wanted, my dad was totally non-present, and all I wanted was to get out and away. All the colleges they wanted to me to go to were totally too close to home—I wanted *freedom*. So that night, when I was so fed up, I *had* to break some rules, I headed to Fenton. Fenton's the next town over, but it's light years different from upper-crust Hawthorne, where I live. Fenton is blue collar; Hawthorne is white collar with country-club snobbiness. I was looking for this bar I'd been to once, and when I couldn't find it driving around, I decided to get out and walk. But I couldn't find it. You'd think it wouldn't have been that hard. Fenton's not that big.
Leo:
 All I can think of is Michelle and how she died because I said my folks should let her go with that maniac. And how she ended up with fifty-seven stab wounds and

her throat slashed. And then I see this girl walking around in this skirt up to her ass and I think it should have been her! She's walking around asking for it—not like my sister. She deserves to die—not Michelle!

And before he realizes what he's doing, Leo has Bree in his car with a knife at her throat, ready to kill her. It would only take one swift stroke and her life would be over, just like Michelle's.

MAJOR THEMES AND IDEAS

- Death can shatter a family until it falls apart.
- Some people deal with tragedy and recover. Others are broken by it and are never the same.
- Each of us decides how to handle the bad parts of our lives—survive or crumble.
- It's hard to believe that there are people rotten enough to kill someone you love, until it happens.
- Life can change from good to bad in just an instant. After that, it can take eons to change back again.
- People tell you time heals all wounds, but that's not true. You only heal when you decide that it's time to do it.
- Sometimes parents want to live their dreams through their children, even when their children's dreams are very different.
- Sooner or later, most teens need to rebel. It's part of being a teen—even if it's not always smart.
- Grief can make people crazy, psychotic.
- Sometimes it's easy to get caught up in someone else's psychotic behavior.
- It's easy to fear and distrust a place you've never been, especially when you've been told how frightening and dangerous it is.
- Sometimes you have to be by yourself and responsible for you, even if you get lost now and then.
- Sometimes it's easy to follow a leader and never be responsible for what happens. Sometimes it's just a cop-out.
- No matter how much someone wants to, no one can go back and change what has already happened. Time travel is a fantasy.
- People are not always who they seem to be at first glance.
- It's easier to kill a stranger than someone you know.
- You don't know the consequences of your actions until it's too late.
- When someone dies, everyone in their family changes.
- Acting on the spur of the moment sometimes creates more problems than not acting would have.
- Everyone is responsible for his or her own actions.
- Money is no guarantee of happiness.

- When you tell the truth about yourself to someone, it makes you more real to them and makes them more likely to trust you.
- If you're afraid, you're paralyzed. You have to get beyond fear to take action.
- When your kidnapper listens to you better than your boyfriend, your relationship is probably headed in the dumpster.
- No one wants to take the blame for a tragedy. Everyone blames someone else.
- If you can find someone to blame for a tragedy, if feels safer. It wasn't a random event.
- When you let yourself be real to someone, they become real to you too. And you don't betray someone who's real.

BOOK REPORT IDEAS
1. Discuss Jesse and Bree's relationship. How healthy is it? What effect are her parents having on them? Was Jesse right to split?
2. Bree's mother wants her to have what she herself has. Compare Bree's view of her mother's life with what her mother believes about herself.
3. Leo encouraged his parents to let Michelle go out with Novack. Is he responsible for her death? Is his guilt deserved or not?
4. Discuss why Leo took Bree and what he thought he might gain from it.
5. How are Leo and Bree alike? How are they different? Which is more powerful, the things that unite them or the things that separate them?
6. Examine what Leo says about Michelle and Novack, and speculate on how much she was responsible for her own death.
7. What makes a person go over the edge, beyond what society says is acceptable? What sends Bree? How did it change their lives?
8. Both Leo and Bree feel alone, separated from the rest of the world. Discuss how that feeling both connects and separates them.
9. Speculate about what happens after the end of the book. What is Bree's life like? What is Leo's like?

BOOKTALK IDEAS
1. Write your talk as if you were a reporter interviewing Leo and Bree.
2. Use a dirty bandanna or some rope as a prop.
3. Focus your talk on either Leo or Bree's story—but not both of them.
4. Death changes everything for Leo and his family—use this as a focus for your talk.

RISKS
- Parents who have let tragedy overcome their lives, until they can no longer take care of their children

- Vulgar language
- Controlling parents; distant parents
- Alcoholic parent who is abusive to her son
- Abusive and controlling boyfriend
- Kidnapping
- Parents who refuse to see others realistically
- Parents who teach sexism to daughters

STRENGTHS
- Realistic language
- Flawed characters that react realistically to sorrow and stress
- Characters grow and gain insight
- Intense storyline that draws readers in
- Alternative viewpoints give readers intimate insight into both main characters
- Ambiguous ending leaves room for discussion and speculation
- Realistic characters that readers can recognize
- Depicts addiction and mental illness realistically
- Shows that money and prestige is no guarantee of happiness

AWARD
ALA Quick Picks for Reluctant Young Adult Readers, 2003

REVIEWS
"Wittlinger has a knack for creating interesting characters that captivate and hold attention. Fearing the worst for each of the likeable protagonists, readers will be unable to put this book down. Both reluctant and eager readers will appreciate the alternating voices and short chapters, and end up wondering what happens next." Bette Ammon, *VOYA*, 2/02

"Wittlinger's dependable, solid character development mirrors that of her previous novels. With its strong, believable emotions and direct, clear writing, this novel will speak to young adult readers." Gail Richmond, San Diego Unified Schools, CA, *School Library Journal*, 3/02

"In only a brief moment of time, readers are taken on a compelling psychological journey. . . . This slim volume packs a punch. Wittlinger—always tops at hard-hitting, realistic fiction—delivers another story of teenagers' self-discovery in a difficult world." *Kirkus Reviews*, 1/02

⊞⊞⊞

LOOKING FOR ALASKA. John Green. Penguin, 2005. $15.99. 160p. ISBN10: 0525475060. ISBN13: 9780525475064. Puffin, 2006. $7.99. 256p. ISBN10: 0142402516. ISBN13: 9780142402511. Brilliance Audio, 2006. $29.95. ISBN10: 1423324447. ISBN13: 9781423324447. (unabridged audio CD) Brilliance Audio, 2006. $82.25. ISBN10: 1423324455. ISBN13: 9781423324454. (unabridged audio CD, library edition) Brilliance Audio, 2006. $24.95. ISBN10: 1423324463. ISBN13: 9781423324461. (unabridged audio MP3-CD) Tandem Library, 2006. $16.95. 221p. ISBN10: 1417729155. ISBN13: 9781417729159. (library binding) Realistic fiction. Reading Level: MS. Interest Level: MS, YHS. English, Ethics, Psychology, Sociology, Philosophy.

SUBJECT AREAS
love; friendship; death and dying; self-knowledge; school; family relationships; bullying; crime and delinquency; cliques; dating and social life; grief and mourning; guilt; justice; sex and sexuality; lying and deceit; peer pressure; religion; rites of passage; secrets; suicide; practical jokes.

CHARACTERS
Miles Halter/Pudge: fascinated by famous last words, he goes to boarding school in search of the Great Perhaps
Chip Martin/The Colonel: Pudge's roommate, and a full-ride scholarship student
Alaska Young: the Colonel's partner in school pranks; she loves to read and is totally hot
Takumi Hikohito: Alaska and the Colonel's best friend and pranks participant; he can rap on anything
Mr. Starnes/The Eagle: dean of students and object of many school pranks
Kevin Richman: a Weekday Warrior who hates the Colonel for ratting out two of his friends
Dr. Hyde/The Old Man: he teaches World Religions and leads his students on a search for meaning
Longwell Chase: president of the junior class, Weekday Warrior, and Kevin's best friend
Sara: the Colonel's girlfriend with whom he fights constantly
Lara Buterskaya: she's Romanian, Pudge's girlfriend, and participates in the pranks

BOOKTALK
It happened. We could have stopped it, any one of the three of us. But we didn't, and now we'll have to live with that knowledge for the rest of our lives.

The summer before I was a junior, I decided that I was tired of my safe, boring, uneventful life, and persuaded my parents to let me finish school at my dad's alma mater, Culver Creek Prep, a boarding school in Alabama. He'd had a rep for creating the wildest pranks while acing all his classes. I wanted to see if I could do the same thing and become someone as different as possible from the boring, conventional person I'd been for sixteen years.

But nothing was what I'd expected. My roommate was a short, wise-cracking prankster genius on a full-ride scholarship who told me to call him the Colonel and nicknamed me Pudge because I'm so skinny. He introduced me to Alaska, the hottest girl in all of human history. She was another genius and her room was full of towering stacks of books—her life's library. She was also the Colonel's partner in crime. She thought up their pranks and he figured out how to do them without being caught. Takumi was the third member of the partnership and I was soon the fourth. I learned how to smoke and drink, not to rat out anyone, even your enemies, and how to get revenge for what had been done to me the night before classes started.

Kevin and his Weekday Warriors—rich, cool kids who went home to their air-conditioned McMansions every weekend—had decided to teach the Colonel a lesson by beating up on his roommate. They thought he'd ratted out two of their friends just before school was out in May and gotten them expelled. But it didn't teach the Colonel anything, it just made him and Alaska and Takumi mad and thirsty for revenge.

MAJOR THEMES AND IDEAS

- Endless strings of consequences result from our smallest actions. But we can't know better until we see those consequences, until knowing better is useless.
- "I go to seek a Great Perhaps."—Francois Rabelais
- "How will I ever get out of this labyrinth!"—Simón Bolívar
- The hand you're dealt in life is not the one you wish you'd gotten.
- Everyone has shit to deal with in life, and yours is no better or worse than anyone else's.
- Sooner or later, things fall apart or go away, even our memories of people we've loved.
- Entropy increases. Things fall apart.
- Forgetting someone is having them die all over again.
- If you don't panic, you can frequently get out of situations that, at first, seemed impossible.
- Don't rat out someone who disses you or your friends just to get even.
- Spending your time imagining what the future will be like prevents you from living in the present and from actually attaining that future.
- There are some secrets that can't be shared, even with your best friends.
- Loyalty to your friends is more important than almost anything else.
- It is possible to love someone and still not trust them.
- When getting revenge on someone, you first have to find what they love most.

- Hating someone just because they are who they are takes a lot of energy. It may not be worth it.
- Our lives can be changed and redefined by a single event.
- Most of the mistakes we make in life can't be fixed with regrets and I'm sorrys. Our only choice is to figure out how to survive them.
- People always have reasons for their emotions and actions, even if they never tell anyone what they are.
- Sometimes anger is the only emotion that can hold guilt and sadness at bay.
- The people we love change us, make our life different.
- When grief is contaminated by guilt, there is no comfort, no healing in it.
- Last words are harder to remember when you don't know that someone's about to die.
- Some mysteries are not meant to be solved.
- There is a part of each of us that is greater than the sum of our parts, a part that cannot be destroyed, it cannot begin and it cannot end, and so it cannot fail. Like energy—never created, never destroyed.

BOOK REPORT IDEAS

1. What is the labyrinth and how do you escape it?
2. Compare the Colonel's, Pudge's, and Alaska's parents and discuss how they influenced who their children became.
3. What's the purpose of, or the goal of, Alaska's and the Colonel's pranks?
4. Was Alaska's death an accident or suicide? Base your argument on your understanding of her emotionally and psychologically.
5. Speculate on how her friends would have reacted to Alaska's death had it been clear that she had either committed suicide *or* had an accident because she was driving drunk.
6. Much of the book is centered around the idea of last words. What were Alaska's last words and what do they mean?
7. How do Pudge, Alaska, and the Colonel answer Dr. Hyde's questions on the first day of class? How do you answer them?
8. Is it necessary to figure out every mystery? How do you know whether you'll be more happy or more satisfied because you know the answer or because you don't?
9. Discuss how this novel illustrates the Buddhist understanding of interconnectedness.
10. In your opinion, what is the most important question humans have to answer?
11. In the end, how does the Colonel answer his most important question?
12. What parts of this book have you continued to think about and why?
13. How does Thanksgiving weekend change Pudge and Alaska's relationship?
14. What was Pudge saying about Alaska when he quoted Auden—"You shall love your crooked neighbors/with all your crooked heart"?

15. What does Pudge's final essay mean to you as a person? Do you agree or disagree with him, and why?

BOOKTALK IDEAS
1. Write your talk in first person as Alaska, without giving away her death.
2. Focus on before and after, i.e., "Before, life was. . . " and "After, life was. . . " without explaining the incident that changed before to after.
3. Include current figures on hazing, teen drinking, and smoking as part of your talk—connecting the book to factual information.

RISKS
* Teens drink and smoke
* Teen uses fake ID to buy alcohol and cigarettes
* Hazing type pranks and bullying
* Weak or abusive parents
* Sex discussed in explicit terms
* Masturbation scene
* Teens are sexually active

STRENGTHS
* Realistic language
* Demonstrates the power of friendship
* Three-dimensional characters with strong and authentic voices
* Strong, suspenseful plot line
* Includes deep philosophical questions
* Ambiguous ending doesn't provide absolute answers
* Strong and supportive parents
* Shows the struggle to find meaning in life and death
* Provides many ideas and questions for the reader to consider
* Complex characters who question themselves, their ideas, their actions
* Culver Creek dean of students combines strict discipline with a genuine liking for his students

AWARDS
Kirkus Reviews Editor's Choice, 2005
SLJ Best Books for Children, 2005
Michael L. Printz Award, 2006
ALA Best Books for Young Adults, 2006
ALA Quick Picks for Reluctant Young Adult Readers, 2006
Booklist Editor's Choice, 2005
New York Public Library Books for the Teen Age, 2006

REVIEWS

"Green. . . has a writer's voice, so self-assured and honest that one is startled to learn that this novel is his first. The anticipated favorable comparisons to Holden Caufield are richly deserved in this highly recommended addition to young adult literature." Beth E. Andersen, *VOYA*, 4/05

"The novel's chief appeal lies in Miles's well-articulated lust and his initial excitement about being on his own for the first time. Readers will only hope that this is not the last word from this promising new author." *Publishers Weekly*, 2/05

"The language and sexual situations are aptly and realistically drawn, but sophisticated in nature. Miles's narration is alive with sweet, self-deprecating humor, and his obvious struggle to tell the story truthfully adds to his believability." Johanna Lewis, New York Public Library, *School Library Journal*, 2/05

"What sings and soars in this gorgeously told tale is Green's mastery of language and the sweet, rough edges of Pudge's voice. Girls will cry and boys will find love, lust, loss, and longing in Alaska's vanilla-and-cigarettes scent." *Kirkus Reviews*, 3/05

📖📖📖

LOOKING FOR JJ. Anne Cassidy. Harcourt, 2007. $17.00. 336p. ISBN: 0152061908. ISBN13: 9780152061906. Bolinda, 2007. $48.00. ISBN10: 1740937295. ISBN13: 9781740937290. (unabridged audio CD) Realistic fiction. Reading Level: MS. Interest Level: MS, YHS. English, Psychology.

SUBJECT AREAS
crime and delinquency; problem parents; self-knowledge; dating and social life; gossip; legal system; working; secrets; justice; prejudice; love; friendship; animals; sex and sexuality; depression.

CHARACTERS
Jennifer Jones/Alice Tully: her life is about to be ripped to shreds
Frankie: Alice's boyfriend
Rosie Sutherland: the woman Alice lives with
Kathy: Rosie's mother
Jill Newton: Alice's probation officer
Patricia Coffey: the director at Monksgrove
Sara Wright: she lives downstairs from Rosie and Alice
Carol Jones: Jennifer's mother, who's a top model

Danny: a friend of Carol's
Derek Corker: a detective looking for JJ
Simone: she took care of JJ when her mother was busy
Michael Forrester: he worked at Monksgrove
Gran: Carol's mother and JJ's grandmother
Michelle Livingston: she lives next door to Jennifer in Berwick Waters
Mrs. Livingston: she works in the school office
Lucy Bussell: she lives near Jennifer and Michelle, but is younger than they are
Miss Potts: Jennifer and Michelle's teacher in Berwick Waters
Mrs. Nettles: the head teacher at Jennifer's school
Sonia: a girl in the same class as Jennifer and Michelle
Stevie and Joe Bussell: Lucy's older brothers
Mr. Cottis: a photographer who takes pictures of Carol
Frank Livingston: Michelle's father
Sophie: Frankie's sister
Jan and Peter: Frankie's parents

BOOKTALK

Everyone wants to know where JJ is. The headlines scream that Jennifer Jones is a dangerous criminal and shouldn't be released from prison. Flyers with her picture are plastered everywhere, asking "Have you seen this girl?" Everyone wants to know what really happened that chilly spring day when three children walked to the lake near Berwick Waters, and only two returned.

Alice Tully knows exactly what happened that day. It's burned into her mind. She will never forget. She has so much, a job, a home, and a boyfriend who adores her, a real normal life. A chance to be happy.

But that new life, that new happiness lasts less than a year. Alice has a past that is dark, and violent, and sad. A past that can rip her new life to shreds.

MAJOR THEMES AND IDEAS

- You can't leave your past behind you.
- Someone who betrayed you once will probably do it again.
- You can't own a person like a possession.
- It's not possible to have someone all to yourself.
- Sometimes people don't want to be found.
- Children can be abused by neglect and abandonment just as they can be abused physically or sexually.
- You can't change the past, no matter how much you want to. You can only change the future.
- Your past makes you who you are.
- The past is with you always.

BOOK REPORT IDEAS

1. Compare Jennifer, Alice, and Kate. How are they similar and different?
2. Discuss what you think might happen to Kate. Will she be able to keep her secret?
3. Show how Carol was partially responsible for what happened.
4. Compare various forms of child abuse, including neglect and manipulation, and the impact they have on children's self-image.
5. Describe Carol and what Jennifer meant to her.
6. Is it true that you can't ever escape your own past? Why or why not?
7. Is it necessary to share your past with someone you love?
8. Discuss Sara, and whether she would have been able to tell JJ's story in a positive way.
9. Many people betray Jennifer. Discuss how each of them does it.

BOOKTALK IDEAS

1. Write your talk as if it were a tabloid story about JJ.
2. Write your talk in first person, as Alice.
3. Focus your talk on the scene at the coffee shop when Alice discovers who Derek Corker is and what he's trying to do.

RISKS

- Child kills little girl
- Neglectful mother betrays daughter
- Mother has sex in front of daughter
- Teens are sexually active
- Child is rejected over and over

STRENGTHS

- Strong, likable main character
- Shows how parents can manipulate a child
- Demonstrates the power of the media to disrupt lives
- Ambivalent ending leaves room for discussion and speculation
- Varying viewpoints add complexity
- Characters grow and gain insight
- Powerful central message: the past is with you always

AWARDS

ALA Best Book for Young Adults, 2008
Booktrust Teenage Prize, 2004

REVIEWS

"Readers will come to care about this character and her ability to find her way in the world after a rough start. This book raises questions of identity, responsibility, family, and healing." Erin Wyatt, *VOYA*, 10/07

"Crisply plotted and smoothly written, this gripping book is sure to hold teens' attention." Meredith Robbins, Jacqueline Kennedy Onassis High School, New York City, *School Library Journal*, 10/07

"Cassidy masterfully builds tension and jolts readers with plot twists. She evokes sympathy for a troubled child who becomes a teenager with a grim future and raises questions about who is responsible when a ten-year-old commits a violent crime. Compelling, thought-provoking crime fiction." *Kirkus Reviews*, 9/07

📖📖📖

LUCAS. Kevin Brooks. The Chicken House, an imprint of Scholastic, 2006. $13.74. 368p. ISBN10: 1905294174. ISBN13: 9781905294176. Scholastic, 2004. $6.99. 384p. ISBN10: 0439530636. ISBN13: 9780439530637. Topeka Bindery, 2004. $16.75. 384p. ISBN10: 1417638966. ISBN13: 9781417638963. Recorded Books, 2004. $115.75. ISBN10: 1419373595. ISBN13: 9781419373596. (unabridged audio CD) Recorded Books, 2004. $46.95. ISBN10: 1419300334. ISBN13: 9781419300332. (unabridged audiotape) Recorded Books, 2004. $88.75. ISBN10: 1402599323. ISBN13: 9781402599323. (unabridged audiotape, library version) Recorded Books, 2004. $61.75. ISBN13: 9781428167629. (unabridged audiobook) Realistic fiction. Reading Level: MS. Interest Level: MS, YHS. Creative Writing, English, Sociology, Psychology, Ethics.

SUBJECT AREAS

bullying; friendship; love; family relationships; self-knowledge; evil; manipulation; anger; depression; violence; intimidation; animals; grief and mourning; gossip; guilt; secrets; lying and deceit; rape; suicide; writing.

CHARACTERS

Caitlin McCann: she's fifteen, and this summer will change her life forever
Dominic McCann: back home after his first year of college and very full of himself
John McCann/Dad: he's a writer and a single father
Simon Reed: Caitlin's friend, a lonely, nerdy kid
Rita Gray: the McCanns' neighbor

Bill Gray: Rita's daughter and Caitlin's best friend, who has a crush on Dominic

Jamie Tait: son of the local member of Parliament; he makes Caitlin nervous because of the unsavory rumors about him

Sara Toms: Jamie's insanely possessive girlfriend, and daughter of the local police chief

Robbie Dean: he's young, fat, and has a car and an attitude to match Angel's

Angel Dean: Robbie's little sister, who's sixteen going on twenty-one, with lots of attitude

Trevor and Malc: two boys Bill picks up

Lee Brendell: a friend of the Deans

Joe Rampton: his farm is just across the fields from the McCanns, and he had Lucas do some odd jobs for him

Detective Inspector Bob Toms: Sara's father and head of the local police force

Kylie Coombe: the girl Lucas rescued from the ocean; she tries to convince her mother that Lucas saved her life

Ellen Coombe: Kylie's mother, who firmly believes Lucas was going to hurt or molest her daughter, and refuses to see the truth

Lenny Craine: the local police sergeant who is investigating the accident

Pete Curtis: a young police constable

Derek Hanson: he owns the raft Kylie fell off of and is a friend of her mother's

Jenny Reed: Simon's mother

Shu Patel: he runs the shop in the village and is a friend of John's

Micky Buck: a friend of Lee Brendell's

Tully Jones: a friend of Jamie's

BOOKTALK

"Let the sadness out, Caitie," Dad said. "Let the feelings come out. Cry yourself a story." So I did, and here it is.

Sometimes life is like a roller coaster, all peaks and dips, unexpected turns that catch you off guard, speeding relentlessly, out of control, and all you can do is hang on and wait for it to be over. The summer I was fifteen life was like that, and more. I even know when it started, when the ride began slow and easy, when my life changed forever. It was toward the end of July, the day my brother Dominic called to ask for a ride from the train station. We were driving back, feeling kind of sick, seeing how different Dom was after a year away from home at university. He smoked and cursed and seemed to be looking down on everything and everyone, and especially me. I began to remember why I'd been wary of his coming back, the way he needled me, mocked me, and in general made me feel like a stupid little girl.

We were driving across the Strand, the bridge between the mainland and Hale Island where we live, when I saw Lucas for the first time. He was walking along the side of the road, heading for the island, a figure all in green. Loose-fitting drab green t-shirt, baggy green pants, green army jacket tied around his waist, and a green canvas bag slung over his shoulder. As we passed him, he turned his head and looked at me. I'll never forget that moment. It wasn't just that he was beautiful, although he was, but there was something about his face that was more than that, more than pale blue eyes, tousled sandy hair, sad smile, something beyond all that, something . . . And then the car whizzed by him, and I was left to wonder what had just happened. I felt a funny, buzzy feeling, anticipation and sadness and excitement all mixed up, as if even then I knew what was going to happen.

I've thought over the past year about that moment, and what would have happened if I hadn't seen Lucas that day. If we'd been ten minutes earlier or later crossing the Strand, if Dom's train had been late, so we'd had to wait at the station. What would have happened? Would I be a different person, happier, sadder? And what would have happened to Lucas if I hadn't seen him that day? How would his life have changed? But what-ifs are pointless. They don't change a thing. Reality is, and doesn't change because we'd like it to. The fact is, I saw him that day, and he saw me. And I stepped onto the roller coaster.

MAJOR THEMES AND IDEAS
- When two people can't give each other what they need, sometimes it helps to have someone in the middle to turn to when things get too much.
- Life is about reality, not what-ifs.
- When you aren't used to something, it's harder to put up with.
- You can tell a lot about people from the way they walk.
- Sometimes you just know something's about to happen and that you're right on the brink of something important.
- It's hard to think about growing up when you're right in the middle of it. It's hard to know what you really want.
- You spend half your childhood wishing you were grown, and when you are, you spend half your time wishing you were a child. Give it up, and live for today.
- No one ever kept a secret as well as a child.
- Don't worry about what other people think of you, or what you imagine they think. Just be yourself. That's good enough.
- But being yourself is difficult when it's someone you care about that thinks badly of you.
- Cruelty is a fact of life.
- It's not always easy to avoid the bad things—sometimes you have no choice. You just have to do what you think is best.
- Don't ignore your feelings, whether you understand them or not. Act on them.
- Some things are best left unsaid.
- Life recycles everything it uses.
- There are all kinds of feelings, and you can't control a single one of them.
- Crowds are unpredictable and have minds of their own.
- We all have to be fools sometimes.

- Sometimes a higher power, something beyond your conscious self, takes over, and you find yourself doing things you'd never usually do, things that are wrong, but still feel so right.
- Losing someone you love leaves a hole in your heart and life that never grows back.
- We all do stupid things now and then.
- People don't like things—or people—who don't fit. It frightens them, the unknown, the mystery. It's dangerous.
- The more you lie, the easier it gets. But sooner or later, you start lying to yourself.
- Some people gain pleasure from others' suffering, particularly from those they perceive as a threat, because they are different and do things that are difficult to understand.
- When something makes you feel bad, you either put up with it, learn to like it, or get rid of it. If getting rid of it is easiest, that's the choice you make.
- "Be content with what you are, and wish not change, nor dread your last day, nor long for it."—Marcus Valerius Martialis
- Never give up.
- Violence *can* be a legitimate answer. It *can* solve things.
- You can't predict the future to see the consequences of your actions. You can only do what seems best, most right, in the heat of the moment, and hope for the best.
- Know your own rules, and know when you're breaking them.
- There's always a way out. You just have to find it.
- You can always hope—even when you know it's a waste of time, you can still hope.
- A mob can't be controlled with logic, or restraint, or even the truth. It can only be controlled by violent emotions—anger, fear, hatred, the dark passions.
- Even when you think the world has ended, life still goes on, and eventually you must return to it.
- Grief lasts forever. If it doesn't, it isn't true grief.
- Eventually, you have to get on with your life. That's what happens. There are no endings.

BOOK REPORT IDEAS

1. When Caitlin first sees Lucas, she says he seemed different and special, and looking into his eyes made time seem to slow down. Did that really happen, or is it something she made up in retrospect?
2. When Lucas and Caitlin meet for the first time, Deefer isn't his usual crazy self. He's polite, quiet, and obedient. Explain the sudden change in his behavior.
3. When Kylie's mother pulls her away from Lucas after he saved her from the ocean, why didn't anyone who'd seen the rescue stand up for him?

4. Explain the idea of a crowd having a mind of its own and how just one person could sway its opinion.
5. Lucas says many mysterious things when he and Caitlin are at his shelter. Explain what they mean, as you look back, knowing what will happen. Is Lucas just using common sense, or is something more going on?
6. Even though he was short and frail-looking, Lucas was able to intimidate older, bigger men. Discuss how he was able to do that.
7. There were a number of inexplicable things that Lucas did or said. Examine them carefully, and explain what he might have meant by them.
8. At the end of the chase, Lucas steps off the path in the mudflats and vanishes. Did he commit suicide, or had he figured out a plan?
9. Discuss whether or not a mob can be controlled by someone outside it, using restraint, logic, reasonableness and common sense. Support your hypothesis by using examples from the several mob scenes in the book.
10. Was there any point at which someone could have intervened, and changed the sequence of events? When? Who? Why?
11. Describe Lucas and his life before he came to the island in as much detail as possible. Examine everything he said for examples that support your theory.

BOOKTALK IDEAS

1. Use a small carved wooden dog as a prop.
2. Include the prologue in your talk.
3. Have three or four characters describe Lucas, ending with Caitlin's description, and then starting the story of what happened that summer.

RISKS

- Father drinks to help deal with his wife's death ten years ago
- Teens drink and smoke cigarettes and marijuana
- Substance abuse
- Teens torment stranger just for fun
- Teens torture a cat
- Townspeople form a mob and act as vigilantes, pursuing an outsider they have decided is guilty of rape
- Stranger in town is falsely accused of rape to drive him out
- Teen threatens to rape girl
- Violence

STRENGTHS

- Almost lyrical passages have an otherworldly quality
- Grim portrait of the power of a mob and groupthink
- Three-dimensional characters the reader can identify with

- Shows the power of knowing and believing in yourself
- Shows how easy it is to get caught up in evil
- Ending leaves room for speculation and discussion
- Realistic dialogue including obscenities
- Teen attacks rapist to save his friend
- Loving family relationships
- Ambiguous ending leaves room for discussion
- Addresses difficult topics not often seen in YA literature
- Ending is a hard-hitting, overwhelming shock to the reader, and the impact isn't lessened by time or rereading

AWARD
ALA Best Books for Young Adults, 2004

REVIEWS
"Brooks. . . offers an-edge-of-the-seat story that has overtones of classics such as *The Ox Bow Incident* and *To Kill a Mockingbird*. . . . Teens may pick this up for its sheer intensity, but once they put it down, they'll ponder its meanings." Ilene Cooper, *Booklist*, 5/03

"This is a powerful book to be savored by all who appreciate fine writing and a gripping read."
Sharon Rawlins, Piscataway Public Library, NJ, *School Library Journal*, 5/03

"Brooks's second novel is an ambitious and intricately crafted tale of love and resurrection." *Publishers Weekly*, 5/03.

"One can read this in allegorical terms, with the worst of modern life represented by Jamie and his mindless attacks on Lucas, who is aligned with nature. Readers who appreciate interesting symbolism and fine descriptive writing, and who like to sink into a long mood piece, will find this hard to put down." *Kirkus Reviews*, 5/03

📖📖📖

LUSH. Natasha Friend. Scholastic, 2006. $16.99. 192p. ISBN10: 043985346X. ISBN13: 9780439899215. Scholastic, 2007. $6.99. 192p. ISBN10: 0439853478. ISBN13: 9780439853477. Realistic fiction. Reading Level: MS. Interest Level: MS, YHS. English, Psychology, Sociology, Creative Writing.

SUBJECT AREAS

drug abuse; problem parents; dysfunctional families; self-knowledge; friendship; writing; secrets; bullying; family relationships; fear; anger; gossip; school; homosexuality; intimidation; peer pressure; rites of passage.

CHARACTERS

Samantha/Sam Gwynn: she's thirteen and tired of living a lie to hide that her father is a lush

Patrick Gwynn: Sam's dad; he'd rather drink than breathe

Ellen Gwynn: Sam's mother, who ignores her husband's drinking and has become a yoga fanatic

Charlie Parker: he used to be Sam's best friend and is the only person who knows about her dad

Luke Gwynn: Sam's four-year-old brother

Miss Howe: the local librarian

Angie, Vanessa, Tracy: Sam's best friends since third grade

Jacob Mann: Sam's earth science lab partner

AJK: the person who answers the note Sam leaves for Juliet in the library

Nana Gwynne: Patrick's mother and Sam and Luke's grandmother, who also ignores her son's drinking

Drew Maddox: high school junior and hockey team captain who Sam meets at the library when she goes to exchange notes with AJK

Mr. and Mrs. Parker: Charlie's parents, who step in to help the Gwynns when things get out of control

BOOKTALK

Being thirteen is never easy, but it's worse when your father's a drunk. At 2:35 in the morning, when normal fathers are in bed asleep, Samantha's father staggers in the front door, breaks a vase, and ends up facedown in a plate of cold lasagna. And when he finally gets upstairs, she can hear the thud as he stumbles and hits something solid in the hallway before lurching into his bedroom, demanding that her mother get him an ice pack. She knows that the next morning, there will be bruises on his face, his shin, his elbow, and he won't remember how they got there. He won't remember anything. He never does.

But it's not just his drinking. It's the lying, the hiding, the sneaking around. She's can't tell anyone about her dad, not even her best friends. That means no sleepovers at her house, not telling anyone what life is like at home after her father gets home from work. She never knows what's going to happen—one moment calm, the next cussing, slamming doors, and throwing things. That's what life's like when you have a dad who would rather drink than breathe.

The worst part of it all is that she doesn't have anyone to talk to, no one Sam can tell how horrible her life has gotten. Then, one day, when she can't stand it anymore, she writes a note, and looks for the right person to give it to. She's at the library, and there's a high school girl named Juliet who has red hair and a sense of humor. Maybe she can be the big sister kind of person Sam needs. She leaves the note in the study carrel Juliet always uses and hopes for the best. The next day, she gets the note back, and the conversation on paper begins. But it's not from Juliet. It's from someone called AJK, who has just as many parent problems as Sam does. Sam's broken her promise to keep her father's secret. But can that broken promise make a difference when her dad's a lush, her mom is in denial, and her baby brother will have to spend the rest of his life with a scar that cuts his face in half?

MAJOR THEMES AND IDEAS
- Ignoring a problem doesn't make it go away; frequently, it just makes it worse.
- Just because you love someone doesn't mean you can't hate what they do. Love and hate can be very close together.
- Keeping a secret keeps you apart from everyone who doesn't share it.
- When there's a part of your life you hate, or a situation you can't change, sometimes it's important to just get away so you can forget about it for a while.
- I promise, trust me, you have my word: they all become meaningless when the behavior doesn't change.
- Promises never kept mean lack of trust that may never vanish.
- Parents' behavior impacts their children as kids, as teens, as adults.
- Sometimes it's impossible to forgive and forget. Sometimes it only gets worse and worse and worse.
- Friends can make you crazy, but the world would be a far worse place without them.
- No matter how drunk you are, or how drunk they are, you never have the right to hurt someone else.
- Sometimes sorry isn't enough. The scars of what you did will always be there.
- Rehabilitation is one day at a time.
- People who are addicts don't need someone to ignore or excuse their addiction. They need someone who will make them face it head-on.
- Being drunk doesn't make you cool. It makes you stupid, so you do things you'd never do if you were sober.
- Sometimes when people do stupid things when they're drunk, they should be forgiven. Sometimes they shouldn't.

BOOK REPORT IDEAS
1. Discuss how you would act and feel in Samantha's situation. What could she have done to change things, with three adults denying everything?
2. Many people in this book had secrets. How were those secrets both good and bad, and what happened when they weren't secret anymore?

3. Speculate on what will happen after the end of the book—will the Gwynns go on being a happy family, or will things go back to the way they were for so long?

4. Alcoholism runs in families. Discuss its progress through three generations of the Gwynn family and comment on how the actions of two generations of parents damaged their children.

5. Trust is another theme in this book. What makes one person willing to trust another, and what kinds of things destroy that trust?

6. What character, what situation, or what line in the book had the most impact on you? Why?

7. A number of characters were manipulative or bullying. How did this affect the bullies or manipulators and their victims?

BOOKTALK IDEAS

1. Focus your talk on the idea of secrets, how they can hurt when they're kept or when they're shared.

2. Have Sam tell her story in first person.

3. Introduce your talk with facts about alcoholics that Sam's parents demonstrated.

RISKS

- Alcoholic father with enabling mother and wife, both of whom demonstrate inappropriate behavior in front of children
- Father seriously injures very young son in alcoholic rage
- Realistic and vulgar language
- Bullying and manipulative teens
- Teens drink and smoke
- Teen boys almost rape a thirteen-year-old girl
- Teen forced to keep the secret of her father's addiction
- Mother refuses to acknowledge her husband's addiction
- Homosexual teen character

STRENGTHS

- Clear, authentic, believable voice of main character
- Several strong, functional, loving families
- Strong, supportive, forgiving friendships
- Ambivalent ending provides few answers, allowing reader to speculate
- Teen characters gain insight and learn from their experiences
- Bullying and manipulative teens have to face consequences

AWARDS

ALA Quick Picks for Reluctant Young Adult Readers, 2007
International Reading Association Young Adult Choices, 2008

REVIEWS

"Friend adeptly takes a teen problem and turns it into a believable, sensitive, character-driven story, with realistic dialogue. The cautiously optimistic ending works because Friend has convinced readers that Sam can handle whatever happens. Friend, who clearly understands and empathizes with young teens, is a writer to watch." Debbie Carton, *Booklist*, 11/06

"Sam comes across as a savvy as well as naïve teen who tells her own story with humor, honesty and hope. Realistic family drama." *Kirkus Reviews*, 10/06

"Friend adroitly portrays a weighty topic with touches of humor and grace." Rebecca M. Jones, Fort Myers-Lee County Library, FL, *School Library Journal*, 12/06

📖📖📖

NAILED. Patrick Jones. Walker, 2006. $16.95. 224p. ISBN10: 0802780776. ISBN13: 9780802780775. Walker, 2007. $7.95. 240p. ISBN10: 0802796486. ISBN13: 9780802796486. Realistic fiction. Reading Level: YHS. Interest Level: YHS, OHS. English, Psychology, Sociology.

SUBJECT AREAS

bullying; school; music; friendship; anger; self-knowledge; prejudice; manipulation; family relationships; love; theatre; intimidation; peer pressure; problem parents; rites of passage; secrets; fear; dating and social life; sex and sexuality.

CHARACTERS

Bret Hendricks: he's sixteen years old, tall and skinny, plays bass and sings in a band, and is determined to do things his own way, even if it means he's kind of a loner

Dad: angry, impatient, chauvinistic, he can't figure Bret out and spends his time yelling at him, rather than trying to understand him

Alex Shelton: Bret's best pal, songwriter for the band, smart, funny and a damn good friend

Sean: drummer in the band, shy, blond, blue-eyed and handsome; he could be a jock but would rather do his own thing

Bob Hutchings: head jock, who bullies anyone who's lesser than he is

Mr. Douglas: the high school theatre teacher

Kaylee Edmonds: she's a year older than Bret, goes to a different high school, is sexy, smart, and cynical, and Bret would give anything to hook up with her

Cameron Hendricks: Bret's older brother, who works as a mechanic

Robin Hendricks: Bret's twelve-year-old little sister, who wants to be cool and is embarrassed by her strange older brother

Mr. King: he's a coach and teaches junior English—the former means far more to him than the latter

Principal Robert Morgan: he's clashed with Bret many times over the years and is one of the reasons why the school is such a hostile environment for everyone except the jocks and their friends

Mom: Bret's mother, who tries to build up Bret's self-confidence

Will Kennedy: half-jock, half-jazz band, he likes the sound Bret and his friends have

BOOKTALK

My junior year in high school really sucked. It was the year I found Kaylee, the love of my life, the year I finally realized I was never gonna be good enough for my dad and that he was never going to understand why being an actor and musician were more important than working a dead-end job and watching NASCAR all weekend.

But, mainly, it was the year I decided I didn't want to take all the junk the "jock culture" at school was dumping on me, my friends, and everyone else at school that they saw as being beneath them. Sometimes when you're in a tight spot, the worst thing you can do is keep on doing nothing. My junior year in high school really sucked, but it was the year I quit doing a lot of nothing, and decided to do a lot of something.

MAJOR THEMES AND IDEAS

- The nail that sticks out the farthest gets hammered the hardest.
- People aren't created equal. Some are stronger, some are smarter. And all too often, the stronger like to beat up on the weaker and smarter to prove their superiority to themselves.
- Some teachers live to teach, to make their students better people. Others build themselves up by harassing students who can't fight back.
- High school has a social hierarchy that is very difficult to break out of once you have been typecast.
- When coaches and school administrators support and defend the jocks, their bullying becomes more overt and uncontrollable.
- Going from victim to victor isn't always easy, or even possible.
- Parents frequently know only what they're told about their children and may be completely ignorant of the pain they are enduring.
- When people make fun of you, consider the source before you decide how much those comments actually mean to you.
- What you think of yourself is more important than what others say about you.
- If people don't like who you are, it's their problem, not yours.
- Even if you won't ever be the victor, you can decide not to be the victim any longer.

- What goes around, comes around. Vengeance is unnecessary.
- There's an easy way to live life, and there's a hard way. It's necessary to think carefully about which you'll choose. They both have highs and lows, and can lead to very different results.
- Life isn't fair—count on it. Then figure out how to deal with it. You don't have to just accept it.
- What matters isn't *why* bad things happen, but that when they do, you can pick yourself up and face another day. If you spend time asking why, you'll just stay knocked down.
- Possessions matter more to those who don't have many of them.
- It's easy to pre-judge someone you don't know. Their shell isn't all that they are.
- Life isn't about getting what you want, it's about getting what you need and doing what you should.
- Don't do the crime if you can't do the time.
- When someone's pushing you around, the worst thing you can do is continue to do nothing.
- Life isn't fair. Accept it. Move on.

BOOK REPORT IDEAS

1. Several characters end up paying for mistakes they made. Discuss some of the similarities and differences in their experiences.
2. A book of realistic fiction is supposed to reflect reality. How much does the "jock-archy" at Bret's high school reflect what you and your friends have experienced?
3. Discuss the relationship between Kaylee and the boys in her life—Chad, Bret, Sean, and Alex. How much or how little has she changed during the year?
4. There are a number of "threesomes" in the book, in which one person is caught between the other two. Describe several of them and how the conflict in each is, or is not, resolved.
5. There are also several parent-child groups in the book. Show the different ways Bret, Kaylee, Sean, and Alex interact with their parents and how the results of this teen-parent relationship is played out in each of their lives.
6. "The nail that sticks out the farthest gets hammered the hardest." What does this mean to you? Do you try to be different or fit in? Why? In what ways?
7. How did Bret change over the course of the year? What do you think happens to him after the book is over? How does he define success now and how do you think he will define it in the future? What do you think he'll be doing in five years? In ten? In fifteen? Base your predictions on scenes from the book, what Bret says about himself, and what others say about him.

BOOKTALK IDEAS

1. Have each member of Radio Free Flint introduce themselves, hinting at some of the conflicts that come up in the book.

2. Write your talk as a series of news stories, choosing three to four scenes that would make a good newspaper story (it doesn't matter if they were not actual news stories in the book).
3. Focus your talk on the idea of being different and the "jockarchy" that ruled the school.

RISKS
- Realistic language including obscenities
- Parents who mentally abuse their children
- Premarital sex, with parental permission
- Teens drink and smoke
- Teachers mock and abuse students
- School administration tacitly and overtly supports bullying and harassment
- Teen uses sex to manipulate her boyfriends
- Bullies use physical force to harass and intimidate
- Parents are overinvolved or withdrawn from their teens' lives

STRENGTHS
- Realistic characters teens can identify with
- Frank presentation of high school bullying, a growing problem
- Teachers and school counselors who are concerned about and supportive of their students
- Characters who are able to grow and change based on new insights
- Somewhat unresolved ending allows reader to speculate on various outcomes
- Many and varied topics for book discussion and curriculum involvement

AWARD
Great Lakes Book Award Finalist, 2006

REVIEWS
"It is one of the few teen novels involving a teen male struggling emotionally with both male and female relationships. It belongs in all teen collections." Rollie Welch, *VOYA*, 4/06

"The characters are many-layered and believable, and the frank depiction of sex and violence as teenage commonplaces is graphically honest but never gratuitous. Readers will hurt for Bret when he falls, cheer for him when he triumphs and feel glad for the privilege of getting to know him." *Kirkus Reviews*, 4/06

"Using multidimensional characters, Jones ably explores the dynamics of raising successful, independent children, at the same time exposing the difficulty faced by an

educational system charged with celebrating independent thought and individual differences while enforcing rules and keeping kids safe. A tough, revealing book worthy
of discussion." Frances Bradburn, *Booklist*, 2/06

📖📖📖

NATURE OF JADE.   Deb Caletti. Simon and Schuster, 2007. $16.99. 304p.
ISBN10: 1416910050. ISBN13: 9781416910053. Simon Pulse, 2008. $8.99. 320p.
ISBN10: 141690069. ISBN13: 9781416910060. Realistic fiction. Reading Level:
MS. Interest Level: YHS, OHS. English, Sociology, Sex Education, P.E.

SUBJECT AREAS
unwed teen parents; illness, mental; self-knowledge; animals; friendship; love; lying
and deceit; runaways; family relationships; rites of passage; anger; dysfunctional
families; fear; problem parents; working; therapy; school.

CHARACTERS
Jade DeLuna: she's seventeen and has panic disorder
Bruce DeLuna: Jade's dad, who's a sports nut
Nancy DeLuna: Jade's mom, who is over the top into PTA
Oliver DeLuna: Jade's brother, who doesn't like sports
Chai, Hansa, Bamboo, Tombi, Flora, Onyx: the elephants Jade watches on live zoo
    cams
Sebastian Wilder: an unwed father who brings his toddler son, Bo, to see the el-
    ephants
Abe Breakhart: Jade's psychologist
Mrs. Saudstrom: the school nurse, who realizes Jade is having panic attacks
Michael Jacobs: one of Jade's good friends who's obsessed with getting A's
Jenna: one of Jade's friends, who's very involved with her church
Hannah: one of Jade's friends, who's obsessed with boys
Akillo: a friend of Michael's who hangs out with them sometimes
Dr. Kaninski: Jade's psychiatrist
Damian Rama: the zoo's elephant keeper
Rick Lindstrom: Damian's assistant
Elaine, Lee, Evan: volunteers at the elephant house
Roger Dutton: Jade's high school librarian

BOOKTALK
It started when Jade saw him for the first time, a tall boy with curly brown hair and a
baby boy in a backpack, standing outside the elephant enclosure. There was a moment

when she almost recognized him, a moment when she knew he would be special, important, necessary, a part of her life that had been missing and was now found.

His name was Sebastian, and his little boy was named Bo. He loved the elephants and came whenever he could.

But Sebastian had secrets, secrets he couldn't share with Jade, and she kept him a secret from her friends and family, sharing him only with Abe, her therapist. He's older than she is. He's not married. He has a little boy. She can't take the risk her parents will try to keep them apart. And Jade kept her panic attacks a secret as well, not telling Sebastian why she loved being around the elephants so much—they helped her feel calm, and centered, the way Sebastian himself did.

What Sebastian and Jade didn't realize is that secrets have a shelf life—they can't be kept forever. How will their lives change when their own secrets, and the ones involving their families and friends, aren't secrets any longer?

MAJOR THEMES AND IDEAS

- "Humans may watch animals, but animals also watch humans."—Dr. Jerome R. Clade
- Everyone has their own story, their own patterns of life.
- Sometimes even just seeing someone for the first time, you instinctively know that they will be important in your life.
- Panic attacks have more to do with what's going on inside your head than about the reality of life.
- You have to ignore the dangers of living in order to live. You have to learn to ignore the one big truth—life is fatal.
- Some parents insist on running their children's lives.
- If you must, you can be brave.
- The way a person relates to animals says a lot about the kind of person they are.
- If you don't feel secure and safe, you'll never feel free. But if you aren't free, you can't be secure.
- Animal behavior is a lot easier to understand than human behavior.
- We tend to believe people's high opinion of themselves, whether it is earned or not.
- It's important to care about yourself, but it's also important to care about the other people in your life.
- Sometimes the greatest changes are caused by fear.
- Life has no guarantees. Joy, pain, loss are all possibilities.
- Love does not come without the chance of loss.
- Instinct can be helpful, but it's not perfect.
- Love doesn't follow a plan. It's not a series of steps. It can hit like a force of nature, far beyond your ability to control it.
- When you're happy, you forget about all those things that can change and take that happiness away.

- There is little about life that is black-and-white. Most of it is in shades of gray.
- Everything is so interconnected, that sometimes it's hard to figure out who impacts who, and how, and why.
- Moving forward always means loss as well as gain.
- Secrets have a shelf life. They don't stay secret forever.
- Politeness can mean forgiveness, but it is also the way we stay safe among strangers.
- Life and our love for others is a balancing act between our need to be safe and our drive to flee.

BOOK REPORT IDEAS

1. Focus on the human-animal interaction and discuss how Jade changes as she leans to work with the elephants.
2. Is Sebastian morally, ethically right in keeping Bo from his mother? Why or why not?
3. Examine the issue of causality and how people can impact each other's lives in unexpected ways.
4. Speculate on what happens in Santa Fe. Will Sebastian and Jade stay together, or will one or the other change, so they drift apart?
5. Compare the relationship between Sebastian and Jade with that of Jade's parents when they first started dating.
6. How realistic are Jade's relationships with her friends? Why or why not?
7. How are animal interactions similar to and different from human interactions?

BOOKTALK IDEAS

1. Use a jade elephant or a red jacket as a prop.
2. Let Jade and Sebastian each tell their story in the first person.
3. Center your talk around some of the conversations Jade has with Abe.
4. Focus part of your talk on Jade's panic attacks and how they made her feel.
5. Have Oliver talk about his big sister, their relationship, and the secrets she seems to be keeping (remember, he doesn't know about Sebastian).

RISKS

- Unwed teen father kidnaps his son
- Self-absorbed parents
- Father forces son into year-round sports
- Grandmother helps teen father hide his son
- Mother has an affair
- Self-centered father withdraws from family
- Sexually active teens

STRENGTHS
- Characters reveal themselves gradually
- Characters grow, change, and gain insight
- Three-dimensional characters teens can identify with
- Positive and effective therapist
- Realistic language
- Strong teen relationships
- Close sibling relationship
- Ending is somewhat ambiguous
- Realistic settings and situations readers can identify with

AWARDS
New York Public Library Books for the Teen Age, 2008
Booksense Pick, 2007

REVIEWS
"Sensitive readers will deeply connect with Sebastian's love for his son, Jade's love for the elephants, and the loss of love that her parents are experiencing. . . . Readers will feel every word in this book." Lynn Evarts, *VOYA*, 4/07

"Smart, engaging (and occasionally awkward) first-person narration, genuinely complex relationships and strong secondary characters . . . combine to make this a sure hit. . . . The naturalist element evident in the zoo scenes is an added and original bonus. All in all, a pleasure." *Kirkus Reviews*, 1/07

"The author offers a rather unflinching look at realistically complicated lives; readers will root for Jade as she begins to learn that she can't 'put things into separate compartments: right, wrong, good, bad'—especially when it comes to the people she loves." *Publishers Weekly*, 2/07

ⅢⅢⅢⅢ

NICK AND NORAH'S INFINITE PLAYLIST. Rachel Cohn and David Levithan. Knopf, 2006. $16.95. 192p. ISBN10: 0375835318. ISBN13: 9780375835315. Knopf, 2007. $8.99 192p. ISBN10: 0375835334. ISBN13: 9780375835339. Knopf, 2006. $18.99. 192p. ISBN10: 0375935312. ISBN13: 9780375935312. (library binding) Realistic fiction. Reading Level: YHS. Interest Level: YHS, OHS. English, Music, Sociology, Creative Writing, Poetry.

SUBJECT AREAS
music; dating and social life; substance abuse; family relationships; homosexuality; sex and sexuality; rites of passage; working; love; friendship; self-knowledge; creativity; poetry; secrets; writing.

CHARACTERS
Nick: he's the straight bass player in a queercore punk band with his friends
DW: he sings in the band
Thom: he plays guitar in the band
Tris: Nick's ex-girlfriend, who goes to school with Norah and Caroline
Scot: Thom's emo boyfriend
Norah: she agrees to be Nick's girlfriend for five minutes
Caroline: Norah's friend, who's too drunk to get herself home
Randy: singer Caroline has a crush on
Dad: Norah's father, a fat-cat record company CEO
Crazy Lou: club owner who used to be Norah's godfather til he and her dad started a feud
Hunter: lead singer in Hunter Does Hunter, who wants to hook up with DW
Tal: Norah's Evil Ex, who's back in town
Toni/Tony/Toné: the Playboy girl Bunny bouncer at the Camera Obscura

BOOKTALK
Sometimes love comes slowly. But sometimes it can take only one night, one unexpected, frightening, wonderful, explosive, musical night. It starts when Nick says, "I know this is going to sound strange, but would you mind being my girlfriend for the next five minutes?" Norah looks at him. He's dressed so badly, he has to be from Jersey. But he's the bassist and the equipment geek from the punk queercore band that just finished playing, and that means he'll probably have a van. Norah's got to get her best friend Caroline, who's totally passed out, home somehow, so she reaches up, puts a hand on the back of Nick's neck, and pulls him down into a long, slow kiss.

That's the beginning. And for the rest of that night, they fall in and out and in and out of love, break up, and get together. Discover they always want to be together and never want to see each other again. It includes music, fear, laughter, confusion, passion, mistakes, insights, endings, beginnings, taxi driver wisdom, a jacket named Salvatore, and of course, a killer soundtrack. It's the kind of night you never want to end, that dips and soars like a roller coaster, always unexpected, always riding the thin line between dreams that come true and ones that crash and burn.

MAJOR THEMES AND IDEAS
- Love hurts—at least part of the time.
- Never let your ex see you sweat—or cry.

- The soundtrack in your head doesn't always match what's actually happening in your life.
- Beauty is in the eye of the beholder—what's hot to one person is white trash to another.
- Real punk goes down with a straight edge, the only punk left after the madness—the music is the madness.
- The person who trashes you and the one who loves you are never going to be the same person.
- If someone you love says he loves you but still wants you to change, it's not really love after all.
- Real love is without qualifications or requirements.
- Music is an angry machine.
- When the music gives the two of you the excitement of being here, being now, you can connect in the deepest sense.
- The connection, the twoliness, two people can create, trumps the loneliness, the doubt, and the fear.
- Too much of the time, our memories and mistakes intrude on our present and pull us back to the place we've just escaped from.
- You don't tell someone you love them and then tell them to change.
- Why does anyone open themselves up to someone and risk the pain, the "what-ifs," the easy damage? Is it worth the risk?
- Sometimes life scares people so much, all they can do is run away.
- Connecting with someone doesn't always take a long time, but it does mean taking a risk, being honest even when it's scary, and seeing each other straight, not slant.
- *Tikkun olam* is real. The world is broken and our job is to help put the pieces back together.
- The older we get, the more aware we are of how complex and confusing the world has become.
- The more we connect and come together, the better our world will be.
- We don't live in just one song. We go from song to song, lyric to lyric. It's an infinite playlist.
- By making each moment our own, we render it timeless.

BOOK REPORT IDEAS

1. This novel has created a lot of controversy because of the language it uses. Discuss how you feel about the obscenities the characters used. Was it realistic, or did it distract you from the story? Would it be a better book if it didn't include obscenities? Why or why not?
2. The teens in this book are sexually active, whether they are gay or straight. How realistic is this?
3. The book opens in a club where punk bands play. Norah says they've got the music right. Punk that goes down with a straight edge—just the music and the

message. Is this how punk is generally defined? Is the picture of punk music in the book accurate? Why or why not?

4. Speculate on what will happen to Nick and Norah after the end of the book. Will their personal playlist be infinite, or will it come to an end?

5. Nick and Norah are almost immediately attracted. What is it about each of them that attracts the other?

6. What things about yourself did you discover as a result of reading this book? What things about love, life, friendships, philosophies?

7. What's the most important or significant message in this book? Why did you choose it?

8. Discuss the relationship Norah has with her family and how it changes what she does and thinks that night. How realistic are her parents and those of her friends?

9. Discuss your understanding of the phrase "*Tikkun olam*" and whether or not you think it is descriptive of the world today and why.

10. Describe the person you identified with most and explain why, using quotes from the book.

BOOKTALK IDEAS

1. Use the lyrics from songs in the book as part of your talk.

2. Use a Nick and Norah playlist as a soundtrack for your talk. If your mix includes lyrics that might be offensive, consider clearing it with your teacher before you present it.

3. Use a jacket like Salvatore as a prop.

4. Write your booktalk from both Nick's and Norah's points of view, including what they each think of the other when they meet.

5. Create a song that is your talk—a song about Nick, Norah, and what happened to them that night.

RISKS

- Uses the word fuck on almost every page
- Homosexual characters
- Teens drink and smoke
- Sexually active teens
- Teens hook up sexually very quickly
- Vulgar song lyrics
- Graphic and somewhat public sexual scene
- Extremely permissive parents with a non-conservative attitude about what their children are allowed to do
- Parents let kids do whatever they want to

STRENGTHS
- Realistic dialogue brings the characters to vivid life
- Authentic teen voices
- Accurately portrayed setting/situation
- Written from two first-person perspectives
- Depicts the difficulty teens can have creating intimate relationships
- Teens make smart decisions about when not to have sex
- Shows the fears and hesitations of starting a new relationship
- Characters grow, gain insight, and learn trust from their experience
- Rite-of-passage story
- Shows just how much can happen over the course of only one night

AWARDS
ALA Best Books for Young Adults, 2007
ALA Quick Picks for Reluctant Young Adult Readers, 2007
ALA Popular Paperbacks, 2008

REVIEWS
"Laced with musical name droppings of punk, heavy metal, and even oldies songs and groups (ABBA gets a nod), the accomplished authors create an alternating-points-of-view romance that is edgy, sexual, and oh-so realistic. Hip and bold descriptive phrases highlight this book—a novel that will achieve cult status with older teens." Rollie Welch, *VOYA*, 4/06

"There are many heart-stopping, insightful moments in this supremely satisfying and sexy romance. A first-rate read." Tracy Karbel, Glenside Public Library District, Glendale Heights, IL, *School Library Journal*, 5/06

"There's perfectly captured teen music—geek talk and delicious stuff about kissing and what lies beyond. Sensual and full of texture." *Kirkus Reviews*, 4/06

📖📖📖

NOTHING TO LOSE. Alex Flinn. HarperTeen, an imprint of HarperCollins, 2004. $16.99. 288p. ISBN: 0060517506. ISBN13: 9780060517502. HarperTeen, 2005. $7.99. 304p. ISBN10: 0060517522. ISBN13: 9780060517526. HarperTeen, 2004. $17.89. 288p. ISBN10: 0060517514. ISBN13: 9780060517519. (library binding) Realistic fiction. Reading Level: MS. Interest Level: MS, YHS. English, Psychology, Government, Social Studies, Ethics, Vocational Education, Sociology.

SUBJECT AREAS

working; stepparents; sex and sexuality; justice; legal system; runaways; problem parents; family relationships; abuse, physical; friendship; crime and delinquency; love; rites of passage; violence; anger; dysfunctional families; bullying; fear; self-knowledge; secrets; school.

CHARACTERS

Michael Daye/Birdman: running away took him from being a high school athlete with a promising future to a carny with no future
Cricket/Jason Dietz: a carny who's a friend of Michael's
Tristan: one of Michael's best friends and football buddy
Mom/Lisa Monroe: she refuses to leave her abusive husband
Walker Monroe: Michael's stepfather who's rich, violent, and mean
Kirstie Anderson: a carny Michael loved
Coach Lowery: Michael's football coach
Vanessa DeLeon: a cheerleader who likes football players
Julian Karpe: a long-time friend of Michael's
Angela Guerra: Jason's stepmother and a lawyer
Victor: a carny with an attitude
Tedder Dutton: a football player Michael doesn't really like
Miss Hamasaki: Michael's English teacher
Antonia: a carny who pretends to be psychic
Sherri Mastin: emergency room nurse who looked at Lisa and knew the truth

BOOKTALK

A year ago, he ran away to join the carnival. Now he's back in Miami with that same carnival, reading newspaper headlines and knowing he shouldn't have come back. But the headlines are about his mother. He had to come back. He had to help her.

> Jury Selection Begins in Monroe Murder Trial
> Jury Selection will begin in the case of a Miami woman accused of bludgeoning her husband to death last year.
> Lisa Monroe, 35, a former legal secretary, is charged with murdering her husband, prominent philanthropist and local attorney, last March. Monroe plans to claim a battered-spouse defense at the trial. Her son, Michael Daye, now 17, has been missing since shortly before the alleged homicide took place.

He liked being a carny, running the Mole in the Hall game. But he could never get away from his memories. For two years, he'd watched his stepfather beat up on his mother and listened to her excuses about his temper. There was no way he was going to let his mother go to jail for killing the man who'd been killing her, one beating at a time. He couldn't let her be punished when the real criminal was his stepfather.

MAJOR THEMES AND IDEAS

- No one has the right to hurt you, either mentally or physically.
- Unfortunately, you can get used to anything, even abuse.
- Once you have been betrayed, trusting someone isn't easy. It takes guts.
- Destiny may be worth dying for.
- Having nothing left to lose can be freeing sometimes.
- You can get beaten up on the inside, just like you can get beaten up on the outside.
- Watching someone you love get abused, when you can do nothing to stop it, is toxic and self-destructive.
- Sometimes you have to help yourself because that's the only person you *can* help.
- Worrying about someone who's in trouble or danger doesn't help them and it makes you crazy.
- Scars don't hurt. They're just something you have to live with, because they won't go away.
- You always have a choice.
- When parents have problems their children often blame themselves, but it isn't their responsibility or their fault.
- It's hard to know what people are capable of when, after years of pressure, they just snap.
- When you do it a lot, you get used to leaving, to being alone.
- Don't carry a weapon if you aren't sure you'll be willing to use it.
- No one can make someone leave an abusive situation. They must decide themselves to leave.
- Postponing making a decision *is* a decision.
- You can't run away from your past.
- There's a before and an after, and once you've crossed the line between them, you can never go back, no matter how much you'd like to.
- You have to live with what you've done, how it's changed you, and the knowledge that nothing will ever be the same again.
- The past is behind you. Accept that and move on.
- Everyone has dark parts of their past that they don't talk about.

BOOK REPORT IDEAS

1. Kirstie told Michael that their meeting was destiny. Discuss what you think about destiny. Do you have one? Why or why not?
2. Explain why you think Lisa let Walker abuse her. What did she get from it?
3. Walker is guilty of abuse, but he isn't the only one who's guilty. Who else is, and why?
4. Several times Michael tells Angela something about himself, only to find out she already knew it. Discuss how she knew so much about him, and where and from whom she got the information.

5. Examine the last eight chapters in the book and discuss how realistic they are. If you think they aren't realistic, explain how you would have ended the book.
6. What did Michael learn from his year as a carny?
7. Consider the idea that no one can be forced to leave a situation where they are being abused. What are some other abusive situations, other than spousal abuse?
8. Angela tells Michael that Walker beat him up on the inside. What do you think she meant by that?
9. Speculate on what might have happened if Michael had gone to the police about his mother's abuse. What scene in the book supports your theory?
10. What is the most important thing you learned from reading and thinking about this book?

BOOKTALK IDEAS
1. Use the newspaper and TV stories in the book as the basis for your talk.
2. Write your talk in first person, as Michael.
3. Write your talk from Julian's point of view, and have him introduce Michael.
4. Many people in this book have secrets. Focus your talk on the secrets everyone is keeping, but don't give too much away.

RISKS
- Woman kills abusive husband
- Teens run away from home
- Teens drink and smoke
- Husband abuses wife in varied and violent ways
- Carny life portrayed as fun and exciting
- Teens are sexually active
- Teen retaliates against stepfather
- Weak woman will not leave abusive relationship
- Some characters work as "freaks" in the carnival
- Vulgar language

STRENGTHS
- Story is told from two perspectives, then and now
- Son tries to protect mother from abusive husband
- Suspenseful storyline draws reader in
- Realistic view of carnival life
- Teaches that you can't run away from your past
- Surprise ending means the reader has to view all the action from a new perspective
- Characters grow and gain insight
- Shows that love doesn't always last forever

- Complex characters are realistic, allowing the reader to identify
- Realistic dialogue
- Positive view of lawyers and legal system
- Shows that it is possible to accept the past and go on
- Portrays the strength of long-term friendships
- Ambivalent but positive ending allows for speculation and discussion
- Shows the unfortunate power of the abuser over the abused
- Impact of spousal abuse on children in several families who respond differently

AWARDS
ALA Best Books for Young Adults, 2005
ALA Quick Picks for Reluctant Young Adult Readers, 2005
New York Public Library Books for the Teen Age, 2005
IRA/CBC Young Adults' Choice, 2006

REVIEWS
"Easy, natural dialogue and a suspenseful plot make this book appealing to all levels of readers." Diane Emge, *VOYA*, 6/04

"The complex, well-drawn characters of Michael and his mother convey the psychological effects of abuse with insight and compassion. . . . Flinn does a masterful job of exploring domestic violence, conveying that it's prevalent among all economic classes and destructive wherever it takes hold." *Kirkus Reviews*, 2/04

"The result is a fast-paced, readable mystery that is rooted in the psychology of battered-spouse syndrome and its impact on an entire family." Michael Cart, *Booklist*, 3/04

📖📖📖

OFF-COLOR. Janet McDonald. Farrar, Straus and Giroux, 2007. $16.00. 176p. ISBN10: 0374371962. ISBN13: 9780374371968. Realistic fiction. Reading Level: MS. Interest Level: MS, YHS. English, Sociology, Ethics.

SUBJECT AREAS
school; friendship; music; racism; prejudice; working; secrets; lying and deceit; self-knowledge; anger; elderly; ethnic groups; family relationships; cultural identity; poverty; stereotypes.

CHARACTERS

Cameron Storm: she challenges adults, cuts classes, loves to sing and hang with her friends
Patricia Storm: Cameron's single mother
Paula Levin: Cameron's homeroom teacher
Amanda Vine: the most fun of Cameron's friends; she wants to be a vet
Prudence Darling: she's a great dancer, but is going to nursing school
Crystal Sterick: she's going to be famous for something—she just doesn't know what
Malcolm Siciliano: school counselor who talks to Cameron about cutting class and getting to school late
Elba Oblomova: she owns the nail salon where Patricia works
Valya, Leedmila, Anna, Irina: they also work at Madame Elba's
Ashaka Johnson: she runs the black nail salon where Patricia works after Elba's closes
Langston Robinson: an ex-actor and Cameron's English teacher
Ruth Goldstone: the strictest teacher in school; she teaches world history
Miss Vi/ Elvira B. Hutton: an elderly black woman who lives in the building Cameron and Patricia move into
Sage Brown: Cameron's multicultures teacher
Bambi Thomas, Kali Harris, Collen Kim, Asia Preston: the women Patricia works with at Nubia Nails
Ja'Qualah, Boomshaka, DéWanda Illnana: Asia's friends from the projects
Shamel, Dwayne, Dashawn, Abdullah: boys who date Asia and her friends
Ashford: Miss Vi's grandson, who starts dating Cameron

BOOKTALK

Cameron's your typical Brooklyn teenager—she hangs with her friends, loves her music, and cuts school as much as she can. Her mom hassles her, but not too much, and they're pretty close, 'cause her father's never been in the picture, so it's always been just the two of them. Her best friends always have her back, and even if money's tight, her life is pretty good. Then one day her mother comes home from work in tears—the nail salon where she works is closing. They can't afford the apartment 'cause her mother's new job doesn't pay as well, and they have to move into the projects—public housing—on the other side of Brooklyn.

Cameron's white, with dark hair and blue eyes. How's she gonna survive in the mostly black projects? The black girls who live there are tough and could make her life really hard. But just days after they move in, Cameron finds the secret her mother has kept from her, the secret that makes everything seem unimportant. Suddenly her whole life is completely changed. Will she be able to figure out how to deal with her new life?

MAJOR THEMES AND IDEAS
- Real friends are forever.
- Parents generally do the best they can at the time, even though in retrospect, it wasn't the wisest decision.
- Race can both separate us and bring us together.
- Refusing to talk about a problem you have with someone only makes it worse.
- Prejudice isn't only about race. It's about being different.
- If all you take home from your job is a grumpy mood and too little money, it's time to look for another one.
- Poverty isn't fun, but it can be endured.
- Secrets don't stay secrets forever.
- Some teachers do care about their students.
- If you have one white parent and one black parent, are you white or black?
- The key to survival is resilience. Deal with the crisis and move on.
- It's important to accept all of yourself.
- Your value comes from inside, not from those around you.
- Race is a social and cultural fact, but it may not be a *biological* fact for much longer.
- Trying to protect us, our parents do the opposite of what we'd want.
- At some level, all of us are mutts anyway.

BOOK REPORT IDEAS
1. Discuss the idea that while race is still a social and cultural concept, it may no longer be a biological one. What does this mean to you?
2. Discuss how you and your friends identify someone's race. On what do you base your decision?
3. Explain how you might feel or react if you suddenly discovered what Cameron did—that one of your parents or grandparents was not the same race you have always believed yourself to be.
4. How true is it that blacks and whites live in different worlds, are treated differently? Why?

BOOKTALK IDEAS
1. Focus your talk on characters, and let Cameron and her best friends introduce each other.
2. Center your talk around Patricia's secret, but don't reveal what it is.
3. Use music by Cameron's favorite singers and bands as a soundtrack for your talk.

RISKS
- Unmarried mother
- Biracial teen
- Racial slurs
- Racial stereotypes
- Interracial dating
- Negative portrayal of teacher
- Somewhat abrupt and pat ending

STRENGTHS
- Strong, positive mother-daughter relationship
- Caring and supportive teachers
- Authentic teen voices and dialogue
- Realistic setting
- Fast-moving plot
- Three-dimensional characters
- Addresses issues faced by biracial teens
- Realistic, but not vulgar, language
- Uses humor effectively
- Shows how world is experienced differently by blacks and whites
- Mother likes and accepts daughter's friends
- Little to no racial tension
- Depicts current teens' perspective on racial identity

AWARD
New York Public Library Books for the Teen Age, 2008

REVIEWS
"School libraries might find this book a worthy addition if patrons are clamoring for street lit because it paints a realistic portrait of inner-city urban life but is neither sexually explicit nor full of profanity. Cameron's solid, caring friendships with people of different races inspire her to be comfortable with who she is." Carlisle K. Webber, *VOYA*, 12/07

"Frank conversations will surely get readers thinking as well. . . . Readers will be impressed with Cameron's growing strength, and they'll be swept up in the exuberant writing." *Publishers Weekly*, 11/07

"McDonald dramatizes the big issues from the inside, showing the hard times and the joy in fast-talking dialogue that is honest, insulting, angry, tender, and very funny." Hazel Rochman, *Booklist*, 8/07

⊞⊞⊞

PARANOID PARK. Blake Nelson. Viking, 2006. $15.99. 176p. ISBN 10: 0670061182. ISBN 13: 9780670061181. Puffin, 2008. $6.99. 192p. ISBN 10: 0142411566. ISBN 13: 9780142411568. Realistic fiction; Mystery/Suspense. Reading Level: MS. Interest Level: MS, YHS. English, Ethics, P.E., Psychology.

SUBJECT AREAS
death and dying; sports; legal system; guilt; school; self-knowledge; rites of passage; family relationships; separation and divorce; friendship; sex and sexuality; homelessness; violence.

CHARACTERS
Me/"Prep skater dude": I'm sixteen years old, and I've made a terrible mistake
Macy McLaughlin: she's a good friend and suggested I write her a letter when I can't tell her what happened
Jared Fitch: a senior and one of the best skaters at school; he took me to Paranoid for the first time
Jennifer Hasselbach: we'd hooked up at the beginning of the summer, but she didn't get the mystique of Paranoid
Mom, Dad: my parents, who were fighting and talking about getting a divorce
Henry: my little brother, who throws up all the time because of the yelling and fighting
Kelly: a weird girl Jared's been hanging out with
Scratch: a guy I met at Paranoid who talked me into loaning him my board
Paisley: a friend of Scratch's, but a lot younger, about fourteen
Uncle Tommy: my uncle, who has a beach house, where my dad is staying
Parker, James: two of my friends
Christian Barlow, Paul Auster: Jared's friends and serious skaters
Elizabeth Gould: Jennifer's good friend
Detective Matthew Brady: he's investigating the security guard's death
Aunt Sally: my aunt who came to stay with us when my mom needed to get away

BOOKTALK
I'd heard about Paranoid Park for years. It was, like, the ultimate place for boarders. It was under a bridge, down by the old warehouses, a street park—no rules, no owners, no pay to skate. Some old guys built it years ago, and a lot of the best skaters go there, from California and even the East Coast. It was kind of a street kid hangout, with a dangerous, edgy vibe, and lots of stories about it, including how a skinhead got stabbed there once. That's how it got its name—Paranoid Park.

I wasn't a bad skater, and with Jared's help, I was coming along. But no way was I ready for Paranoid—especially alone. That was my first bad decision—going to the park alone after Jared bailed on me. The second bad decision was talking to Scratch and his friends after he borrowed my board. The third bad decision was going with him when he hopped the ten-twenty train to go get some beer. Three strikes and you're out in a ball game. But this was no game, this was life, and it was that fourth strike that changed my life completely, and led me to where I am now, at my Uncle Tommy's beach house, trying to write out what I can't talk about—the way that security guard looked when I hit him over the head with my skateboard and he fell to the ground beside the moving train. The way he got up and his coat got caught by the train, and he was dragged along beside it, and then under it, where the wheels cut him in two. It seemed like years while Scratch and I watched it, but it couldn't have been more than a few seconds.

Scratch bolted—I never saw anyone move so fast in my life. But I just stood there. I picked up my skateboard. I felt like I should do something—but what? The train passed, and there was the body, cut in half. A body that had been alive just seconds ago. Blood was everywhere, on the tracks, on the gravel under my feet. I didn't know what to do—call the police?—but we'd been breaking the law. And I was the one who hit him, made him dizzy or careless so he got caught by the train. What if they told me it wasn't an accident—it was murder?

So I left. I skated away. I didn't tell anyone. Not then, not when the cop came to my school, asking questions, not even when Macy started asking questions about why I was acting so weird. I never said anything to anyone—til now.

MAJOR THEMES AND IDEAS

- No matter how bad your life seems, it's no comparison to the true outcasts, the guys who had to be tough enough to survive life on the streets.
- Do the right thing, or everything will get worse.
- It only takes one bad move to blow your whole life and lose everything you've worked for.
- What if telling won't really help anyone and could make things a lot worse for you?
- Extreme stress is dangerous. It can warp your thinking and point you in dangerous directions that make sense only at the time.
- Crying is one way the body releases tension and stress.
- When you have a secret, you can forget it for hours, but then suddenly, you'll remember it, and it just blindsides you from outta nowhere, and it's all you can think about.
- Being able to function while keeping the worst possible secrets may be what makes you a man.
- When you're lying about something, the hardest thing to do is keep your story straight.

- Character is fate.
- Once your innocence has been stripped away, you can never get it back again.
- Life only moves in one direction—there are no do-overs.
- Secrets isolate you, separate you from everyone around you.
- In most situations, the truth comes out sooner or later.
- Mostly, people do what they think they're supposed to do.
- What does freedom really mean? Any place can be a prison if your head's not in the right place.
- The older secrets get, the deeper they get buried, and the harder they are to dig up.
- Digging up an old secret that's been buried by the daily routines of life destroys a lot more of your life than a secret you've just begun to bury.
- Time may heal all wounds, but it sure doesn't erase the scars.
- Dark secrets, big, intense ones, change who you are and how you relate to other people.
- Knowing there's one person out there on your side, one person who's got your back, can be enough to keep you sane.

BOOK REPORT IDEAS

1. Speculate on what might have happened if the narrator had reported the accident from the security guard's car. Would his story have been believed? How might Scratch have reacted?
2. How did the narrator's life change because of his guilty secret?
3. Discuss why the narrator didn't tell anyone about the accident. He didn't want to tell family, friends, or the police—but why didn't he find someone else to call?
4. Discuss the idea of an 800 number that you could call and talk to someone who would listen and tell you what your options were.
5. Speculate on what happens after the book is over. Does the security guard's death remain unsolved? Does the narrator ever learn to trust again? How will this incident impact his adult life?
6. Examine the concept of guilt. What is its function? Is it valuable? Why or why not?
7. If the Streeters had beaten up the narrator without police intervention, would he have gone to the police? If his mother had called the cops about it, what would he have done and what would he have told them? Would he have kept his secret?

BOOKTALK IDEAS

1. Write your talk as a letter.
2. Include excerpts of the news stories as part of your talk
3. Build your talk around what the narrator's friends might say about him.
4. Base your talk on the idea of guilt and how it can eat away at you.

RISKS
- Teen participates in fatal accident
- Teen doesn't report accident and tries to hide his involvement
- Angry and separated parents are unaware of son's problems
- Skateboarders stereotyped as dangerous
- Teens drink and have sex
- Teen girls plan for and then brag about their loss of virginity

STRENGTHS
- Realistic dialogue and narration
- Characters readers can identify with
- Few curse words
- Shows the impact of intense guilt on thoughts and behavior
- Ambiguous ending
- Shows the power of friendship
- Realistic, three-dimensional characters
- First person narration enhances authenticity of the voice

AWARD
ALA Quick Picks for Reluctant Young Adult Readers, 2007

REVIEWS
"The reader spends the entire book in the narrator's head as he struggles mainly with the guilt of the death and how this guilt changes his outlook on everything he experiences. . . . The novel feels quite genuine, especially the ending in which Nelson does not resolve the main plot, preferring instead to allow the narrator to come to terms with his guilt." Steven Kral, *VOYA*, 10/06

"This novel, which probes the cultural divide separating the narrator from the rough-and-tumble 'Streeters,' examines the chasm separating moral responsibility from the eternal damnation of keeping a horrible secret. . . . Many teens will relate on one level or another to this teen's terrible dilemma." Joel Shoemaker, Southeast Junior High School, Iowa City, IA, *School Library Journal*, 11/06

"Readers will have a visceral reaction to this story, but on a literary level, they'll also appreciate Nelson's clever plotting and spot-on characterizations: the boy's parents' acrimonious divorce . . . seems depressingly real. Nonstop page turning until the surprising conclusion." Ilene Cooper, *Booklist*, 9/06 ᴒᴒᴒ

PARROTFISH. Ellen Whittlinger. Simon and Schuster, 2007. $16.99. 294p. ISBN10: 1416916229. ISBN13: 9781416916222. Realistic fiction. Reading Level: YHS. Interest Level: YHS, OHS. English, Sex Education, Health, Sociology, Psychology.

SUBJECT AREAS
GLBTQ; self-knowledge; rites of passage; peer pressure; family relationships; bullying; sex and sexuality; school; problem parents; ethics; stereotypes.

CHARACTERS
Angela/Grady Katz-McNair: Angela has never felt comfortable as a girl and decides to become Grady, a boy

Mom/Judy Katz: Grady's mother, who doesn't understand her son at all

Dad/Joe McNair: Grady's father, who takes everything in stride

Aunt Gail: Mom's sister, who just had a baby, Michael

Laura Katz-McNair: Grady's younger sister

Charlie Katz-McNair: Grady's spoiled little brother

Eve: Grady's ex-best friend

Susan: Eve's mother

Sebastian Shipley: he's into cable TV, shooting, editing, and programming the local access cable TV channel

Mr. Reed: the TV production teacher

Mrs. Norman: Grady's English teacher, who refuses to call him Grady

Ms. Marius: Grady's Spanish teacher

Ms. Unger: girls' P.E. teacher who knows about transgendered teens and sympathizes

Dr. Ridgeway: the high school principal

Danya Seifert: she's a bully and lots of girls are afraid of her

Melanie, Zoe: they'll do anything to be Danya's friends

Kleinhorst, Whitney: two guys who try to harass Grady

Russ Gallo: he's in TV production and stands up for Grady

Kita Charles: Russ's gorgeous girlfriend

Wilma: sales clerk at the pharmacy

George Garrison, Ben London: co-captains of the basketball team

BOOKTALK

His mother said, "Angela, what do you mean, you're Grady now? You can't be my son, you're my daughter!"

His ex-best friend said, "Angie, this is too confusing. I need to have friends, but I don't want people to think I'm a weirdo."

The school geek said, "Wow, Grady, that means you're just like the parrot-fish—they go from female to male, too!"

The principal said, "Teenagers rarely know what's good for them. Take my advice, Angela, and forget all about this."

The freshman bully said, "That is so sick! I've never heard of that! Stay away from me—you're disgusting!"

His father said, "I want you to know you're still my kid no matter what I call you, whether you're my son or my daughter."

The girl he is in love with said, "You have more courage than a whole football team of those idiots."

The Monday after Thanksgiving Angela Katz-McNair didn't go to school. Grady Katz-McNair did. Angela had always felt like a boy, even though she was a girl. Changing her gender, looking like the boy she'd always felt like, seemed like the right thing to do. But Grady hadn't anticipated how everyone around him would react. People could change lots of personal things, and no one said anything—they dyed their hair, gained or lost weight, changed jobs or religions or political parties. They got implants and nose jobs, did botox and lasix. Why was gender the one sacred thing that could never change?

What makes a person male or female? How they look? How they act? How they think? How they are raised? Changing from a girl to a boy means Grady will have to find his own answers to all those questions and more.

MAJOR THEMES AND IDEAS

- Gender identity is whether, in your mind, you see yourself as a boy or a girl.
- Gender identity starts in early childhood, long before puberty or sexual identity.
- Transgendered people see themselves as one gender, while their body is a different gender, rather than the one in their mind.
- You can only lie to yourself about who you are for so long without going crazy.
- Telling the truth, and being who you are, will probably make people feel uncomfortable, even your family and closest friends.
- Sometimes people are great, sometimes they're jerks.
- Some adults believe that teens really don't know what's good for them.
- Nature creates many variations; there are fish that can change their gender in response to their environment.
- Being different makes you stand out in a crowd.

- Many times, people are uncomfortable around someone who's different, and this discomfort expresses itself as ridicule and anger.
- Gender is a label and doesn't affect what's inside.
- Coming out about being transgendered can be very scary, because you have no way of predicting what anyone will do in response to the news.
- Change one little thing in a situation and everything else responds and changes.
- Spending all your time working and making money can be a poor choice. You should also have time to do what you love and enjoy.
- You can't ignore bullies. They'll never change unless you call them on it.
- Gender is the first thing people want to know about you, and it divides the world into two groups—male and female. There's no place for anyone who doesn't fit in either gender.
- A friend is someone who likes you, believes in you, and stands up for you when anyone puts you down.
- Being angry at everyone all the time is exhausting.
- People talk about something because it's important to them. They're thinking about it, not ignoring it.
- Oddballs are frequently the most interesting people.
- People usually recognize courage, even if they do not acknowledge it.
- Mean people generally hate themselves as much as they do others.
- No one ever knows what really goes on between two people when they're alone. All you know is what people tell, and most don't tell. And a lot of what people *do* tell isn't necessarily true.
- It's hard to be totally mad at someone who's been your best friend.
- Some people are stronger than others and are able to fight back against their enemies.
- Knowing you have friends who will help you roll with the punches makes life a lot more exciting and easier to deal with.
- What makes you miserable today will someday be a good story to tell your friends.
- We spend a long time trying to figure out how to act like ourselves, and then, if we're lucky, we figure out that being ourselves has nothing to do with acting.

BOOK REPORT IDEAS

1. Sebastian takes Grady at face value, doesn't treat him like a freak, and stands up for him. Explain why he doesn't see Grady as anything but normal.
2. Discuss why females respond more negatively to Grady's gender shift than males do.
3. Discuss the effect on others of Grady's outward change to being male. Why do they see him as a different person, when all he's changed is the surface? He's still the same person on the inside.

4. Analyze the scene in the gym when co-captains dressed as women, and Grady's thoughts about why macho males enjoy dressing as women.
5. Discuss the idea gender of identity as a football field, and what people would look/act like at the two ends compared to people located more towards the center of the field. What makes people male or female, aside from body parts?
6. Explain why changing gender is such a big deal, based on Grady's thoughts on it in chapter 11.
7. Explain Eve's feelings about Grady. She doesn't want to be seen with him, yet calls to warn him about Danya's plans.
8. What have you learned while reading this book? What scenes, situations, and characters were most important to you and why?
9. Does each man have a sense of himself as "leader of the pack," who gets the last word and makes the decisions? Why or why not?

BOOKTALK IDEAS
1. Have two or three different characters introduce themselves and Grady, ending with Grady himself.
2. Use a picture of a supermale parrotfish to illustrate your talk.
3. Have Grady tell his own story.

RISKS
- Transgendered character
- Realistic language including obscenities
- Transgendered teen is mocked, bullied, and ridiculed by other teens and adults
- Frank and honest tone may be offensive to some
- Detailed discussions of sex and sexuality
- Presents GLBTQ teens as normal

STRENGTHS
- Shares what transgendered teens experience
- Presents being transgendered as a physical condition present from birth
- Includes GLBTQ teens within the normal spectrum of human sexuality
- Explains the difference between transgendered and homosexual
- Includes several supportive teen and adult characters
- Provides many opportunities for discussion
- Allows reader to experience what it means to be transgendered and understand what they or someone they know is going through
- Depicts a loving, yet volatile family that works to make the family succeed and that shares love even when members don't agree

- Grady is a character who is easy to like and identify with, because he is so much more than his gender
- Explains the differences between gender identity and sexual identity
- Deals with gender identity in an open and honest manner
- Three-dimensional characters that grow and gain insight
- Positive portraits of geeky or oddball characters who sometimes win out over the "popular" crowd

AWARDS
Lambda Literary Award Finalist, 2007
New York Public Library Books for the Teen Age, 2008

REVIEWS
"Peopled with wonderfully wacky characters and scenes, this narrative snaps and crackles with wit, even while it touches the spirit of the sensitive reader. Wittlinger scores another success with this highly recommended novel." Jamie S. Hansen, *VOYA*, 8/07

"The book is an excellent resource for building awareness about, and serving the increasing number of, transgendered teens. Helpful resources include Web sites and further-reading material. The lack of similar titles available. . . , and Wittlinger's captivating storytelling ability combine to make this a book that most libraries should stock." Cara von Wrangel Kinsey, New York Public Library, *School Library Journal*, 9/07

"[Wittlinger] has also done a superb job of untangling the complexities of gender identity and showing the person behind labels like 'gender dysphoria.'" Michael Cart, *Booklist*, 4/07

ඕඕඕ

PERFECT CHEMISTRY. Simone Elkeles. Walker, 2008. $16.99. 368p. ISBN10: 0802798233. ISBN13: 9780802798237. Walker, 2008. $9.99. 368p. ISBN10: 0802798225. ISBN13: 9780802798220. Realistic fiction. Reading Level: YHS. Interest Level: YHS, OHS. English, Foreign Language, Psychology, Sociology.

SUBJECT AREAS
school; love; ethnic groups; peer pressure; gangs; substance abuse; family relationships; self-knowledge; mental illness; rites of passage; anger; bullying; violence;

survival; secrets; crime and delinquency; dating and social life; creativity; friendship; fear; revenge; prejudice; problem parents; poverty; guns; gossip; death and dying.

CHARACTERS

Brittany Ellis: she's blonde, beautiful, rich, and her life isn't nearly as perfect as she pretends it is

Shelley Ellis: Brittany's older sister, who is mentally handicapped and has cerebral palsy

Bagha: Shelley's new caretaker

Patricia Ellis/Mom: she needs everything to be perfect, all the time

Alex Fuentes: a gangbanger from the wrong side of the tracks, who wishes he could get out of the Latino Blood

Luis Fuentes: Alex's eleven-year-old brother

Carlos Fuentes: Alex's fifteen-year-old brother

Mrs. Fuentes/Mamá: a single mother; she's a grocery store checker, and she keeps a close eye on her sons

Carmen Sanchez: Alex's ex-girlfriend and next door neighbor, who's tough and wants Alex back

Colin Adams: Brittany's boyfriend, whom she hasn't seen all summer

Dr. Aguirre: the new principal, who's determined to run a tight ship and cut the gangbangers no slack

Paco: Alex's closest friend, who's also in the Blood

Mrs. Peterson: she teaches senior chemistry and is one of the toughest teachers in school

Darlene Boehm: co-captain of the varsity pom squad with Brittany

Isabel: a friend of Alex's who's on the pom squad

Morgan, Madison, Megan: Brittany's friends, the M-factor

Ms. Small: gym teacher and pom squad sponsor

Caitlin: another pom squad member

Doug: he's dating Sierra

Sierra: another member of the pom squad

Bill Ellis: Brittany's dad, who owns a computer chip manufacturing company and is a workaholic

Blake: Alex is going to make sure he pays his debt to Hector

Hector Martinez: he's the leader of the Latino Blood, the gang Alex is a member of

Lucky: Alex's friend and fellow gang member who makes a bet with him about Brittany

Enrique: Alex's cousin who owns the body shop where Alex works; he's also in the Blood

Wil, Mario, Chris, Javier, Raul, Sam: they're all members of the Blood

Miss Koto: she's the school nurse

Dr. Meir: Shelley's doctor

Elena and Jorge: Alex's cousin and her new husband

Gary Frankel: a white geek that Alex meets in jail
Lexie: Brittany's roommate at the university
Georgia Jackson: she works at Sunny Acres, where Shelley lives

BOOKTALK

They couldn't be more different. Brittany's a blonde cheerleader with a BMW convertible, who dates the football team captain and lives in a mansion on the north side of town. Alex is a Latino gangbanger, with a motorcycle he built himself; his mom's a grocery store checker and he lives with her and his two little brothers in a small house near the railroad tracks on the south side of town. His reputation says he's a drug dealer and an addict. Her reputation says she's little miss perfect, and most of the girls at school hate her because of the way she looks.

But they're very alike under the skin. They're both playing the game, hiding their real selves behind the image they protect. They both want out of the lives they feel they're forced to live. They both want someone they can be real with. The last time a northerngirl tried to date a *Mexicano*, she lost everything. And Alex is not just a guy from the wrong side of the tracks; he's the enforcer, the debt collector, for his gang, and they want him to stick to his own kind.

Which are stronger—their differences or their likenesses?

MAJOR THEMES AND IDEAS

- Your history defines who you are.
- Just because it looks like you have a perfect life doesn't mean it really is perfect.
- Outward appearances mean everything.
- Do something for mankind or the planet you live on—then you'll be a success.
- Diversity may bring knowledge, but it can also breed hatred, prejudice, and ignorance.
- In some towns, where you were born defines you more than your ethnicity.
- Once you're in a gang, you're in for life.
- A gang member rarely avoids the cops, or jail.
- The mean streets are only three blocks away from mansions and million-dollar homes.
- Either you're in a gang, or you're against them.
- It's not fair to use somebody to make yourself feel better when you're hurting.
- It's easy to hate someone who has everything, who has a perfect life.
- Everyone has secrets they're dying to share with the right person.
- We're all actors in our lives, pretending to be who we want people to think we are.
- Sharing your secrets draws you closer. Trust allows you to take a chance and share.
- Problems don't go away by ignoring them or hiding from them.

- You have to live for the moment, the day, the here and now. It can all be taken away from you in only a moment.
- Gangs have their own rules and expectations about their members. Follow the rules or pay the consequences.
- A guy who cheats once will cheat again.
- If you ask someone for a favor, you're going to owe him one. A bigger one.
- Sometimes good men need to, have to, do things that aren't good.
- Even the most unlikely guy can become your ally.
- Never let them see you sweat—or scared shitless.
- Sometimes getting too close to the fire does actually burn you.
- Kids just want parents to love and accept them for who they are.
- Your best friend tells you the truth and has your back.
- You can change the world. The world is what you make it. There are lots of paths. Some are just harder than others.

BOOK REPORT IDEAS

1. Compare the book to *West Side Story* or *Romeo and Juliet*.
2. Compare the way Brittany treats Shelley to the way their mother does.
3. Explain why Brittany is so afraid of Shelley's being put in a residential facility.
4. Discuss why Brittany keeps her home life a secret. What might happen if people found out about it?
5. Brittany falls apart when she realizes she hurt Alex. Why does she react like that, and why is she so concerned about her friends finding out.
6. How are Alex and Brittany different and alike? What do they have in common?
7. Why is Brittany so concerned about being in control of her life? What will happen if she loses control?
8. Discuss Brittany's relationship with her mother. Why is Brittany so concerned about not upsetting her? What does she think might happen?
9. Explain why Brittany's reputation as a good girl and Alex's reputation as a bad boy are so important to them.
10. Speculate how much influence/impact Alex's and Brittany's relationship had on the town, and on their contemporaries. How different is the high school when Paco is a senior from what it was like when Alex and Brittany were seniors?

BOOKTALK IDEAS

1. Have Alex and Brittany introduce each other.
2. Have Sierra and Isabel introduce Brittany and Alex.
3. Use the book trailer from the author's website as part of your booktalk.

RISKS

- Gangs and gangbangers
- Interracial dating and love

- Graphic violence, gang wars
- Mother is unable to cope with handicapped daughter
- Father ignores fights between mother and daughter
- Parents put enormous pressure on daughter to be perfect
- School administration harasses student only because he's a gang member
- Teens drink, smoke, curse, and are sexually active
- Gang members commit murder

STRENGTHS

- Three-dimensional, realistic characters teens can identify with
- Accurate, realistic dialogue, including English and Spanish slang and obscenities
- Plot line pulls reader into story immediately
- Multiple narrators give two perspectives and make novel more complex
- Beautiful, evocative love story
- Shows love and strong ties between siblings
- Main characters look beyond each other's surface to see the real person inside
- Friendships cross the lines of social class
- Rite-of-passage story
- Much for teens to identify with
- Shows a perspective not often presented in YA lit
- Main characters learn to stand up for themselves and don't take the easy way out
- Offers many discussion options and opportunities

AWARDS

Title published too recently to be eligible for awards.

REVIEWS

"Alternately narrated by Brittany and Alex, this compelling story portrays complex teens whose manufactured personas hide personal problems. Their contradictory lives and reactions to each other's provide conflicts and character insights." Lisa A. Hazlett, *VOYA*, 2/09

"Brittany's controlling parents and sister with cerebral palsy are well drawn, but it is Elkeles' rendition of Alex and his life that is particularly vivid. Sprinkling his speech with Spanish, his gruff but tender interactions with his family and friends feel completely genuine. . . . This is a novel that could be embraced by male and female readers in equal measure." Daniel Kraus, *Booklist*, 11/08

"Elkeles pens plenty of tasteful, hot scenes—including one where Brittany loses her virginity to Alex—that keep the pages turning. . . . The author definitely knows how to write romance." *Kirkus Reviews*, 12/08

ⅢⅢⅢ

RAG AND BONE SHOP. Robert Cormier. Delacorte, 2001. $15.95. 160p. ISBN10: 0385729626. ISBN13: 9780385729628. Laurel Leaf, 2003. $6.50. 176p. ISBN10: 0440229715. ISBN13: 9780440229711. Delacorte, 2001. $17.99. 160p. ISBN10: 0385900279. ISBN13: 9780385900270. (library binding) Recorded Books, 2002. $20.75. ISBN10: 1402510284. ISBN13: 9781402510281. (unabridged audiotape, library version) Recorded Books, 2002. $30.75. ISBN10: 1402519656. ISBN13: 9781402519659. (unabridged audio CD, library version) Recorded Books, 2002. $51.75. ISBN13: 9781428168213. (unabridged audiobook) Realistic fiction. Reading Level: MS. Interest Level: YHS, OHS. English, Ethics, Government, Psychology, Sociology.

SUBJECT AREAS
manipulation; lying and deceit; secrets; legal system; crime and delinquency; death and dying; justice; ethics; fear; intimidation.

CHARACTERS
Carl Seaton: he's seventeen years old and has just confessed to murder
Trent: a detective who interrogates Carl and hears his confession
Jason Dorrant: he's twelve years old and his summer has just begun
Emma Dorrant: Jason's eight-year-old sister who likes to follow him around
Kim Cambridge: a friend of Emma's
Brad Bartlett: a friend of Jason's who likes to play practical jokes
Alicia Bartlett: Brad's kid sister
Norma and Laura Bartlett: Brad and Alicia's parents
George Braxton: the detective in charge of the investigation
Harold Gibbons: a senator whose grandson had been in Alicia's class
Alvin Dark: the D.A. eager to take over for Braxton
Boho Kelton: a bully who picks on Jason
Rebecca Talland: a girl Boho picks on
Mr. Hohart: the middle school principal
Mrs. and Mrs. Durrant: Jason and Emma's parents
Greg Chavin and Marc Galehouse: Brad's friends
Adolph Califer: he confessed his murder to Trent
Henry Kendall: the police officer who takes Jason in for his interrogation
Jack O'Shea and Tim Connors: jocks who were questioned during the investigation
Danny Edison: an outsider who sometimes ate lunch with Jason
Jimmy Orlando: a regular kid
Sarah Downes: she's with the D.A.'s office and gives Trent background information on the investigation

BOOKTALK

It was the first day of summer vacation and when Jason woke up, he lay in bed thinking about how he'd spend his day. He'd swim at the Y in the morning, and Brad Bartlett had invited him over to swim in his pool that afternoon. Jason didn't like Brad all that much—he liked to play practical jokes and Jason didn't trust him. But he liked Alicia, his seven-year-old sister who was into jigsaw puzzles. Jason thought he might go by to see Alicia, but he wouldn't take his swim trunks.

Trent was tired, tired of his job, tired of himself, tired of all the confessions he's had to listen to as an interrogator, the sick, vile, unspeakable acts committed by the person sitting across the table from him. And they always confessed. Trent had the "magic Trent touch" that finally got to them, every time. Jason was his third case this week. First had been a seventeen-year-old who killed a whole family, just because he could. Then it had been a middle-aged man who strangled his next-door neighbor. And now it's Jason, a twelve-year-old who was the last person to see Alicia Bartlett alive. The detective in charge of the case was sure he'd done it, and needed a confession because he didn't have any physical evidence. The boy's father was out of town, and his mother fell for the story the cop who came to get Jason told her. Trent has three hours to get Jason to confess.

Jason knows he's innocent. Alicia was alive when he left her house. And he liked Alicia—he'd never hurt her. Why was this man acting like he was a murderer?

MAJOR THEMES AND IDEAS

- Telling the truth is not always enough to convince someone of your innocence.
- The truth has many layers.
- You reveal more of yourself than you might realize through facial expression and body language.
- It isn't difficult to manipulate someone who is naïve, confused, and trusting.
- We each choose our own path in life and make our own decisions, good or bad.
- Doing what you're told to do isn't always the best thing to do. Doing what's right usually is.
- Once a person is completely broken psychologically, it may not be possible for them to heal.
- Acting without honor can cause you to lose the respect of others and also of yourself.
- Confessing guilt does not change the fact of one's innocence.
- With enough time and pressure, almost anyone can be made to confess to something they are innocent of.
- "You are what you do." True or false?
- Seeing a person as a role—the perpetrator—makes them less human, easier to blame.
- We must all live with the decisions we've made.
- The evidence frequently doesn't reveal the whole story.

BOOK REPORT IDEAS

1. Discuss why Trent was brought into the case. Was it legal? Was it ethical?
2. Most of the characters have their own behind-the-scenes agenda. Describe what they are and how they impact Jason.
3. Describe Trent's state of mind and explain why he hates himself. How have all the confessions he's heard affected him?
4. Lottie says Trent is what he does. How true do you think her comment "You are what you do" is? Do you agree with it? Are we all what we do?
5. Did Jason tell the truth during his interrogation? How much of the truth?
6. Discuss Trent's view or opinion of Jason. How correct or incorrect are his deductions?
7. Why do you think Jason confessed?
8. Discuss Jason's actions and emotions after he was released. Why did he feel not there?
9. Who is more responsible for Jason's actions at the end of the book: Jason himself, or Trent?
10. Trent did what he was told to do. He got a confession. When did he decide to do that, rather than looking for the truth, and why?
11. Speculate about Jason and Trent—what will their futures be like? How did their meeting change them and their futures?
12. Jason was determined not to cry. If he had cried during the interview, how might that have affected Trent?
13. Trent manipulates Jason. How is he himself manipulated?
14. When the book begins, Trent is tired of being an interrogator and thinking of getting out. Discuss whether this underlying emotion might or might not have influenced his decision to force Jason to confess. He ultimately got what he'd wanted at the beginning.
15. The law says a suspect is presumed innocent until proven guilty. List the people who didn't do this and describe why they didn't.

BOOKTALK IDEAS

1. Use a red piece of a jigsaw puzzle as a prop for your talk.
2. Write your talk as if it were a news story.
3. Tell only the very first part of the story, as Jason daydreams in bed. Suggest the terrible things that will happen to him only a few hours later.
4. Focus your talk on the ethical concerns in the book.

RISKS

- Adults make snap decisions about a boy's guilt to close a troublesome murder case
- An adult deliberately coerces a confession of murder from a boy he knows to be innocent

- Frightening portrayal of the amount of power the police can hold
- Child is not held innocent until proven guilty
- Child's and parents' rights are flagrantly denied and ignored
- Parent allows twelve-year-old to be questioned by police alone

STRENGTHS

- Multiple points of view relate to the events from both Trent and Jason's perspectives
- Taut writing maintains suspense
- Ambiguous ending allows for speculation
- Many opportunities for discussion
- Powerful contrast between innocence and greed
- Realistic yet not vulgar language
- Very short, but asks large and important questions
- Characters are forced to deal with the consequences of their actions
- Presents reader with knotty ethical dilemma

AWARDS

ALA Popular Paperbacks, 2006
ALA Best Books for Young Adults, 2002

REVIEWS

"This final offering by a beloved author is entertaining and provocative—the hallmark of a Cormier novel. Bravo again, and farewell to the master." Florence H. Munat, *VOYA*, 10/01

"The chilling results will leave an indelible mark on readers and prompt heated discussions regarding the definition of guilt and the fine line between truth and deception." *Publishers Weekly*, 5/03

"Highly discussible, the ethical questions contained are intricate and absorbing, but detract not at all from the increasing tension as the story unfolds. Chilling." *Kirkus Reviews*, 10/01

ⅢⅢⅢ

RAIDERS NIGHT. Robert Lipsyte. HarperTeen, an imprint of HarperCollins, 2006. $15.99. 240p. ISBN10: 0060599464. ISBN13: 9780060599461. HarperTeen, 2007.

$6.99. 256p. ISBN10: 0060599480. ISBN13: 9780060599485. HarperTeen, 2006.
$16.89. 240p. ISBN10: 0060599472. ISBN13: 9780060599478. (library binding)
Realistic fiction. Reading Level: YHS. Interest Level: YHS, OHS. English, Ethics,
P.E., Government.

SUBJECT AREAS

ethics; fear; handicaps; sports; intimidation; peer pressure; school; problem parents;
dysfunctional family; self-knowledge; illness, mental; bullying; violence; sexual
abuse; drug abuse; rites of passage; physical abuse; anger; dating and social life;
friendship; gossip; lying and deceit; secrets; revenge; manipulation; prejudice; suicide.

CHARACTERS

Matt Rydek: football player, hero, team co-captain: he's got it all—or does he?
Brody Heinz: quarterback and Matt's best friend on the team, who's a juicer
Tyrell: running back, best in conference, he glides like a phantom and refuses to
    juice
Monty: he owns the gym and provides the juice for the Raiders
Pete: the fourth member of the Back Pack; he hates the juice's side effects
Lisa: Pete's girlfriend
Ramp: one of the linemen, who's co-captain with Matt and loves the power
Larry Rydek/Dad: Matt's father, who coaches men's softball and pressures Matt
    constantly
Jody Rydek/Mom: Matt's mother, who takes care of Junie and helps run Rydek Cater-
    ing
Junie: Matt's brother, who is mentally disabled
Freddy Heinz: Brody's older brother, who's on the softball team
Mandy: Matt's girlfriend and a cheerleader
Lexie: a football groupie
Terri: Matt's ex-girlfriend who's dating Brody
Patel: the team kicker
Sarah Ringe: she's making a play for Matt
Heller and Conklin: wide receiver and running back
Boda and Hagen: two of Ramp's linemen
Chris Marin: a sophomore transfer who plays tight end; he's good, he's fast, and he's
    got it in for Ramp
Coach Mac: Raiders' head coach
Coach Kornbauer: offensive coordinator
Villanueva: he plays center
Coach Dorman: defensive backfield
Coach Sims: works with quarterbacks and wide receivers and is the only black
    coach

Pastor Jim: team chaplain and youth minister at Rydek's church
Mr. Koslo: a lawyer who's a big Raiders fan
Paul Barry: nosy reporter for an independent school paper
Mr. Rampolski: Ramp's father
Dr. Jaffe: high school principal

BOOKTALK

This is a banned book. Your parents, your teachers, your coaches, your principals don't want you to read it. They don't want you to read it because it tells the truth, straight, flat-out, without pulling any punches.

Robert Lipsyte wrote it to show the negative side of Jock Culture, to create a football player who has to make a painful decision, to go deep inside himself to find the right moves.

Matt lives in a pressure cooker. Everyone pushes him to be the best—his father, his coaches, his girlfriends, his teammates. It's his senior year, he's one of the co-captains of the football team, and this is the year they might go to State. Coaches from the Division One schools are scouting him. All he's got to do is make it through the season and it'll be a free ride and a career in the pros. But he pays a price— nightmares, killer headaches, and body aches, he has to deal with the vicodin and booze, pimples on his back and intense, almost uncontrollable fits of anger from the steroids he's been using since he was a sophomore, and a crushing sense of responsibility for the younger kids on the team.

And after a new kid transfers in to challenge Ramp, the other captain, at training camp, Ramp takes the annual Raiders Night hazing over the line.

Matt knows that what happens inside the team, stays inside the team, but this is explosive enough to tear the team apart. Ramp doesn't have Matt's back, so why should Matt protect his? But what about the rest of the team?

MAJOR THEMES AND IDEAS

- It's not enough to be good, you have to be the best.
- Never let them see you hurt.
- It's dangerous to make a bully angry.
- It's not about you, it's all about the game.
- Making your teammates look bad is never a good idea.
- Missed plays can be a sign that something's not right with your head, not your body.
- When the world starts to close in on you, sit back and take some deep breaths.
- You aren't responsible for everything—just yourself.
- It's not all about you—especially the bad stuff.
- The captain is a role model. He needs to be there for the other players, especially the younger ones.
- A warrior depends on his teammates when the going gets tough.

- We're a band of brothers and we watch each other's backs.
- To get to the future, you have to get past the past.
- Think team. What happens inside the team stays inside the team.
- A captain takes care of his team.
- A man does what it takes to get the job done.
- A parent pressuring a kid to excel does it for himself, not for the kid.
- Being a jock is one way to prove you're a man.
- If you have to put down someone weaker than you to make yourself look good, you are not much of a human being.
- Knowing the right thing and doing it are two different things.

BOOK REPORT IDEAS

1. Was there a point at which Matt could have controlled what happened on Raiders Night? What was that point, and what could he have done?
2. Do you think this could happen at your school? Why or why not?
3. Being a jock is the best way to prove you're a man—true or false? Why?
4. Speculate on what happens after the end of the book, to Matt, to the Magnificent Seven, to the Ramp, to the coaches, the school, and the town.
5. Discuss the roles girls and women play in the book. How positively or negatively are they portrayed?
6. Could Matt's mother have done anything to ease her husband's pressure on Matt? If so, why did she do nothing?
7. Discuss Mandy's relationship to Matt. Does she really care about him? Why or why not?
8. Why do you think the author included Junie in the book? What impact did his presence have on the family?
9. Discuss Matt's dad and the relationship he had with his son. What do you think that relationship will be like after the end of the book?
10. Gossip helps move the action of the book along. Who started the rumor that something had happened at camp?
11. Describe the kind of person Ramp was. How do you think he saw himself? What forces or experiences might have helped make him who he was?
12. Is there a way to reduce the adulation that star jocks of all ages get?
13. Describe some of the positive parts of jock culture and contrast them to the negative parts.

BOOKTALK IDEAS

1. Use a football helmet as a prop.
2. Make Matt the focus of your talk, and have several characters introduce him from their points of view; for instance, Brody, Ramp, Coach Mac, Mandy, or Sarah.
3. Let Matt tell the story in first person.
4. Use some of the information at the back of the book as part of your talk.

RISKS
- Jocks rule high school culture
- Teens take steroids
- Father puts tremendous pressure on his son
- Teens drink and smoke pot
- Teen has breast enhancement surgery
- Homophobic slurs
- Realistic language, including vulgarities
- Coaches put extreme pressure on players
- Cruel and extreme hazing of younger players
- Coaches and parents encourage steroid use
- Team members allow sexual abuse of new player
- Father harasses officials at son's game
- Father encourages son to keep quiet about hazing for the sake of the team

STRENGTHS
- Accurate, vivid portrayal of high school jock culture
- Authentic voices of teens
- Shows the effects of steroids
- Shows the intense pressure put on jocks to get bigger and better
- Teens use condoms
- Teen is able to stand up for what he believes is right
- Shows the power of peer pressure
- Provides many opportunities for discussion
- Publicizes the increasing drug use among high school athletes
- Characters teens, including jocks, can identify with

AWARDS
ALA Popular Paperbacks, 2008
New York Public Library Books for the Teen Age, Winner, 2007

REVIEWS
"Veteran author Lipsyte knows sports and his book's football scenes are spot on. More important, a believable tone describing the reckless macho behavior penetrating high school athletics weaves throughout the novel." Rollie Welch, *VOYA*, 4/06

"Lipsyte exposes the underbelly of high school sports where racism, drug use, misogyny and bullying are shrugged off so long as the team wins. Matt has a soul-crushing choice to make and Lipsyte's careful rendering of the world in which Matt moves gives his story an awful and terrifying ring of truth." *Publishers Weekly*, 7/06

"An important work for the high-school athlete and anyone concerned about what sports might be doing to today's kids." *Kirkus Reviews*, 6/06

"Lipsyte paints an ugly picture of a corrupt high-school athletics world ruled by arrogance, homophobia, sexism, and a pathological obsession with winning. Readers will feel Matt's pain as he struggles between turning his back on his team and listening to his conscience." Ed Sullivan, *Booklist*, 5/06

📖📖📖

RIGHT BEHIND YOU. Gail Giles. Little, Brown, 2007. $15.99. 292p. ISBN10: 0316166367. ISBN13: 9780316166362. Little, Brown, 2008. $7.99. 320p. ISBN10: 0316166375. ISBN13: 9780316166379. Realistic fiction. Reading Level: YHS. Interest Level: YHS, OHS. English, Psychology, Creative Writing, P.E.

SUBJECT AREAS
rites of passage; secrets; self-knowledge; family relationships; violence; anger; therapy; school; friendship; bullying; peer pressure; substance abuse; gossip; sports; self-destruction; revenge; dating and social life; love; mental illness.

CHARACTERS
Kip McFarland: he's living a lie, hiding what he did when he was nine years old
Bobby Clarke: a seven-year-old with a new baseball glove
Dad/Mr. McFarland: an outsider who won't conform; he's still done all he could to help his son
Aunt Jemma: Kip's aunt, who argues constantly with his dad
The Frown/Don Shofield: Kip's psychiatrist when Kip decides to talk again
Two Fer: a ten-year-old Kip meets in the mental hospital
Cowboy: a school shooter
Slice 'n' Dice: he killed neighbors' pets
Loon Platoon: nickname for the hospital residents
Ward Nazis: what the residents call the nurses
Orderly of the Day/OOTD: one of the staff at the mental hospital; he understands Kip
Klepto: he couldn't stop stealing cars
Carrie: she loves Kip's father
Belinda: an orderly who teaches Kip to play chess
Jack, Carrie, and Wade Madison: the McFarland's new identities in Indiana
Ms. Bales: Wade's first English teacher in Indiana

Justine, Brandon, Amber, Anthony: kids that are curious about how Wade lived in Alaska

Dave: he clues Wade in on the way to survive at high school

Mr. Schultz: Wade's algebra teacher and Dave's father

Lindsay/Absolutely Cutest: a really cute girl who likes Wade

Three B's in a Pod: Brett, Brandon, Brenda

Coach Tully: he teaches gym and respects Wade

Dr. Lyman: Wade's therapist

Grant: Carrie's stepfather, who's like a father to her

Clint Jons: leader of the pack of jocks that stole Wade's clothes the first day of school

Coach Redmon: swimming coach

Kelley Hamilton: she has tattoos and lots of piercings

Sam: she and her parents live next door to Carrie's house at the beach

Dr. Martin: Wade's therapist in Texas

Jessica: she works in the bookstore with Carrie

BOOKTALK

When I was nine, I killed Bobby Clarke. He was seven and was showing off the baseball glove he'd gotten for his birthday from his mom. I didn't have a glove, my mom had just died, and I was afraid my Aunt Jemma would take me away from my dad. I wanted to ruin that glove. I remember throwing the gasoline on the glove, lighting the lighter and throwing that too, and seeing the flames. But that's where my memory shuts down. It doesn't start up again for five weeks, when I opened my eyes in the hospital and saw my dad.

I know what happened. People have told me, and eventually, years later, when I was still in a locked-down ward for the criminally insane, I read all the newspapers and saw hours of TV reports.

I'm fifteen now, and I know it's time for me to share my story, what I remember, what they told me about, and what happened afterward. But nothing can take away the truth I have to live with. When I was nine, I killed a boy. He was seven.

MAJOR THEMES AND IDEAS

* There are stages of understanding the major tragedies in your life.
* It's not always easy to forgive yourself.
* Cartoons have do-overs. Life doesn't.
* Turning points in life can be hard to handle.
* The obvious victim in a crime isn't ever the only one.
* Death touches everyone involved, not just the person who died.
* Guilt and shame go hand in hand with acknowledging you've done something wrong.

- When you can't face the horrors of what you've done, your mind shuts down until you're ready to face it, piece by piece.
- Since you can't undo anything, no matter how much you want to, you have to figure out how to cope with life now.
- Even if you change your name, move away from home, invent a new past for yourself, you still know who you are and what you did.
- Learning how to live outside an institution takes time. There's a whole new pattern of behavior to learn.
- Giving the pond scum of a high school attention isn't cool.
- The truth is the only thing that will calm the hungry ghost and give you peace.
- Life isn't like a straight road. It has unexpected twists and turns, and it's usually never easy.
- Someone's life might look easy from the outside, but if you walk in their shoes for a bit, you'll see that that's not true.
- Asking someone for help makes them feel good, smarter, maybe even a little superior.
- Sometimes not making waves and staying can earn you major cool points.
- You can't ever relax when you're living a secret.
- When you feel guilty, you're likely to feel like you need to be punished. If you do too well or get too happy, you may sabotage yourself as punishment.
- Just like breakthroughs, bad things take you by surprise.
- Be careful not to let your passion become your demon.
- You do things when you're drunk that you'd never consider doing sober.
- Losing your temper and spilling your guts without thinking can have disastrous consequences.
- Learning that you deserve to be happy and successful can be a long and difficult process when you're haunted by guilt, deserved or not.
- Forgiving or liking yourself before asking or expecting others to forgive or like you isn't a cliché. It's the truth, and it's necessary.
- When you hurt yourself, you also hurt your family.
- Hatred is toxic. It damages everything it touches, the one who hates and the one who is hated.
- Waves crashing on the shore have a savage yet soothing music that is engrossing.
- If you think you don't deserve respect, think about the people who have loved and supported you for years. Can you really be that awful if they've known what you did and have still had your back?
- If you worry about being a bad person, you probably aren't one. Bad people don't care about it.
- Our experiences in life make us who we are. If those things hadn't happened, you'd be a different person.
- If you like and accept who you are today, you have to accept the past that made you that person.

- If you can't forget or forgive what you've done, you have to live with it, like the way you live with a limp or a scar. You live with it, one day at a time.
- We're all walking wounded, in one way or another.
- No matter what you've done, and especially if you regret it, you deserve love.

BOOK REPORT IDEAS

1. Discuss Carrie's comment about the differences between Kip and Wade, one too grown-up with a therapy mind-set and vocabulary, the other naïve because he's never lived in the real world.
2. Think about what your life was like from nine to thirteen or fourteen, and give examples of some of the things Kip missed while spending five years in a mental hospital.
3. There are many people with secrets in this book. What are they concealing and why?
4. Compare the person Kip is in Alaska, in Indiana, and in Texas. How does he change? How does he stay the same?
5. Discuss the questions Sam asked herself after she finished reading Wade's story. What do you think the answers to them would be?
6. Kip/Wade was changed by his guilt in many ways. Discuss both the positive and the negative ways he was changed.
7. Given the way phone calls can be traced, speculate on whether or not Mrs. Clarke will be able to find Kip and his father again.
8. Comment on what Mrs. Clarke said to Sam, and compare the way she dealt with the tragedy to the way Kip and his father did.
9. Speculate on what happens after the book ends. What will Wade be like in ten years? Where will he be and what will he be doing? What would he say if someone asked about Bobby and the rest of his childhood?

BOOKTALK IDEAS

1. Write your talk as if it were a news story.
2. Write your talk from one of the main characters' point of view, say Dr. Schofield or Dave, and have them introduce Kip/Wade and his story.
3. Use a notebook like the ones Wade used to tell his story as a prop for your talk. If you use part of his words for your talk, you could read from the notebook, as if it really was his notebook.

RISKS

- A nine-year-old boy kills a younger child
- Teens are sexually active
- Teens drink and smoke marijuana
- Teen is heavily medicated with prescription drugs

- Teen is violent and self-destructive
- Vulgar language
- Somewhat negative picture of conservative religion
- Town violently rejects family when their past becomes known
- Threats of revenge and violent retribution

STRENGTHS
- Shows the effect of overwhelming long-term guilt
- Shows the impact of a good therapist
- Characters grow and gain insight
- Characters learn to forgive themselves
- Strong, supportive parents
- Positive family relationships
- Three-dimensional character readers can identify with
- Ambiguous ending leaves room for speculation
- Vividly depicts an individual's journey to mental health
- Realistic dialogue
- Shows the power of hate and fear
- Value of trust and acceptance

AWARD
ALA Quick Picks for Reluctant Readers, 2009

REVIEWS
"In Kip's case, ultimate redemption comes not in the form of self-forgiveness but in letting go of regret and self-sabotage. And as the title tells readers, it is often what is right behind that can be the most difficult to see." Ria Newhouse, *VOYA*, 8/07

"This story explores, with sympathy and compassion, the nature of guilt, atonement and forgiveness. As Giles delicately handles these . . . issues and questions . . . , readers should be glued to Wade's story, hoping for his redemption." *Publishers Weekly*, 6/07

"This powerful and moving novel of self-discovery gives no easy answers, except inasmuch as it's too easy to have Kip be an entirely sweet, well-intentioned young man, unscarred by anything but guilt after four years of incarceration. Thought-provoking and heart-wrenching." *Kirkus Reviews*, 8/07

ᘢᘢᘢ

A ROOM ON LORELEI STREET. Mary Pearson. Holt, 2005. $16.95. 272p. ISBN10: 0805076670. ISBN13: 9780805076677. Square Fish, 2008. $7.99. 288p.

ISBN10: 0312380194. ISBN13: 9780312380199. Realistic fiction. Reading Level: YHS. Interest Level: YHS, OHS. English, Sociology, Vocational Education, Ethics.

SUBJECT AREAS

rites of passage; working; elderly; self-knowledge; addiction; problem parents; school; anger; bulling; dysfunctional families; ethics; family relationships; friendship; manipulation; poverty; secrets; handicaps.

CHARACTERS

Zoe Buckman: a seventeen-year-old girl who wants to escape her family
Mama/Darlene Buckman: Zoe's alcoholic mother
Aunt Patsy: she told Zoe about her name, and used to be Mama's best friend
Uncle Clint: Mama's older brother; he's married to Aunt Patsy
Grandma: the Buckman matriarch, who is demanding and controlling
Opal Keats: a tough old lady, who's Zoe's landlord
Murray: he owns Murray's Diner, where Zoe's a waitress
Mrs. Garrett: Zoe's English teacher, who doesn't know how to pronounce her name
Mrs. Tarantino: Zoe's school counselor
Reid: a friend of Zoe's, who's into the theatre
Carly: Reid's sister, who's also a long-time friend
Monica Hernandez: a friend of Zoe's who's in Mrs. Garrett's English class
Jorge Hernandez: Monica's twin brother

BOOKTALK

Zoe was careful, very careful. She was careful to never be late. She was careful to get her assignments in on time. She was careful to save as much money as she could. And she was careful to take care of Mama. Mama needed her. What would Mama do if Zoe wasn't there to clean up after her, fix her meals, pay the bills, and everything else that Zoe does?

But Zoe is tired of the cooking and cleaning, the smell of cigarettes, and the atmosphere of depression and hopelessness. Then one day she sees a sign—"Room for Rent." That's what she needs. A place of her own, a place where she can be herself, and not have to worry about anyone else.

So one day, after years of thinking about it, Zoe goes home from work, packs her things, and tapes a note to her mother on the TV—"There's Chinese in the refrigerator. The dishes are done. The utility bill is paid. I don't live here any more. I live at 373 Lorelei Street. Love, Zoe."

Zoe is seventeen. It's time she started living for herself. Lorelei is the first step.

MAJOR THEMES AND IDEAS

- Being on time, being dependable is important.
- Sometimes the only person you can depend on is yourself.
- Saying everything will be all right doesn't make it so.

- Some people in powerful roles make themselves feel better by making those they have power over feel worse.
- If you take care of someone who is codependent, she'll never learn to take care of herself.
- People who don't feel confident of themselves will frequently blame someone else for their mistakes, treating them as a scapegoat.
- Some scars are on the outside, where they're easy to see. But the scars in your brain and heart are much deeper and long-lasting.
- Sometimes silence and indifference are more painful than harsh words and angry confrontations.
- People can make you feel inferior only if you allow them to.
- Sooner or later, it's time to take off on your own.
- Take care of yourself first.
- You can't go back and fix your mistakes. You can only do your best to survive them.

BOOK REPORT IDEAS

1. Discuss what home means to Zoe at the beginning and at the end of the book. Compare it to what you think home means to you.
2. Explain how Zoe was helping support her mother's alcoholism and the effect on the family when she stopped.
3. Speculate about what Zoe might be like in five years, or ten years.
4. Compare Zoe's budget to your own life. Would you be able to survive on the same amount of money?
5. Discuss Opal and her carefree attitude. How realistic do you think she is? Is she crazy, or just eccentric?
6. Examine Mrs. Garrett and the way she treats Zoe. What do her actions say about herself?

BOOKTALK IDEAS

1. Have several characters introduce Zoe showing different parts of her personality: for instance, Grandma, Mrs. Garrett, Murray, Opal, Reid, or Monica.
2. Use a hand-lettered sign, "Room for Rent," as a prop.
3. Focus your talk on the scene where Zoe leaves, including the note on the TV.

RISKS

- Teens smoke
- Alcoholic mother
- Codependent family
- Overbearing, controlling grandmother
- Grandmother is physically and emotionally abusive
- Teens are sexually active

STRENGTHS

- Strong female main character
- Three-dimensional characters teens can identify with
- Characters grow, gain insight, and succeed
- Ending doesn't resolve all problems, leaving reader to speculate on what the future holds
- Realistic situations, and realistic solutions
- Shows the power of standing up for yourself
- Characters have to deal with the results of their bad decisions
- Demonstrates the effects of codependency

AWARD

ALA Best Books for Young Adults, 2006

REVIEWS

"The portrayal of alcoholism and abuse is realistic but not melodramatic. . . . Teenage girls will enjoy reading this book, and it might provide good material for classroom discussions." Jenny Ingram, *VOYA*, 6/05

"The third-person narration is at times lyrical, vividly expressing the teen's feelings and motivations. This book is a good read and the message—while powerful—is not overpowering." Sharon Morrison, Southeastern Oklahoma State University, Durant, OK, *School Library Journal*, 8/05

"All literary elements—characters, setting, mis-en-scene—seamlessly and poetically coalesce into her ephemerally hot and cold teenage persona whose tough outer shell masks enough skeletons in the closet to eat her alive." *Kirkus*, 5/05

📖📖📖

THE RULES OF SURVIVAL. Nancy Werlin. Dial, 2006. $16.99. 272p. ISBN10: 0803730012. ISBN13: 9780803730014. Puffin, 2006. $7.99. 288p. ISBN10: 0142410713. ISBN13: 9780142410714. Listening Library, 2007. $30.00. ISBN10: 0739349082. ISBN13: 9780739349083. (unabridged audio CD) Reading level: MS. Interest level: YHS, OHS. English, Psychology, Sociology, Family Studies.

SUBJECT AREAS

family relationships; violence; child abuse; abuse, physical; abuse, emotional; mental illness; problem parents; secrets; intimidation; friendship; fear; anger; divorce and separation; love; dysfunctional families; lying and deceit; manipulation; self-knowledge; survival.

CHARACTERS

Matthew Walsh: he's grown up trying to protect himself and his two younger sisters from their violent and unstable mother

Callie Walsh: two years younger than Matthew; she also understands the danger of their situation and their need to be out of it

Emmy Walsh: the youngest of the Walsh children; she remembers the least of the horrors they had to endure

Nikki Walsh: beautiful, manipulative, selfish, and dangerous, their mother regards them not as individuals, but as her property and the focus of much of her rage

Ben Walsh: Matthew and Callie's father, who fears Nikki and refuses to help the children escape from her

Roberta O'Grady/Aunt Bobbie: Nikki's sister, who's been tormented by Nikki her whole life, fears her sister, and ignores the whole situation between Nikki and her children

Murdoch McIlvane: a quiet, loving man who does what he can for the children while dating Nikki and refuses to help them after he and Nikki break up

Rob Borodetsky: one of the men Nikki dates after Murdoch breaks up with her

Officer Brooks: he became involved with the Walshes when Nikki was beaten up and later worked with Murdoch to get the children away from her

BOOKTALK

Fear changes you when you live with it 24/7. It reshapes your thoughts, your ideas, maybe even affects you as far down as the cellular level. It makes you into someone different from who you would have been without it. Fear eats you up inside like acid, and takes away your ability to act against it, instead of just running away or giving in.

Matthew has lived with fear ever since he can remember. He was only four when he realized that it was his job to protect his little sister from their mother when she was angry. It was his job to hide them, to be quiet so their mother wouldn't notice them. It was the only way to stay safe, to stay alive, and uninjured.

He was fourteen and Callie and Emmy were twelve and six when their mother started dating Murdoch, a man who made all of them feel safe, until Nikki's crazy behavior drove him away. Murdoch seemed like a miracle, but Matthew and Callie already knew that miracles didn't last long. When Murdoch left, the family was even more broken than it had been before he came. Matthew could see how crazy their life was, now that he had the normality of their life with Murdoch to contrast it. He knows he has to get the three of them away from Nikki, but one by one, the adults he turns to refuse to help. And as Nikki's behavior becomes more and more frightening and dangerous, Matthew and Callie begin to wonder how long they have before their beautiful, angry, and evil mother kills them in one of her uncontrollable rages.

📖📖📖

Emmy,

You're too young now to understand what really happened, or the danger we were all in. But someday, you might wonder what the real story is, and have questions. So I'm going to write down everything that happened, from the time I was just four and first understood what my job was in our frightening and unpredictable family, until now, when I'm eighteen, getting ready to leave you and Callie for the first time.

It's hard to remember, Emmy, because it means that I have to live through the horror and the pain and the fear all over again. But I need to do it, not just for you, but also for me. If I can understand what happened to me, to us, and how our mother changed all our lives, if I can understand where I came from, what shaped me, maybe I can understand who I am now, and who I have a chance of becoming.

For me, it all started when I saw Murdoch stare down an angry father twice his size who was about to start whaling on his son. I heard him tell the little boy that no one had the right to hurt him, no one, not even his father. I'd never heard anyone say that before. I was thirteen years old, and what I'd learned was that no one could be trusted, and that sometimes the people who hurt you the most, like our mother, were also the ones who said they loved you, like our mother.

You're old enough now to remember the end of our story, Emmy, but I want you to hear the beginning of it, the parts you didn't live through, the parts you didn't understand when you did live them, and the parts that Callie and I never told you about. I protected you from the frightening and evil parts of our lives for as long as I could. Callie and I both did. But in case someday I decide that protection isn't helping you any longer, I'm writing down the whole story for you.

Maybe the story should start when I first realized the danger we were all in, but like I said, for me the story starts the night we met Murdoch. I was thirteen, Callie was eleven, and you were five. It was a stifling summer Saturday night in Southie, where we grew up, and our mother, Nikki, had locked us into the apartment when she left for a date. You were asleep, and Callie and I snuck out for a popsicle and a breath of fresh air. . . .

MAJOR THEMES AND IDEAS
- There are people in the world who mean you harm, and sometimes they are also the ones who say they love you.
- It's wrong for anyone to hurt a kid, no matter who they are, and even if they're family.
- Fear isn't always a bad thing. It's a primitive instinct that warns you of danger and makes you pay attention to what's going on around you.

- Fear is a gift, and if you respond to your fear instead of ignoring it, you will be safer.
- Living with fear all day, every day, changes you mentally, physically, psychologically, and makes you into someone different from the person you would have been without it.
- Living with constant fear means it is no longer a gift, but your master, and you are its slave.
- Kids don't need adults to be superheroes. They just need someone who will act for them when they ask for help.
- When you're living your life in endurance mode, you don't expect good things to happen.
- When someone is living a crazy life, they get used to it, and don't see the craziness until they get a glimpse of how normal people live and contrast it with their own life.
- The human instinct for self-preservation is strong. Everyone has the right to survive.
- Children are not always safe with their parents.
- Many times, adults see what they want to see, rather than seeing what is really happening.
- Sometimes, charming lies can be more convincing than the truth.
- All humans have evil desires and impulses, and can decide to reject them, or let them into their heart and soul, and allow that evil to control them completely.
- Jealousy can make you do crazy things you wouldn't usually consider doing.
- Too many times when we look at someone we see every day, we don't notice the changes in them. Instead we see what we want to see, what we've always seen, until something opens our eyes and forces us to look more closely and discover what we have been missing.
- Not giving in to fear and deciding we can act against it is a choice we can each make, no matter our age or situation.
- Evil never gets home free. Somehow, sometime, somewhere, payment must be made.
- We all choose our actions. Life isn't random.
- The survivors get to tell the story.
- Your present and future are affected by your past, but you can choose to examine and understand it, and then go on with your life. The past doesn't have to control your life.

BOOK REPORT IDEAS

1. There are many ways to survive in a dangerous situation. What are some of the ways Matthew, Callie, and Emmy survive?
2. Explain why Emmy prayed for Murdoch. Do you think she realized the effect that it would have on her mother? How might their lives have been different if she had just gone to bed that night?

3. Matthew describes Nikki as evil. In what ways do you think she exhibited this quality?

4. How did Matt and Callie's protecting Emmy endanger her instead? Speculate on how you think Emmy thought about their mother, both before and after they were separated from her.

5. Discuss the scene when Matthew and Callie saw Murdoch for the first time, and what characteristics he showed them in their brief interaction with them, and how that meeting changed their lives.

6. Compare Matthew's first view of Murdoch with the way he sees him at the end of the story. What are some of the key events that changed Matthew's perception of Murdoch?

7. Why are those you love the most able to inflict the most pain on you?

8. Discuss how the children's lives were different from and similar to the life of the POW in the movie they watched with Murdoch. In what ways were they prisoners?

9. Describe how Matthew and Callie felt when no one would help them. How did those refusals affect them mentally and emotionally?

10. Speculate on what might have happened if Ben, Bobbie, and Murdoch had intervened sooner. Would Nikki have been able to stop them as Ben feared?

11. Nikki knew her children very well, and knew exactly what buttons to push to manipulate them. Give several examples of her ability to do this.

12. What were some of the reasons behind Nikki's eccentric and dangerous behavior? What did she gain by acting that way?

13. In what ways was Ben a good father? In what ways did he let his children down?

14. A number of adults in the book seemed to be afraid of Nikki. What did she do to each of them to make them fear her? What about her frightened them? What about her frightened you?

15. There are several turning points in the book where the children's lives get significantly better or worse. Describe several of them and discuss what caused them and what the results were.

16. Why was it so important for the children to pretend the summer with Murdoch had never happened? What might Nikki have done if they hadn't?

17. Why did Nikki take Emmy away? Whom was she punishing? How?

18. Discuss what Murdoch's quote means: "Some are born great, some achieve greatness, and some have greatness thrust upon them." Give examples from the books of each of these kinds of people.

19. Why did Aunt Bobbie and Ben suddenly decide to start protecting the children? What caused them to start acting differently?

20. Why did Nikki enjoy tormenting Bobbie, both as a child and an adult? What did she gain? How did it affect her children, Bobbie, and Nikki herself?

21. On page 126, Matthew describes the scene when Murdoch commits himself to helping the children. Why did he make that decision at that point? Speculate on

what might have happened to him earlier in his life that caused him to come to that decision at that moment.

22. Matthew says he never really learned to trust Aunt Bobbie. Why not? What prevented that bond from forming? What would have had to happen for Matthew to come to trust her completely?

23. Every time Matthew realizes nothing has changed in his family, he gets more and more depressed and hopeless. Discuss how future disappointments might change the man he will someday become.

24. Compare Matt, Murdoch, and Bobbie's lives after Nikki got out of jail to living in enemy territory or an active war zone. How would those situations be physically and emotionally similar to what they had to endure?

25. Matthew said he changed in the boatyard when he came face to face with Nikki. What caused that change, and why did he say that it was irreversible?

26. Discuss Matthew's queen bee/mosquito theory. How did the change occur? Are there "queen bees" in your life that you might be able to change to "mosquitoes"?

27. How would Matthew's life have changed if he had killed or seriously injured Nikki? How would his sisters' lives have changed?

28. Speculate on what will happen to the Walshes, Murdoch, and Aunt Bobbie in the future, in five years, in ten years? What kind of people will Matthew, Callie, and Emmy grow up to be? How will their childhood experiences affect them as adults? Will Nikki come back? If she does, what effect will that have on her family and their friends?

BOOKTALK IDEAS

1. Use the letter at the opening of the book as part of your talk.
2. Focus your talk on the convenience store scene.
3. Describe each of the four main characters—Nikki and her children.
4. Focus your talk on how the children fear their mother.

RISKS

- Abusive, violent, and manipulative mother constantly endangers her children physically and psychologically
- Distant and uninvolved father
- Adults choose to lie to or ignore children in a dangerous situation who are asking for help
- Children have to protect themselves from their mother
- Mother is sexually active and uses drugs in front of her children
- Mother abandons her children for days at a time without warning or explanation
- Children learn from an early age that adults are not to be trusted
- Mother exhibits various types of criminal behavior

- Several male characters are easily manipulated into harming others
- Social agencies such as police are not always portrayed positively

STRENGTHS
- Strong, resilient children
- Children protect each other
- Nonsequential storyline
- Realistic language
- Three-dimensional characters readers can identify with
- Characters have authentic voices that ring true
- Unresolved ending allows reader to speculate on what might happen in the future
- Adults work together to rescue children from a dangerous and potentially deadly situation
- Provides opportunities for discussion of difficult topics, such as abuse or evil and how to survive it, what constitutes a family, and how sometimes children must be protected from their families
- Plot and format draw reader into story quickly
- Complex characters portrayed as having both positive and negative qualities
- Short chapters make it more accessible to reluctant readers
- Unusual writing style, as narrator recounts past events to unseen listener

AWARDS
SLJ Best Books for Children, 2006
ALA Best Books for Young Adults, 2007
ALA Notable Children's Books, 2006
National Book Award Finalist (Young People's Literature), 2006
VOYA's List of "Perfect 10's," 2006

REVIEWS
"The plot moves swiftly and unrelentingly to a climax that visits themes common to some of Werlin's earlier works and offers an uneasy recognition of the same conclusion David Yaffe voiced in *The Killer's Cousin* (Delacorte, 1998/*VOYA* October 1998), 'Anyone in this world can have the power of life and death over someone else. It's horrible, but true.'" Amy S. Pattee, *VOYA*, 10/06

"Edgar Award–winner Werlin delivers another suspense-filled thriller that is sure to spark discussion. Though there is ample foreshadowing, readers never know what is coming next from the psychotic Nikki, or what the kids' response to her will be." *Horn Book Magazine*, 9/06

"The characters captivate readers from the beginning, and short, terse chapters move the plot along with an intensity that will appeal to seasoned Werlin fans and reluctant readers alike. Teens will empathize with these siblings and the secrets they keep in this psychological horror story." Kim Dare, Fairfax County Public Schools, VA, *School Library Journal*, 9/06

"Werlin reinforces her reputation as a master of the YA thriller, pulling off a brilliant departure in this dark but hopeful tale, with pacing and suspense guaranteed to leave readers breathlessly turning the pages." *Booklist*, 8/1/06

SANDPIPER. Ellen Wittlinger. Simon and Schuster, 2005. $16.95. 240p. ISBN10: 0689868022. ISBN13: 9780689868023. Simon Pulse, 2007. $6.99. 288p. ISBN10: 1416936513. ISBN13: 9781416936510. Realistic fiction. Reading Level: MS. Interest Level: YHS, OHS. English, Sex Education, Health, Psychology.

SUBJECT AREAS
sex and sexuality; friendship; gossip; self-knowledge; secrets; bullying; death and dying; mental illness; rape; anger; problem parents; rites of passage; love; depression; dysfunctional family; divorce and separation; lying and deceit; homelessness; guilt.

CHARACTERS
Sandpiper Hollow Ragsdale: a good girl with a bad reputation
Walker: a loner, mysterious, who walks wherever he goes
Andrew: one of Sandpiper's most recent exes
Melissa: one of Sandpiper's friends, who figured out how to get guys to like her
Allie: Sandpiper's other best friend
Colleen Ragsdale: Sandpiper's mother, an ex-hippie who gave her her unique name
Nathan: he and Colleen are about to get married
Daisy Ragsdale: Sandpiper's little sister, who's very like Colleen
Rachel: Nathan's daughter, who lives with her mother in San Francisco
Claire: Rachel's mother, Nathan's ex
Rags Ragsdale: Sandpiper and Daisy's dad, who introduced Colleen and Nathan and is also an ex-hippie
Adrienne: Colleen's best friend and maid of honor
Derek and Hamilton: friends of Andrew, who give Daisy a hard time
Sam: Daisy's boyfriend
Mrs. Humphries: Sandpiper's English teacher

Grandma Edie: Colleen's mother, who's a no-nonsense person, unlike her o⌐
Mark Conrad: a boy Rachel meets on the beach
Gil Steinhart: Nathan's best friend and best man, and a really nice guy

BOOKTALK

My name's Piper, Sandpiper, actually. My parents were hippies back in the old days, and met at a place on the beach called Sandpiper Hollow. That's my name. My sister Daisy is named after the flowers my mother wore in her hair during her hippie wedding. But all that's several lifetimes ago. In this lifetime, my mom and dad are divorced, but while she hasn't dated a lot, he's changed women about as often as he's changed shirts. So it's kind of surprising that she's the one getting married—to Nathan, a shrink, of all things—and having a huge white formal wedding.

But this story isn't about that wedding—it's just playing in the background. This is my story, mine and Walker's. I met him three weeks before the wedding. Everyone in town knew who he was—Hammond's not exactly a big town. He was tall and skinny with hair that flapped in his face, and he wore an old brown leather jacket with his arms sticking four inches out of the sleeves. He never talked to anyone. He just walked—alone.

That's what he was doing when he walked up to Andrew and me. I'd hooked up with Andrew a few days before, and even though I generally get tired of guys pretty quickly and move on, I got tired of Andrew in just about three days. He wasn't real happy about it, and that afternoon, he'd cornered me in the park to tell me how much of a slut he thought I was. I just wanted to get away, so when I saw Walker coming our way, I hollered at him, and told Andrew I was busy and couldn't talk to him. For someone who didn't know what was going on, Walker was really cool and stepped right up like he was my new boyfriend.

That was the beginning of the strangest four weeks of my life. There was Andrew, who knew my secret; Derek, who was so mad at me that he'd hurt anything I cared about—my friends, my family, my house, and finally me. There was Walker, who had a terrible secret that was the reason why he was all alone, and Daisy, who had a secret of her own, but also knew way more about my secret than I'd ever imagined. And Rachel, my new stepsister, also had her own secret hidden behind her smile and perfect size-two body. What will happen as we all begin the countdown to the wedding, and people's secrets and angers are suddenly not so well hidden any longer?

MAJOR THEMES AND IDEAS
- Being needed by someone else can give you a feeling of control.
- Understanding yourself can be very difficult.
- Everyone is entitled to their secrets.
- Sometimes it's good to be quiet with your friends. Friendship doesn't always require conversation.

- Most people don't stop and think before they react; they just react, and later they can't take it back.
- Most bullies like to hurt other people because they don't feel good about themselves.
- Sometimes it's easier to share secrets about yourself with a stranger than with your friends.
- Your reputation isn't who *you* say you are. It's what everyone else says you are, and it isn't necessarily true.
- Even when you're a teenager, there can be some things you need to deal with yourself, if you can, rather than tell your parents.
- Take care of yourself. You're worth something, even when you feel worthless.
- A tragedy or a crisis frequently wipes out the bad feelings between people, because such a catastrophe highlights how small the disagreements really were.
- Knowing that someone you like likes you back can make it easier to like yourself.
- Before you judge someone, find out the real story behind the words she's been labeled with. Her story may be far different than the labels.
- No one *ever* deserves to be raped or blamed for attempted rape. No one—*ever*.
- When a girl or a woman says no, it means no, no matter how she's dressed or what she's done. It still means no.
- When someone is raped, it is *never* her fault. No one asks to be brutalized.
- The rapist is the criminal. The victim is the *victim*. The rapist is to blame, the one who's at fault, *not* the victim.
- It's easier to be strong when you have people backing you up.
- We aren't perfect. People hurt each other without meaning to. But when someone hurts someone deliberately, it's their fault, and no one else's. No one *asks* to be hurt, mentally or physically.
- When someone who cares about you reaches out to help you, let them do it, let them in, no matter how scary it is.

BOOK REPORT IDEAS

1. Discuss, compare, and explain the poems Sandpiper wrote. Explain what they mean to you and what they say about Sandpiper and the people in her life.
2. Several characters go through a series of changes in the book. Explain how and why those changes happen, and how each person is different.
3. Discuss the ways Sandpiper feels alienated from her family. What characteristics make her feel that way—theirs and hers?
4. What does Sandpiper get from relationship with Walker? How does walking with him give her insight into her own life?
5. At one point Sandpiper wonders how well you have to know someone to really know what they're like inside. What do you think?
6. Rags described Walker as "damaged." Who are some other people who are damaged, and how or why?

BOOKTALK IDEAS

1. Focus your talks on Sandpiper's poetry and what her words say about herself.
2. Write your talk from several different perspectives and have Sandpiper introduce herself, and then have three or four other people introduce her briefly, some who see her as a good girl, and some who don't.
3. Focus at least part of your talk on Derek and his escalating criminal behavior, but don't go any further than the incidents with the cat and Daisy, and just imply that his behavior might get much worse.
4. Many people in this book have secrets. Point them out in your talk, and explain just a little of their secrets without giving them all away.

RISKS

- Teen girls specialize in blow jobs and teach each other how to do them
- Family abandons teen after he causes accidental death
- Father is embarrassed about daughter's large bust line
- Good friends reject girl because she goes from one boy to another
- Oral sex is not considered "real" sex
- Difficult and judgmental mother/grandmother
- Teen boys, angry at protagonist, bully and harass her and her little sister to dangerous levels
- Battery and attempted rape
- Sociopathic teen commits assault, battery, and vandalism
- Father sets bad example by dating one woman after another in a series of casual relationships
- Mother prevents daughter from seeing her father after bitter divorce

STRENGTHS

- Three-dimensional characters with strengths and flaws
- Characters teens can identify with
- Positive, supportive relationship between divorced parents
- A crisis unites family members and friends
- Adults reach out to help homeless teen
- Characters, both adults and teens, grow and gain insight and understanding
- Adults and peers reach out to damaged homeless teen
- Satisfying ending, in spite of uncertain future
- Parents affirm and support and love their kids

AWARDS

ALA Best Books for Young Adults, 2006
New York Public Library Books for the Teen Age, 2006

REVIEWS

"Wittlinger is at her best with this latest offering that tells an edgy and compelling story exploring the danger of suppressed emotions and pent-up guilt. A recent and disturbing trend among teenagers to discount oral sex as 'real sex' is also portrayed, but the ultimate message conveys the value of human connections and how the strength of friendships can save lives." Valerie Ott, *VOYA*, 8/05

"Wittlinger takes on tough teen issues with candor, humanity, humor, and grace." Hazel Rochman, *Booklist*, 6/05

"Secondary characters are faultlessly multidimensional, and Wittlinger tackles the subject of the 'school slut' with compassion, balancing Piper's unapologetic self-ownership and defensive wit with her intrinsic empathy to create a unique, compelling heroine." *Horn Book Magazine*, 11/05

ᗕᗕᗕ

SHATTERING GLASS. Gail Giles. Simon Pulse, 2003. $7.99. 224p. ISBN10: 0689858000. ISBN13: 9780689858000. Tandem Library, 2003. $16.95. 215p. ISBN10: 0613733940. ISBN13: 9780613733946. (library binding) Realistic fiction. Reading Level: MS. Interest Level: MS, YHS. English, Sociology, Psychology.

SUBJECT AREAS

school; friendship; intimidation; secrets; peer pressure; bullying; power; anger; manipulation; problem parents; dating and social life; stereotypes.

CHARACTERS

Rob Haynes: he's king of the school, and the one who comes up with the idea to transform Simon
Jeff Cooper/Coop: a star athlete, but not an intellectual
Bobster/Baby DeMarco: a player who likes to brag about his latest conquests
Lance Ansely: he's a jerk who likes to bully Simon and used to be the king of the school, before Rob
Simon Glass: an uber-geek; he's bullied by everyone in school
Mr. Cooper: Jeff's fat father, who sneers at his son's dreams
Young Steward: part of Rob's posse; he's the book's narrator
Blair Crews: she's queen of the school and dates Rob, but she doesn't trust him
Ronna Perry: smart and intelligent; Young has a crush on her
Caroline Davids: one of the A-list girls; she's friends with Blair, Ronna and Sherry

Todd: he's a friend of Lance's and part of the popular crowd
Ginger Donalson: the girl Bob takes to Homecoming

BOOKTALK

Simon Glass was easy to hate—there were lots of reason. I guess we each hated him for a different reason, but we didn't realize it until the day we killed him.

How could it happen? How could something that was almost a joke turn so dark and deadly? They decided to turn the school nerd into a popular kid—and they did. Suddenly, Simon Glass wasn't the geek everyone picked on—he was one of the guys everyone looked up to, everyone liked. But just as suddenly, he was the one who was dead. What happened in the high school gym that night and could anyone have stopped it?

MAJOR THEMES AND IDEAS

- People aren't always what they appear to be.
- Bullying is about power and making yourself look good at someone else's expense.
- Someone who tortures an animal may also be likely to torture a human, who is vastly more easy to damage than an animal.
- Writing a story about your own experiences allows you to see them from a different perspective.
- It's easy to be blind to the faults of someone who appears to be your friend, someone you trust and admire.
- Helping someone can make them feel supported or patronized. Not all help is appreciated.
- Actions not carefully considered from all perspectives can have unexpectedly negative consequences.
- Just because someone's a geek doesn't mean he's not smart or aware of what's going on around him.
- Does making someone look better make everyone else look worse?
- A mean person, when cornered or threatened, will get vicious, striking at anyone in the way, not caring who's hurt.
- Don't turn your back on someone you have publicly angered and humiliated. You might find a knife in it.
- When someone you love and trust betrays you, it leaves a hole that's hard to fill.
- When you hurt someone deeply, you can't always go back and fix it.
- Don't ask someone to choose between you and someone else. You might be surprised by the result.
- Everyone has a dark side, and sometimes it's tempting to let it out to do whatever it wants to do.
- If you don't do what you know is right, anyone can manipulate you.

- If you do what's right only because someone told you to, sooner or later you'll do something wrong for the same reason.

BOOK REPORT IDEAS

1. Compare Young's relationship with his father and with Rob. How are they similar and different?
2. Discuss how your image of Young changed as you got deeper into the story.
3. Discuss the roles that parents, especially fathers, played in their sons' lives. How much are they to blame for what happened?
4. Explain why it was so important to Rob for Simon to be popular. What did Young mean when he said, "What hole was in Rob that only the triumph of Simon Glass could fill?" (p. 127, paperback edition)
5. Discuss what Young means when he refers to *The Book of Bob*.
6. Young made a number of mistakes, but was he really on a one-way street, or were there times when he might have turned everything around by making a different decision?
7. Discuss why Young let Rob manipulate him so completely. What need did Rob's approval fill?
8. How much of what happened to Simon was his own fault? Why do you think he had to taunt the others to the point of violence? What did he get from ruining Rob's plans?
9. Why didn't Young either join Rob and Bob or help Coop? Why did he do nothing?
10. We knew Young was paroled and planned to live with Coop for awhile. Speculate on what the rest of his life will be like.
11. Look at the different views of popularity in the book. What does it mean to the different characters? How do you define it?

BOOKTALK IDEAS

1. Use some of the quotes to add mystery and suspense to your talk.
2. Focus your talk on the five boys—perhaps have them describe each other as they are when the plan begins.
3. In this book, you know the ending on the first page. Be careful not to give away so much that your audience guesses too much of the final chapters. Consider stopping before chapter 10, or not including the quote from the prison chaplain in your talk.
4. Write your talk as if it were one of the newspaper stories about the murder.
5. Use pictures that could be of the five main characters as props.

RISKS

- Bullying and intimidation
- Wealthy, distant, and uninvolved parents

- Alcoholic father sneers at son's dreams
- Demanding and controlling father
- Teens manipulate and then murder another teen
- The boy who didn't participate in the beating is the only one punished for it
- Vulgar language

STRENGTHS

- Authentic teen voice draws in reader
- Quotes at the beginning of each chapter are hooks, pulling the reader along
- Characters' personalities are revealed slowly, piece by piece
- Ensemble cast allows reader to see each character from a variety of perspectives
- Abrupt ending is shocking and memorable
- Blame is assigned to every member of the group
- Characters are realistic, neither black nor white, and respond to situations in genuine ways
- Very moral story
- Teaches lessons on multiple topics and at various levels
- Encourages discussion, speculation, and self-reflection

AWARDS

ALA Best Books for Young Adults, 2003
ALA Quick Picks for Reluctant Young Adult Readers, 2003
ALA Popular Paperbacks, 2005

REVIEWS

"As the suspense begins to build, readers will find it hard to put down the book. . . . Giles's novel is also a chilling portrayal of manipulation leading to tragic consequences. Teens in upper middle school and high school will relate to the characters and, sadly, to some of the events in this book." Linda Roberts, *VOYA*, 6/02

"The plot is fast-paced and compelling and there is power in the brewing violence and shocking end; the language is raw and the behavior is brutal." Vicki Reutter, Cazenovia High School, NY, *School Library Journal*, 4/02

"The pacing is superb, and the story's twists are unexpected and disquieting. Heading the chapters are the comments of those involved, five years after the event. This conceit extends the story and will keep readers wondering." Ilene Cooper, *Booklist*, 3/02

⊞ ⊞ ⊞

SHOOTER. Walter Dean Myers. Amistad/HarperCollins, 2005. $7.99. 256p. ISBN10: 0064472906. ISBN13: 9780064472906. HarperChildrensAudio. $22.00. ISBN10: 006074765X. ISBN13: 9780060747657. (unabridged audio CD) HarperTempest, 2004. $17.89. 240p. ISBN10: 0060295201. ISBN13: 9780060295202. (library binding) Thorndike Press, 2004. $22.95. 247p. ISBN10: 0786269693. ISBN13: 9780786269693. (large print) Realistic fiction. Reading Level: MS. Interest Level: MS, YHS, OHS. English, Psychology, Creative Writing.

SUBJECT AREAS
anger; bullying; crime and delinquency; dysfunctional families; guns; secrets; legal system; justice; revenge; suicide; self-destruction; school; bullying; friendship; manipulation; family relationships; substance abuse; problem parents.

CHARACTERS
Cameron Porter: a seventeen-year-old black student at Madison High School.
Dr. Richard Ewings: a senior county psychologist and a member of the Harrison County School Safety Committees
Elizabeth and Norman Porter: Cameron's parents
Leonard Gray: one of Cameron's friends since they were sophomores
Dr. Brendal: Cameron's psychologist
Mr. Anders: high school baseball coach
Carla Evans: girl at school who hung out with Cameron and Len
Victoria Lash: FBI Special Agent, Threat Assessment Analyst
Dr. Franklyn Bonner: he's the President of Spectrum Group, Threat Assessment Specialists
Sheriff William Beach Mosley: head of the Harrison County Criminal Bureau
Dr. Jonathan Margolies: Superintendent, Harrison County Board of Education

BOOKTALK
Another school shooting. Another outsider dead. Another jock dead. Newspaper headlines. Depositions. Theories. Assumptions. Clues. Questions.

Everyone knows what happened—Leonard Gray brought guns and ammunition to school. At 8:03 AM, he started shooting. By 8:33, it was over. Brad Williams was dead, shot multiple times; some shots were fired after he was dead. Leonard Gray was also dead. He was found on the third story of the school. It was obvious from the evidence at the scene that he had put the barrel of one of his guns in his mouth and pulled the trigger. Cameron Porter was found on the second floor, with a loaded gun in the same room. He was taken into custody. More guns and ammunition were found in the library. Carla Evans was also found on the second floor, hiding in a closet. She was also taken into custody.

Yes, everyone knows, and no one knows. What made Len come to school and start shooting? How did he choose his targets? What had happened to him that made him that desperate? Read the transcripts of the interviews, the opinions of the experts, the police reports, and Len's journal, and find out how a shooter was created.

MAJOR THEMES AND IDEAS

- Just because it appears in the media news stories doesn't make it true.
- Being a teenager is all about comparisons—who's smarter, who's better at sports, who has the best car or best date.
- Kids measure each other against themselves—even if they say they aren't doing it.
- When you have to put part of yourself aside in order to fit in, it's painful, like you are betraying that part of you.
- It can mean a lot when you're into something with someone, like you're tight with them, and wouldn't betray them.
- Once you become a target for bullies, it's almost impossible to remove the target from your back.
- A lot of kids are doing things that are dangerous or illegal, but no one rats them out.
- Whoever bullies you does it because he knows you're nothing and he knows you know it too.
- Big events don't happen by themselves. There are many small events that lead up to the big one, that make it happen, that make it impossible to avoid.
- Ignoring danger signs can lead to a more drastic or devastating tragedy.
- Ignoring a troubled teen who has been bullied or marginalized in some way is *never* a good idea.

BOOK REPORT IDEAS

1. Discuss the sequences of events that led to Len's final confrontation. What were the turning points that sent Len off in a new and more dangerous direction?
2. Evaluate the various interviews and explain what significant information is revealed in each of them.
3. Compare the Final Report and the Dissent. Determine which is more valid and explain why.
4. Was there a point (or points) when Len could have been steered away from violence, rather than toward it? Explain how this might have been worked out.
5. Examine the three sets of parents/foster parents, and determine what they might have done to decrease the risk of a shooting incident. If you decide they could not have changed the outcome of the events, explain why.

6. What role did bullying play in the sequence of events. Could anyone have done anything to either prevent the bullying or reduce its impact on Len, Carla, and Cameron?
7. If you were in a position of power so far as the school was concerned (i.e., superintendent, principal, school board member), what would you do to ensure that this kind of situation didn't happen again?
8. Which events leading up to the shootings were the most significant and most likely to have resulted in change, had they been resolved differently?
9. Which of the characters are more like you and why?
10. Examine the various reports that were made about the shootings and explain which you think are the most accurate and why.
11. What would you have done if you'd been Cameron? Carla?

BOOKTALK IDEAS
1. Write your talk as if it were a newspaper article or TV news story.
2. Let Cameron and Carla take turns introducing Len and his story.
3. Have Len tell his own story, in his own words.
4. Base your talk on Len's journal and some of his conversations with Cameron and Carla.

RISKS
- Entire book is based on school shooting scenario
- Teens shoot guns, including target shooting at live targets
- Realistic language including obscenities
- Teens are into "the dark culture"
- Teen makes a list of his enemies
- Crime and delinquency
- Defacing a church
- Teens abuse prescription drugs
- Deliberately cruel and hurtful acts to take revenge
- Multiple points of view can made novel choppy and disconnected
- Parents are distant and uninvolved or irresponsible and neglectful
- Parents and school officials ignored warning signs from Len and Cameron
- Teacher is threatened by student
- Gives the perspective of the outsiders involved in the incident
- Students perceived as outsiders are bullied by jocks and other insiders
- Students don't report the violent behavior of their friends—"code of silence"

STRENGTHS
- Story is told from multiple perspectives and points of view
- Court documents, newspaper articles, and journal entries are used to reveal the story gradually
- Examines a shooting investigation from the "inside out"

- Maintains tension and suspense even though ending is known from the very first scene

AWARDS
ALA Quick Picks for Reluctant Young Adult Readers, 2005
New York Public Library Books for the Teen Age, 2005

REVIEWS
"This novel is a powerful, intriguing, and imaginative fictional exposé of a teen crying out for emotional and mental relief. It draws the reader in with its unique format . . . and its unfortunately recognizable setting of high school violence, leaving a wake of unsettling emotions." Diane Tuccillo, *VOYA*, 6/04

"In addition to young adults who will find this story intensely readable as well as intense, adults working with teens should read and discuss the questions and implications that the tale reveals." Francisca Goldsmith, Berkeley Public Library, CA, *School Library Journal*, 5/04

"Readers will find themselves racing through the pages, then turning back to pore over the details once more." *Publishers Weekly*, 3/04

ᗰᗰᗰ

SIDE EFFECTS. Amy Goldman Koss. Roaring Brook Press, 2006. $16.95. 144p. ISBN10: 1596432942. ISBN13: 9781596432949. Realistic fiction. Reading Level: MS. Interest Level: MS, YHS. English, Psychology, Art.

SUBJECT AREAS
illness, physical; family relationships; self-knowledge; school; friendship; death and dying; anger; fear; gossip; art; rites of passage; survival.

CHARACTERS
Isabelle Miller/Izzy: she gets cancer, gets treatments, and survives
Mom/Helen Miller: she falls apart when she learns about Izzy's cancer
Dad/Mr. Miller: Izzy's dad; he does his best to help his wife and daughter
Max Miller: Izzy's little brother, who is honest with Izzy
Kay: Izzy's best friend
Dr. Pasner: Izzy's doctor who diagnoses her cancer
Dara: Dr. Pasner's nurse

Jared Peterson: Izzy has a crush on him
Lucy: Izzy's aunt, who doesn't fall apart and helps Izzy stay strong
Carrie: Izzy's roommate at Children's Hospital who has sickle cell anemia
Marilee: another teen with sickle cell
Sam: he's about Izzy's age and has leukemia
Pamela Anne Carter: a psychiatric social worker assigned to Izzy
Tanya White: the nurse who gives Izzy her first chemo
Amanda: a girl at school who's not one of Izzy's friends, but who pretends to be to get attention
Dr. Seacole: Izzy's oncologist
Heather: Izzy's caseworker, who bonds with her mom
Andy Siegol: a guy in one of Izzy's classes who treats her like a normal person
Larry Rodriguez: Izzy's tutor, who has low expectations of her

BOOKTALK

There was no doubt about it, my life sucked. Ever since they day I found out I had cancer, it was just chemo and puking, chemo and more puking til I thought I'd puke up my insides. And getting the chemo was like shooting up with poison. I had no idea a human being could be in so much pain and feel so bad and not die.

And then they sent me home. First thing I did was run to the bathroom and celebrate with a big, noisy puke. Then I slept for a day and a half. It seemed like a nightmare I couldn't wake up from. Tests, scans, chemo, puking. And through it all, my mom crying and freaking out, 24/7. I was the one with cancer; I was the one being tortured; so why did I have to take care of *her* as well as me?

Even Kay, my best friend, was getting weird on me. She was angry all the time, but at least she was *there* and not in tears. And she told me what was going on at school—everyone knew what had happened, and I was like the school cancer kid. And she was right. When my mom finally forced me to go back to school, everyone was all nicey-nice, and all my teachers said I didn't have to do any work if I didn't feel like it.

Andy, a guy who sat in front of me in fifth hour, asked if he could loan me some notes; I said no, I was just gonna dare them to flunk me. He laughed and gave me a thumbs up, just like I was the old Izzy, not the cancer kid. Turns out his sister had to have chemo when she was in high school, so he knew I was still Izzy on the inside. I wondered why I hadn't noticed him before.

Having cancer sucks, and I hate it. But like my Aunt Lucy said, you don't have to like what's happening to you. You just have to keep going, push on through, til you can come out on the other side. Not everyone who has cancer dies. Maybe I'll be one of the survivors.

MAJOR THEMES AND IDEAS

- Life can change forever in only a minute: first when you learn you have cancer, and then when you find out you're cancer free.

- People make lots of assumptions about someone who has cancer, many of them wrong.
- Not everyone who has cancer dies from it.
- Having cancer doesn't make you someone else—you're still you.
- Treating a cancer patient like a person instead of a disease is the best thing you can do for them.
- Cracking jokes can be a way to cover up anxiety.
- When kids get really sick, most people won't be honest with you. Instead, they're really fake-nice.
- It's hard to be everyday normal with a person who has cancer.
- Having cancer is bad enough, but on top of that, it means most things and most people are either a little weird or a *lot* weird.
- Sometimes saying the wrong thing beats saying nothing at all
- Having cancer/being sick is just about getting through it, any way you can.
- Humor helps, even black humor.
- The more chemo you have, the worse you feel.
- There is life and love after cancer.
- You don't have to like what's happening to you. You just have to keep going and push on til you can come out on the other side.

BOOK REPORT IDEAS
1. Compare and contrast Izzy as she appears on the first and last pages of the book.
2. Discuss the way people treated Izzy after she got sick. Why were some people able to see her as more than a cancer patient? Why could others not do this?
3. People in this book used different coping mechanisms to cover up their fear of Izzy's death. Explain how several of them did this.
4. Discuss the relationship between Izzy and her mother and how it changed after Izzy got sick.
5. Show how Kay and Izzy's relationship changed over the six months Izzy was sick.
6. Discuss Amanda's video. Why did she make it and what did it mean to her? How would you have felt if you'd been Izzy watching it?

BOOKTALK IDEAS
1. Write your talk from Kay's point of view, in first person.
2. Use a picture of some of the equipment for chemo as a prop.
3. Use one of Izzy's pictures as a prop.
4. Izzy used humor as a way to keep going. Include some of her jokes and sarcastic remarks in your talk.

RISKS
- Shows what happens during and after chemotherapy in vivid detail
- Ineffectual mother
- Realistic and vulgar language
- Depicts the experience of having cancer very vividly
- Medical use of marijuana
- Defiant teen rebels against authority figures

STRENGTHS
- Authentic voice of a teen
- Skilled writing draws in reader
- Teen gets cancer and survives
- Could be used as bibliotherapy with friends and/or parents of a teen cancer patient
- Educates reader about cancer and chemotherapy
- Three-dimensional characters readers can identify with
- Honest, yet with a touch of hope

AWARD
ALA Best Books for Young Adults, 2007

REVIEWS
"This novel is not the typical kid-with-cancer book. Izzy is bitingly sarcastic, not even letting cancer dull her razor-sharp tongue. She swears, makes witty and morbid (although inappropriate, says her mother) jokes about the circumstances, and maintains a sense of humor about something that is difficult to find funny . . . Vibrant and authentic, Izzy's narrative voice is unique and refreshing, as is Koss's unforgiving look at a topic that too often has no happy ending." Amanda MacGregor, *VOYA*, 10/06

"Koss refuses to glamorize [her protagonist's] illness or treatment. Instead, she settles for an honesty and frankness that will both challenge and enlighten readers." Frances Bradburn, *Booklist*, 9/06

"This tale will certainly open readers' eyes to the tribulations of young cancer patients and how to offer support." *Publishers Weekly*, 12/06

"The book has realistically typical teenage characters and apparently solid research into various Childrens Hospital patients and their treatments, but it's not too heavy, complex, or long." Rhona Campbell, Chevy Chase Neighborhood Library, Washington, D.C., *School Library Journal*, 9/06

⊡⊡⊡

SOLD. Patricia McCormick. Hyperion, 2006. $15.99. 272p. ISBN10: 0786851716. ISBN13: 9780786851713. Hyperion, 2008. $8.99. 272p. ISBN10: 0786851724. ISBN13: 9780786851720. Topeka, 2008. $18.75. 263p. ISBN10: 1417818107. ISBN13: 9781417818105. (library binding) Realistic fiction, Verse novel. Reading Level: YHS. Interest Level: YHS, OHS. English, Sex Education, Psychology, Geography, Ethics.

SUBJECT AREAS
sex and sexuality; poverty; child abuse; sexual abuse; working; addiction; anger; betrayal; ethnic groups; fear; friendship; manipulation; lying and deceit; other countries; rape; secrets; self-knowledge; suicide.

CHARACTERS
Lakshmi: at thirteen, she travels from her home in Nepal to find a job to help support her family
Ama: Lakshmi's mother
Gita: Lakshmi's best friend before she went to work in the city
Krishna: the boy to whom Lakshmi is promised in marriage
Stepfather: he takes in Ama and Lakshmi when her father dies; he spends all their money gambling
Bajai Sita: the old trader woman in the village
"Auntie" Bimlo: she buys Lakshmi from her stepfather and then sells her to a man in the city
"Uncle Husband": after he pays for Lakshmi, he takes her across the border to India
Mumtaz: she runs Happiness House
Shahanna: one of the other girls at Happiness House
Habib: the first man who lies with Lakshmi
Anita: her scarred face makes her look angry
Pushpa: a widow who tries to support her two children as a prostitute
Shilpa: Mumtaz's spy
Monica: she's more aggressive with men and brags she will soon pay off her price and go home
Jeena and Harish: Pushpa's children

BOOKTALK
Once, long ago, I was thirteen and I lived in a small village in the mountains of Nepal. We were poor, and my stepfather couldn't work because of his crippled arm. Instead, he sat in the tea shop and gambled away the money that I and my mother earned. I

had a goat named Tali and a baby brother. I thought I knew many things, but now I know that I was an ignorant child. When our crop of rice washed away during the monsoon, my stepfather decided I should go to the city to work. The journey was long, four days of walking and riding, leaving my country and traveling into India, to a place called Happiness House.

It was not a real house of happiness, at least not for me and the other girls who worked there. We were forced to take men to our beds every night, and to let them do to us whatever pleased them. If we refused, Mumtaz made us take drugs that made us sleepy and calm, so we would not object to what the men did to us.

The only way we could get out was to pay Mumtaz back for our purchase price, and even lying with six men each night, it was impossible. Soon, I was no longer an ignorant child, but a girl who has seen far too much to ever return to the bliss and confidence of ignorance.

MAJOR THEMES AND IDEAS
* Simply to endure is to triumph.
* Daydreams—a luxury that costs nothing.
* Any man is better than no man at all.
* Promises from a stranger mean little—they could too easily be lies.
* Looking back is futile—you can't change the past. Look ahead instead. Anything can happen in the future.
* It is better if you show no one how frightened you are.
* When life is a nightmare, the truth can be unbearable. It's easier to believe the nightmare instead.
* If life is too hard to deal with, pretending is the only possible escape.
* There are far too many bad people in the world—including some of the ones who are supposed to be good.
* When life gives you little opportunity for laughter, take advantage of every one.
* Never give up hope, for without it, you die.
* Reaching for what you want takes courage and determination. Not everyone has enough of either.

BOOK REPORT IDEAS
1. Focus on the real statistics about the youngest prostitutes in Calcutta.
2. Illustrate your work with a map tracing Lakshmi's journey from the Nepali Mountains to Calcutta.
3. Discuss the children at Happiness House. What are their lives like? How much do you think they know about the truth of their lives?
4. Why do the girls at Happiness House pretend so hard? What do they gain from it?

5. Examine the advice Lakshmi gets on how to act around men: what does this show about the girls' relationships?
6. Discuss the friendships among the girls at Happiness House. Why are they so important?
7. Discuss how difficult it must have been for Lakshmi to continue to believe in people when the promises made to her weren't kept.
8. Speculate about what Lakshmi's life might be in the future. Will she ever be able to go back to her village? Where else might she go?

BOOKTALK IDEAS
1. Illustrate your talk with a map that traces Lakshmi's journey.
2. Create your talk from several of Lakshmi's poems.
3. Use some of the author's statistics as a way to introduce your talk.
4. Let Lakshmi tell her own story. End the talk before she understands what she will have to do.
5. Focus your talk on the friends Lakshmi made—why they were important and necessary—but don't give away the information that they are prisoners and prostitutes.

RISKS
- Sexism—boys are worth more than girls
- A thirteen-year-old girl is forced into prostitution
- Rape of a minor, described vividly and graphically
- Girl is drugged so she won't fight the men who've paid to have sex with her
- Ending comes too quickly and easily

STRENGTHS
- Shows a culture and lifestyle unfamiliar to most teens
- Narrator's voice is clear and poignant
- The horror of life at Happiness House is stark and real
- Strong narrator's voice draws in the reader
- Stark, spare writing conveys the poverty of life both in the mountain village and at Happiness House
- Shows the sexual slavery trade that supplies prostitutes for the red light district of Calcutta
- Unflinching examination of the lives of young prostitutes
- Hopeful ending doesn't give anything away—reader is left to speculate on what happens to Lakshmi
- Shows girls' determination to be free and willingness to take chances to attain her goal

- Portrays characters and settings not often found in teen and YA literature
- Encourages discussion of sex and sexuality versus love and nurturing

AWARDS
ALA Best Books for Young Adults, 2007
ALA Quick Picks for Reluctant Young Adult Readers, 2007
Booklist Editor's Choice, 2006
Bulletin Blue Ribbons, 2006
National Book Award Finalist (Young People's Literature), 2006
Publishers Weekly Best Children's Books, 2006

REVIEWS
"McCormick tells Lakshmi's story in brief, poetic scenes, painting a haunting and thought-provoking picture of helplessness and hope. . . . This novel is not to be missed, and readers will find themselves thinking about Lakshmi and the real girls whose lives inspired this stunning novel long after they turn the last page." Vikki Terrile, *VOYA*, 12/06

"In beautiful clear prose and free verse that remains true to the child's viewpoint, first-person, present-tense vignettes fill in Lakshmi's story. The brutality and cruelty are ever present ('I have been beaten here, / locked away, / violated a hundred times / and a hundred times more'), but not sensationalized. An unexpected act of kindness is heartbreaking . . . An unforgettable account of sexual slavery as it exists now." Hazel Rochman, *Booklist,* 9/06

"The author beautifully balances the harshness of brothel life with the poignant relationships among its residents. . . . Readers will admire Lakshmi's grit and intelligence, and be grateful for a ray of hope for this memorable heroine at book's end." *Publishers Weekly*, 8/06

"McCormick provides readers who live in safety and under protection of the law with a vivid window into a harsh and cruel world—one most would prefer to pretend doesn't exist." *Kirkus Reviews,* 9/06

📖📖📖

SPLINTERING. Eireann Corrigan. Scholastic, 2004. $16.95. 192p. ISBN10: 0439535972. ISBN13: 9780439535977. Push, 2005. $7.99. 192p. ISBN10: 043948992X. ISBN13: 9780439489928. (library binding) Verse novel. Reading Level: MS. Interest Level: MS, YHS, OHS. English, Creative Writing, Psychology.

SUBJECT AREAS
violence; family relationships; child abuse; anger; crime and delinquency; dysfunctional family; sex and sexuality; survival; self-knowledge; secrets; poetry; lying and deceit; love; guilt; depression; fear.

CHARACTERS
Paulie: she's fifteen and is angry a lot of the time, partly because her mother slaps her around

Mimi: she's the perfect one and moves back with her family when her marriage falls apart

Jeremy: the middle kid; Paulie thinks he's a pest

Mom: she's one of the ladies who lunch

Dad: he's over-involved in his career

Matthew: Mimi's husband, who's less than perfect

Evan: Paulie's boyfriend

Mr. Fitzpatrick: Paulie's history teacher, who says she's got potential

Dr. Sutter: the high school guidance counselor

Nina: a girl Jeremy has a crush on

Gigolo Joe: he owns the bagel shop where Evan works on Sundays

BOOKTALK
It takes only one crackhead and one night of terror to splinter a family for what could be forever.

From the outside, Paulie's life looks pretty good—successful, married older sister; pest of an older brother; a mother who's one of the ladies who lunch; a father who rides the train into the city every day and pays the bills; and of course, tons of friends to laugh and gossip with every day. But when you turn her life around and look at it from the inside, it's not all that great.

> . . . Ever since I could first name things, I've known the shape of my mother's fist. There's an uglier way to say that—she's slapped me around. In the car, in the kitchen. In front of my dad. And never once has he stepped forward, with his hand held up like a school crossing guard, and said Stop. So she might whack you in the back of the neck with the hairbrush. She might narrow her eyes and say You little shit. She may punch. But the backhanded half of punishment was my dad and his retreating back. Silent. And almost worse, somehow.

And that was before the night that changed everything, before their family splintered apart the way doors and windows splintered when the crackhead broke into Mimi's house screaming, waving a machete, ready to kill them all. That was when Mimi's marriage splintered, when she refused to live in the shattered house, and moved back with her family. That was before everyone realized that after Mom, Paulie, and Mimi barricaded themselves in an upstairs bedroom, Jeremy didn't stay and help Dad fight off the madman, but instead, hid under the basement stairs with all the dogs and prayed no one would find him. That was before Dad nearly died that night from the heart attack that could have splintered the family even more. And that was before the realization came of what that night had really done to them, and how they were all stuck in the feelings and emotions they'd experienced that night: Dad weakened, Mimi hurting, Paulie raging in futile anger, Jeremy afraid and withdrawn, and Mom trying to put back together what was damaged beyond repair.

Listen to Paulie and Jeremy's voices as they remember that night and try to figure out how to survive its aftermath and go on with their lives.

MAJOR THEMES AND IDEAS
- You can't be afraid forever. Sooner or later you have to let go and move on.
- You can't ever go back. Life doesn't have do-overs.
- Sometimes you just want someone's arms to hold tight and keep away the fear, if only for a moment.
- You can get caught in a moment when you see your most honest, wretched self, and you can't go any further or see anything else.
- In a crisis, time slows down, and everything seems to happen very slowly.
- When a family splinters apart, even the closest friendships may not survive.
- Having to survive a life-and-death crisis forces you to grow up faster and suddenly see how little you have in common with your friends.
- After a crisis that turns your life upside down, your daily goals can become very specific: keep your mouth shut and don't kill yourself.
- Not sharing the personal hell you are trying to survive, keeping it inside you, can mean that it is free to eat you up, from the inside out.
- Having someone you can trust completely, can relax with, and just be yourself with, can be the one thing that keeps you sane.
- In a family where secrets are important, swift, unguarded glimpses are all anyone has to show them who their mothers, fathers, sisters or brothers really are.
- An unexpected moment of sibling unity can help make you realize how much you love them, in spite of everything.
- You shouldn't trade being careful for being cared for.
- When you find out that the world holds worse people and better reasons to be afraid, enemies you've fought with for years suddenly seem less frightening and deranged, closer to human, if not humane.
- Sometimes things hurt all over again like the first time whenever you share them. But you still need to share them, and let the acid seep away, drop by drop.
- Reciting the facts of a traumatic situation can sound like you're telling everything about it, when actually you've said nothing that really matters. The facts don't begin to encompass the enormity of what has happened or how you are still struggling to deal with it.

- Love unmasks us, and we stand naked, open, real, before the one person who matters most.
- Everyone's got their story, some private grief they guard like a secret scar.

BOOK REPORT IDEAS

1. Describe the family before the attack—who each family member was and how they interacted. Compare them to the people they became afterwards.
2. Explain why you think neither Paulie nor Jeremy told anyone, including their friends, about what had happened.
3. Discuss how the family dealt with Paulie being abused by her mother. What reasons did each of them have to justify their behavior?
4. What did the family members learn about because of the attack? How did they change?
5. Speculate about what might have happened if the whole family had challenged the crackhead as a group, a united front.
6. How does Paulie protect herself after the attack? How do the other family members?
7. Why doesn't anyone ever comment on what Jeremy did and didn't do? It becomes a family secret that no one's allowed to mention. Explain how this affects Jeremy.
8. Why would their father send Paulie and Mimi upstairs and face an armed man alone, and yet not defend Paulie in the anonymity of their own house? Discuss how he did and didn't show his bravery.
9. Discuss how each of the family members is stuck in whatever he or she was feeling that night.
10. In "The Surrealist," Jeremy draws what he thinks is "priceless and crucial" in the lives of his family members. They each get a box of sharp, shining knives. Why does he give each of them weapons—the same weapons? How does he imagine each of them using those weapons?
11. What's the source of her mother's anger at and abuse of Paulie? It's been going on for as long as she can remember, and no one has ever done anything to stop it.
12. Discuss why Paulie pushes Evan away in "The Ball Breaker," "The Sensitive Man," and "Not Exactly Low Maintenance." Where does her need to hurt him come from, and what does she gain from it?

BOOKTALK IDEAS

1. Write your talk in the same style as the book, alternating between Paulie's and Jeremy's voices. Make sure you let your audience know who is speaking by starting each section with "Paulie's Story" or "Paulie Speaks" or something similar.

2.   Write your talk from a third person perspective, talking about the attack.
3.   Describe the attack from all five perspectives, letting each of the family members tell their part of it.

RISKS

*   Mother physically abuses younger daughter—rationale/source of the abuse is not made clear, nor is the rationale for its stopping
*   Father, sister, and brother ignore abuse in spite of physical signs
*   Teens drink and smoke marijuana
*   Fifteen-year-old has secret sexual relationship with a young man in college
*   Family members draw apart as a result of the attack
*   Ending resolves few issues
*   Realistic language, including obscenities

STRENGTHS

*   Shows how a trauma can divide or unite a family
*   Different fonts indicate points of view—a shift in the narrator
*   Verse format makes emotions very real, allowing reader to identify with narrative more closely
*   Three-dimensional characters the reader can identify with
*   Several characters do not speak, so their perspectives are not seen, creating opportunities for discussion
*   Ending not completely resolved, allowing for speculation and discussion
*   Demonstrates the different ways people react to trauma and its aftermath
*   Realistic language helps make characters come alive

AWARD
ALA Best Books for Young Adults, 2005

REVIEWS
"The two teen characters and their family members are very realistic. They have the usual sibling rivalry, but the way that they care for each other also comes through strongly. Teens who enjoy novels in poetry form will be happy to see another book by Corrigan." Cindy Faughnan, *VOYA*, 8/04

"The poems offer insight into sibling relationships, rivalries and misunderstandings. . . . Although this novel captures several kinds of splintering, its climax imparts hope of a solid healing." *Publishers Weekly*, 4/04

"A culminating event brings the strands and family together in a satisfying dénouement. Effective and affecting." *Kirkus Reviews*, 4/04

"A work of fiction, told through poetry, this is a powerful story of a family splintering apart because of an act of violence. A brother and a sister share the narrative in alternating poems. . . . Obscenities are frequent, and absolutely appropriate as the traumatized Paulie and Jeremy try to put words to their confusion and misery. . . . For sophisticated adolescents." Claire Rosser, *KLIATT*, 3/04

STONER AND SPAZ. Ron Koertge. Candlewick, 2002. $15.99. 176p. ISBN10: 0763616087. ISBN13: 9780763616083. Candlewick, 2004. $6.99. 176p. ISBN10: 0763621501. ISBN13: 9780763621506. Tandem Library, 2004. $15.80. 176p. ISBN10: 0613748204. ISBN13: 9780613748209. (library binding) Listening Library, 2003. $18.00. ISBN10: 0807212458. ISBN13: 9780807212455. (unabridged audiotape) Realistic fiction. Reading Level: MS. Interest Level: MS, YHS. English, Psychology, Art, Drama, Filmmaking.

SUBJECT AREAS
handicaps; friendship; love; grandparents; school; drugs; addiction; sex and sexuality; substance abuse; self-knowledge; gossip; dating and social life.

CHARACTERS
Ben Bancroft: he's sixteen, has cerebral palsy, no parents, and an overprotective grandmother
Mrs. Sterzgarden: she works the ticket window at the Rialto Theatre
Reginald: he owns and manages the theatre
Colleen Minow: she's a doper with ripped tights, tattoos, and an attitude
Mrs. Bancroft/Grandma: Ben's very conservative, proper grandmother
Ed Dorn: the school dealer, who's dating Colleen
Stephanie Brewer: reporter for the school paper
Danny and Robert: the school anarchists
Ms. Johnson: sociology teacher and resident feminist
Marcie Sorrels: the Bancrofts' new neighbor
Chana, Debra, Molly: three black students with babies
Oliver: a high school student who's been openly gay since he was in sixth grade

BOOKTALK
You've heard the saying, "opposites attract." Well there couldn't be two people more opposite than Ben and Colleen—the Stoner and the Spaz.

Ben's an orphan who lives with his very proper and uptight grandmother. He has cerebral palsy and one side of his body doesn't work very well. He's kind of quiet and doesn't have any real friends. He's smart, so grades are no problem, and he loves movies. He loves to watch them and he loves to analyze them, looking at camera angles and editing, and what the director did to get the effect he wanted.

Colleen is a druggie who sells to support her own habit, and goes with Ed, the biggest dealer at school. She has tattoos, piercings, and major attitude. She also sees people for who they are, as Ben finds out when they meet at the theatre Ben goes to regularly. She's the first person who treats him like a regular person, not someone who's disabled. She talks to him, touches him, and since she's pretty loaded, she throws up all over Ben's grandmother's car when they offer to take her home. That's it, so far as Mrs. Bancroft is concerned. Colleen is definitely *not* the kind of girl Ben should be associating with.

But Ben has other ideas, and likes the way Colleen sees *him* and not his body. They go clubbing; she gives Ben his first joint. Even the kids at school start to really notice him, and before long, Ben's in love with Colleen. The only problem is, Colleen's in love with anything she can smoke, snort, swallow, or shoot.

Can such an unlikely couple ever survive? Succeed?

MAJOR THEMES AND IDEAS
- A lot of the time, everyone avoids a disabled person, treating him as if he were invisible.
- People like to be touched, but are sometimes hesitant to touch someone who's disabled.
- People see someone's disability before they see the person. Then they don't mention it or joke about it, they pretend that it doesn't exist.
- Sometimes people need a little help letting out their inner bad child.
- Take responsibility for yourself and your vices and don't blame them on anyone else.
- Try. You don't know what will happen until you do.
- Others see us through their own filters and draw their own conclusions—which can be very far from reality.
- You are what you say you are.
- Don't let them see you sweat.
- Everybody stands in front of the mirror and wishes they were different.
- Bodies are interesting—they reflect your life.
- Some people like their vices too much to let them go.
- Life is what *you* make of it. You create your own life.

BOOK REPORT IDEAS
1. What is Colleen's motivation for befriending Ben? What does she get from it?
2. Discuss the relationship between Ben and his grandmother and how it changes during the book.

3. Discuss how hard it is to give up your vices. Drugs were Colleen's vice. What was Ben's?
4. Compare Ben on the first and last pages of the book. How has he changed? How has he stayed the same?
5. Speculate on what happens after the book ends, to Ben and to Colleen.
6. What is the most important thing Ben learned? What do you think is the *most* important?
7. Explore Ben's relationship with Marcie. What influence does she have in his life?

BOOKTALK IDEAS

1. Write your talk as if it were one of Ben's favorite movies.
2. Make a video booktalk, and interview people to talk about Ben and Colleen.
3. Write your talk in first person, as Ben or as Colleen.
4. Focus your talk on what you think is the most important scene in the book from the first 25 percent, or the first 50 percent, of the book.

RISKS

- Obscene language
- Teens smoke cigarettes and marijuana
- Teens use drugs
- Over-controlling and hypochondriac grandmother
- Scenes show teens having sex
- Drug-addicted teen gets straight, and then goes back to drugs

STRENGTHS

- Realistic, genuine portrait of a teen with cerebral palsy
- Three-dimensional characters
- Realistic dialogue
- Girl treats disabled boy as if he wasn't disabled
- Pulls reader into story immediately
- Wry, sarcastic tone
- Characters grow and gain insight
- New experiences and new people change teen's self perception
- Teens practice safe sex
- Realistic ending

AWARDS

ALA Popular Paperbacks, 2005
ALA Best Books for Young Adults, 2003
ALA Quick Picks for Reluctant Young Adult Readers, 2003

REVIEWS

"Language and subject matter, including sex and heavy drug use, target this novel for high school students, who undoubtedly will find truth not only in the struggles of Ben and Colleen but also in those of the other high school students that Ben interviews for his film." Mary Ann Darby, *VOYA*, 4/02

"Koertge displays his usual flair for creating believable characters, genuine dialogue, and some wonderfully humorous moments. Ben's apprehension and awkwardness with Colleen and her almost complete obliviousness to everything in the world around her rings true. Their need for a sense of belonging and their efforts to find it in one another are themes to which readers will certainly relate." Edward Sullivan, White Pine School, TN, *School Library Journal*, 4/02

"The first-person narrative is Ben's, but the human face, the fully developed personality of Ben Bancroft, is revealed through Colleen's drug-enhanced innocence and acceptance. Didactic? No. Revealing and consciousness raising? Absolutely. Buy several copies." Frances Bradburn, *Booklist*, 5/02

📖📖📖

TANTALIZE. Cynthia Leitich Smith. Candlewick, 2007. $16.99. 336p. ISBN10: 0763627917. ISBN13: 9780763627911. Candlewick, 2008. $8.99. 366p. ISBN10: 076364059X. ISBN13: 9780763640590. Walker Books, 2008. $10.23. 336p. ISBN10: 1406315605. ISBN13: 9781406315608. Fantasy/Supernatural fiction. Reading Level: YHS. Interest Level: YHS, OHS. English, Sociology, Vocational Education.

SUBJECT AREAS

occult/supernatural; working; family relationships; school; friendship; love; secrets; revenge; self-knowledge; rites of passage; animals; betrayal; cooking; manipulation; mystery/suspense; prejudice.

CHARACTERS

Quincie Morris: she's seventeen, and trying to open Austin's first vampire-themed restaurant, Sanguini's

Kieran Morales: Quincie's best friend; he's a hybrid werewolf, who doesn't like vampires

Vaggio Bianchi: the Italian chef of Sanguini's

Davidson Morris: Quincie's uncle and guardian, who came up with the vampire theme

Roby Kitahara: Uncle Davidson's girlfriend, who is a living vampire
Officer Walker, Officer Rodriguez: they responded to Kieran's 911 call
Detective Bartok: she did the initial interviews after Vaggio's murder
Ms. Morales: Kieran's mother, who's a werewolf
Mitch: the town character
Henry Johnson/Bradley Sanguini: the new chef Davidson hired
Travis, Clyde: two of Kieran's friends who want to work at Sanguini's and aren't exactly human
Winnie Gerhard: senior class gossip
Quandra Perez: tall, dark, and zowie
Vice Principal Harding: better known as "Hardass"
Mrs. Levy: Quincie's English teacher
Detective Sanchez: he's investigating Vaggio's murder
Mr. Wu: Quincie's economics teacher
Keio, Jamal, Mercedes, Simone, Sebastian, Sergio, Yanira/Yani, Ian, Jerome: Sanguini's wait staff

BOOKTALK

Sanguini's was going to be Austin's first vampire-themed restaurant—classy, elegant, unique. It had been the best Italian restaurant in town, but a new place with more parking and lower prices had sent it skidding into the red. That was when my Uncle Davidson had his bright idea about the undead. He hired a contractor to expand into the empty space next door, doubled the size of the dining room and almost doubled the kitchen. A bigger space and a bigger concept should put us back in the black in no time.

But that was before our chef Vaggio, whom I'd known all my life, was murdered in our newly remodeled kitchen. And not just murdered, but savaged, his throat torn out, a claw mark ripping open his chest. It looked like he'd been attacked by an animal, maybe by a werewolf or some other kind of shapeshifter. There weren't a lot of shapeshifters in Austin, but I'd practically grown up with a whole family of them. Kieran, my best friend and love of my life—although he didn't know about the last part—was a half werewolf, although he'd never been able to shift all the way yet. But he could have shifted enough to kill Vaggio. And he was the one who'd found him. When I saw him, he had blood all over him, his t-shirt, his jeans, even his boots. But the idea of Kieran killing anyone was so foreign to me, I rejected it almost as soon as I thought of it. Let the police figure out who killed Vaggio, and why. I had a restaurant to open, a new chef to find, and a menu to create. Opening day was Friday, September 13, and it was just a few short weeks away.

Step into Sanguini's, peruse the menu of bloody favorites, and drink a toast to the Dark Count at midnight. It will be a meal and an occasion to remember for the rest of your life—whether that's a few years or a few centuries. Sanguini's is truly A Very Rare Restaurant, indeed.

MAJOR THEMES AND IDEAS

- One instant everything's normal, then in another instant nothing would ever be the same.
- First love seems more significant because you don't have anyone to compare it with.
- Changes, especially big ones, are almost always painful.
- The villain of the story may be the very person you had no reason to suspect.
- First love is almost never comfortable.
- Vampires may not fit all the myths we have about them. Neither do the shape-shifters.
- People are attracted to what is elegant and beautiful, especially if it's just slightly dangerous as well.

BOOK REPORT IDEAS

1. Examine myths and legends of vampires and shapeshifters, and explain why the author used the ones she did. Discuss some others she might also have included.
2. List the steps that led to the discovery of the killer. When did you first suspect s/he was the killer, and why?
3. Speculate on what Quincie's life might be like after the book ends.
4. Create more menus for the restaurant, for vampires, and for shapeshifters.
5. Determine how many people die in this book, who killed them, and why.

BOOKTALK IDEAS

1. Wear a black cape for your talk.
2. Write your talk as if it were a newspaper article on Sanguini's.
3. Write your talk from Quincie's point of view, in first person, and have her introduce/talk about each of the main characters.

RISKS

- Vampires and shapeshifters
- Teens drink, and are encouraged to drink by adult
- Irresponsible guardian of teen girl
- Vampire-themed restaurant and menus

STRENGTHS

- Unusual and interesting characters
- Tongue-in-cheek writing style
- Suspense is drawn out, keeping readers interested
- Well-crafted murder mystery plot line
- Unique restaurant setting

- Clever menus for prey and predator
- Realistic dialogue

REVIEWS

"This offbeat vampire romance mystery offers both comic and creepy elements. Sanguini's, for example, has two menus, one for predators and one for prey—chilled baby squirrels simmered in orange brandy, anyone? . . . [An] entertaining, intriguing, and original story." Sarah Flowers, *VOYA*, 6/07

"Quincie must make a terrifying choice in a heart-pounding climax that will have teen readers weeping with both lust and sorrow. The storytelling is straightforward but elegant and will hold infinite appeal to the vampire-loving crowd." *Kirkus Reviews*, 2/07

"Readers will be tantalized by this dark, romantic, and disturbing fantasy of vampires, werewolves, and a strong no-nonsense heroine. Fans of Stephenie Meyer and Annette Curtis Klause will eat it up." Donna Rosenblum, Nassau Boces School Library System, NY, *School Library Journal*, 5/07

ꕤꕤꕤ

TEACH ME. R. A. Nelson. Razorbill/Penguin, 2005. $16.99. 272p. ISBN10: 1595140840. ISBN13: 9781595140845. Razorbill, 2007. $8.99. 272p. ISBN10: 1595140859. ISBN13: 9781595140852. Realistic fiction. Reading Level: YHS. Interest Level: YHS, OHS. English, Ethics, Sex Education, Health, Creative Writing.

SUBJECT AREAS

sex and sexuality; school; anger; love; betrayal; friendship; obsession; lying and deceit; manipulation; poetry; revenge; secrets.

CHARACTERS

Carolina/Nine Livingstone: she's smart, six feet tall with fuzzy brown hair, and invisible to boys but not to men
Richard Mann: Nine's English teacher, to whom she is immediately attracted
Schuyler Green: Nine's best friend and practically part of her family
Alicia Sprunk: Mr. Mann's petite bride
Mr. Livingstone: Nine's engineer father
Mrs. Livingstone: Nine's mother, who just wants her daughter to act more normal
Hub Christy: a tackle on the football team who's Nine's lab partner

Ms. Larimore: Nine's lab teacher
Mr. Deason/Zeb Greasy: high school principal
Beezle Bob: shift manager at the burger place where Nine and Schuyler work
Mary Katie, Country, Threatt: they work with Nine and Schuyler
Peggy Foster: the high school counselor
Ms. Jackson: school secretary
Mr. Perdergraff: assistant principal
Barb and Vince Mann: Richard Mann's parents

BOOKTALK

Nine's world changes forever when she sees him walk into her English class. Mr. Mann. Younger than most teachers. Trim. Black Dockers and a crisp white shirt, broad back, long arms and legs. His eyes are pale blue, and his dark hair hangs partly across his face. In moments, Nine is in love with him.

She can't wait to get to class, see him, talk to him, feel special in a way she's never felt before. He is the most important thing in her life. When her best friend Schuyler calls to remind her about the work day at his old elementary school, Nine tries to get out of it. Schuyler's not going because of a chess tournament and Nine won't have a partner at the work day. Schuyler wins. She goes. And the only other person without a partner is Mr. Mann. They spend the whole day together. Nine digs holes, Mr. Mann plants trees. Nine plants hope, hope that blossoms when she leaves work a few nights later and finds Mr. Mann waiting by her car. They park behind the Super Wal-Mart and hold each other close. And Nine's life changes again. Now she has a secret, a wonderful secret that she wants to hold close and shout to the world at the same time. He says he didn't mean for it to go so far, but he is so fascinated by her, he can't help himself.

Nine doesn't know what to say—she's six feet tall, has bushy brown hair, and she's smart. She's always been invisible to boys. "But not to me," he says. "I can see your mind. It dazzles me. It's luminous. I'm supposed to be good with words, but I'm speechless. I'm lost."

How could something with such a magical, powerful beginning, fall apart so quickly? It's May, a Sunday, two weeks before Nine's senior prom. It's the day Mr. Mann and Alicia Sprunk, his petite bride, are getting married. Nine wakes up strangely peaceful. She knows what she's going to do. She has a plan. Simple, and she hopes, effective.

What will Nine do today? What will it mean, and how will her life change because of it?

MAJOR THEMES AND IDEAS

- When you're holding back a secret, you don't want to be with people who are important to you. You're too used to telling them everything, and secrets struggle to be told.

- Sometimes, just screaming as loud as you can feels like a release, cleansing, freeing.
- Boyfriends are people you break up with. Friends are people you keep forever.
- Everyone's here for a reason; we aren't supposed to just waste our lives messing around—there are too many fantastic things to do.
- The longer a deception goes on, the worse it gets.
- There is more than one kind of love.
- Doing the right thing has a very good chance of hurting someone you don't intend to hurt.
- Sometimes the need to find the why behind the act can become an obsession.
- A coward dies many times, a hero dies but once.
- A real friend doesn't give up, no matter how strange, painful, or confusing things get.
- Hell hath no fury like a teen girl scorned, when she doesn't know the reason behind it.

BOOK REPORT IDEAS

1. Discuss the significance of Nine cleaning Richard's apartment and making his bed.
2. Emily Dickinson's poetry seems to frame the story and its chapters. Explain why you think the author chose this poet, rather than someone else.
3. Explain why Richard started the affair with Nine. What did he think he might gain? What did he ultimately lose?
4. The title of this novel is *Teach Me*. What did the various characters learn, and who were their teachers?
5. Answer Nine's question to Schuyler: "Can you really make a new life just by throwing out all the junk from your old one?"
6. What is the most important scene in the book? Why did you choose it and what does it mean to you?
7. Discuss and compare Schuyler and Nine's relationship, Richard and Nine's, and Ricky and Alicia's. Include how they see each other, positive and negative aspects, and what the future might hold for each of them.
8. Discuss your emotional reaction to the book. With whom did you most identify? Which scenes made you feel happy? Sad? Angry? Afraid? What other emotions did you feel?
9. Speculate on what each of the main characters will be like in five years? In ten?
10. If you were Nine, would you have fought back the way she did, or would you have chosen another way? What did her fighting accomplish? What did she want it to accomplish?
11. Was Richard's choice to marry Alicia the decision of a brave man or a coward? What would have happened if he'd chosen not to marry her?

12. When someone says they decided to do the right thing, is it usually a wise or a foolish decision?

BOOKTALK IDEAS

1. Use a volume of Emily Dickinson as a prop for your talk. You could also read some of the poems from it.
2. Introduce Nine by having Richard and Schuyler describe her, then have her talk about her relationship with them. (This should be while everything is right for Nine and Richard.)
3. Focus your talk on the scene when Richard tells Nine it's over. Make sure your audience understands that they are both in pain, and suggest that Nine isn't satisfied and will continue to obsess about Richard.
4. Base your talk on the idea of right and wrong, and how those concepts were interpreted by Nine, Richard, and Schuyler.

RISKS

- Teacher seduces his student
- Out-of-control, vengeful behavior
- Realistic language
- Teen puts herself and others in danger
- Parents are unable to see their daughter's pain
- Shows that marriage is the only way out of an unmarried pregnancy, even when it hurts more people than it helps
- Teen is obsessed with her teacher

STRENGTHS

- Powerful portrayal of the impact and influence of an adult having an affair with a teen
- Shows the positive effect of strong and long-term friendship
- Characters grow and gain insight
- Three-dimensional characters that have flaws as well as strengths
- Involving plot teens will identify with
- Presents a scenario that many teens are curious about and can identify with
- The conclusion has endings for some characters, while readers are left to speculate about others
- Opens a forum for debate on the question of teacher-student romances
- Tension created in the first eight pages never lets up, pulling the reader through the book

AWARDS

Booksense Fall Kids' Pick, 2006
New York Public Library Books for the Teen Age, 2006

REVIEWS

"This standout debut novel owes much to the engaging narrative voice of Nine. Her wry humor, quick wit, and constant obscure references make an already interesting story even more compelling. The loaded subject matter will draw in readers, and the stellar writing and careful pacing will keep them reading. Nine's voice echoes long after the story is finished, making this novel one not to be missed." Amanda Mac-Gregor, *VOYA*, 12/05

"Ultimately, this is a doomed love story complete with the usual trappings of passion and betrayal, but made more gripping because it mirrors real-life cases. . . . Contemporary and compelling." *Kirkus Reviews*, 8/05

"The story is juicy and cautionary without being preachy, which gives it wide teen appeal." Jane Cronkhite, Cuyahoga County Public Library, OH, *School Library Journal*, 10/05

THEORIES OF RELATIVITY. Barbara Haworth-Attard. Holt, 2005. $16.95. 240p. ISBN10: 0805077901. ISBN13: 9780805077902. Realistic fiction. Reading Level: YHS. Interest Level: YHS, OHS. English, Psychology, Sociology.

SUBJECT AREAS

homelessness; family relationships; friendship; survival; problem parents; substance abuse; physical abuse; mental illness.

CHARACTERS

Dylan Wallace: he's sixteen, homeless, and determined to survive
Jenna: she's new to the streets, and works for Vulture
Vulture/Brendan: a dangerous man, a predator who specializes in street people
Amber: she also worked for Vulture and helped Dylan when he ended up on the street
Mom: Dylan's mother, who kicked him out and refuses to help him or let him go home
Granddad/Edward Wallace: Dylan's paternal grandfather; he and his wife wanted to help raise him, but his mother refused
Pete: Dylan's stepdad and his brother Jordan's father
Phil: Dylan's father
Jordan: Dylan's mouthy little brother, who gets into trouble

Twitch/Aaron: a homeless kid who's tall, thin, and can't keep still; he frequently creates chaos and won't leave Dylan alone
Brad: he lives in an old church converted to apartments and lets Twitch sleep there
Micha: Dylan's six-year-old little brother
Harley: Micha's father, from Jamaica, who was there for two years before Mom kicked him out
Don: Mom's new boyfriend
Mr. Crowe: Dylan's teacher
Glen Matthews: a computer geek who sometimes buys Dylan a sausage roll
Lurch: an ex-con who's one of Vulture's enforcers
Ainsley: she works at the youth center
Jack Cody: a friend of Dylan's grandfather's in Murdock
Miriam Collins: she works for the home Dylan's grandfather lives in
Amy: she also works at the home

BOOKTALK

Dylan has a theory about panhandling—every fourth person he asks for money drops something in his cup. But on this day, the fourth person, a geeky looking guy, gives him a lecture instead. But later he comes back with a sausage roll. So maybe the theory works after all.

It's been three weeks since Dylan's mother kicked him out of the house. Her new boyfriend is a good guy, and she didn't want Dylan messing things up, and telling him all three of her kids have different fathers. Living on the street isn't easy, but Dylan's making it, just barely. But as Christmas gets nearer and the weather turns frigid, Dylan begins to wonder if he has any place to turn. His mom won't let him in the house. He doesn't have any other family that can help him, and the other street kids he knows are just as bad off as he is.

Beaten, broken, everything he owned stolen, Dylan is about to give up. If this were TV, someone would rescue him. But this isn't a TV show, it's real life, life on the streets, where there are no happy endings.

MAJOR THEMES AND IDEAS
- No one gives something for nothing.
- Panhandling is all about appearance and timing.
- Every fourth person gives money.
- Folks on the street might be curious, but they generally don't ask questions, to give each other at least a little privacy.
- If you look someone in the eye, it looks like you're telling the truth. Most of the time it works.
- A shrug can take the place of answering questions and the person asking them can interpret it any way they want to.

- It's dangerous to be in debt to a predator.
- Libraries are generally forgiving places as far as street people are concerned, as long as they don't make a scene.
- When you carry all you own, yourself, in a backpack, you'll do almost anything to protect it.
- On the streets time is measured by light and dark, relief and fear.
- Once you do something, it can't be undone. Think before you act in anger.
- Once you get a street name, it means you belong there, and it's harder to leave if you get a chance.
- There are no friends when you're on the street. Even people who claim to be your friends will betray you. You have to watch your own back.
- You can't help someone who doesn't want to be helped.
- Sometimes life at home is worse than surviving on the streets.
- Somehow, we always recognize the people we love, no matter how much they've changed.
- You can get off the streets—you just have to want it and work for it.
- You can think you have the illusion of control of your life, but no one can control everything.
- If no one treats you as though you matter, it's almost impossible to believe that you do.

BOOK REPORT IDEAS
1. Look up figures on the homeless teens in your area, and include them as part of your report.
2. Discuss the character of Dylan's mother. What signs do you see that she will be able to change her life? What signs that she won't?
3. Speculate on what Dylan's future might be like. What roles might Vulture and Lurch play? Glen? Ainsley? His mother and stepfather?
4. If you were Dylan, would you move back in with your brothers, mother, and stepfather? Why or why not?
5. What is the most important idea in the book? Why did you select it?
6. Discuss what you think is the most frightening thing that happened to Dylan. Why did you select it?
7. It takes something to get off the streets—strength and determination are necessary, but what else means the difference between success and failure?

BOOKTALK IDEAS
1. Work local statistics on homeless teens into your talk.
2. Find pictures that could be of the other street people in the book as props.

3. Write the talk from several perspectives as people describe Dylan—his mother, his brothers, Jenna, Amber, Twitch, Glen, Ainsley, Vulture, and others.
4. Let Dylan tell his own story in first person.

RISKS
- Sixteen-year-old boy is kicked out of his home and forced to live on the street
- Teens panhandle, drink, smoke, work as prostitutes, and do drugs
- Mother has three illegitimate sons by three different men
- Sexual abuse of a fourteen-year-old girl by her father
- Predators take advantage of homeless teens
- Teens' own sense of worthlessness prevents them from accepting help
- Few adults willing to reach out to teens on the street

STRENGTHS
- Graphic depiction of street life
- Shows the difficulty of getting off the street
- Realistic language
- Genuine teen voices
- Three-dimensional characters
- Some sense of hope of a better life
- Shows different reasons why teens and adults become homeless
- Street teens gain insight and must decide to fight for their lives or give in
- Ambiguous ending leaves room for speculation

AWARDS
The Stellar Book Award from British Columbia, 2006
Finalist Governor General's Award, 2003
Nominee CLA YA book of the Year Award, 2004

REVIEWS
"This gritty, slice-of-life novel from Canada is a page-turner. It will captivate both male and female readers. Characters are presented realistically, with no sugarcoating, as fully realized people." Mike Brown, *VOYA*, 2/06

"This is indisputably a problem novel, but it's one that shows the realities of the streets (not every homeless teen depicted finds a mentor, as Dylan does, in a corporate

executive) while suggesting brighter times ahead for its strong-willed protagonist."
Jennifer Mattson, *Booklist*, 11/05

"A beautifully written work on a gritty subject." *Kirkus Reviews*, 7/05

📖📖📖

TITHE: A MODERN FAERIE TALE. Holly Black. Simon and Schuster, 2002.
$17.99. 320p. ISBN10: 0689849249. ISBN13: 9780689849244. Simon Pulse, 2004.
$7.99. 336p. ISBN10: 0689867042. ISBN13: 9780689867040. Tandem Library,
2004. $15.80. 331p. ISBN10: 0613734564. ISBN13: 9780613734561. (library
binding) Thorndike Press, 2003. $22.95. 368p. ISBN10: 0786256494. ISBN13:
9780786256495. (large print) Fantasy. Reading Level: MS. Interest Level: YHS,
OHS. English.

SUBJECT AREAS
supernatural; homosexuality; friendship; death and dying; addiction; problem parents; war; revenge; betrayal; manipulation; drug abuse; dysfunctional families; fear;
secrets; self-knowledge; rites of passage.

CHARACTERS
Kaye Fierch: sixteen and in very dangerous faerie trouble, as in real, not imaginary
Ellen Fierch: Kaye's mother and a member of the band Stepping Razor
Lloyd: a member of Stepping Razor and Ellen's lover
Frank: Stepping Razor's drummer
Janet Stone: Kaye's friend from childhood, who's kept in touch by email
Doughboy: he went to school with Janet and Kaye
Kenny: Janet's boyfriend
Marcus: Kenny's friend
Cornelius Stone: a gay computer genius geek and Janet's brother
Spike, Lutie-loo, Gristle: faeries Kaye played with when she was a little girl and who
    need her help now
Roiben: a faerie Kaye helps when he's injured and an emissary from the Seelie Court
    to the Unseelie Court
Gram: Ellen's mother and Kaye's grandmother
Fatima: a friend of Janet, Kenny, and Doughboy
Liz and Sue: friends of Ellen's who used to be in a band with her

Thistlewitch: a faerie who tells Kaye what her destiny is
Lady Nicnevin: Queen of the Unseelie Court
Nephamael: emissary from the Unseelie to the Seelie Court

BOOKTALK

Kaye has been a wanderer for six years, as her mother does everything she can to become a rock star. Until she was ten, they lived with her grandmother on the New Jersey shore, and Kaye was known as the weird girl who talked to faeries. But Gristle, Lutie-loo, and Spike were real to Kaye. She played with them and they told her all kinds of stories about the faerie folk.

But Kaye's sixteen, no longer a child, when she and her mother go back to New Jersey. The faeries are gone. But then she gets a message from Lutie-loo and Spike warning her of danger, and a few nights later, they wake her up and take her to see Thistlewitch, who tells Kaye her true identity and her destiny. The two faerie courts are at war, and Kaye is caught squarely in the middle.

In the real world, a tithe is a payment to the church. But in the twisted, dangerous, and evil world of the faerie courts, a Tithe is something quite, quite different. And it isn't paid in money—it's paid in blood.

MAJOR THEMES AND IDEAS

- We are not all that we appear to be. Some are more, others are less.
- Few things drive a person harder than an obsession unmet or a dream unfulfilled.
- Magical ability gives cruel people more ways to show that cruelty.
- Everything has consequences. You just have to decide which ones you prefer before you act.
- Adoration that is magically created is meaningless.
- Not all those who appear to be friends actually care as much as they appear to.
- Those whom you are closest to have the power to hurt you the most deeply.
- Problem parents can be survived.
- Some people grow up when they have kids. Some do not.
- Kids whose parents act like children frequently have to learn to parent themselves and their parents.
- You can break a thing, but afterwards may not be able to force it into the shape you want.
- Action taken before considering its consequences may have devastating and unexpected results.

BOOK REPORT IDEAS

1. Analyze the relationship between Kaye and Janet. Why have they stayed friends? What do they each gain from their friendship?

2. Discuss how it would feel to have someone obsessed with you the way Kenny is obsessed with Kaye. How would that make you feel? Why did Kaye torment Kenny before she released the spell?
3. Compare the two faerie courts. How were they alike and different? Compare the two Queens and how they ran their courts.
4. Imagine what it might have been like if there had been a respected member of one court sent for life to the other one. Explain your understanding of how Roiben and Nephamael changed after they left their home courts. How did their new queens influence them?
5. Speculate on what happens to Corny, Kaye, and Roiben after the end of the book. If you were to write a sequel, what would you include?

BOOKTALK IDEAS
1. Write the talk from Corny's perspective as he gets more and more involved with faeries.
2. Have Janet, Kaye, Corny, Kenny, and Roiben or another group of characters introduce each other.

RISKS
- Teens smoke and drink
- Irresponsible, single mother lets daughter raise herself
- Realistic and vulgar language
- Characters steal and shoplift
- Teens are sexually active
- Includes faeries and other supernatural beings
- Openly homosexual character who is sexually active
- Magic is real

STRENGTHS
- Compelling plot line
- Three-dimensional characters
- Scenes and settings teens can identify with
- Characters grow, gain insight, and mature
- Characters discover and grow into their own power

AWARDS
ALA Popular Paperbacks, 2005
ALA Best Books for Young Adults, 2003

REVIEWS
"Although this story is not for the squeamish, teens who enjoy violent fantasy with romantic overtones will undoubtedly provide an eager audience for this disturbingly

lurid tale. Its dark tone, sex, violence, and language place it in the realm of older teens." Mary Ann Darby, *VOYA*, 10/02

"Black has an eye for the telling detail that brings the most minor character to life. A labyrinthine plot with Goth sensibility makes this a luscious treat for fans of urban fantasy and romantic horror." *Kirkus Reviews*, 9/02

"Dark, edgy, beautifully written, and compulsively readable, this is sure to be a word-of-mouth hit with teens, even a few usually unmoved by magic and monsters." Gillian Engberg, *Booklist*, 2/03

📖📖📖

TOMORROW, MAYBE. Brian James. Push/Scholastic, 2003. $6.99. 248p. ISBN10: 0439490359. ISBN13: 9780439490351. Topeka, 2003. $16.45. 248p. ISBN10: 0613666755. ISBN13: 9780613666756. (library binding) Realistic fiction. Reading Level: MS. Interest Level: YHS, OHS. English, Sociology.

SUBJECT AREAS
homelessness; fear; anger; survival; self-knowledge; problem parents; friendship; sexual abuse; addiction; poverty; runaways; drugs; depression; rites of passage; secrets; physical abuse.

CHARACTERS
Chan/Gretchen: she's fifteen and has been on the street for two years
Jef: Chan's friend, who gave her her nickname and treats her like a little sister
Scott and Lily: two street kids who are never apart and like to get high together
Tip: a friend of Jef's; he's in his twenties
Eric: he came from L.A. and complains about the cold
Marc: he's black, with scary eyes
Elizabeth: a ten-year-old who is too small and young and frightened to be on the street, with dark bruises from her dad; she and Chan stick together
Jay: he knows Chan and likes to make people laugh
Eva: she's cool and gorgeous
Billy: his parents are rich, and he goes to a private school, but likes to party with street kids
Candy: she's been on the streets awhile and likes to hang with Billy

BOOKTALK

I never asked for this life, this life on the street, this not-knowing life, with no one to care about. I never asked for it; I don't want it, but I don't know how to get out, how to live any other way and still be real for myself.

When I look around, I wonder how these became the people I have in my life. Who are they? Who am I? This isn't happily ever after. This isn't what the TV promised. This isn't my dream come true. When I wrote essays in school about what I wanted to be when I grew up, I never said I wanted to be homeless. I never said I wanted to be living on the street when I was only fifteen.

And now, I live with the other kids who don't have a place to go, like Jef, who gave me my nickname—Chan—no one ever calls me Gretchen any more. Scott and Lily, always together, looking like twins. Eric, who came from L.A. a few months ago and is always colder than the rest of us, always talking about California. Ty, with his red hair and his stories of all the places he's been and the things he's done. Marc, with the strange eyes, who makes me nervous. And the others, Candy, Eva, Jay . . . and then there's Elizabeth. She's tiny, with black hair and blue eyes, bruised and scarred from her father's fists and cigarette butts. Only ten, too young to be on the street, too young to be all alone. Ty tries to chase her out of our building, but I won't let him. I make him let her stay, but I know we have to find another place. Ty's right, it's dangerous to keep her with us. The cops don't like little kids living on the streets. They look the other way when it's adults, and even I look old enough to get by. Elizabeth doesn't.

We find another tenement, and move in. The kids squatting there are younger than my friends, more my age. They leave us alone. We beg on the street for money to buy food, saying Elizabeth is my little sister, and that we ran away from our parents who abused us. But we have to be careful. We can't sound too desperate, or someone will start looking for the police. Things were going pretty well until the Saturday of the party. Billy is one of the rich kids that hangs around with us sometimes, pretending he'd like to be on the street. His folks are out of town, and he's got the whole brownstone to himself. Everyone's welcome. It's good to see Jef and Eva and Jay and the rest. The house is beautiful, full of wonderful furniture, looking just like something out of a magazine. Elizabeth says it's just like her old home. Billy scored some drugs for us, but I don't get high, and shake my head at Elizabeth when Ty offers her some. I spend most of the day sleeping, but when I wake up, Elizabeth isn't there. She's up in one of the bedrooms, crying. I persuade her to stop, and we take a shower and wash our hair. I dress in one of the fabulous designer dresses in Billy's mom's closet, but Elizabeth wants to wear my favorite t-shirt, so I let her.

When we go downstairs, someone's found the liquor, and folks are passing out. I want to get out for a while, so I persuade Jay to take me for a walk. People stare at us, Jay so filthy and smelly, and me all clean, in an expensive dress. We walk and talk for hours before we go back to Billy's to crash. I wake up with Eva screaming at me, saying I have to get upstairs right away, they're killing him. Suddenly, I know what happened, but seeing it is worse than just knowing it. One of Billy's school friends tried to do something with Elizabeth. Jef and Eric are holding him while Ty beats him up. Billy's trying to stop them, but Scott's holding him back, until Billy gets away and runs to another bedroom and locks the door. We know he's calling the cops, but I jump on the kid on the floor, hitting him as hard as I can and screaming things I can't even remember. All they want to do is use us, play with us like they used to play with toys. I hate myself for thinking it was anything else, for thinking that we were their friends, or that they were ours. And then we hear sirens, and all we can do is run. Run and hide. We're criminals now. No longer invisible. Beat up a rich kid, and suddenly we're alive to them.

Later, Elizabeth explains what Billy's friend did to her, and falls asleep in my arms. I wonder how we ever ended up here. Why bad things always have to happen. Why even good things go bad so often. Why bad things happen to people who don't deserve them. I never asked for this life. Neither did Elizabeth. It's just the one we ended up with.

What will happen to us now?

MAJOR THEMES AND IDEAS
- Life isn't what we thought it would be when we were kids.
- No one ever writes essays on what they want to be when they grow up and says they want to be homeless and living on the street.
- Even homeless kids can find things to be happy about, if they look for them.
- When you're fifteen and a girl, it's dangerous to be on the streets alone.
- It's difficult to understand why life has to include so many bad things.
- If you're going to survive on the street, you have to watch your back and follow the rules.
- It's easy to live on the street when you know you have a home to go back to whenever you want to.
- Street kids can get used to anything—they have to, to survive.
- You don't always understand how much you need a person until they aren't there.
- Everything is easier when you have someone there to help you through it.
- What do you do when everything you've been afraid of comes true?
- Sometimes it's nice to be taken care of, so you aren't responsible for everything all the time. It's nice to have someone you could go to for advice and support.
- You can't have do-overs in life.
- Sometimes it seems like memories of home are the most important thing in the world. Other times, you'd give anything to forget them.
- It's hard to be homeless in a big city, where no one cares.

BOOK REPORT IDEAS
1. Discuss some of the rules about living on the street that Chan follows.
2. How accurate is the book when it shows you what life on the street is really like? Explain how and why it seems—or doesn't seem—realistic.

3. Chan shares some of her dreams. What do they think they mean? How do her dreams both help her and hold her back?
4. Discuss the most important thing about living on the street, the one thing you have to have, or have to know.
5. Discuss the last fight between Chan and Elizabeth, and explain what you think Elizabeth was thinking and feeling about their situation and about Chan. Why does she leave with all their money? Where is she going?
6. Speculate on Chan's life after the book ends. Does she stay with her dad? Does she continue to look for Elizabeth?
7. People come and go in Chan's life. Do you see a pattern in this? Discuss how she connects with people and why they leave.
8. Would Chan have called her father if Elizabeth hadn't left? Why or why not?

BOOKTALK IDEAS

1. The book is written in a choppy style, part Chan's train of thought, part dialogue. Write your talk in the same style.
2. Have several of the people Chan cares about talk about her, from their points of view.
3. Focus your talk on a specific scene, one that is important and pivotal, such as the scene when the cops break into the squat where Chan, Elizabeth, and Jay are staying, and she and Elizabeth have to get away.
4. Write your talk as if it were a series of news stories on radio or TV.

RISKS

- Homeless teens and children live on the streets
- Realistic language
- Teens beg for money and steal whenever they can
- Mean stepmother harasses stepdaughter
- Teens drink and use drugs
- Father ignores daughter and her problem with his second wife
- Police are unsympathetic characters—the enemy
- Teens are sexually active

STRENGTHS

- Shows what street life is really like
- Choppy sentences mimic real speech
- Strong protagonist, determined to survive
- Bleak, realistic view of homeless teens with little or no hope for the future
- Father is glad when runaway daughter calls
- Strong friendship between two girls makes life as street kids bearable
- Girl puts money aside to get off the streets

REVIEWS

"Gritty and honest, James's writing about life on the street pulls readers closer to hear the story that no one tells." Michelle Winship, *VOYA*, 8/03

"James has created a believable world for these two girls, a harsh and scary yet often tender place. The language is raw yet poetic; Chan's voice is appropriate and fresh. The author has done a fine job of presenting the issues surrounding teen homelessness." Angela J. Reynolds, Washington County Cooperative Library Services, Hillsboro, OR, *School Library Journal*, 6/03

"With a conclusion both sorrowful and satisfying, Chan's story is truly worthwhile." Deborah Kaplan, *KLIATT*, 5/03

TRIGGER. Susan Vaught. Bloomsbury, 2006. $16.95. 304p. ISBN10: 1582349207. ISBN13: 9781582349206. Bloomsbury, 2007. $8.95. 320p. ISBN10: 1599902303. ISBN13: 9781599902302. Realistic fiction. Reading Level: YHS. Interest Level: YHS, OHS. English, Psychology, P.E.

SUBJECT AREAS

suicide; illness, mental; self-knowledge; anger; friendship; rites of passage; school; family relationships; divorce and separation; therapy; depression; elderly; fear; guns; grief and mourning; violence; sports; self-destruction; lying and deceit; love; handicaps.

CHARACTERS

Jersey Hatch: he shot himself in the head, survived, and now must figure out how to put his broken life back together
Mom/Sonya Hatch: she's pulled away from her son, because she doesn't know what to do about him
Dad/Mr. Hatch: he tries hard to help his son, but there's very little he can do
Todd Rush: he used to be Jersey's best friend, but now he won't speak to Jersey
Mama Rush: Todd's grandmother, who came to see Jersey in the hospital
Leza Rush: Todd's little sister
Elana Arroyo: the reason Todd is so angry with Jersey
Kerry Brandt: he played golf with Jersey Before it happened
Zero: a jock who hassles Jersey
Big Larry: a friend of Mama Rush's; he had a stroke and can't speak
Alice Wenchel/The Wench: Jersey's helper at school

Carl: he lives at the Palace where Mama Rush lives, and used to be her boyfriend
Mr. Sabon: Jersey's math teacher
Ms. Chin: Jersey's earth science teacher
Maylynn: Todd's girlfriend
Nicholas: Leza's boyfriend

BOOKTALK

There are five things I know. They are my To-Do List, the one the shrink made me write before I left Carter: Carter Brain Injury Center, my fourth and final hospital. But there's one thing I don't know, that the doctors told me I will never know, and that is why. Why, when I was fifteen years old, did I put on my ROTC dress blues, load my dad's pistol, and shoot myself in the side of the head? They've told me that's what I did, and how my mom found me, but I don't remember any of it. A whole year of my life is gone, leading up to the day I did it, and seventy-one days afterwards, when I woke up in the hospital and discovered that the person I'd been before was gone. All I had left was a broken brain, a broken life, a broken family, and too many questions I had no answers for.

Some things can be so broken they can't be fixed. Am I one of them?

MAJOR THEMES AND IDEAS

- There's a Before and an After, and once you've crossed the line between them, you can't go back.
- If you can't remember the last year or so before you shot yourself in the head, there's no way to know why you did it.
- There's no such thing as down time if you use it to get stronger.
- It's hard to feel normal when everyone around you treats you like a freak.
- Own up to your choices. You have to admit and accept what you did before you can go on.
- Some things can be fixed, but some are just too broken.
- Talking trash about yourself makes you trash. If you don't think good things about yourself, no one will.
- Fear's natural when you don't understand something.
- Everyone's life sucks sometimes, some more than others. Deal with it.
- "You're so self centered I bet you think I'm mad at you."
- When you try to kill yourself, you kill your family and friends too.
- It's hard to see the person behind the scars and chaotic speech.
- No one can make your choices for you. If they do, the choices won't stick, and you'll just have to make the same choices again.
- Don't make small things seem so big and important that you forget how small they really are.
- Don't kill yourself over nothing.
- Don't sweat the small stuff, and remember, it's *all* small stuff.

BOOK REPORT IDEAS
1.   Compare the ways different people treat Jersey. What are their reasons for acting the way they do?
2.   Speculate on Jersey's life after the book ends. What will he be like in five years? Ten?
3.   Discuss the motivations Leza had for befriending Jersey. If you had been in her situation, what would you have done?
4.   The high school had several assemblies to tell students about Jersey, after his suicide attempt and before he went back to school. Was this a good idea, and did it help or hurt him? Why or why not?
5.   Is there anything anyone could have done to stop Jersey from committing suicide?
6.   If you had the mental, social, and physical handicaps that Jersey did, what are some of the things you might want people to know about you? How would you want them to treat you?
7.   Discuss the influence of Mama Rush on Jersey, both Before and After.

BOOKTALK IDEAS
1.   Use Jersey's recurring dream as part of your talk.
2.   Write your talk as if you were Jersey, with his chaotic speech patterns.
3.   Use a picture of a gun, a football player, or a golfer as a prop.
4.   Have several characters introduce Jersey from their point of view; for example, Todd, Leza, Mama Rush, one of the shrinks from Carter, or one of Jersey's parents.
5.   Build your talk around the idea of a Before Jersey and an After Jersey.
6.   Write your talk as if it's a letter from Jersey to his friends and family, explaining who he is After.
7.   Focus your talk on his list called "Why?"

RISKS
- Teen tries to commit suicide
- Teen boys bully brain-damaged teen
- Occasionally vulgar language
- Mother can't handle the aftermath of son's suicide attempt

STRENGTHS
- Shows the reader the chaotic thought processes of someone whose brain has been severely damaged
- Three-dimensional characters
- Suspense and mystery keep readers involved
- Realistic portrayal of how a different teen is treated
- Teen is able to overcome some of his disabilities
- Demonstrates how to see a person, not a handicap

- Realistic teen voices
- Jersey's inner dialogue pulls reader into his world and allows reader to identify with him
- Ambiguous ending leaves room for speculation
- Shows the impact of a suicide attempt on the person's family, friends, and classmates
- Shows that suicide attempts aren't always because of something big but can be the result of making something small *seem* big

AWARD
ALA Best Books for Young Adults, 2007

REVIEWS
"Drawing from her work as a neuropsychologist, Vaught includes extensive heartwrenching descriptions of a brain-damaged person's struggle to re-enter society. Teen readers' blood will run cold, however, when Jersey perceives that once again his life is not worth living." Rollie Welch, *VOYA*, 10/06

"The portrayal of brain damage is precise, comprehensible (but never condescending), and seamlessly woven into Jersey's narrative voice, itself a masterful reflection of his internal chaos that conveys both emotional and neurological stumbling blocks by embedding them in the language itself. Poignantly affirming of life and love even in the face of overwhelming loss, this is a haunting tragicomic drama of grief and renewal." *Horn Book Magazine*, 9/06

"Vaught's tightly focused story never deviates from its exploration as to what would drive a teen to suicide. Readers who ever wondered what could happen if their suicide attempt failed may find this to be a powerful cautionary tale." *Publishers Weekly*, 11/06

"The interior landscape revealed through Jersey's unreliable yet sympathetic narration is dense, repetitious, and fragmented, granting readers entree into a damaged mind. Despite its somber character, the story, both engrossing and excruciating, never descends into heavy-handed messages and has nicely placed touches of humor. An original and meaningful work that provokes thought about action, consequence, redemption, and renewal." Holly Koelling, *Booklist*, 12/06

📖📖📖

TWISTED. Laurie Halse Anderson. Viking, 2007. $16.99. 272p. ISBN10: 0670061018. ISBN13: 9780670061013. Puffin, 2008. $9.99. 272p. ISBN10:

0142411841. ISBN13: 9780142411841. Listening Library, 2007. $35.00. ISBN10: 0739348841. ISBN13: 9780739348840. (unabridged audio CD) Realistic fiction. Reading Level: MS. Interest Level: MS, YHS, OHS. English, Psychology, Vocational Education

SUBJECT AREAS

crime and delinquency; self-knowledge; legal system; school; peer pressure; bullying; family relationships; problem parents; dating and social life; substance abuse; anger; dysfunctional families; ethics; gossip; revenge; friendship; intimidation; suicide.

CHARACTERS

Tyler Miller: he's just finished a summer of hard labor
Dopey, Toothless, and Joe: they're on the school maintenance team
Bethany Millbury: the most beautiful girl in school
Dad/Bill Miller: a hard-nosed businessman who doesn't cut his son any slack
Mom/Linda Miller: Tyler's mother, who's trying very hard to make the family happy
Hannah Miller: Tyler's little sister
Brice and Doreen Millbury: Dad's boss and his wife—very rich and very snobbish
Chip Millbury: Bethany's evil twin, who beat up on Tyler on a regular basis
Calvin Hodges/Yoda: Tyler's friend who also works at Pirelli Landscaping
Mr. Pirelli: Tyler's boss
Mr. Hughes: the high school principal who's just waiting for Tyler to make a mistake
Parker: a J.V. player who harassed Yoda
Mr. Benson: Tyler's probation officer
Josh Rawson: with his parents out of town, he hosted the annual Halloween party

BOOKTALK

It was my senior year, and all the work I'd had to do over the summer had turned me from Nerd Boy to 6'1" worth of ripped muscles and six-pack abs. The problem was, everyone saw me as I had been—including me. Because of what I'd done last year—the Foul Deed—I'd lost my car, my driver's license, and my cell phone. I had to work to pay for the damage and do community service at school all summer. That was the source of my new body.

But just as soon as there was any problem, or any rules got broken, I was the automatic suspect. And every time, Dad got more and more angry. Pretty soon, he was blaming me for just about everything, whether or not it actually had anything to do with me or not. Sneaking out to a party (which I did do), having sex with a drunk girl (which I didn't do), taking naked pictures of her (not a chance) and posting them on the web (absolutely not), were all my fault, just like the problems Dad was having at his job.

How did life get so twisted that nothing made sense, that the truth looked like lies and lies looked like the truth, that suicide looked like a viable alternative to living? Join me for my senior year, and I'll tell you.

MAJOR THEMES AND IDEAS

- Be an asset not a liability—make me look good.
- Men are disciplined, tough. They follow the rules, and they come out on top.
- Bullies are usually not brave.
- Stress and worry don't make it okay to take your fear out on your family.
- A**holes frequently beget a**holes.
- Standing up to a bully will frequently make them back down.
- Sometimes it's better not to tell the powers that be exactly what you are thinking about or what your plans are.
- If you think too long and hard about doing something really big and really stupid, you feel like you actually have done it, and it's hard to tell where your limits are.
- Fear of litigation can turn the wild and craziest celebration into an event that's a pathetic shadow of its former glory.
- If you get knocked down enough, you begin to believe that you are what the world says you are.
- Killing yourself is the one thing you shouldn't screw up.
- Don't be a baby. Quit whining 'cause your parents are jerks. Grow up and live your own life.
- A real man faces his conflicts on his own.
- Doing the right thing is frequently doing what's the hardest.

BOOK REPORT IDEAS

1. Discuss how Tyler's changed appearance affected the other teens around him.
2. Tyler took a very deliberate stance or course of action after the big party. How effective do you think it was? How would you have handled the situation?
3. Examine the character of Bethany. What kind of person is she? Does her image in the eyes of the kids around her accurately reflect the person she really is?
4. There are a number of adults, most of whom fall into three categories: parents, school faculty/staff, and coworkers. How do the members of each group interact both within their group and with members of other groups. (Note: some are members of more than one group.)
5. Tyler learns a number of things during the course of this book. What are they and which do you consider his most important lesson?
6. Speculate on where the Miller family will be in about five years, when Tyler and Hannah are in their senior years in high school and college.

7. Discuss Tyler's thoughts and actions about suicide and why he thinks it would be a good idea. Speculate on his family's and his friends' reactions if he had killed himself. Who might have felt sad, or guilty, or glad?

BOOKTALK IDEAS

1. Use a twisted pen or pencil, like the one on the cover, as a prop.
2. Start with the Foul Deed, describe it and what happened afterwards, ending before school starts, and hinting at some of the issues Tyler would have to deal with.
3. Write your talk from Hannah's point of view, as she describes her brother and what he has to deal with.
4. Write your talk from Tyler's perspective, including the various things he got blamed for.

RISKS

- Realistic language
- Angry and demanding father who sees his children only as extensions of himself
- Meek, placating wife/mother doesn't ever confront abusive and controlling husband/father
- Husband is angry and disparaging about wife in front of their children
- Teens drink and party without supervision
- Teens are sexually active
- Bullying of one person by a group of jocks, both physically and mentally
- Teen is bullied and ostracized at school
- Suicide is considered as a serious option
- Father chooses to believe hearsay about his son, rather than the truth that the son tells

STRENGTHS

- Realistic, three-dimensional characters that teens can identify with
- Characters grow and gain insight
- Boy decides not to have sex with drunk girlfriend
- Depicts one boy's rites of passage to adulthood
- Many situations provide for good discussions
- Shows how one person's personal ethics/philosophy developed
- Demonstrates how far apart family members can get before they realize it
- Son has the courage to confront his father
- Shows some of the thought patterns of suicidal youth
- Teen decides to not commit suicide and takes positive steps to keep himself from doing it

- Positive ending still leaves room for speculation
- Character seen as "loser" becomes a winner by thinking for himself and doing what he considers right

AWARDS
ALA Best Books for Young Adults, 2008
ALA Quick Picks for Reluctant Young Adult Readers, 2008

REVIEWS
"Anderson again presents readers with a sympathetic protagonist surrounded by a deftly drawn cast of characters. . . . This compelling novel of growth and maturity will be eagerly received by readers awaiting another story from this talented author." Heather Pittman, *VOYA*, 4/07

"Teenage concerns with sex, alcohol, grades, and family are all tackled with honesty and candor. Once again, Anderson's taut, confident writing will cause this story to linger long after the book is set down." Erin Schirota, Bronxville Public Library, NY, *School Library Journal*, 5/07

"What works well here is the frank, on-target humor . . . the taut pacing, and the small moments, recounted in Tyler's first-person voice, that illuminate his emotional anguish. Writing for the first time from a male perspective, Anderson skillfully explores identity and power struggles that all young people will recognize." Gillian Engberg, *Booklist*, 1/07

TYRELL. Coe Booth. Scholastic, 2006. $16.99. 320p. ISBN10: 0439838797. ISBN13: 9780439838795. Push, 2007. $7.99. 320p. ISBN10: 0439838800. ISBN13: 9780439838801. Reading Level: MS. Interest Level: MS, YHS, OHS. English, Sociology, Psychology, Music.

SUBJECT AREAS
family relationships; love; poverty; friendship; working; problem parents; rites of passage; survival; homelessness; music; crime and delinquency; sex and sexuality; self-knowledge; drugs; substance abuse; secrets; teen parents; unwed mothers.

CHARACTERS

Tyrell Green: his family is living in a roach motel, 'cause his pops is in jail and his moms thinks the world owes her a living and won't get a job

Novisha Jenkins: Tyrell's girlfriend, who wants more than Tyrell has to give

Bonelle Jenkins: Novisha's mother; she feels sorry for Tyrell and his brother and always sends him home with food when he comes to see Novisha

Mr. Jenkins: he walked out on his family two years ago, but he still shows up every so often

Dante: he says he's friends with Tyrell's pop, but he's still making moves on Tyrell's mother

Jasmine: she and her sister end up at the Bennett Motel along with Tyrell, his little brother, and his moms, and she starts putting moves on Tyrell as soon as she knows his name

Reyna: Jasmine's big sister

Lisa Green/Moms: Tyrell's mother, who's never done a thing but sit around waiting for folks to take care of her

Troy Green: Tyrell's seven-year-old brother

Calvin: Tyrell's friend, who's into dealing drugs

Greg and Andre: Cal's older brothers, who are also dealers

Emiliano: Reyna's boyfriend

Miss Niles: she was Tyrell's and Troy's foster mother when they were in foster care

Patrick: he sells bootleg CDs and has stuff Tyrell needs for his party

Regg: a friend of Tyrell's father, who used to help him at his parties

Leon: he helped Tyrell's father find places to have his parties

Wayne: one of the boys staying at the Bennett Motel who will be working at Tyrell's party

Rafael: he's staying at the Bennett Motel and is going to work Tyrell's party

Mr. Mendoza: the night manager at Bennett

Yolanda: the school counselor at Jasmine's alternative high school

BOOKTALK

Tyrell's pops is in jail again, his moms thinks the world owes her a living, and his girl Novisha wants more than he can give. Tyrell, his moms, and his little brother Troy got kicked outta their apartment 'cause his moms refused to look for a job, and they couldn't pay the rent. All she wants to do is party with her friends and rag on Tyrell all the time, blaming him for all their troubles, when it's a clear as the nose on your face that it's really her fault. Now they've stayed in the shelter as long as they can, and they're gonna have to live in Bennett Motel, the worst roach motel in the worst part of the Bronx. Tyrell's worried about his little brother Troy, and their moms ignores him most of the time, letting him eat whatever he wants and leaving him to stay alone with the roaches, even though he's only seven.

Tyrell's gotta get some money somehow. The only time he gets real food, not junk food from machines, is when he eats at Novisha's. Her moms always feeds him good, and sends him home with the leftovers for Troy and their moms. But now that he's living at Bennett, he's not just across the parking lot from Novisha, but two train rides and a long walk away, so he can't see her every day like he used to. And now she's got some guy from her school stalking her, leaving notes in her locker, calling her at home, and saying all kinda things, in spite of the fact that Novisha keeps telling him she already has a man and is gonna be true to him. So Tyrell worries about her, and Troy, and getting some money, and how he's ever gonna get ahead. Tyrell knows he could hook up with his best friend Cal and sell stuff on the street and make a ton of money. But he can't be doing anything illegal, because if he went to jail, Troy would end up in foster care again, and they've been there, done that, got the scars to prove it. And their moms is way too into herself to keep it from happening again.

But his pops is a mad good DJ, and he taught Ty how to years ago. Ty's almost as good as his pops now, and he has the key to the storage shed with all his pops' equipment, and knows a lot of his contacts. Maybe he could get a party together, just for teenagers, with no drugs and no booze, charge admission, and make a bundle, and get them outta that roach motel and into a decent place to live. But on the bad streets of the Bronx, with the hos and the dope and the weed, nothing is ever easy, especially when you want cool and legal. Ty's under a lot of pressure. Will he be able to pull it off, or will he end up in jail on Rykers Island, just like his pops?

MAJOR THEMES AND IDEAS
- Everybody has a reason why they can't get and keep a job and take care of their family—it's never their fault. It's always someone else's fault.
- No matter how bad their husbands treat them, some women keep letting them come back, over and over.
- If you expect everyone to take care of you, and don't try to do it yourself, you're gonna hit bottom sooner and stay there longer.
- What kind of man doesn't take care of his family? What kind of mother refuses to work to support her children?
- It's up to parents to take care of their children, not the other way around.
- Don't depend on anyone other than yourself, and you won't get hurt.
- Hurt sometimes looks and sounds like anger.
- When parents set a bad example for their kids, it's harder to stay strong and stay clean.
- It's important for a man to take care of the people he loves.
- You have to be strong and tough to survive where the living is hard.
- When a man finds himself in a situation that needs correcting, he's got to find the easiest way to get out of it, and make it right.
- The right music can help you deal with your problems and your anger.
- If you keep on taking risks and not thinking about the consequences, those consequences are going to show up sooner or later.
- Smart girls don't want a man to take care of them—they want to take care of themselves and be independent.

- Sometimes it's nice to just relax with someone who knows what's going on with you, so you don't have to pretend that life isn't as awful as it really is.
- When you work for yourself, all the profits are yours.
- Women always think they know what men need—and sometimes they do, but not always.
- No one's going to come to your dance if you don't promote it and let everyone know what a good time it's going to be.
- You can never have too many people who care about you.
- If you love someone, you'll be willing to do stupid or crazy things if it makes them happy.
- A big brother can make up for not having your dad around all the time.
- Once you have to shoulder adult responsibilities and take care of your family, because your father isn't there to do it, you can't go back to being a kid when he shows up again.
- Sometimes you have to put all your problems out of your mind and do what you need to do, what's right for you.
- When you find out that the one person you trusted not to hurt you has been lying from the day you met, it's not something that can be made better with "I'm sorry," or "you don't understand." When some things break, they can't be repaired.
- Hardly anyone gets to have a childhood when you grow up in the hood.
- Everyone needs time to just be with themselves, free, not having to worry about anyone else, responsible only for themselves.

BOOK REPORT IDEAS

1. Discuss Tyrell's mother, explaining what kind of a person she is and why, and whether or not she will be able to change enough to keep her sons out of the system and with her.
2. Tyrell talks about how much pressure he is under. Who or what is putting pressure on him and why?
3. There are several characters in the book who have secrets. Who are they and what are their secrets? How do those secrets change the relationships between or among characters?
4. How does Tyrell change during the book? Compare and contrast who he was on the first page of the book with the person he is at the end of it.
5. There are several women in the book who have negative or difficult relationships with the men in their lives. How do their children respond to these conflicted messages and relationships?
6. Describe and discuss the relationship between Tyrell and Jasmine. How is it both similar and different from the relationship he has with Novisha?
7. Troy is in special ed at school because his mother gets extra money when he is. Explain how you think he feels about this, using some of the things he does as examples.

8. Speculate what might happen to Tyrell in the future. His father is in prison, his brother is back in the welfare system, and his mother refuses to take any responsibility for herself. He just found out that his girlfriend has been living a lie the entire time they've been together. He's living with drug dealers, because he doesn't have any other place to go. He has a *lot* of strikes against him, and not much in his favor. Will he be able to do more than just survive, one day at a time, or will he be able to escape the projects and make something of himself?

9. Discuss what you think is the most important part of the book and why you chose it. Explain how it made you think and how it made you feel.

10. Tyrell's best friend Calvin sells drugs on the street and just became a fifteen-year-old father. Discuss how he and Tyrell are different and alike.

BOOKTALK IDEAS

1. Introduce several of the main characters and explain their relationships, for instance, Tyrell, Novisha, Jasmine, Calvin, and Lisa, Tyrell's mother.

2. Write your talk as if you were Tyrell, using the black English and slang he uses.

3. Focus your talk on one of the scenes early in the book, perhaps the scene when the bus drops off Tyrell, his little brother, and his mother at the Bennett Motel.

4. Base your talk on some of Tyrell's dreams and hopes for the future, and contrast them with the reality of his life right now.

RISKS

- Written in black dialect, including obscenities
- Teens are sexually active
- Homelessness
- Mother convicted for welfare fraud
- Irresponsible mother ignores her sons, doesn't take care of them
- Mother parties with her friends, and drinks and smokes marijuana, leaving her sons alone
- Mother refuses to get a job and tells her older son it's his responsibility to support her and his little brother
- Substance abuse
- Sexual abuse of a teen girl
- Drug dealing is an acceptable way to support yourself
- Father is in and out of prison
- Teens smoke
- Graphic descriptions of several different kinds of violence
- Homeless families are forced to stay in squalid motel that's home to thousands of huge roaches
- Mother encourages fifteen-year-old son to become a drug dealer

STRENGTHS

- Authentic voice of the narrator makes it easy for reader to identify with him and his situation
- Settings and situations are genuine, frank, and described in excruciating detail that brings them to vivid life, so they become real for the reader
- Shows the desperation and shame of homelessness, when there is little left to hope for, when you are as low as you can get
- Narrator is determined to not emulate his father and resists selling drugs or doing anything illegal in order to take care of his little brother when their mother won't be responsible for him
- Shows that there's a way up and out of poverty, if you are willing to work hard and stay strong
- Dialogue is accurate, written in authentic black English
- Introduces people, places, and situations not often seen in young adult literature
- Ending is ambiguous, leaving room for discussion and speculation
- Author resisted making "quick fixes" or happy endings
- Focuses on the downward spiral of poverty and how difficult it is to escape
- Characters are so realistic that they could be people the reader recognizes from his/her own life

AWARDS

ALA Best Books for Young Adults, 2007
ALA Quick Picks for Reluctant Young Adult Readers, 2007

REVIEWS

"This tiny epic is a glimpse at a place many readers will never visit, and others will never leave. Everything is captured and held up to the light, not for judgment but to show readers that life like Tyrell's actually happens. Booth's undertaking is a monumental one, and let the record show that she provides the definitive tale of the modern African American urban youth." Matthew Weaver, *VOYA*, 2/07

"This is a thrilling, fast-paced novel whose strong plot and array of vivid, well-developed characters take readers on an unforgettable journey through the gritty streets of New York City's South Bronx. At its heart is the painful choice the teen must make as he realizes the effect of his mother's failure to do right by their family." Caryl Soriano, New York Public Library, *School Library Journal*, 11/06

"Booth, who was born and raised in the Bronx, is now a social worker there, and her first novel is heartbreakingly realistic. . . . Unlike many books reflecting the contemporary street scene, this one is more than just a pat situation with a glib resolution; it's filled with surprising twists and turns that continue to the end." Hazel Rochman, *Booklist*, 11/06

꙲꙲꙲

UNDER THE WOLF, UNDER THE DOG. Adam Rapp. Candlewick, 2004.
$16.99. 320p. ISBN10: 0763618187. ISBN13: 9780763618186. Candlewick, 2007.
$8.99. 320p. ISBN10: 0763633658. ISBN13: 9780763633653. Realistic fiction.
Reading Level: MS. Interest Level: YHS, OHS. English, Psychology, Sociology,
Ethics, Creative Writing.

SUBJECT AREAS
illness, mental; writing; self-knowledge; substance abuse; suicide; therapy; death
and dying; school; family relationships; anger; homelessness; problem parents; grief
and mourning; addiction; sex and sexuality; homosexuality; self-destruction; love;
dysfunctional family.

CHARACTERS
Steve Nugent: he's sixteen, tall, skinny, gifted in math, and seriously depressed
Mrs. Leene: she's Steve's lead counselor and asked him to write a journal
Silent Starla: tried to kill herself with kitchen cleanser
Rory Parker: he's homosexual and sleeps only with men who have AIDS, trying to
    get infected
Shannon Lynch: former heroin addict and trained cellist who likes punk rock
Amanda Pelt: she has trouble feeling pain, so she hurts herself deliberately
Welton Nugent: Steve's brother, who hanged himself several months ago
Grace: Steve's cousin
Aunt Ricky: Steve's aunt, who's into the family thing
Jimmy Smallhorn: he believes he was a wolf in a former life
Dad/Richard Nugent: seriously depressed after his wife's death, he ignored Welton's
    drug use
Dantly: a friend of Welton's who's a total burnout
Lyman Signer: Richard's business partner
Mary Mills: a girl Steve had a crush on
Gary Ship: he hung himself with an extension cord
Dr. Shays: one of the counselors at Burnstone
June: a little girl Steve meets in a diner
Steve: a little boy Steve meets in the hospital

BOOKTALK
Steve Nugent is sixteen, tall, skinny, and a math geek. He's also a resident at Burn-
stone Grove, a facility for kids who are druggies or want to kill themselves, or both.
The junkies are the Red Groupers, the suicide kids are the Blue Groupers, and the

kids like Steve, who don't fit in either group, are the Gray Groupers. There are only about seven of them. So how does a math geek who spent the last two years at a gifted school end up in a nuthouse? His therapist, Mrs. Leene, thinks that since he won't talk about his past, he should write about it, to see if he can figure out what's going on with him.

The last few years, Steve's family has gotten way off track. His mother got cancer, and because it was inoperable, she was sent home to die. His dad got so depressed, he basically checked out. His older brother got fired from his job and hardly ever left his room. Only a few months after their mother died, he hung himself in the basement. Steve found him.

Steve's life was falling apart, and there was nothing he could do to hold it together. The gaps in his memory got worse and worse, and nothing seemed to make any sense any more. He couldn't live with his father; he couldn't live on his own. Burnstone seems like the only option, even if he's not a druggie or a suicide kid. Maybe it's a place where Steve can figure out what's going on with him, who he is, and what he can do now.

MAJOR THEMES AND IDEAS
- If you want to kill yourself badly enough, you won't stop trying til you're dead.
- Grief makes people do strange things.
- Dealing with the death of someone you love is a different process for everyone.
- The smallest victory can impact a lot of things.
- Rumors are like roaches—they're hard to kill and they feed on garbage.
- Grief and anger manifest themselves in strange ways because our minds are designed to protect us from those feelings.
- You have to deal with your own stuff any way you can.
- Sometimes children have more insight than adults.
- Therapy can help you understand yourself.
- Very few things in life are simple.
- Almost everything in life is connected.
- Some things in life can be fixed, but many things cannot, and you just have to deal with them.
- Depression can kill you, just as surely as cancer can.

BOOK REPORT IDEAS
1. Several of the people in this book are self-destructive. Discuss the various ways they are hurting themselves and why.
2. Steve's memories of the time when he was homeless are somewhat confused. Make a timeline of the action in the book, starting with the earliest sequences before his mother's death and ending with his father's visit to Burnstone.
3. Describe several of the turning points in Steve's journey and explain why you think they are significant.

4. Speculate on the kind of person you think Steve will be in fifteen years.
5. What was the most significant idea, lesson, or perspective you will take away from this book? Why did you choose it?
6. There are a number of deaths in this book. Explain your understanding of what death means to Steve and how or what he feels about all the people around him who have died. How are these deaths similar and dissimilar?
7. Imagine what Steve might have left unsaid to his mother and brother, and write each of them a letter including those things.

BOOKTALK IDEAS
1. Write your talk in first person, as Steve.
2. Use an empty bottle of Robitussin as a prop.
3. Focus your talk on Steve's gradual disintegration, as his life keeps falling apart.
4. Write your talk as the book is written, partly in the present, partly in the past.

RISKS
- Set in mental institution
- Teen substance abuse
- Teen suicide
- Teen homosexuality
- Vulgar language
- Teen vandalizes his father's store
- Teen breaks into and steals from a friend's home
- Teen are sexually active
- Mother neglects elementary school-age daughter
- Teen deliberately hurts himself
- Father withdraws from his sons into grief
- Teen find his brother's body after he killed himself

STRENGTHS
- Authentic teen voice
- Realistic depiction of residential mental health facility
- Terse, gripping narrative draws in the reader
- Characters learn about themselves and gain insight
- Ambiguous ending leaves room for speculation
- Ending leaves some hope of recovery
- Graphic picture of impact of death, depression, and drug addiction on a family and on individuals

AWARDS
ALA Best Books for Young Adults, 2005
Schneider Family Book Award Winners, 2006

REVIEWS

"Rapp continues to titillate and shock his readers with his no-holds-barred style. Steve is a likeable character, one to whom readers may not relate in every way because of the multitude of hardships he has had to face. Yet it is very easy to sympathize with him and easier still to feel hopeful that he will be okay in the end. Rapp is a master when it comes to crafting relationships, both brutal and loving. . . . Rapp balances these elements with smatterings of humor and a great deal of hope." Kimberly L. Paone, *VOYA*, 12/04

"Rapp offers teens well-constructed peepholes into harsh circumstances, with a bit of hope tinting the view." Francisca Goldsmith, Berkeley Public Library, CA, *School Library Journal*, 10/04

"Steve Nugent is a character as distinctive and disturbing as Salinger's Holden Caulfield. . . . This is not for timid readers or those easily offended or shocked by rough language or graphic descriptions, but teens will root from their hearts and even laugh a little as Steve struggles to fight his way out from under the dog of depression that has him pinned down." Cindy Dobrez, *Booklist*, 11/04

ꤥꤥꤥ

UNDONE. Brooke Taylor. Walker, 2008. $16.99. ISBN10: 0802797636. ISBN13: 9780802797636. Realistic fiction. Reading Level: MS. Interest Level: YHS, OHS. English, Ethics, Psychology, Music.

SUBJECT AREAS

friendship; love; school; death and dying; secrets; family relationships; dysfunctional families; guilt; anger; fear; problem parents; sex and sexuality; drugs; self-knowledge; dating and social life; computers; music; gossip; peer pressure; rites of passage.

CHARACTERS

Serena Moore: she's just an average girl until Kori helps her find her wild side
Kori Kitzler: bold, wild, daring—she dares to do it all, and everyone else can't wait to talk about it
Destiny Moore/Mom: Serena's mother who got pregnant at seventeen and still cares too much about what other people think
Josh Krivvy: a computer gaming geek with a crush on Serena
Parker Walsh: he's into pot and other addictive things
Señora Rosa: she teaches Spanish
Kyle Kitzler: Kori's perfect older brother

Kieren Kitzler: Kori's older brother who just pretends to be perfect and is into skate-boarding

Lexi Devlin: Serena's friend and her mother's biggest advocate

Mrs. Talabar: she teaches English

Cole Blakely: she's one of Serena's best friends

Mr. and Mrs. Blakely: Cole's parents, who are wealthy and busy with their own lives

Mr. and Mrs. Kitzler: Kori's parents, who are very wealthy and self-involved and care more about what the community thinks of them than about what their children do

Chelsea Westad: blonde dingbat, head cheerleader, and the mayor's daughter

Marci Mancini: one of the cheerleaders

Heath: one of Chelsea's boyfriends

Mrs. Patterson: the Moore's nosy next door neighbor who has way more cats than she needs

Dr. Ramsey: he teaches social psychology and encourages his students to tempt fate

Anthony Beck: a junior, who used to be a geek and is now hunky in the extreme

Mr. Click: he teaches history

Adrian17: the quarterback for the football team

Brittany DeSalvo: she's on the cheerleading squad and is the police chief's daughter

Mrs. Krivvy: Josh's mother

Shay Miller: he's the man Kori IM'ed with online

Samit: the clerk at the Mini-Mart

Catherine Giles: the high school counselor

BOOKTALK

Kori was gone. Even while it seemed impossible, there it was. She was gone.

I stared at the words in her social psych notebook, the words she'd written after Doc Ramsey's tempting fate assignment—five things you would never dream could happen to you this term. Five ways of tempting fate. Five things Kori had left undone. Five things I could feel her daring me to do. When we played truth and dare, she always took the dares. I always took the truth. But this time, I'd have to take the dares. She wouldn't let me do anything else. Five dares. Five fates

1. Sing with Bleeder Valve
2. Get a tattoo
3. Work things out with Shay
4. Confront D
5. Tell Serena

I didn't understand. What did she mean? What was she going to tell me? I didn't have any idea who D was, but I thought I knew who Shay was. Kori had used my computer to IM him, and his screen name was Shaym. He would be my starting point. I'd have to figure it out one step at a time.

MAJOR THEMES AND IDEAS

- "Discretion is knowing how to hide that which we cannot remedy."—Spanish proverb
- Some people don't have to pretend to be dark and mysterious, they carry their darkness inside them.
- Everyone has secrets, something they can't or won't share even with their closest friends.
- Sometimes you just have to poke at a bruise or pick at a scab, just to see if it's healed or not.
- "To punish me for my contempt for authority, fate made me an authority myself."—Albert Einstein
- If you think it, you can be it. Create your own life.
- Life can't kill you—when it's your time, it's your time. It's fate. And if you think it came too soon, too bad.
- "Wait until it is night before saying it's been a fine day."—French proverb
- There are no coincidences in life. Everything has a purpose.
- "There is no shame in not knowing; the shame lies in not finding out."—Russian proverb
- Some things you never really recover from. The death of your closest friend is one of those things.
- People say, "What would I ever do without you," never thinking that one day they would have to figure out how.
- Love is about pushing aside all the stupid stuff that's gotten between you, no matter who started it or why, and embracing what's really important.
- Sometimes when people love each other, they don't always show it or say it.
- "A turkey never voted for an early Christmas."—Irish proverb
- Everyone handles death differently. It's not right to criticize someone for not doing it the way you do.
- Everyone should have someone who worries about her.
- People we love and who love us are always with us. No matter how long or short their time is, they have changed our lives and left their fingerprints all over our souls.
- Bravery isn't having no fears, but recognizing them and overcoming them.
- "Do not employ handsome servants."—Chinese proverb
- Sometimes it's hard to see the purpose in life when you've lost someone you loved.
- "A lie runs until it is overtaken by truth."—Chinese proverb
- Sometimes being wild and doing crazy things can make you forget, make the pain go away for a while.
- The more I pretend to be shiny and bright, the darker I feel inside.

- It is choice, not chance, that determines your destiny.
- Friends don't abandon you. They give you another chance, many more chances, that sometimes you don't deserve.
- Secrets are like Band-Aids that never allowed the cut beneath them to heal.
- We carry around burdens for other people, and give our burdens to someone to carry around for us. And we never stop to think about what we are carrying around or why.
- "A camel never sees its own hump."—African proverb
- People who are scared to be alone don't push people away, they hang onto them instead.
- It's not because you're scared to be alone, it's because you're scared to *not* be alone, and have to open up to someone who cares about you, and show the real you inside.
- You can't control fate. It presents you with opportunities, and you decide how you react to them.

BOOK REPORT IDEAS

1. Serena said that Kori always looked after her, and Cole looked after Lexi. Discuss what that means. Why did Serena and Lexi need to be taken care of?
2. Explain and compare the way different characters respond to Kori's death and grieve for her.
3. Discuss what happened in Doc Ramsey's class when they discussed the Secret Postcard website. What would you have said if you had been in the class? Explain what you think it means when you tell your secrets anonymously but in public.
4. Discuss what Doc said about carrying other people's burdens for them and never asking why you're doing it.
5. Discuss how fullfilling Kori's five ways to tempt fate also fulfilled Serena's.
6. Parker told Serena that Doc knew the wreck happened because of the flour babies. What do you think—did he know or not? Support your discussion with examples from the book.
7. How does Serena change by the end of the book? Compare and contrast the "old Serena" and the "new Serena."
8. Serena says Kori left her fingerprints all over Serena's soul. Explain what you think Serena is talking about, and describe what some of those fingerprints might be.
9. Almost every main character in the book has secrets of some sort. Why do they keep their secrets? What do they get as a result of keeping their secrets?
10. Describe and explain Anthony and Serena's relationship, showing what attracts them to each other, and what tears them apart.
11. Speculate about what happens after the novel is over, to Serena, her mother, Cole, Lexi, Anthony, and Parker. Include what might happen in the next few months, or in five years, or ten.
12. Explain what your five ways to tempt fate are, and why you chose them.

BOOKTALK IDEAS
1.   Have each of the four girls introduce herself or introduce one of the others.
2.   Focus your talk on the idea of secrets, and who has them.
3.   Focus your talk on Serena's and Kori's ten ways to tempt fate.

RISKS
- Teens smoke cigarettes and pot
- Fifteen-year-old gets fake ID
- Parents are uninvolved in their children's lives
- Teen pursues older men, looking for a father figure
- Teens drink alcohol
- Teen drives drunk and high
- Mother has affair with married man
- Teens are killed while driving high after smoking pot
- Teens are sexually active
- Father doesn't believe his daughter when she says she was raped by the son of one of his business partners, sides against her and punishes her
- Teen gets tattooed

STRENGTHS
- Realistic language including obscenities
- Authentic voice of teen narrator
- Appropriate use of teen slang and brand names
- Shows the pain of losing the person you love the most
- Examines how people grieve in different ways
- Shows the reasons people choose to keep secrets and how their motivations can vary
- Portrays the strength of both love and friendship
- Well-rounded, full-developed characters that the reader can identify with
- Pulls reader into the story from the first page
- Author resisted writing a pat ending, and left threads dangling for the reader to consider and question

AWARD
ALA Quick Picks for Reluctant Young Adult Readers, 2009.

REVIEWS
"Told with appropriately coarse language and depicting realistic risky situations, the story unfolds layer by layer. . . . Readers drawn to *Looking for Alaska*

by John Green will immerse themselves in this book too." Diane Tucillo, *VOYA*, 10/08

"Numerous plotlines intertwine to create an underlying mystery that unfolds in tandem with Serena's self-actualization. Replete with the requisite . . . witty banter that characterizes many an angst-ridden, teen-narrated tale, this absorbing novel will fit well in most contemporary fiction collections. Readers will empathize with Serena's struggle to figure out who she is and which friendships are truly valuable." Jill Heritage Maza, Greenwich High School, CT *School Library Journal*, 8/08

📖📖📖

UNWIND. Neal Shusterman. Simon and Schuster, 2007. $16.99. 352p. ISBN10: 1416912045. ISBN13: 9781416912040. Science fiction. Reading Level: MS. Interest Level: MS, YHS, OHS. English, Science, Psychology, Biology.

SUBJECT AREAS
friendship; betrayal; problem parents; family relationships; self-knowledge; rites of passage; survival; legal system; justice; homeless; grief and mourning; adventure; anger; ethics; crime and delinquency; music; death and dying; peer pressure; manipulation; secrets; terrorism; violence; war.

CHARACTERS
Connor Lassiter: he's sixteen and his parents have signed an unwind contract for him
Ariana: Connor's girlfriend, who says she'll run away with him and then changes her mind
Mr. and Mrs. Lassiter/Dad and Mom: Connor's parents, who may be regretting the unwind contract
Josias Aldridge: a trucker who understands Connor's desperation
Andy Jameson: a kid Connor knows who's also being unwound
Risa Megan Ward: an orphan from a state home, who's also a talented pianist
Mr. Durkin: Risa's piano teacher and the closest thing she has to a parent
Headmaster Thomas: he's the head of the state school where Risa lives
Mr. Paulson: the school's legal counsel
Ms. Something-or-Other: a social worker who evaluates Risa for unwinding
Samson Ward: a scrawny kid who's also an Unwind
Levi-Jedidiah Calder: he's being unwound because he's the tenth child and is a tithe for his family's strict religion
Marcus Calder: Lev's oldest brother, who makes a scene at Lev's tithing party

Pastor Dan: a family friend Lev talks to when he needs advice
Mr. and Mrs. Calder: Lev's parents, who had him only to be a tithe
Officer JT Nelson: he's spent twelve years working Juvenile
Mother: she's nineteen and has just had a baby she plans to stork
Alexis: a girl with a baby that Connor and Risa meet on the school bus
Ms. Hannah Steinberg: a teacher who helps Unwinds when she can
Sonia: she runs an antique shop and helps Unwinds escape
Didi: the baby that was storked and that Connor decided to keep
Hayden: he's an Unwind because of his parents' bitter divorce
Mai: the youngest of four girls, she's an Unwind because her parents didn't want her
Roland: he beat up his stepfather to protect his mother and was sent to be unwound
Cyrus Finch/CyFi: a runaway who teaches Lev to live on the street
Emby/Mouth Breather: one of the Unwinds that shares a packing crate with Connor and Hayden
Diego: a quiet kid, who's also in the crate
Tina: one of the three girls Risa shares a crate with; she was a ward of the state also
Admiral Dunfee: he rules the Graveyard
Amp: one of the kids greeting newcomers to the Graveyard
Tyler: the Unwind who was the original owner of CyFi's temporal lobe
Cleaver: the pilot who works for the Admiral and has earned his trust
Jeeves: the Admiral's driver
"The Goldens": the Admiral's five most trusted kids, and the ones in charge
Blaine: a member of the secret group creating chaos
Dalton: a kid Connor meets at the Happy Jack Harvest Camp

BOOKTALK

The Second Civil War was fought over only one issue: abortion. It ended with the Bill of Life, which satisfied both the pro-life and the pro-choice armies. It stated that life is sacred and is to be protected from the moment of conception to the individual's thirteenth birthday. From that day on, until the individual's eighteenth birthday, parents can retroactively "abort" a child by unwinding. The child's body is harvested for all its body parts, which are made available for anyone who wants or needs them. Because the child is still "alive" in those transplanted parts, unwinding is not considered murder or even death, and it is an accepted part of society.

That's how it sounds in polite legalese, but what it really means is that when you're a teenager, your parents can legally throw you away, kill you, for any reason whatsoever. Get into a fight, spend too much money, crash the car—anything at all—and they can sign an unwinding contract. One day, the juvey cops show up at your door and take you away, like somebody taking out the garbage.

And that's what would have happened to Connor, if he hadn't been looking for a stapler in his dad's home office and found the contract. He couldn't believe his parents were going to have him unwound just because he didn't always keep a lid on his temper. The only thing he could do to stay alive was to leave, and so that's what he did, in the middle of the night, with no goodbyes to anyone.

Risa was an orphan, a ward of the state, and was scheduled for unwinding because of budget cuts.

Lev had always known he'd be unwound. He was a tithe, a tenth child created only so he could be unwound when he was thirteen.

There's little hope for any of them to escape unwinding. Everyone knows that teens on the run are probably escaped Unwinds, and there's a $500 bounty on them. But they have to try, and they have to keep moving, stick to the shadows, try to blend in, until their eighteenth birthday ends the race.

What does life mean? When does it begin and end? Who has the right to say that someone else will live or die?

MAJOR THEMES AND IDEAS
- Most of life is better when it's shared with a friend.
- No good deed goes unpunished.
- Change is frequently scary and uncomfortable.
- Everyone is entitled to only thirteen years of life.
- Kids who are troublemakers can be recycled.
- Strict religions can be cold and heartless, with many rules that must be followed.
- Knowing your destiny can give life a purpose.
- Scamming is stealing with style.
- Some people make bad decisions, but the ones to watch out for make dangerous decisions.
- This isn't a perfect world, and the problem is people who think it is.
- It's hard to ignore something you've believed in all your life. It's even harder to change your mind about it.
- Life is so full of rules and regulations that sometimes we forget we're all human beings and forget compassion in favor of expediency.
- There is no desperation like being betrayed by the ones you love most.
- Necessity is the mother of compliance.
- In a desperate situation, people are likely to forget what's right in favor of what's necessary.
- Sometimes being sorry just isn't enough.
- It's not difficult for frustration to turn into anger and get out of control.
- Small victories are better than none.
- If you're a teen who's unwanted, or too much trouble, or creates uncomfortable situations, you can be thrown away.
- Saying what's in your heart is freeing, even if you're just saying it on paper and not in person.
- People aren't all good or all bad. We spend our lives moving in and out of the darkness and light.

- Survival depends on how observant you are. Even small things can trip you up.
- Sadness or despair may frequently be expressed as anger.
- No one can tell you what you have in your heart. You have to figure it out yourself.
- Everyone has a right to exist.
- Survival may sometimes mean putting your emotions aside to be coldly calculating.
- If you're fighting the same enemy, you're on the same side.
- Chaos can be intriguing and even addictive.
- We have the right to live our lives, and to choose what happens to our bodies.
- There are no accidents. Everything happens for a reason.
- We are all connected. Every day we touch the lives of everyone around us.

BOOK REPORT IDEAS

1. Do donated body parts really retain the characteristics of their original owner?
2. Discuss why Sonia and Hannah worked together to rescue Unwinds.
3. Discuss the concept of souls and where they are located. If you were unwound, where would your soul go?
4. Discuss the admiral's explanation of the Heartland War and the Bill of Life, and how the concept of unwinding changed as it was debated.
5. Discuss the concept that a part of our consciousness resides in every part of our body, even when it is separate from that body.
6. Compare the concept of transplanting body parts in the book and in today's society.
7. Discuss the ethics of unwinding, storking, and tithing as they are described in the book.
8. Risa, Connor, and Lev go through many changes during this book. Explain what you think their most significant change is and why.
9. Many people who get organ transplants today want to meet the family of their donor. Explain why you think this happens, and whether or not Harlan's twenty-sixth birthday party might really happen.
10. Explore how much of this science fiction title is really science fact.
11. Describe the most powerful scene in the book and why you chose it.
12. Speculate about what you think happened to the major characters during the next five to fifteen years.
13. Explain why you think Lev became a Clapper.
14. Compare the Unwinds to other minority groups in today's society.
15. Discuss your answers to these two questions: When does life have value? Who determines whether someone will live or die?

BOOKTALK IDEAS

1. Write your talk as the book was written, each character speaking in turn. Let Connor, Risa, and Lev explain how they were picked for unwinding.

2. Write your talk from the point of view of only one of the three major characters.
3. Write your talk as if it were a news story.
4. Focus your talk on the idea of unwinding and replacing body parts.

RISKS
- Parents unwind their children for typical teen behavior and rebellion
- Unwanted children can legally be thrown away at thirteen
- Runaways are homeless, forced to survive on their own
- Children are killed and their body parts are harvested for transplants
- Various kinds of criminal activity by teens
- Bullying and manipulation
- Suicide bombers
- Society has condoned murder
- Parents sacrifice their children if they are too much trouble, or unwanted, or for religious reasons
- Parents are universally portrayed negatively
- Only those younger than thirteen and over eighteen are protected from unwinding
- Many graphic scenes are difficult to read
- Religiously conservative parents are portrayed negatively

STRENGTHS
- Writing style pulls the reader into the book
- Reader is able to see the action from the perspective of almost every character
- Encourages discussion and speculation on difficult topics and concepts
- Characters learn, gain insight, and mature
- Characters are realistic, neither all bad nor all good
- Forces readers to confront their ideas on life and death
- Plot moves swiftly, with many twists and surprises
- Could be compared to *Fahrenheit 451* or *1984*
- Deals with many important social issues: life, death, religion, free will, trust, and betrayal
- Characters are forced to make difficult decisions, and don't always make the "right" choice

AWARDS
ALA Best Books for Young Adults, 2008
ALA Quick Picks for Reluctant Young Adult Readers, 2008

REVIEWS

"The novel begs two questions: When does a life have value? Who determines whether it is worth keeping? . . . Poignant, compelling, and ultimately terrifying, this book will enjoy popularity with a wide range of readers beyond its science-fiction base." Courtney Wika, *VOYA*, 10/07

"There is evenhanded, thoughtful treatment of many issues, including when life starts and stops, consciousness, religion, free will, law, trust and betrayal, suicide bombers, and hope. . . . Characters live and breathe; they are fully realized and complex, sometimes making wrenchingly difficult decisions. This is a thought-provoking, well-paced read that will appeal widely." Amy J. Chow, New York Public Library, *School Library Journal*, 1/08

"Characters undergo profound changes in a plot that never stops surprising readers. The issues raised could not be more provocative—the sanctity of life, the meaning of being human—while the delivery could hardly be more engrossing or better aimed to teens." *Publishers Weekly*, 11/07

"Well-written, this draws the reader into a world that is both familiar and strangely foreign, and generates feelings of horror, disturbance, disgust and fear. As with classics such as *1984* and *Fahrenheit 451*, one can only hope that this vision of the future never becomes reality." *Kirkus Reviews*, 10/07

📖📖📖

VALIANT. Holly Black. Simon and Schuster, 2005. $16.95. 320p. ISBN10: 0689868227. ISBN13: 9780689868221. Simon Pulse, 2006. $7.99. 320p. ISBN10: 0689868235. ISBN13: 9780689868238. Thorndike Press, 2006. $21.95. 335p. ISBN10: 0786282266. ISBN13: 9780786282265. (large print) Fantasy. Reading Level: YHS. Interest Level: YHS, OHS. English.

SUBJECT AREAS

friendship; supernatural; runaways; secrets; poverty; rites of passage; betrayal; family relationships; sex and sexuality; anger; homelessness; drug addiction; revenge; love; death and dying; violence.

CHARACTERS

Valerie Russell: a seventeen-year-old runaway who finds new friends squatting in the city's subway system
Ruth: Val's best friend

Mom/Mrs. Russell: Valerie's mother, who's beauty-queen beautiful
Tom: Val's boyfriend
Lollipop and Dave: two teens Val meets in a coffee shop, who live in a deserted subway station
Luis: Dave's brother, who sees things no one else can
Derek and Tanya: two teens who have come back to sleep in the subway squat
Ravus: a troll who lives under the Manhattan Bridge and enslaves Val for one month
Greyan: another faerie
Officer Montgomery: he looks for Val when her mother reports her missing
Maybre: a faerie woman with goat feet
Lord Roiben: the Lord of the Dark Court of the faeries

BOOKTALK
It was like a nightmare she couldn't wake up from. Her mother leaning down to kiss Tom, her wine-red lipstick smeared on his face. How could he cheat on her with her own *mother*? Val turned and ran as fast as she could. She didn't know if she could ever live at home again. She'd been betrayed by the three people she loved most—her mother; Tom; and Ruth, her best friend, who'd known what was going on and didn't bother to tell her.

Maybe if she hadn't met Lollie and Dave, if she hadn't gone to the deserted subway station where they lived with Dave's brother Luis, if she hadn't met Ravus, the troll, or any other of the faerie folk, maybe Val's life would have been different. But she'd done all those things, she'd used Never, a faerie drug that healed faeries but was as addictive to humans as heroin. She'd been drawn too close to the faerie world and to the faerie she'd fallen in love with. The world of faerie is dark and dangerous. A misstep could be fatal, and trusting the wrong person could send Val down the wrong road, with no way to predict the dangers that waited for her.

MAJOR THEMES AND IDEAS
- Some things cannot be forgiven.
- You can't make someone change. Change happens only when he or she decides to change.
- No one else changes you. You can change only when you decide to.
- Drugs can make you feel new and powerful.
- It's hard to protect people from themselves.
- Sometimes you end up in situations where you have to do crazy things you'd never usually do.
- Survival, staying alive and safe, can make you act in ways that normally would seem crazy.
- You can't go back. When you run away from home, it changes you, what you do and how you live, and you can't go back.

- "Reality is that which, when you stop believing in it, doesn't go away."—Philip K. Dick
- When a man tells you he's going to hurt you, believe it. They always warn you and they're always right.
- If you choose to step off the path of everyday normality, and into the darkness that surrounds it, anything can happen.
- People see only what they choose to see.
- It is all too true that love can quietly become hate and vice versa.
- Coincidences are very convincing, even when they are wrong.
- To fight effectively, you must let go of your anger and concentrate on what you are doing.
- Perhaps imaginary problems require imaginary solutions.
- Even if you have all the clues, you still have to figure out how they fit together to make sense of them.
- It's easier to get forgiveness than permission.

BOOK REPORT IDEAS

1. Which mortal and which faerie characters did you connect with most, and why?
2. Many of the characters change during the course of the story. Trace the changes in several of the characters, and discuss the causes of those changes.
3. Speculate on what might have happened had Val not met Lollie and Dave.
4. There are many unfinished plot lines in the story. Take one or two of them and discuss the various endings they might have had.
5. What lies in the future for Val, Lollie, Luis, David, Ruth, and Ravus? Speculate on what they might be like and what they might be doing in a year, or two, or five.
6. What would you do if you saw your mother and your boyfriend making out? Is this something you could forgive? How would you handle it?
7. Consider the wide variety of things Lollie, Luis, Dave, and Val had to do to survive, and discuss what kinds of things a homeless teen in your town or city would have to do to survive. How long do you think you would survive?

BOOKTALK IDEAS

1. Use pictures of a subway station squat or a bottle of dark powder to help make your booktalk more real.
2. Have several characters introduce themselves and Val.
3. Focus your talk on the faerie world, what it was like, and what parts did mortals get to see.
4. Write your talk in first person as Val, showing how she's drawn into the faerie world.

RISKS
- Involves magic and the supernatural
- Mother seduces daughter's boyfriend
- Teens drink, smoke, steal, and take drugs
- Homeless teens live in deserted subway station
- Realistic language, including obscenities
- Teens cut themselves
- Faerie/supernatural characters
- Teen kills her own kitten
- Teens have unprotected sex

STRENGTHS
- Strong female lead character
- Friends protect, take care of each other
- Engrossing plot, with many unexpected developments
- Completely realized fantasy world
- Friends are willing to fight for each other
- Friends believe in each other, in spite of betrayal
- Love exists, and is able to overcome evil, or at least, some part of it
- Characters grow and gain insight
- Characters change loyalties, and are not always who they appear to be at first

AWARDS
ALA Popular Paperbacks, 2008
ALA Best Books for Young Adults, 2006
ALA Quick Picks for Reluctant Young Adult Readers, 2006
New York Public Library Books for the Teen Age, 2006
SFWA Andre Norton Award, 2005

REVIEWS
"This novel's appeal to teen readers is undeniable. It is escapist fantasy complete with romance and a happy ending. It is likely to circulate regularly, especially if teens at your library enjoy fantasy and if the author's last book has been popular." David Goodale, *VOYA*, 8/05

"This dark fantasy includes drug use and strong language, but beneath its darkness readers find well-rendered characters, a gripping plot, and pure magic." Tasha Saecker, Caestecker Public Library, Green Lake, WI, *School Library Journal*, 6/05

"As in Black's companion novel *Tithe* (2004), the plot matters far less than the exotic, sexy undercurrents (including a scene where Val overhears teens having sex), the deliciously overripe writing, and the intoxicating, urban-gothic setting, where 'everything was strange and beautiful and swollen with possibilities.'" Jennifer Mattson, *Booklist*, 7/05

ᗡᗡᗡ

VENOMOUS. Christopher Krovatin. Illustrated by Kelly Yates. Anatheum, an imprint of Simon & Schuster, 2008. $16.99. 336p. ISBN10: 1416924876. ISBN13: 9781416924876. Realistic fiction. Reading Level: YHS. Interest Level: YHS, OHS. English, Psychology, Sociology.

SUBJECT AREAS
anger; violence; self-knowledge; love; friendship; family relationships; depression; separation and divorce; therapy; rites of passage; mental illness; death and dying; betrayal; bullying; homosexuality; secrets; dating and social life; revenge; manipulation; drugs; school.

CHARACTERS
Locke Vinetti: he's a loner who tries to keep his anger locked inside
Charlotte Vinetti/Mom: Locke's mother, who worries about him and his anger
Randall Elliott: Locke's best friend who isn't bothered by the venom
Lou Vinetti: Locke's ten-year-old little brother; he's smart, and gets things done
Tommy Ferraro: he bullied Locke one too many times when he was eight and released the venom for the first time
Alan Raskowitz: in fifth grade, he pulled out a chunk of Locke's hair and let the venom loose
Rick Vinetti/Dad: he left because of Locke's venom and is remarried with two children
Tallevin the Tower: tall black kid with a Mohawk who's the lookout during Locke's first night at the Rock
Renée Tomas: she's a beautiful Goth pixie, and Locke falls for her at first glance
Casey: he's the Emperor of the kids who gather at the Rock, who also has anger problems
Marie: Renée's aunt, who lives with her and her brother
Andrew Tomas: a sadist and a bully in Locke's grade at school who hates Locke, and who's also Renée's older brother
Brent: a friend of Casey's
Dr. Laura Yeski: a friend of Charlotte's who is a psychologist
Bethany Vinetti: Locke's half sister, who lives with his dad and stepmother
Millie Vinetti: Locke's stepmother

Brian Vinetti: Locke's half brother
Shelby Waters: a girl who goes to Locke's school and is also seeing Dr. Yeski
Terry and Omar: friends with both Andrew and Randall

BOOKTALK

Locke doesn't just have anger issues, he has the venom. Ever since he was eight years old, when he gets too angry, something breaks free inside, pure liquid hate bubbles up inside him and spills free, uncontrollable, overpowering, overflowing. It burns in his veins and makes him feel alive. And he loves it, and he hates it. Then, when it's gone, he's left tired, drained, and shaky. But that's not all the venom does. It's turned Locke poisonous—venomous. He poisons everything he's a part of—his dad walks out; he has no friends; girls never last. He's almost totally alone, except for Randall, his best friend. Randall doesn't understand the venom, but he deals with it and he doesn't leave.

But the venom is getting stronger, bubbling just beneath the surface of Locke's mind, waiting for the right moment to explode outward. And when someone gets in his face, the venom takes over. He's losing track of who's running the show of his life—him or it.

And then Randall invites Locke to meet Casey and Renée, and his life changes.

Casey has the same venom bubbling under the skin that Locke does, only he calls it the black. Renée is a beautiful Goth pixie, and Locke falls for her at first glance. Perhaps, he now has three friends, not just one. But the venom is always there, and it would be all too easy to ruin everything.

MAJOR THEMES AND IDEAS

- The only demons darker than the ones around you are the ones inside you.
- The road is long and life is short, so drive like hell and don't look back.
- Better to be lonely than to screw up someone else's life.
- Sometimes the bad stuff just forces itself to the surface, and it's hard to stay in control. But losing control just makes everything worse.
- Rich, preppy kids drink and do drugs more than anyone else.
- Once your anger bursts free, it's hard to rein it in until it has run its course.
- Getting tormented for who you are is worse than being tormented for what you can do.
- You always have a choice. Be who you want to be.
- A father is the man who raises you, not the one who supplies you with genetic material.
- Doing something outside your comfort zone is worth a try if it keeps you from hurting people who love you.
- Hurting someone you care about because you are in pain isn't ever right or a good thing to do. And if the person you hurt is your friend, it's worse.
- No matter how much you regret doing or saying something, you can't go back and fix it. All you can do is try to put the pieces back together.

- Love hurts. But it also heals.
- Forgiveness takes time and work. But eventually, it happens.

BOOK REPORT IDEAS

1. If Locke had not flipped out in the bookstore, would he have been able to figure out a way to buy the books?
2. Explain what you think the venom is, and why Locke says he's poisonous.
3. Discuss how the venom is gradually taking over Locke's life, and why.
4. Explain the meanings of the Tarot cards assigned to Casey and the others, including Locke, and why these cards fit them so well.
5. Define the venom and the black. Were they separate from Locke and Casey, or just their own uncontrollable rage?
6. What was the effect of Locke and Casey's fight?
7. What did Locke mean when he said that after all the insanity they couldn't help but be friends—who else would they want to spend time with? Without each other, what did they have?
8. Compare the text of the novel with the text of the superhero story between chapters. How do the excerpts and Locke's story fit together?

BOOKTALK IDEAS

1. Focus your talk on describing the venom and what it makes Locke do and feel.
2. Include information from Locke's superhero story in your talk.
3. Use a copy of *Spiderman and Venom* as a prop for your talk.
4. Center your talk around describing the central characters—let Locke introduce Randall, Renée, Casey, and Tallevin.

RISKS

- Graphic violence
- Verbal abuse
- Homosexual characters
- Teens smoke, drink, and are sexually active
- Graphic descriptions of sex
- Teen party is unsupervised by adults

STRENGTHS

- Realistic dialogue, including obscenities
- Lead character struggles to control himself
- Portrait of a loyal, nonjudgmental friend
- Cute, quirky younger brother
- Strong mother-son relationships
- Teen learns to control his anger

- Two broken teens are able to connect and help each other
- Bully is willing to change his behavior for the sake of his sister
- Teens party and still drink responsibly
- Teens practice safe sex

AWARD
ALA Quick Picks for Reluctant Young Adult Readers, 2009

REVIEWS
"Locke is a hero in the tradition of Holden Caulfield. Both find themselves in worlds in which they do not really fit yet try to adapt in somewhat haphazard and marginal ways. . . . High school readers will find it a fast-paced and enjoyable read. Yates's illustrations add to the book's graphic novel flavor and may draw in otherwise reluctant readers." Steven Kral, *VOYA*, 12/08

"Revealed in first-person chapters interspersed with graphic-novel-style illustrations mirroring Locke's ongoing battle with his inner self, this is an authentically voiced story that includes sex, drugs, drinking, violence, and, ultimately, Locke's move toward maturity through self-knowledge and subsequent self-control." Jeffrey Hastings, Highlander Way Middle School, Howell, MI, *School Library Journal*, 8/08

"Krovatin's writing is steeped in aching intensity and includes characteristically graphic articulations of sex, violence, and redemption. Nothing is gratuitous, though, as Locke draws the reader into the heart of each venomous attack, making palpable every outburst, loss, and success." Thom Barthelmess, *Booklist*, 9/08

📖📖📖

WHAT HAPPENED TO CASS MCBRIDE? Gail Giles. Little, Brown, 2006. $16.99. 224p. ISBN10: 0316166383. ISBN13: 9780316166386. Little, Brown, 2007. $7.99. 240p. ISBN10: 0316166391. ISBN13: 9780316166393. Topeka Bindery, 2007. $16.95. 211p. ISBN10: 1417780673. ISBN13: 9781417780679. (library binding) Mystery. Reading Level: MS. Interest Level: MS, YHS, OHS. English, Psychology, Ethics, Communication.

SUBJECT AREAS
suicide; death and dying; secrets; crime and delinquency; self-knowledge; family relationships; divorce and separation; revenge; school; peer pressure; manipulation; problem parents; anger; bullying; child abuse; depression; dysfunctional families; fear; friendship; violence; lying and deceit; mental illness; gossip.

CHARACTERS

Kyle Kirby: he plans revenge for his brother's death
Cass McBride: pretty and popular, Kyle thinks she's the reason his brother killed himself
Dad/Ted McBride: a salesman who has taught his daughter well
Detective Ben Gray: he's the lead officer investigating Cass's disappearance
Roger Oakley: first officer on the scene at Cass's house; he's a good, sharp cop
Big Cop, Young Cop: they interrogate Kyle
Scott Michaels: Ben's partner, who's young and green and excited about his first Amber Alert
Tyrell Ford: Roger's partner
Erica: a friend of Cass's who thinks Kyle's a hottie
Leatha McBride: Cass's mother, who lives in Louisiana

BOOKTALK

The whole school was freaked out. Tuesday, this kid hanged himself, and on Friday, one of the most popular girls in school was kidnapped and the cops were questioning everyone who knew her. There hasn't been a ransom demand, and the cops have no clues to identify the kidnapper. In an Amber Alert situation, the first forty-eight hours are critical, and those hours keep ticking away.

But for Cass, there's no sense of time passing. She doesn't have any idea how long she's been kidnapped. Her world is now very, very small and very, very dark. The walls of her prison are just inches away from her shoulders, her head, her feet. The ceiling is inches from her face. There is no light at all. The darkness is total and complete. There's something taped to her right hand. It feels like a remote control, and her right thumb is taped to one of the buttons. There is no noise, it is completely silent.

Long, narrow, shallow box. Total darkness. Total silence. No room to move. Very little air. It's everyone's nightmare come true. Cass McBride has been buried alive.

MAJOR THEMES AND IDEAS

- Set your sights high, see it happening in your head, and then go for it.
- Some families bury things, shove them away, so they won't have to look at them or think about them.
- When a deal goes sour, stop selling and accept. You can't win *every* time.
- Fear is your enemy's weapon. Don't shoot yourself with his gun. Accept the fear and deal with it.
- Even if someone else controls you physically, you can still get mental control. You are the only one who controls what's in your head.
- The rhyme about "Sticks and stones may break my bones, but words can never hurt me" is a lie. Words can hurt. They can even kill.

- Act and speak with authority and confidence. People will believe you.
- You don't sell the product, you sell the customer his own self-doubt. You sell his shortcomings.
- Mental strength can take you only so far. If you are unable to escape from the situation, you will reach your breaking point.
- There's always a deal to be made. It just takes the right person and the right time.
- Never underestimate your opponent. If you do, you'll lose.
- Your enemy's weakness is your advantage.

BOOK REPORT IDEAS
1. There are a lot of control issues in this book. Discuss how Kyle was in control and how Cass was in control.
2. Describe Cass, how she looked, acted, thought. Is she someone you'd want for a close friend? Why or why not?
3. When the book ends, how long has Cass been in the hospital? Do you think she will ever leave? Why or why not?
4. Describe Kyle's mother. Discuss whether or not she will ever accept responsibility for her actions.
5. Discuss how her father helped Cass survive.
6. Explain what the most important theme is in the book, and describe several scenes that illustrate it.
7. Discuss the clues that led Ben to Kyle.

BOOKTALK IDEAS
1. Write your talk as if it's a news story.
2. Write your talk from Ben's point of view, showing how he got to know Cass by talking to everyone around her.
3. Focus your talk on the scene when Cass realizes that the only way she can get out is to talk her way out.
4. Focus your talk on things people are most scared of, leading up to claustrophobia and the fact that Cass is buried alive.

RISKS
- Controlling, angry mother is cruel to her sons
- Girl is thoughtlessly mean and petty
- Father trains daughter rather than loving her
- Teen kidnaps girl and buries her alive
- Teen commits suicide
- Mother's persecution drives teen to suicide
- Ineffectual father allows his wife to persecute their sons
- Father escapes while leaving sons at the mercy of their mother

STRENGTHS
- Typefaces change when different characters are narrating the story
- Realistic characters readers can identify with
- Presents the situation from a variety of perspectives
- Vividly portrays what mental discipline and determination can accomplish
- Ending leaves room for speculation and discussion
- Suspense never lets up
- Plot moves swiftly

AWARDS
ALA Best Books for Young Adults, 2007
ALA Quick Picks for Reluctant Young Adult Readers, 2007

REVIEWS
"Over and above plot. . . and intertwined with Cass's fate, are complex issues of responsibility and scapegoating that even the most black-and-white thinkers will ponder long after they close the book. . . . Often brutal, this outstanding psychological thriller is recommended for older teens." Mary E. Heslin, *VOYA*, 12/06

"This book will disturb readers, frighten them, and make them feel as though they are trapped like the characters. It is a thrilling, one-sitting read that they won't be able to put down." Sherry Quinones, Frederick County Public Libraries, MD, *School Library Journal*, 2/07

"If the plot alone isn't disturbing enough to yank readers up by their bootstraps and catapult them headfirst into the horrors that are about to befall the two, Giles's jagged, terse, just-the-facts narrative only amplifies their claustrophobically dire situation. There is no light shed on the human condition, no touching moments of patient understanding. There are hardly any characters for teens to look up to, and, in true Giles form, nothing ties up neatly. It's just plain chilling, and that's what makes it brilliant. A damn scary read." *Kirkus Reviews*, 10/06

📖📖📖

WHAT HAPPENED TO LANI GARVER? Carol Plum-Ucci. Harcourt, 2002. $17.00 307p. ISBN10: 0152168133. ISBN13: 9780152168131. Harcourt, 2004. $6.95. 336p. ISBN10: 0152050884. ISBN13: 9780152050887. Tandem Library, 2004. $15.75. 307p. ISBN10: 1417618302. ISBN13: 9781417618309. (library binding) Realistic fiction. Reading Level: MS. Interest Level: YHS, OHS. English, Sex Education, Health, Ethics, Sociology, Communication.

SUBJECT AREAS
addiction; bullying; religion; runaways; illness, physical; family relationships; sex and sexuality; homosexuality; substance abuse; problem parents; prejudice; friendship; supernatural; music; creativity; eating disorder; cancer; homelessness; lying and deceit; death and dying; rites of passage; manipulation; anger; school; violence.

CHARACTERS
Claire MacKenzie: she has a lot to cope with and needs a friend
Lani Garver: no one knew much of anything about him, not even if he was a she
Macy Matlock: one of Claire's best friends
Mary Beth Matlock: Macy's older sister
Myra Whitehall: another of Claire's friends
Mom: wants her daughter to follow her footsteps as cheerleader and Homecoming Queen
Chad MacKenzie/Dad: he's a musician who lives in Philadelphia and wants Claire to live with him and his new wife, Suhar
Eli Spellings: a popular girl with a mean mouth
Geneva Graham: another popular girl
Albert Fein: a dorky kid who makes fun of Lani
Ms. D'Angelo: she runs the cheerleading squad
Sydney: she owns the café where Claire plays and sings on Saturday nights
Lyda Barone: a girl no one is nice to because she smells
Scott Dern: the boy Claire's dating
Ginny DeGrassa: she lives next to Sydney and is a friend of Claire's mom
Vince Clementi, Mike Mayer, Phil Krilley: guys from the fish frat
Tony Clementi: Vince's older brother
Marcus: a medic at the clinic in Philadelphia who tells Claire about angels
Dr. Lowenstein: doctor at the Philadelphia clinic
Dr. Haverford: Claire's doctor at Children's Hospital
Ellen, Cooper: friends of Lani's who go to the Creative and Performing Arts High School in Philadelphia
Dr. Erdman: a psychiatrist who knows a lot of musicians and kids from CAPA
Calcutta: rock band whose members are all HIV positive
Jule: Eli's younger sister
Kaitlin: Jule's best friend

BOOKTALK
I may be a Hackett Island native, born and raised here, but in some ways I've always been an outsider. My dad's a musician, not a fisherman like most of the men who live here. He lives on the mainland, in Philadelphia. He moved out when I was in the sixth grade, just before we found out I had leukemia and my mom turned into a drunk. I

was out of school for a year and a half, which really made me feel different, even if my hair had come back and I was in remission.

I was sixteen, one of the popular girls, when Lani Garver walked into the island high school and changed everything, challenged everything. At first glance, you couldn't tell if he was a boy or a girl. He said his name like a boy—Lonny—but he spelled it like a girl—Lani. He was over six feet, skinny, with broad shoulders, but he had long eyelashes, and hair that wasn't just cut, it was styled. The digs about his being gay started immediately, but he didn't pay a lot of attention to them, just let it all flow over him. It was like nothing bothered him, not even when I told him what I'd never told anyone—that I was afraid my cancer had come back. He just told me where I could go to get tests done and get the results the same day, and offered to go with me. Not even my best friend would have done that!

After that trip, when I met some of Lani's friends, I began to feel more at home with him than I did with the kids I grew up with. I started seeing me and them in a whole different light: a light that showed the ugliness of their hearts and minds, not their average or even attractive bodies and faces. And I began to wonder how their surface appearance could hide the foulness they held inside themselves.

It's in the past now, and I've moved on. But sometimes I find myself at the end of the wharf, searching the darkness, hoping for a sign, and wondering about him.

Why did he come to Hackett? Why was I the only one to make friends with him? Why were the others so threatened by him? Did I watch them drown him, or did he get away somehow? Who was Lani Garver—a boy? A man? Or an angel?

MAJOR THEMES AND IDEAS

- Even people who are attractive have ugliness inside them that they can't always hide.
- If you can understand human behavior, it can't hurt you nearly as much.
- Bullies were once bullied, and they depend on your fear to make them strong.
- Be careful about letting people know how well you understand them. Some people don't like you looking at their hidden garbage.
- It's easier to deal with people if we know which boxes they fit into.
- A life-threatening disease changes your perspective.
- Dangerous stunts and dares will sooner or later end up with someone hurt or dead.
- People create the hells that they live in.
- People say they want to help you, be there for you, but when you need them the most, they turn their backs.
- There are times in life to grow, and times in life to shine. You can't do both at the same time.
- Even if you're surrounded by people who care, you still have to do the impossible things yourself.
- Sometimes complete happiness can feel so much like complete terror, it's hard to tell them apart.

- You have to pay the dues to sing the blues.
- Everyone dies, but most of us don't get to say when.
- Pain can be useful. It can help you see yourself more clearly.
- We see what we want to see, what we expect to see, not necessarily what's real.
- You can change what you do, you can change what you say, but you can't just decide to change what you believe.
- Eyewitness testimony is frequently tempered by "convenient recollection," and is partly truth and partly fiction, even though the speaker believes it to be totally true.
- The truth will set you free, and then you shall be free indeed.
- People are always moving, changing, leaving the boxes others try to fit them into.
- Those who look too hard for the truth are considered crazy.
- Sometimes it has to feel worse before it feels better.
- People admire you for your strength, but they love you for your faults, the imperfections that make them more comfortable with their own flawed selves.
- Be kind to everyone. You never know if you're meeting an angel unaware.
- Life is full of strange experiences and looking for ways to explain them doesn't always work out.
- Lots of times people edit their memories, edit reality, so they'll look good and fit in.
- It's always possible to outgrow your friends, if you change and they don't.
- Learning about and changing yourself isn't easy and is frequently quite painful.
- Whenever parents betray you over and over, it's hard to have hope.
- Crumbled realities can create paths to purer, clearer truths.
- There's no going back in life. You can only go forward.
- If you don't like your reality, choose to think about and experience it differently, and it will change.

BOOK REPORT IDEAS

1. Was Lani an angel? Was he anything more than human?
2. Discuss the idea of convenient recollection. How would you know if someone was doing it?
3. Is Lani alive or dead at the end of the book? Explain why you believe one way or the other.
4. In your reality, are floating angels real? Why or why not?
5. Gender is an important issue in our society. It's a box we can never entirely escape from. Explain why you think Lani wanted to blur his gender.
6. Lani doesn't want to be put in any of the boxes we usually slot people into. Compare the ways different people reacted to that.
7. What boxes do you put yourself in? Why? What are the advantages and disadvantages of living in boxes, rather than outside them?

8. Discuss the idea of convenient thinking and what it means to you. Is it something you've done?

BOOKTALK IDEAS
1. Illustrate your talk with a picture of an angel who might be Lani in costume.
2. Have several different characters describe who they think Lani is.
3. Focus your talk on the scene when Claire and Lani meet.
4. Focus your talk on the secrets in the book—who was hiding what, and why?

RISKS
- Alcoholic mother, distant father
- Teens play dangerous games and dares
- Homophobic characters
- Teens drink
- Vulgar language
- Homosexual characters
- Anorexic teen
- Gay bashing
- Physical abuse
- Girl manipulates her friends
- Characters hide from themselves, constructing their own reality

STRENGTHS
- Realistic dialogue
- Authentic voice
- Intense suspense
- Shows power of friendship
- Characters are three-dimensional and realistic
- Shows the length to which people will go to maintain their own view of reality
- Therapeutically appropriate advice and insight
- Characters mature and gain insight
- Graphic depiction of the impact of homophobia
- Shows how easy it is to manipulate your own or someone else's belief of what they saw and heard
- Unbiased glimpse of HIV positive men
- Suspense never relents
- Immature teens who haven't had to take a clear, honest look at themselves are in stark contrast to those who have and who see themselves and their world more honestly
- Information on anger management
- Characters who see themselves clearly and honestly

AWARDS
ALA Best Books for Young Adults, 2003
ALA Popular Paperbacks, 2005

REVIEWS
"Mature readers who love intriguing mysteries without neat solutions already appreciate Plum-Ucci. . . . This novel should cement her reputation as a writer whose stories keep readers turning pages and whose books contain a mystery that lingers long after the last page." Teri Lesesne, *VOYA*, 12/02

"Outstanding writing, strong characterization, and riveting plot development make this title rise above many recent coming-of-age stories." Lynn Bryant, Great Bridge Middle School, Chesapeake, VA, *School Library Journal*, 10/02

"Ucci is a pro at teen dialogue, worries, and thought processes. The characterizations are superb, from Claire's troubles to her over-the-top friends' shallow concerns to Lani's fierce individualism and his artsy, eclectic city friends. The hint of supernatural only adds to the appeal. Successfully raising many valid issues, this should appeal to teens from the popular to the marginalized." *Kirkus Reviews*, 9/02

📖📖📖

WILD ROSES. Deb Caletti. Simon and Schuster, 2005. $15.95. 296p. ISBN10: 0689867662. ISBN13: 9780689867668. Simon Pulse, 2006. $6.99. 320p. ISBN10: 0689864752. ISBN13: 9780689864759. Simon Pulse, 2008. $8.99. 320p. ISBN10: 1416957820. ISBN13: 9781416957829. Bt Bound, 2006. $15.80. 296p. ISBN10: 1417773502. ISBN13: 9781417773503. (library binding) Realistic fiction. Reading Level: MS. Interest Level: YHS, OHS. English, Psychology, Music.

SUBJECT AREAS
music; family relationships, mental illness; creativity; friendship; stepparents; problem parents; divorce and separation; love; mental illness; school and social life; rites of passage; self-knowledge; secrets; self-destruction; music; obsession; anger; bullying; creativity; depression.

CHARACTERS
Cassie Morgan: her life changed when her mother married a world-renowned violinist and composer
Ian Waters: Dino's student and Cassie's love

Dino Cavalli: famous musician and formidable bully
Siang Chibo: she is in awe of Cassie and Dino
Zebe Rawlinson: Cassie's best friend, who also has a stepfather
Dad: Cassie's father and Daniella's first husband, who's an accountant
Daniella Morgan Cavalli/Mom: Cassie's mother, who married Dino five days after the divorce was final
Dr. Mieton: Dino's psychiatrist
Nannie: Dad's mother
Sophie Birnbaum, Nate Frasier, Brian Malo: friends of Cassie's
Zach Rogers: he's a little weird and is in all of Cassie's classes
Courtney Powelson: Cassie's next door neighbor, and a Popular Girl
Alice: Danielle's closest friend, who also plays in the orchestra
Janet Waters: Ian's mother, who's determined that her son will become a professional musician
Bunny: Ian's older stepbrother, who looks like he should be a biker
Chuck: Bunny's best friend, who also looks like a biker

BOOKTALK

The first time Cassie saw Ian, she fell in love before she even knew his name. Both of them felt the pull, the attraction, the awareness between them. But they were the only ones who wanted them to be together. Dino, Cassie's musical genius/insane/paranoid jerk stepfather, wanted his student to concentrate on his music. Danielle, Cassie's mother, wanted Dino to be happy. Janet, Ian's mother, wanted her son to go to the best music school in the country, and he had only three months to prepare.

Dino also had only three months to prepare. His first concert in years was coming up and he had to compose three new pieces for it. But they weren't coming easily, and Dino's manic rages and his paranoia were getting worse and worse. It was like living with a time bomb, never knowing when it was going to explode.

The only time that Cassie felt safe and calm was when she was with Ian. Even just listening to him play could help her relax. But with Dino's demands and schedules, Ian didn't have time to spend with Cassie, and whenever she caught a glimpse of him, he looked more and more tired and unhappy. She was sure all Ian needed was a day off, time to relax and think about something other than music. But what happened on that day changed everything—it tore Cassie's family apart, and left Ian's career in tatters. Because, once you've gone too far, you can't go back again.

MAJOR THEMES AND IDEAS

- Sometimes our dreams depict what we cannot do or say in reality.
- You never know when you'll find a kindred spirit.
- Sometimes madness comes with great genius.
- Being a genius doesn't give you the right to be a bully.
- The true musician lets a part of his soul show through the music he plays.

- Blame is so satisfying that you can forget it's actually useless.
- Horrible, scary things happen in almost everyone's life. We all have our secrets that are too scary to share.
- Even if a mean person is attractive, sooner or later their spirit shows through, making their outside match their inside.
- There's no way to avoid change.
- People don't go crazy all at once. There can be days or weeks when they're normal and sane. But gradually, those times get further and further apart and the crazy times get closer and closer together.
- Insanity is deadly serious.
- Depression or paranoia is a farce, and affects everyone around it, trying to draw them in.
- Control is easier to relinquish when you have no control.
- When you think about it, most of life is absurd.
- Destroyed hope is the most profound loss of all.
- Letting your passions control your life can be painful and destructive.
- When you love too deeply, it can destroy you.
- It's hard to feel safe when you have to live with someone who's an eruption waiting to happen, or a bolt of lightening about to strike.
- Do what you fear. Embrace the unknown. Growth is in the feared places.
- Life is a banquet. Approach it with hunger.
- When things are falling apart all around you, headphones can help you find a temporary peace.
- Right can be steady, stable, but wrong feeds upon itself, getting larger and more intense.
- Nothing is ever 100% good or bad.
- Love isn't something you can measure scientifically. Love just *is*.
- Love is a force with its own reasons and can bring either pleasure or pain.
- In the world of insanity, nothing is sacred.
- Music can draw powerful emotions from us.
- You can't reason with insanity. It's a frightening tyrant when it's in control.
- Fear can distort what is real to the point that the damage is real.
- Madness and genius can be two sides of the same coin.
- Love makes the ordinary seem special.
- Mental illness is embarrassing, and hard to conceal for long.
- It's better to live in the moment and be happy, than to worry about what might happen in the future.
- Sometimes, in a stepfamily, you have all the pieces, but they don't add up to a family. A lot of times there's no love, and everyone is just faking it, living with strangers who have family-like names.
- Once you've gone too far, you can never go back again, back to the before.
- Being part of an unhappy household means you are always on edge, assessing your danger.
- Self-destruction can create a desperate, ever-increasing momentum.

- You never know when you might find your kindred ones, with whom you are home and safe.
- Fragile things can come undone with frightening speed.
- Your own small universe moves in surreal ways when you feel a crisis building and your sanctuary's gone.
- The most honest, deepest and purest forms of thought and creation seem to make their owners pay a price.
- In geniuses, sometimes there is a tremendous outpouring of creativity before their final breakdown.
- The heart, and all its love, is as vast and wide as the universe, but we must stay anchored, stable, and safe, as we begin to explore it.

BOOK REPORT IDEAS

1. Compare and contrast the parents in the book, and the different ways they tried to control their children.
2. Speculate on what might have happened had Ian not been in the book.
3. Examine the various definitions of love in the book and how it meant different things to different people.
4. Discuss the idea that the greatest creative gifts cause their owners pain.
5. This book tells what it's like to live with a person with bipolar disease. How does Cassie cope? How does her mother?
6. Several people in this book use manipulation or intimidation to get their way. Identify them, how they do it, and who they are doing it to.
7. Describe what Cassie has learned from the four years she spent with Dino.
8. Describe what Danielle learned from her marriage to Dino.

BOOKTALK IDEAS

1. Use music that Dino might have written as a soundtrack.
2. Build your talk around the "sound bites" Cassie lists about other crazy geniuses.
3. Use an old violin or violin case as a prop.
4. As the time for the concert nears, Dino gets worse and worse. Build your talk around that timeline. Three months away, two months, six weeks—describe what's happening at each step.
5. Write your talk as if it were Cassie's journal.

RISKS

- Stepfather who's an emotional bully, mean and cruel
- Stepfather enjoys making others feel small
- Occasional curse words

- Divorced father obsesses about second husband
- Wife overlooks signs of mental illness
- Links mental illness and extreme creativity
- Frightening and very detailed picture of a gradual mental breakdown
- Genius self-destructs
- Stepfather has a frightening, uncontrollable temper

STRENGTHS

- Strong, authentic voice of a teen
- Powerful portrait of what living with a manic-depressive is like
- Protagonist's pain is lightened by her sense of humor
- Shows an individual's downward spiral into insanity
- Strong and supportive friendships
- Depicts the power of love
- Authentic dialogue
- Immediately involves reader in the protagonist's problems and family
- Subtle foreshadowing of final breakdown
- Suspense and uneasy anticipation increase as the story progresses
- Unresolved ending leaves room for discussion and speculation

AWARDS

ALA Best Books for Young Adults Nominee, 2006
RT Book Club Magazine's finalist for Best Y/A Book of 2005
New York Public Library Books for the Teen Age, 2006

REVIEWS

"Caletti crafts a fine story of a girl finding her way while coping with her parents divorce, her own fears, and an unstable home. . . . It builds tension, resolves conflicts in a real-life, sloppy manner in which the reader's heart knows that the story continues, and yet leaves the reader satisfied that the characters one has grown to love—or at least empathize with, such as Dino—will persevere." Mary Ann Harlan, VOYA, 12/05

"With its profound observations and vivid, if occasionally profane, language, this multifaceted and emotionally devastating novel will stick with readers." Susan Riley, Mount Kisco Public Library, NY, *School Library Journal*, 11/05

"In the end, readers will empathize with each trapped character, even Dino himself." *Publishers Weekly*, 11/05

⊞⊞⊞

WINTERGIRLS. Laurie Halse Anderson. Viking, 2009. $17.99. 288p. ISBN10: 067001110X. ISBN13: 9780670011100. Brilliance Audio, 2009. $29.99. ISBN10: 1423391861. ISBN13: 9781423391869. (unabridged audio CD) Brilliance Audio, 2009. $39.97. ISBN10: 142339181896. ISBN13: 9781423391890. (Unabridged MP3, library edition). Realistic fiction. Reading Level: MS, YHS. Interest Level: YHS, OHS. English, P.E., Psychology, Sociology, Health.

SUBJECT AREAS
eating disorders; self-knowledge; secrets; illness, mental; family relationships; rites of passage; self-destruction; therapy.

CHARACTERS
Lia Overbrook: she is driven to see how thin she can get
Cassie Parrish: Lia's best friend, who succumbs to the demons that haunt them both
Jennifer: Lia's stepmother, who's determined to make her eat and gain weight
Dr. Nancy Parker: Cassie's psychologist
Emma: Lia's little stepsister, who's in the third grade
Dr. Chloe Marrigan: Lia's mother, who's a heart surgeon
Professor David Overbrook: Lia's father, who's a history professor
Jerry Parrish: Cassie's father and an elementary school principal
Cindy Parrish: Cassie's mother
Elijah: he works at the Gateway Motel and found Cassie's body
Ms. Rostoff: Lia's high school counselor
Detective Margaret Greenfield: she's one of the cops investigating Cassie's death
Melissa: one of Dr. Marrigan's nurses, who babysits Lia when she gets out of the hospital

BOOKTALK
Jennifer tells me during breakfast, while I watch words dribble out of her mouth like the crumbs of the muffin she's eating—I eat nothing until I hear her say I'll have to take my little sister Emma to soccer practice. Food is fuel. I have to eat enough so I won't pass out. I need to keep Emma safe. I drink my black coffee and eat ten raisins, five almonds, and a pear. That equals 172. Emma will be safe.

Later, two spoonfuls of Jennifer's leftover Thanksgiving stuffing with ketchup squirted on top, heated in the microwave long enough for it to splatter all over. The open microwave door lets the smell pollute the kitchen as I scrape the plate into the disposal and turn it on. The smell and the dirty plate are enough to convince Jennifer I've eaten, and I'm excused from dinner.

Now finally, I'm alone. The words Jennifer said to me, the words from the newspaper story I read, come rushing back to haunt me.

Cassie is dead, and it is my fault. She died cold and alone in room 113 of the Gateway Motel. She died after she called my phone thirty-three times. Thirty-three cries for help that I didn't answer.

She hadn't called me in six months, not since I got out of the hospital for the second time, and she told me that what we did together was my fault, and she didn't want me in her life anymore. But it wasn't true—I was the one who kept her sane on the crazy roller coaster ride that was our lives. I'm the one she dared to get skinnier than she was. I'm the one who understood her better than anyone else. That's why it hurt so much when I saw her in the ballet school, her new BFF's arm draped around her neck. She wiped me out of her life the way I used to wipe up her puke after she'd stuck her finger down her throat, so she wouldn't get fat.

That's why I didn't answer the phone when she began calling sometime between Saturday night and Sunday morning. That's why I threw the phone across the room when I was tired of its ringing and too tired to turn it off. She was just drunk dialing or prank dialing, and she wasn't going to sucker me into being her friend again just so she could turn around and crush me all over again.

But today is Monday and I know those calls were calls for help. Help she didn't get, because I didn't answer, and I was the only person who would have understood.

📖📖📖

From the day Cassie moved in across the street when we were in third grade, we were best friends who did everything together. We even starved together, to see who could be the skinniest. If she'd been driving that morning a year ago, things might have been different, but she was painting her toenails, so I was driving. Of course, I hadn't had breakfast, or dinner the night before, or days before that. I saw the brake lights ahead of us, but everything was so fuzzy, I just couldn't get my foot on the brake quick enough.

The next thing I knew, I was in the ER, and the nurses were finding out just how hard I'd been trying to win, to be thinner than Cassie. I spent the rest of the summer in a jail called New Seasons, where they stuffed me full of anything fattening, and asked me to spill my guts in therapy groups.

And when I got home and called my best friend, she told me that everything had been my fault, and she didn't want me in her life. I was alone in a way I never had been.

That's why, six months later, when my phone rang, and I saw Cassie's number, I didn't answer it, even though she called and called and called. I finally threw the phone across the room 'cause I was tired of hearing it. No way Cassie was gonna sucker me into being her friend again. I didn't find out until a day later that those calls had been her thirty-three cries for help. Calls to let me know she was going to win our game—she was going to be the skinniest, because she was going to be dead.

MAJOR THEMES AND IDEAS

- Parents may not see or hear their children's pain, ignoring their cries for help even when they are most desperate.
- Everyone has ghosts who stare at them in the dark, ghosts they are too afraid to talk about.
- Where you run out of answers, death may seem like the only alternative.
- There can be no safer when there is no safe.
- Even families that look perfect can be broken and crumbling inside.
- Hiding the scars and flaws doesn't make them go away or reduce their pain.
- Saying the right words, parroting them back to the proper people, doesn't mean you really believe them, or that you're on the road to recovery. They're just sound bites, just the surface.
- Where you've had a skewed self-image for too long, you can forget what you really look like.
- Believing that something is true doesn't make it so.
- You become who you think you are, even if it's only in your own head.
- Negative self-talk pulls you even farther into guilt and despair.
- Sometimes being adult means doing the right thing, even if it's not what you really want to do.
- Cutting yourself is a way to cope with the pain.
- Once you have seen or heard something, it can't be unseen or unheard.
- "Why?" is the wrong question. Ask "why not?" instead.
- Sometimes cries for help are hard to hear and hard to understand.
- An anorexic's eyes see her body differently from everyone else's. It's as if her eyes don't work anymore.
- If you starve yourself for too long, your body forgets how to process food.
- There are two ways of starving yourself to death—either eat nothing, or eat and then throw it up. Or you can do first one and then the other.
- Believing you don't deserve to live is sometimes enough to kill you.
- Not believing in yourself and your worth makes it almost impossible to ask for help in a clear, direct way.
- Anorexics obsess about food, rather than forgetting about it. They think about it all the time. They just don't *eat* it.
- No matter how much you try to get better, your obsession can be stronger than any of your promises.
- If you cannot control your obsession, it controls you, and takes over your life.

- Doing something difficult is easier when you have a best friend to back you up.
- To an anorexic, the numbers don't really matter—they are never low enough. The only number that's good enough is zero.
- It's hard to get better if you really don't want to have a life.
- Severe illness means that the whole family is sick, the whole family is affected.
- We create our own ghosts and haunt ourselves so well, we lose track of what's reality and what's the world the ghosts created.
- Be careful what you wish for. There's always a catch.
- Food is life.
- When you're alive, people can hurt you. It's easier to lock them out. But it's a lie.
- Living is the hardest thing you'll ever do.
- In order to get well, you must first decide to live, and then figure out how.

BOOK REPORT IDEAS

1. How real is Cassie's ghost? Why does she haunt Lia?
2. Both Lia and Cassie cried for help many times. Discuss what those cries were and why they weren't answered.
3. Lia's decision to live came very suddenly. What is real about that, and what isn't real?
4. What was different about Lia, very near the end of her life, and Cassie, at the end of hers? Why do you think Cassie died and Lia didn't?
5. If your best friend was refusing to eat, what kinds of things might you do, based on Lia's story?
6. Lia covered up the weight loss and anorexic behavior in a variety of ways. Discuss these cover-ups and how effective they were.
7. What was unique about each of the times Lia went to New Seasons?
8. Explain what it might have been like to be Lia's friend. What might you do, or not do, to help her?
9. Lia does a lot of negative self-talk. Explain what effect it has on her and why.
10. Why does Cassie's ghost try to persuade Lia to continue her self-destructive behavior?
11. What part of Lia is Cassie's ghost? What role does she play in Lia's thoughts, and how does that role change?
12. Explain what the term "wintergirl" means to you?
13. Why did Lia create Cassie's ghost? Where does she come from?
14. What event or insight makes Lia realize she wants to live?

BOOKTALK IDEAS

1. Write your talk as a dialogue between Lia and Cassie.
2. Have Lia's family members introduce her, each one showing how they think or how they feel about her.

3. Focus your talk on the idea of "wintergirls," explaining how to become one.
4. Write your talk in first person, as Lia talks about her need to be thin, and what she does to make people think she's eating.
5. Use props for your talk—pictures of the amount of food she'd allow herself to eat, pictures of anorexic girls, a half-finished knitted scarf, a size zero t-shirt, or other clothes.

RISKS
*   Divorced, bitter parents don't acknowledge their part in Lia's illness
*   Girl starves herself to death
*   Parents are distant, uninvolved
*   Two girls bond over their competition to see who can weigh the least
*   Shows the variety of tricks anorexics will use to appear they aren't losing weight
*   Anorexia completely controls girls' lives
*   Therapy is ineffective (therapist fooled by girls' tricks/lies)
*   Parents don't see/hear their daughters' cries for help
*   Parents use their arguments to avoid dealing with their daughters' illness
*   Girls starve, binge and purge, and obsess about being thin
*   Shows a potential anorexic exactly what to do
*   Parents' flaws and weaknesses are examined in clear detail

STRENGTHS
*   Shows the impact of an eating disorder on family
*   Written from multiple points of view
*   Scratched out words make Lia's thoughts immediate
*   Detailed self-talk takes reader into Lia's mind
*   Examines the power and pervasiveness of anorexia
*   Characters teens can identify with
*   Interior point of view draws in readers
*   Teaches about anorexia by *showing* the reader its seductiveness
*   Includes some of the causes of anorexia
*   Shows the subtle seduction of eating disorders
*   Three-dimensional characters readers can identify with
*   Writing style draws reader into the book
*   Formatting and positioning of Lia's inner dialogues makes them stand out
*   Tension and suspense are maintained from the first page

REVIEWS
"A devastating portrait of the extremes of self-deception in this brutal and poetic deconstruction of how one girl stealthily vanishes into the depths of anorexia. . . . Anderson illuminates a dark but utterly realistic world . . . this is necessary reading."
Daniel Kraus, *Booklist*, 12/08

"As events play out, Lia's guilt, her need to be thin, and her fight for acceptance unravel in an almost poetic stream of consciousness in this startlingly crisp and pitch-perfect first-person narrative. . . . What happens to her in the end is much less the point than traveling with her on her agonizing journey of inexplicable pain and her attempt to make some sense of her life." Carol A. Edwards, Denver Public Library, *School Library Journal*, 2/09

"Anderson perfectly captures the isolation and motivations of the anorexic without ever suggesting that depression and eating disorders are simply things to 'get over.' Due to the author's and the subject's popularity, this should be a much-discussed book, which rises far above the standard problem novel" *Kirkus Reviews*, 2/09

"The intensity of emotion and vivid language here are more reminiscent of Anderson's *Speak* than any of her other works . . . an almost poetic stream of consciousness in [a] startlingly crisp and pitch-perfect first-person narrative." *School Library Journal*, 3/08

📖📖📖

ZIGZAG. Ellen Wittlinger. Simon and Schuster, 2003. $16.95. 272p. ISBN10: 0689849966. ISBN13: 9780689849961. Simon Pulse, 2005. $6.99. 288p. ISBN10: 0689849982. ISBN13: 9780689849985. Realistic fiction. Reading Level: YHS. Interest Level: YHS, OHS. English, Psychology, Geography.

SUBJECT AREAS
family relationships; travel; rites of passage; self-knowledge; problem parents; friendship; love; grief and mourning.

CHARACTERS
Robin Daley: she goes on a road trip that changes her life
Chris Melville: Robin's boyfriend, who's on his way to Rome for the summer
Dr. Ransom: a friend of Chris's dad
Dr. Melville: Chris's mom, a pediatrician
Franny: one of Robin's best friends
Liz and Bill: Franny's divorced parents who fight over her custody
Karen Daley/Mom: Robin's mother, a single parent and a nurse
Michael Evans: a man Mom is dating
Jerry Daley: Robin's father, who left when she was about a year old
Esther: a friend of Robin's mom, who works with her
Aunt Dory: Robin's aunt and her mother's younger sister, whose husband was just killed

Iris Tewkesbury: she's Robin's wealthy thirteen-year-old cousin
Marshall Tewkesbury: Iris's ten-year-old brother, who also looks down on their "country cousins"
Allison Daley: Robin's stepmother
David Daley: Robin's half brother
Des Sanders: the boy Franny's dating
Glen: a cowboy that just might be able to make Robin forget about Chris
Jackson, Joe, Mel: other cowboys from the Lazy River Dude Ranch
Savannah: a college student with a summer job in New Mexico, who helps out in an emergency
Roland and Sukey: artists who run a motel and Savannah's parents, who take care of Robin, Iris, and Marshall while Dory's in the hospital
Cesar: Savannah's brother, who is very attracted to Robin
Tony: Savannah's youngest brother, who's the same age as Iris

BOOKTALK

It wasn't the summer Robin had expected. She wanted to have two months with her boyfriend Chris. But when Chris's parents surprised him by sending him to Rome for the summer, Robin's plans come crashing down around her. At least she won't have to stay in town all summer—after her husband is killed suddenly, Robin's Aunt Dory decides to take a road trip across the country with her two kids and wants Robin to go along and help with the driving. Robin's never been out of Iowa, and a wandering trip to California, with a stop in Arizona to see the father she hardly knows, sounds like a good idea, even if she hates her snobby, bratty cousins.

Robin has no idea how much her life will change before she gets back to Iowa. Her cousins are out of control, her aunt doesn't have a clue how to deal with them, and soon Robin is doing a lot more than sharing the driving. She's also a part-time therapist, an art critic, and a big sister to the two biggest brats she's ever met. And most of the time, she's too busy to even think about Chris, especially after she meets not one, but two cute cowboys.

So climb into the minivan, separate the two battling siblings, and discover all the adventures an Iowa farm girl can have when she visits South Dakota, Wyoming, Colorado, New Mexico, and all points west.

MAJOR THEMES AND IDEAS

- Kids in an abusive home don't always realize how awful it is because they're used to it.
- When parents get divorced, they shouldn't divorce their kids as well.
- Love is more difficult when you are from different social classes or don't have similar backgrounds.
- You make your own luck.
- Everyone handles grief differently—meanness or anger can cover up sorrow.

- People generally have good reasons for their behavior, even if they aren't willing to share them.
- Sometimes getting angry is a way to stop the pain you're feeling. Unfortunately, it doesn't help you handle the pain, just cover it up.
- Sometimes it's more about the trip than the destination, the process more than the product.
- Once someone you love dies, the more tightly you want to hold onto the other people you love.
- Money can get in the way of happiness sometimes. People with millions are usually no happier than people who merely have enough money.
- Being rich isn't the most important thing in life. Many important things are free.
- Sometimes it's best not to look too far ahead into the future. What you might worry about today might never happen, or if it did, might turn out to be a good thing.
- Life can change completely in just a moment.
- It's foolish to worry about something that may never happen.
- Things happen for a reason. The trick is figuring out what that reason is.
- Being the one in charge can be frightening, but it can also make you realize how strong and capable you truly are.
- Life changes you, it's inevitable. The only way to survive is to take one day at a time and go with the flow.
- First love doesn't have to be forever. People change, and so does love.
- If you feel like you're no one without the one you love, you need to spend some time apart and figure out who you are, because you *are* someone!

BOOK REPORT IDEAS

1. Robin changed in many ways over the summer. Compare the person she was at the beginning of the book to the one she was at the end.
2. Speculate on what might happen when Robin and Chris are together again. Will their time apart draw them closer or separate them more completely?
3. There were several points along the trip when Iris and Marshall had to make significant changes. Examine those points and explain what the changes were and why they happened.
4. Illustrate your book report with a map of the trip. Be sure to show their route all the way to L.A. so you don't reveal that it stopped in New Mexico.

BOOKTALK IDEAS

1. Tell your talk in first person, as Robin, Dory, Iris, and Marsh, letting each of them introduce him/herself.
2. Illustrate your talk with a map of their trip.
3. Write your talk as if it's letters Robin wrote to her mother, Franny, and Chris.

RISKS
- Parents are alcoholic
- Parents physically and psychologically abuse daughter
- Teens are sexually active
- Distant and uninvolved father
- Boy reacts to his father's death by becoming very violent and lying
- Girl reacts to father's death by being mean and cruel
- Children are rude, thoughtless, and self-centered
- Mother is indulgent and ineffective
- Teen's bulimia is ignored by her mother

STRENGTHS
- Genuine teen voices
- Characters are vividly drawn, easy to identify with
- Teen has positive, supportive relationship with mother
- Characters mature and gain insight
- Realistic male-female relationships
- Shows the importance of accepting changes in yourself and your world
- Ambivalent ending leaves room for speculation and discussions
- Shows that relationships can sometimes survive time and distance

AWARD
ALA Best Books for Young Adults, 2004

REVIEWS
"Wittlinger delivers another stellar performance with this story. . . . In this realistic novel, resolution comes neither easily nor neatly although Wittlinger leaves room to imagine what Robin calls 'all the possibilities.'" Amy S. Pattee, *VOYA*, 10/03

"With gentle wisdom and remarkably true characters, Wittlinger's writing conveys a fundamental truth: life is a nonlinear journey that everyone takes and it is the simple choices that define a person." Jane Halsall, McHenry Public Library District, IL, *School Library Journal*, 8/03

"Wittlinger elevates the familiar into a moving, realistic exploration of first love, class issues, girls' self-confidence, and the process of healing. Teens will easily hear themselves in Robin's hilarious, sharp observations and feel her excitement as she travels through new country and discovers her own strength." Gillian Engberg, *Booklist*, 9/03

📖 Appendix One 📖
Censorship: What It Is, Why It Is, and How to Deal with It

Censors. We all know they exist. We all know what they do. But why do they do it? Censorship is a fact of life, something that affects us every day. We censor what we say and what we do, fitting our actions to the situation. We say what is tactful rather than what is absolutely true. We select one action and reject another. We decide that someone else is too young or too old to understand something, and prevent that person from seeing or hearing or having something, and by doing so, make the world a safer place—at least in our own opinion. The censor in all of us helps keep us and those we care about safe, perhaps even moral. But sometimes that censor gets out of control and decides to control the environment more than is appropriate, trying to make safe not just immediate surroundings, but the whole world—on its own terms. That's when the censor, in an effort to completely control its environment, moves from being a positive to a negative force.

The American Library Association defines censorship in the following way: "Censorship is the suppression of ideas and information that certain persons— individuals, groups, or government officials—find objectionable or dangerous. It is no more complicated than someone saying, 'Don't let anyone read this book, or buy that magazine, or view that film, because I object to it!'"

The *ALA Intellectual Freedom Manual* states: "Although an attempt to stereotype the censor would be unfair, one generalization can be made: Regardless of the specific notices, all would-be censors share one belief—that they can recognize 'evil' and that other people must be protected from it. Censors do not necessarily believe their own morals should be protected, but they do feel compelled to save their fellows."

The psychology of censors is composed of fear: fear of loss of power and control, over themselves, their families, their children, and their situations. Censors are not necessarily logical when they are afraid or on a moral crusade. They attempt to exert their authority over others in order to have the situation resolved the way they want.

413

Censors are filled with fear, and use that fear to try to persuade others to think the same way they do.

Censors mask their concerns with semantics filled with emotions. Books become power tools that can turn young adults into serial killers or sex fiends. The language of censorship surrounds the protection of our young, the protection of family, and deciding what is morally appropriate for our culture. Censors want to remove all the objectionable materials so that no one else can judge for themselves whether the subject matter is appropriate. They don't trust young people to decide for themselves whether the material is harmful. Censors are afraid that exposure to the objectionable subject matter will result in the loss of control over their children or children in general. But censors who believe they are protecting children are also acting out their personal agenda. If they are against abortion, they will not want young adults reading books about teenagers grappling with the issue. If the censors are deeply religious, then any book dealing with something that is deemed inappropriate by the church will be challenged.

Censors believe that they seek the highest moral ground, and believe everyone should have the same vision of morality, removing what doesn't fit into that vision. Censors typically object to specific scenes or pages, taking them out of context and ignoring the overall message or theme of the material. They may circulate copies of these to friends or read them aloud in a meeting. Censors also assume that the librarian, library, school, or teacher endorses the entire work, including what they are objecting to. In a school situation, even when alternative materials are available for children of parents who object to the work, censors want the work unilaterally banned. The most frequent reasons for banning a book are sex, violence, profanity, supernatural elements, inappropriate family values or structures, abuse of various kinds, and racist comments or slurs. Censors believe that exposing children to this subject matter will be dangerous and confuse them about the values and ethics their parents are teaching them. The larger issue of control is masked by the idea of protecting children from the ideas expressed in books. Ideas and words are power, and censors are afraid of them.

Suzanne Fisher Staples (*ALAN Review*, Winter 1996) speculated on why certain parents become censor zealots: "They feel helpless sending their children into a world that seems increasingly plagued with hazards over which they have no control. They see the books available to their children as an area where they can have control."

Unfortunately, parents don't realize that kids have already heard the language and experienced or been exposed to a great deal more in school and through television, radio, the Internet, and video games than parents are aware of. Furthermore, these parents are doing their children a disservice. Children develop good judgment when allowed the freedom to find and select materials for themselves. Parents who make their children aware of what behaviors are acceptable and what are not build accountability into their children instead of fear.

Librarians and teachers do consider what is age-appropriate as they build their collections or curricula. However, the need to control and have power over individuals who have access to children is a strong force within the censor. After all, words like child, young adult, and appropriate can be defined in a wide variety of ways.

Most people agree that it is the parents who are ultimately responsible for what their children watch, read, and come into contact with. The American Library Association states: "The primary responsibility for rearing children rests with parents. If parents want to keep certain ideas or forms of expression away from their children, they must assume the responsibility for shielding those children. Governmental institutions cannot be expected to usurp or interfere with parental obligations and responsibilities when it comes to deciding what a child may read or view."

Censors need to understand that this control extends only to their children, not all the children of the entire community. The issue of protecting all children from witchcraft, sexual issues, AIDS, obscenities, abuse, and a wide variety of other subjects in print and nonprint media should not be a governmental concern. Ideas and freedom of expression are part of the Constitution for all citizens. Parental control must stay within the family or organizational boundaries.

Some of the best reasons for young adults to read the edgy, controversial literature when it is age appropriate for them to do so is to allow them to deal with issues they face in a private, nonthreatening manner. If a child is being abused at home and afraid to tell anyone, books such as *Staying Fat for Sarah Byrnes, Dreamland, Learning to Swim,* or *Breathing Underwater* might be an outlet for their fears and help them make a decision about their situation. If nothing else, these titles tell them that they are not the only one enduring an abusive situation.

If schools are charged with preparing students for life, then studying controversial subjects in the classroom is necessary. AIDS, drug and alcohol abuse, sexuality, homosexuality, ethics, gangs, self-reliance, anorexia nervosa/bulimia, prejudice, and self-esteem are just a few of the topics that teachers and librarians must educate students about during their time in school. Subjects like these are all controversial, "hot" subjects. They are loaded with emotions and prejudices. Parents or censors are often afraid to discuss these issues with their own children and usually do not want anyone else to do so either. If censors are afraid of the topics presented in the classroom and supported by materials in the library, a challenge is a very strong possibility.

This is a group of people who knows what is right, not only for themselves, but for everyone. They do not deal well with confrontation, and when confronted tend to dig in and defend their position even more strongly. They are ruled by fear, fear of losing power and control. When making a challenge, they may also be angry or frustrated. The library staff must be trained to deal with them effectively and positively.

For this reason, strong reconsideration and challenge policies and procedures need to be present in every library. Staff must be trained to deal with challenges and be educated about guidelines and procedures. Written policies and an educated staff form a solid foundation of support for the teacher or librarian who wants to keep the more edgy, realistic young adult fiction in their collections and in the hands of young readers.

It is important to know how to make challenges less difficult and traumatic for both the challenger and the librarian. These tips offer suggestions for what to do before a challenge occurs, how to deal with a challenger face-to-face, and what kinds of policies and procedures need to be in place to support you in facing the challenge.

The first thing to remember in dealing with challenges is to accept the fact that sooner or later someone will object to something in your collection. It may or may not be about an item that you thought would be challenged, and it may or may not be about a part of that item that you thought would be controversial—in fact, it will probably be something you never expected a challenge about. Given this, it is important to prepare ahead of time so you already know what steps to take.

Of course a written selection policy, including reconsideration procedures, is essential. This policy is a general one, covering the whole library collection. Smaller departments, especially children's and young adult departments, should have their own written policies tailored to their customers' specific needs, but the procedures and forms used should be consistent throughout the library. The general policy should first clearly define the goals and philosophy of the library and then include sections on selection of materials, intellectual freedom issues, reconsideration procedures and forms, and any curriculum guidelines that apply to the library. (Other sections not having to do with challenges have been omitted here, for brevity's sake.)

The reconsideration form should be concise, but should include several key pieces of information.

- Has the customer read the whole book or just a part?
- If the latter, how did the customer find out about that section in the book?
- Is the customer affiliated with any organization seeking to challenge the book?
- Has the customer read any reviews of or articles on the book?
- What action does the customer want the library to take?

The form should help the customer clarify his thoughts about the book and formalize his concerns.

The selection policy is the library's first line of defense. It should be backed up by additional "ammunition" on the titles and authors that are most likely to be challenged. This ammunition can include a wide variety of materials, for instance:

- A file of reviews, including the full text of each review and a citation to its source
- A list of honors that the book has won (the cover or dust jacket may help you get started with this)
- Articles written about the book, either by the author or critics
- A rationale supporting the book, containing bibliographic information, intended audience, a brief summary of the plot, a statement on the value of the book and how it might be used, the impact of the book and the new perspectives it could open up, the potential problems or risks with the book and how they might be handled, and alternative titles that might be less objectionable

- A list of other challenges to the book and information on how they were handled
- Statements from customers who support the book, especially from members of the intended audience for the book or from influential community members
- Books or websites on how to deal with censors
- Information on how to contact the Office for Intellectual Freedom at the American Library Association and at your state or regional library association
- And of course, this book is designed to help you defend the titles in it!

These are only a few of the kinds of ammunition you can collect about a book that you expect will be challenged. Almost anything can be grist for this mill.

A third line of defense is a well-trained library staff that knows how to handle a customer and a situation that can quickly become explosive. Training classes that include role-playing and lists of tips on how to handle customers' complaints are very helpful. Some things that are important to remember when faced with a challenge are:

- First of all, remember to breathe! Pay conscious attention to maintaining a relaxed body posture and to staying calm.
- If you are in a public area, ask the customer to go to a less public or less crowded area, so you can devote all your attention to their complaint without the distraction of other customers. This also prevents others from getting involved in the situation and helping to escalate it.
- Invite the customer to sit down with you. It's harder to maintain a high level of emotion when you are sitting rather than standing. Do not sit across the table from the customer, which is a confrontational posture. Rather, sit on the same side of the table, or at one end, while the customer sits at right angles to you.
- Make eye contact but don't stare.
- If you choose to take notes, make sure the customer can easily see what you are writing.
- Watch your body language. Your posture should be open and relaxed; your facial expression should be polite, calm, attentive, and receptive.
- Keep your voice low. The louder the customer gets, the more quietly and softly you should respond.
- Respond to what the customer is saying by nodding and using verbal encouragers such as "I see. . . . Yes. . . . Right. . . . Um-hum. . . . I understand. . . . "
- Listen to the content of the complaint and also to the subtext behind it. "I can't believe you have this smut in the library where children can find it!" "It sounds like you really care about your kids." Work to change the interaction from a confrontation to a dialogue.
- Agree with the customer as much as you can, so that he or she doesn't have to become defensive.
- Find something positive to say, some kind of praise you can give. "It's really great to see a parent willing to go to so much trouble for their children."

- Let the customer tell the story over and over, as many times as he or she wants to. It may take several retellings before the customer has vented enough to be ready to go on to the resolution stage of the interaction. Remember, these people are angry, anxious, nervous, and need to defend themselves and their points of view and try to convince you of the rightness of their cause before thinking about how to solve the problem.
- Really listen to the customer without planning ahead what you are going to say or do. Be in the moment with the customer at all times.
- Once the customer is ready to move into the resolution stage, explain the library's policies and procedures and what the next steps will be.
- Have copies of the reconsideration form, the Library Bill of Rights, and the Freedom to Read Statement available for the customer to have.
- If necessary, or if requested by the customer, refer him or her to someone higher in authority, and when possible, take the customer to that person and introduce them, rather than just giving the customer a name and phone number. If the staff person being referred to is in another building, offer to call them for the customer and introduce them over the phone.
- Finally, follow the procedures given in the reconsideration policy if the customer wishes to continue with the challenge.

📖 Appendix Two 📖
How to Write a Rationale

Note: The information in this appendix comes from the website http://ncte.org/censorship/write_rationales.shtml and is adapted from SLATE Starter Sheet, NCTE, April 1994, Jean E. Brown, Saginaw Valley State University, Michigan, Region 4 Representative to the SLATE Steering Committee (SLATE stands for Support for the Learning and Teaching of English and is the intellectual freedom network of the National Council of Teachers of English).

WHAT IS A RATIONALE?

We frequently hear the term rationale defined as a justification for doing something. Certainly that perspective is a vital one as we explore the need for developing rationales for books or other instructional material. Both Diane Shugert (1979) and Margaret Sacco (1993) advocate writing and keeping a file of rationales in advance as a defense against potential censorship. We will frame the discussion in a broader context, describing the overriding role of rationales in classroom planning. Teachers must make decisions about what they will teach and how they will then teach it, decisions that will achieve their purposes and address their students' needs. The value of developing a rationale is that it provides a framework for this planning.

A rationale is the articulation of the reasons for using a particular literary work, film, or teaching method. Minimally, a rationale should include a bibliographic citation and the intended audience; a brief summary of the work and its educational significance; the purposes of using the work and how it will be used; potential problems with the work and how these can be handled; and alternative works an individual student might read or view. Shugert (1979) identifies criteria for assessing rationales. Among these guidelines are that they are well thought out, avoid specialized technical jargon, are specific and thorough, and are written so that they will be readily understood by teachers who use the work. These and other components of rationales will be explored in the section on Guidelines for Writing a Rationale.

WHY DEVELOP A RATIONALE?

Rationale development should be part of thoughtful planning for classroom instruction. If we have not reflected on the "whys" of what we teach, we will be unprepared to meet the needs and challenges of our students and to respond to potential complaints, either from parents or from others in the community who seek to influence the curriculum. While rationales are important in every aspect of teaching, we will focus here on the need for well-developed rationales for books used in the classroom—whether in whole-class instruction, small-group work, or classroom libraries. Teachers who make curricular decisions based upon mere expediency leave themselves vulnerable. Problems can be averted by carefully analyzing the audience (the students), the school, and the community and taking into full account the most effective means for meeting students' interests and educational needs.

HOW DO WE DEVELOP RATIONALES?

Teachers are frequently advised to have a written rationale for every book that they use. Realistically, this issue might be better addressed in a less absolute way by exploring four levels of rationale development. In an ideal situation, teachers would automatically write a rationale for every book that they teach, assign, include on a reading list, or keep in their classroom libraries. But mandating teachers to take on such a task when they are already overburdened is unrealistic and unreasonable. If teachers were required to write rationales for every book, many might simply stick to their literature anthologies and even avoid potentially controversial selections in those books. So while Shugert (1979, 190–91) rightly cautions about using shortcuts to rationales, we do suggest options in the belief that the circumstances and conditions will determine what the teachers will do at any time.

1. A brief written statement of purpose for using a particular book—the "why" for using it and where it will fit in the curriculum. This is prepared by individual teachers based on the students, school, and community noted above and on curricular and instructional objectives and needs. At this level of rationale writing it is essential for teachers to have a written statement. Just thinking about the reason is not enough to demonstrate thoughtful planning if a protest should arise, nor does it provide teachers with opportunities to be reflective about their decisions.
2. The second level involves a more detailed accounting through use of forms. Pages 424–27 of this appendix [in original document; sample forms not provided] show sample forms from the Connecticut Council of Teachers of English (Shugert, 1979, 192–93). These samples provide two approaches—the first for an individual teacher to complete and the second for department members to fill out together. Of course, both forms can be modified to meet the needs of particular school situations.

3. The third level provides for the development of fully constituted rationales by individual teachers, departmental or district-wide committees, or the district English language arts coordinator or supervisor in cooperation with teachers. These rationales include many of the elements discussed above and will be explored further in the next section.
4. The fourth level calls for the collection of existing rationales that have been developed by other teachers or by professional organizations. By their nature these rationales are often comprehensive because they are developed as a service for schools that have challenges.

GUIDELINES FOR WRITING A RATIONALE

The guidelines below will promote consistency as well as provide direction and support for writing rationales individually, in small collegial groups, or in departments. Sacco, in a paper prepared for the Assembly on Literature for Adolescents (ALAN) Intellectual Freedom Committee, and Shugert (1979) are among those who have presented systematic views of how to put together a rationale. Sacco uses a highly structured format in developing rationales with her undergraduate students; Shugert provides a more open-ended approach based on the following questions posed by Donelson (1979, 166):

1. For what classes is this book especially appropriate?
2. To what particular objectives, literary or psychological or pedagogical, does this book lend itself?
3. In what ways will the book be used to meet those objectives?
4. What problems of style, tone, or theme or possible grounds for censorship exist in the book?
5. How does the teacher plan to meet those problems?
6. Assuming that the objectives are met, how would students be different because of their reading of this book?

Fundamentally, Sacco, Shugert, and Donelson concur that the role of the rationale is to provide a written statement of teachers' best professional perspective on their curriculum. The following guidelines for preparing rationales draw upon and synthesize their ideas.

The bibliographic citation. A rationale should begin with a complete bibliographic citation, including author's name, complete book title, publisher, publication date, and edition.

The intended audience. The rationale should articulate the type of class and the range of grade levels at which the book will be used. The rationale should indicate whether the book is going to be used for individual study, small-group work, or whole-class study, along with an explanation of reasons for why the book is being used.

A brief summary of the work. There are a number of reasons for summarizing a book in the rationale. Writing a summary requires an in-depth look at the book. The summary provides an overview of the book for anyone who chooses to read it, and it can also reflect aspects of a work that the teacher considers most important and aspects that relate to its educational significance.

The relationship of the book to the program. Reading a book is not an isolated educational experience; as a part of the total program, the book should be consistent with the ongoing objectives of the class. Regardless of the quality of a book, if it does not make sense within the broad goals of the program, it is an inappropriate choice in that particular classroom. Any discussion of objectives should also include an examination of how a book will be used, including the teaching methodology and methods of assessment.

The impact of the book. One of the significant arguments for any work is the ways in which it will open new perspectives to its readers. In determining the reasons for using a book, teachers should also consider the potential impact it will have on students' behavior or attitudes.

Potential problems with the work. Teachers and districts are often blindsided by complaints that they never anticipated. The reflective process of developing a rationale is an opportunity for anticipating uses of language, actions, and situations in a work that might be the source of challenges. Additionally, as teachers examine potential problems, they have the opportunity to make decisions about how to address the problems, establishing a framework that supports the book's quality and strengths. For example, a teacher might anticipate an objection to the language in Walter Dean Myers's *Fallen Angels*. The issue can be addressed within the context of the realistic portrayal of young men fighting in Vietnam; the language, while inappropriate in many settings, helps build the portrait of the war's horrors. The language quite simply adds to the book's credibility.

Collection of information about the book. It is useful to collect references about the book, especially published book reviews. Professional journals and booklists from various associations (e.g., NCTE, the International Reading Association, American Library Association), journals like *ALAN Review*, *Horn Book*, and *New Advocate*, as well as non-school sources like the *New York Times Book Review* and *Time* magazine, are rich resources that can be searched via various databases for reviews of particular books. Reviews that address any controversial issues in the book are particularly helpful. These materials should be kept in a file with the rationale.

Collection of supplementary information. Teachers should collect additional materials such as biographical information about the author, especially if it includes any critical assessment of the author's work.

Collection of books of rationales. Books of rationales such as *Rationales for Commonly Challenged/Taught Books* (*Connecticut English Journal*, Vol. 15, 1983), *Celebrating Censored Books!* (Wisconsin Council of Teachers of English, ed. Nicholas J. Karolides), and *Hit List* (Intellectual Freedom Committee, American Library Association, 1989) are valuable as part of the teacher's individual library or as part of the English department's professional library.

Alternative works an individual student might read. For each book they use, teachers should have a list of related titles that might serve either as an alternative or as a supplement to the book. The list of alternatives is useful when parents exercise their right to choose what their child will read. Additionally, the list may be used when students are choosing books from several options, or when they want to read related works. In other words, the listing can be useful in a number of ways, not just in response to a challenge.

REFERENCES

American Library Association. Young Adult Services Division's Intellectual Freedom Committee. *Hit List: Frequently Challenged Young Adult Titles: References to Defend Them.* Chicago: ALA, 1989.

Donelson, K. "Censorship in the 1970s: Some Ways to Handle It When It Comes (and It Will)." *Dealing with Censorship*, ed. James Davis. Urbana, IL: NCTE, 1979.

Karolides, N. J., and L. Burress, eds. *Celebrating Censored Books!* Racine, WI: Wisconsin Council of Teachers of English, 1985.

Sacco, M. T. "Writing Rationales for Using Young Adult Literature in the Classroom." Unpublished manuscript.

Shugert, D. "How to Write a Rationale in Defense of a Book." *Dealing with Censorship*, ed. James Davis. Urbana, IL: NCTE, 1979.

Shugert, D., ed. "Rationales for Commonly Challenged/Taught Books." *Connecticut English Journal*, Vol. 15, 1983.

Teacher's Rationale Form

This form is a model that is intended for individual teachers to fill out. You may wish to print this form and make as many copies as you need or amend it to suit your own situation. It is designed to be used primarily to assist teachers with specific local situations.

School:

Teacher:

Author:

Title:

Grade or course:

Approximate date(s) a book will be used:

This book will be (check one or more):

- Studied by the whole class
- Studied by small groups
- Placed on a reading list
- Placed in a classroom library
- Recommended to individual students

Part of a larger study of (explain):

Other (explain):

Ways in which the book is especially appropriate for students in this class:

Ways in which the book is especially pertinent to the objectives of this course or unit:

Special problems that might arise in relation to the book and some planned activities which handle this problem:

Some other appropriate books an individual student might read in place of this book:

English Department Rationale Form

This form is a model that is intended for department members to fill out together. You may wish to print this form and make as many copies as you need or amend it to suit your own situation. It is designed to be used primarily to assist departments with specific local situations.

Submitted by:

Email:

School:

Title:

Author Name:

Recommended grade(s) or course(s):

Ways in which the book is appropriate for students in this school:

Ways in which the book is pertinent to the objectives of this curriculum:

Special problems that might arise in relation to the book:

Ways that a teacher might handle those problems:

Some other appropriate books an individual student might read in place of this
book:

📖 Appendix Three 📖
Sources of Support for Resisting Censorship

ORGANIZATIONS AND WEBSITES

Anti-Censorship Home Page
    www.best.com/~cgd/home/anticens.htm
Archive of [Censorship] Cases
    (sorted by date, location, medium, and grounds for censorship) http://fileroom
    .aaup.uic.edu/FileRoom/documents/CategoryHomePage.html
Banned Books and Censorship
    www.booksatoz.com/censorship/banned.htm
Banned Books and Censorship: Information and Resources
    www.luc.edu/libraries/banned/
Banned Books Online
    www.cs.cmu.edu/Web/People/spok/banned-books.html
Banned Books on the Internet
    www.lhup.edu/~rparker/advcomp/papers/bressle.htm
Book Banning, Burning, and Censorship
    www.banned.books.com/
Censorship and Intellectual Freedom Page http://ezinfo.ucs.indiana.edu/~quinnjf/
    censor.html
Censorship in the Library?
    www.rightnow.org/censorship.html
Cyberliberties: Teens Affected by Online Censorship Speak Out
    www.aclu.org/issues/cyber/trial/teens.html
The File Room's Exhibit of Banned Books http://fileroom.aaup.uic.edu/FileRoom/
    documents/Mliterature.html
Free Expression (American Booksellers Association)
    www.ambook.org/abffe/
Free Expression Clearinghouse
    www.FreeExpression.org/

Freedom, Discipline, and Censorship
   www.cudenver.edu/~mryder/itc_data/censorship.html
Freedoms Under Fire
   www.uniontrib.com/reports/bill_of_rights/bill_of_rights_1st.html
Index on Censorship
   www.oneworld.org/index_oc/index.html
Joint Task Force on Intellectual Freedom of the National Council of Teachers
   of English and the International Reading Association. 800-336-READ.
   www.reading.org
Know Your Enemies
   www.eff.org/pub/Groups/BCFE/bcfenatl.html
National Coalition Against Censorship
   www.wlma.org/intfree/first.htm
National Council of Teachers of English (Standing Committee Against
   Censorship, SLATE—Support for the Learning and Teaching of English).
   800-369-6283. www.NCTE.org/censorship/
Office for Intellectual Freedom, American Library Association. 312-280-4223.
   www.ala.org/alaorg/oif/index.html
   • Coping with Challenges: Kids and Libraries www.ala.org/alaorg/oif/
      kidsandlibraries.html
   • Coping with Challenges: Strategies and Tips www.ala.org/alaorg/oif/coping
   • Top 100Banned or Challenged Books of 1990–1999 www.ala.org/alaorg/
      oif/top100 bannedbooks.html
Outpost Culture
   www.coolbooks.com/~outpost/
Peacefire: Youth Alliance Against Internet Censorship
   www.peacefire.org/
ProjectCensored
   http://censored.sonoma.edu/ProjectCensored/
See/Hear/Speak No Evil
   www.xnet.com/~paigeone/noevil/noevil.html

JOURNALS

Newsletter on Intellectual Freedom. ALA.

BOOKS

Dealing with Censorship in the 21st Century: A Guide for Librarians and Teachers,
   by Eliza Dresang and John Simmons. Greenwood Press, 2000.
The Hit List II: Frequently Challenged Books for Young Adults. American Library
   Association, Second ed., 1996.

Intellectual Freedom Manual. American Library Association, Fifth ed., 1996.
Rationales for Teaching Young Adult Literature, edited by Louann Reid.
  Calendar Islands, 1999.

PAMPHLETS

Censorship: Don't Let It Become an Issue in Your Schools. National Council of
  Teachers of English (NCTE).
Common Ground. Joint Task Force of NCTE and International Reading
  Association.
Guidelines for Dealing with Censorship. NCTE.
Intellectual Freedom Packet. American Library Association/Association for Library
  Service to Children.
The Student's Right to Know. NCTE.
The Student's Right to Read. NCTE.

CD-ROM

Rationales for Challenged Books. Joint Task Force of NCTE and IRA, 1998.

📖 Appendix Four 📖
Bibliography

Bott, C. J. "Why We Must Read Young Adult Books That Deal with Sexual Content." *The ALAN Review*, Summer 2006.

Bowler, Tim. "Let the Young Decide What They Read." *New Statesman*, July 17, 1998.

Brown, Jennifer M. and Cindi Di Marzo. "Why So Grim? Awards and Controversy Focus Attention on a Recent Burst of Dark-themed Fiction for Teens." *Publishers Weekly*, February 16, 1998.

Budlong, Tom. "'For "Sex" See Librarian': Censorship and Intellectual Freedom in Libraries." *Atlanta-Fulton Public Library System Symposium on Freedom of Speech*, November 10, 1999. Retrieved March 19, 2008, from www.faculty.de.gcsu.edu/~dvess/ids/freedom/budlong.html.

Carroll, Pamela Sissi. "Today's Teens, Their Problems, and Their Literature: Revisiting G. Robert Carlsen's 'Books and the Teenage Reader' Thirty Years Later." *The English Journal*, March 1997.

Cart, Michael. "Bold Books for Innovative Teaching: A Place of Energy, Activity, and Art." *The English Journal*, September 2003.

Clark, Ruth Cox. "Get Controversial! Edgy Novels for Older Teens." *Library Media Connection*, April 2007.

Coeyman, Marjorie. "Teachers Tackle 'Uncomfortable' Books Head On." *Christian Science Monitor*, May 19, 1998.

Cohn, Rachel. "Teens, Teachers, and Controversial Texts." *The ALAN Review*, Summer 2004.

Crowe, Chris. "Defending YA Literature: Voices of Students." *The English Journal*, September 2002.

Curry, Ann. "Where is Judy Blume? Controversial Fiction for Older Children and Young Adults." *Journal of Youth Services in Libraries*, Spring 2001.

Davis, Terry. "A Healing Vision." *The English Journal*, March 1996.

Enriquez, Grace. "The Reader Speaks Out: Adolescent Reflections about Controversial Young Adult Literature." *The ALAN Review*, Winter 2006.

FitzGerald, Frances. "The Influence of Anxiety." *Harper's Magazine*, September 2004.

Fitzpatrick, Betty. "Young Adult Literature." *School Libraries in Canada*, 2005.

Gable, Craig. "The Freedom to Select." *American Libraries*, March 2007.

Gallo, Don. "The Boldest Books." *The English Journal*, September 2004.

———. "Censorship, Clear Thinking, and Bold Books for Teens." *The English Journal*, January 2008.

———. "How Classics Create an Aliterate Society." *The English Journal*, January 2001.

Glenn, Wendy J. "Trusting Texts That Trust Students." *The English Journal*, November 2006.

Hanny, P. "How to Survive High School & Home." *Book Report*, May/June 1992.

Hart, Melissa. "Attract Teen Readers with an Edgy Plot." *The Writer*, October 2004.

Hebert, Thomas P. and Richard Kent. "Nurturing Social and Emotional Development in Gifted Teenagers through Young Adult Literature." *Roeper Review*, April 2000.

Hipple, Ted. "It's the THAT, Teacher." *The English Journal*, March 1997.

Joiner, Whitney. "The Gloom and Doom Canon." *Salon.com*, October 18, 2004. Retrieved March 19, 2008, from http://dir.salon.com/story/mwt/feature/2004/10/18/lizard_motel.

Juozaitis, Vida. "Sex and Censorship in School Libraries." *School Libraries in Canada*, 2006.

Lancto, Craig. "Banned Books; How Schools Restrict the Reading of Young People." September 2003. Retrieved March 19, 2008, from www.worldandi.com/special report/2003/September/Sa23320.htm.

Lent, ReLeah Cosset. "Facing the Issues: Challenges, Censorship, and Reflection through Dialogue." *The English Journal*, January 2008.

Mackey, Margaret. "Risk, Safety, and Control in Young People's Reading Experiences." *School Libraries Worldwide*, January 2003.

Marler, Regina. "Youth Fiction Grows Up." *Advocate*, June 21, 2005.

Martinson, David L. "School Censorship: It Comes in a Variety of Forms, Not All Overt." *The Clearing House*, May/June 2008.

Meyers, Elaine. "Give 'Em What They Want." *School Library Journal*, June 2006.

Mires, Diane. "Censorship and the Freedom to Read." *Pacific Northwest Library Association Quarterly*, Spring 2003.

Norton, Terry L. and Jonathan W. Vare. "Literature for Today's Gay and Lesbian Teens: Subverting the Culture of Silence." *The English Journal*, November 2004.

Patee, Amy. "Rethinking 'Racy Reads.'" *School Library Journal*, January 2007.

Peck, Richard. "From Strawberry Statements to Censorship." *School Library Journal*, January 1997.

Prater, Mary Anne, Marissa L. Johnstun, Tina Taylor Dyches, and Marion R. Johnstun. "Using Children's Books as Bibliotherapy for At-Risk Students: A Guide
for Teachers." *Preventing School Failure*, Summer 2006.

Scales, Pat. "Alice Doesn't Live Here Anymore: What to Do When a Good Series
Contains Explicit Language." *School Library Journal*, January 2007.

——. "Freedom for All?" *School Library Journal*, December 2007.

Schreur, Greg. "Using Bibliotherapy with Suspended Students." *Reclaiming Children
and Youth*, Summer 2006.

Stallworth, B. Joyce. "The Relevance of Young Adult Literature." *Educational Lead-
ership*, April 2006.

Stone, Tanya Lee. "Now and Forever: The Power of Sex in Young Adult Literature."
VOYA, February 2006.

Swing, Georgia Hanshew. "Choosing Life: Adolescent Suicide in Literature." *The
English Journal*, September 1990

Wasserman, Emily. "The Epistolary in Young Adult Literature." *The ALAN Review*,
Spring 2003.

Whelan, Debra Lau. "A Dirty Little Secret: Self-Censorship." *School Library Journal*, February 2009.

Younker, J. Marin. "A Classic Argument." *School Library Journal*, August 2007.

📖 Author Index 📖

📖 Subject Index 📖

441

ANIMALS

ART

BETRAYAL

BULLYING

CANCER

CENSORSHIP

CHILD ABUSE

DEPRESSION

DIVORCE AND SEPARATION

DRUGS

DYSFUNCTIONAL FAMILIES

EATING DISORDERS

ELDERLY

EMOTIONAL ABUSE

ENVIRONMENTAL ISSUES

ETHICS

ETHNIC GROUPS

EVIL

FAMILY RELATIONSHIPS

FEAR

FOSTER CARE

FRIENDSHIP

GANGS

GLBTQ

GOSSIP

GOVERNMENT

GRANDPARENTS

GREED

GRIEF AND MOURNING

GUILT

GUNS

HANDICAPS

IRRESPONSIBILITY

JUSTICE

LEGAL SYSTEM

LOVE

LYING AND DECEIT

MANIPULATION

MENTAL ILLNESS

MENTORING

MUSIC

PHYSICAL ILLNESS

POETRY

POLITICS

POLYGAMY

POVERTY

POWER

PRACTICAL JOKES

PREJUDICE

ROMANCE

RUNAWAYS

SCHOOL

SCIENCE

SECRETS

SELF-DESTRUCTION

SELF-KNOWLEDGE

SEX AND SEXUALITY

WAR

WORKING

WRITING

📖 Curriculum Area Index 📖

ENGLISH

ETHICS

FAMILY STUDIES

FILM

FOREIGN LANGUAGE

GEOGRAPHY

RELIGION

SCIENCE

SEX EDUCATION

SHOP

SOCIAL STUDIES

SOCIOLOGY

VOCATIONAL EDUCATION

📖 Genre Index 📖

SCIENCE FICTION

SUPERNATURAL FICTION

SUSPENSE

VERSE NOVELS

Reading and
📖 Interest/Age Level Index 📖

📖 About the Author 📖

Dr. Joni Richards Bodart, internationally known as the leading expert on booktalking, is on the faculty of the School of Library and Information Science at San Jose State University and is the coordinator of the Youth Librarianship specialization. Her two booktalking series from H. W. Wilson, the Booktalk! Series and the Booktalking the Award Winners series, are considered to be the standard in the field. She is well known as a speaker and workshop leader on booktalking, YA literature, adolescent culture and development, and promoting and defending controversial literature for teens.